THE GOD OF SHATTERED GLASS

For Jim,

    With gratitude for your gentle presence
& wise counsel — to be sure, shards
of light within the shattered glass.

[signature]

Epiphany, 2011

The God of
SHATTERED GLASS

Frank Rogers Jr.

An EMERALD CITY  Book

THE GOD OF SHATTERED GLASS: A NOVEL

Resource Publications
An Imprint of Wipf and Stock Publishers
199 W. 8th Ave., Suite 3
Eugene, OR 97401

ISBN 13: 978-1-60899-324-6

Cataloging-in-Publication date:

Rogers, Frank.

    The God of shattered glass : a novel / Frank Rogers Jr.

    xii + 370 p.; 23 cm.

    ISBN 13: 978-1-60899-324-6

    1. Los Angeles (Calif.)—Fiction. 2. Child abuse—Fiction. I. Title.

Manufactured in the U.S.A.

Contents

Acknowledgments

T HIS NOVEL CAME TO me as a vision in the night. In a two o'clock in the morning burst,
I scribbled twenty pages of notes. Several characters, Tony and Carey in particular,
were so fully formed I was sure I knew them; and the storyline of their time together
was etched in such vivid clarity I imagined that writing it would be more like transcription than creative composition. Whatever spirits brew in the depths that inspire artistic
imagination, I hold you with awe and gratitude. This novel has been an extravagant gift of
creative vitality and personal healing. What writing did for Tony, you did for me.

The novel's vision also came with a surge of passionate conviction: I *had* to write this
novel. Of course, I had never written fiction before, had never taken a writing class before,
but Goethe declared, and Julia Cameron's *The Artist's Way* confirmed it, that the moment
one leaps, the universe mobilizes to meet you. By week's end, I had resigned my tenured
faculty position determined to write full-time. I am grateful to Dean Jack Fitzmier and
the faculty of the Claremont School of Theology for talking some sense into me. *Some*
sense. For I still resigned my faculty position, but with the help of Scott Cormode, I found
funding that enabled me to teach part-time and direct the Narrative Pedagogies Project,
a project through which I could research the narrative practices around which the novel
revolves. I am also grateful to the source of that funding—Craig Dykstra, Chris Coble,
and the Lilly Endowment. You believed in the power of this work, and supported it in
ways beyond the financial.

A wide array of persons trained me in the use of narrative for nurturing meaning
and healing in the lives of troubled young people. Steve Greenstein introduced me to the
liberating power of drama for embattled youth in Watts and East Los Angeles. Augusto
Boal, through his writings and workshops, taught me how the stage can be a source of
social and cultural empowerment. Drama teachers Fran Montano, William Alderson, and
John Ruskin taught me the emotional and spiritual catharsis possible through Sanford
Meisner's approach to acting. And Richard Gardner, Christine Neuger, Michael White, and
Dan MacAdams contributed to my understanding of narrative therapy and the construc-
tion of narrative identity. One scholar-practitioner, however, influenced me like no other.
Daniel Judah Sklar was more than a teacher, he was my mentor. His book, *Playmaking:
Children Writing and Performing Their Own Plays*, remains to this day the only book that,
upon reading, it, I immediately wrote the author like a groupie in the making. Daniel

Judah not only responded, he trained me, he worked with my students, and he became a steadfast friend and unfailing advocate for my fictionalization of work we both now do. Daniel Judah, your inspiration, generosity, and pedagogical genius breathed form and life into my scribble-scrabble dream of working narratively with young people.

Without a doubt, my research would have been only academic if not for the hundreds of young people who participated in the Narrative Pedagogies Project. Participants from the Westmont Community Center in Pomona, 'Acting 4 Change,' the Youth Discipleship Project, the McKinley Boys' Home, the Leroy Haynes Center for Boys, Willard Elementary School in Long Beach, Peppertree Elementary School, and Rosary Catholic High School in Fullerton—you are the embodiment of narrative's promise for personal vitality. I hold as sacred the stories you risked sharing and creating with me. Your stories are now a part of my own.

Finally, I am grateful to Ralph 'Doc' Roberts who so believed in this work that he endowed a permanent faculty position to secure its future, a position I now hold with tenure restored. When the universe mobilizes, it comes full circle.

Researching a novel and writing one are as different as mapping a journey and leaving one's hearth for the dark woods. My early illusions that writing would feel like transcription were quickly shattered. The first draft of this novel took five years; editing took another two. I was self-aware enough to know that writing would demand a descent into the shadows of my own experience. I was not aware, however, that the demons that haunt this Underworld would have such soul-stealing strength. Self-doubt, mistrust of my truth, writer's resistance (far more insidious than writer's block), and the sheer repulsive horror of the terrain being uncovered, assaulted me like guard dogs to hell. Without Mark Reaves for a guide, I would have withered. If writing this novel, Mark, was a voyage through the Inferno, you were my Virgil. Therapist, spiritual counselor, unequivocal cheerleader, and unflinching advocate for the truthfulness of the stories and passions within me, you kept me sane and steered me toward the light on the far side of darkness.

After five years of insisting I was but a few months from completion, I fully emerged from the shadows. I had a draft. Mark Yaconelli, Michael Hryniuk, Deb Arca Mooney, and the staff at the Youth Ministry and Spirituality Project—you were there when I arrived at our meeting with the ecstatic exhaustion of a mother having just given birth. One of the stars that shone in the night sky of finishing a draft was your joy, your toasts, and your insistence that we have a party to celebrate the new arrival. Thank you for that evening's respite.

The respite, however, was brief. Now came the time for editing. My first draft was painfully rough, more in need of sandblasting than sanding and polishing. I am grateful to all my friends and colleagues who read the text, graced me with their reactions and critiques, and offered unique gifts from their particular perspectives. Thank you: Andy Dreitcer, Carol Lakey Hess, Ernie Hess, Lori Anne Ferrell, and Lou Ruprecht—members of our monthly book group—for reading my manuscript as if it belonged in the company of any other book we read, and for teaching me that one can claim a vocation as a writer long before one has published; Doug Frank—for your incisive list of questions, spiked with sangria at Cha Cha Cha's, and your compassionate eyes both tearful and dry; Mark

Yaconelli—for recording so precisely where you couldn't put the novel down, and where you could; Frank Alton—for tearing through the text, peppering me while we hiked, and passing on the Neruda poem about the artist who transforms pain into beauty; Ellen Marshall—for naming Jen as the feminist theologian she is; Marjorie Suchocki—for getting the theology and feeling the horror so acutely; John Cobb—for writing the theology and finding Tony's credible; and Daniel Judah Sklar—for your pitch-perfect sensibilities around engaging young people through narrative.

In addition to great friends, I had great editors. Marie Pappas, Dudley Delffs, Julianne Cohen, and Kathryn Helmers—you were the first professional readers of my manuscript. You know the craft. You love the art. You strengthened not only the manuscript, but me as a writer. The final draft bears each of your imprint.

I thought that completing a final draft would land me but a step away from the Paradiso of publication. Little did I know that a Purgatorial mountain still loomed. I bought my books on query letters; I agonized over synopses; and I collected my rejection letters. It became quite clear, without a literary angel, the cliffs would be too steep to scale. Ulrike Guthrie was sent from the sphere of the sun's luminescence. Uli, as a literary representative, you radiate. Your unadulterated enthusiasm for truthful fiction, your unequivocal honesty free of both cynicism and sentimentality, your unerring wisdom of both the craft and the business, your undying hope, your tireless devotion, your unheard-of promptness, and above all, your unswerving commitment to relationships over the bottom line are beams of sunshine in an all too dark world. Both literally and metaphorically, you bring manuscripts to light.

And I am grateful for the vehicle through which this novel has finally stepped into the public's light. K. C. Hanson at Wipf and Stock—thank you for remembering me from our cabin days on Mt. Baldy, and for not being too scared by what you remember to give my manuscript a chance. This novel was borne from the rages of the forest—it is uncannily appropriate that you should oversee its publication.

Framing my novel's journey—from inception to publication—as a Dantean pilgrimage is misleading in one respect. I have been blessed with loved ones who, throughout the journey, steadily mediated heaven's grace. Steven Otto, Steven Cope, Raza Rasheed, and David Falkinburg—your delight in me writing a novel rivaled your joy in constructing Legos and playing Bull. And your desire for autographed first editions is as satisfying as the Wheat Thins and M&Ms that always await you. Even if not by blood, you will always be Justin's brothers and my sons.

Dad—when I gave you a copy of my manuscript, I knew that, with the exception of the Bible, you had not read a book in the last thirty years. I expected you would display it perhaps, but not that you would read it. The night you phoned me, eighteen months later, to tell me you not only read it, you skipped a day at work because you were so consumed, was like a gospel parable for me. The prodigal son could not have felt more embraced than I did.

Michael and Sammy Daugherty, my soon to be step-sons—thank you for the champagne flutes of sparkling cider, the silly string on the ceiling and walls, and your flammably exuberant participation in the party your mom threw when my publishing contract was signed. As festively as you celebrated my joy, I celebrate the two of you joining my life. You know what I mean when I say this: You are now my boys as well.

Alane, my purpled partner for life. Like Beatrice with her Dante, you entered my life near the top of this Purgatorial mountain, and you ushered me into Paradise. You knew that reading my novel was coming to know me. The days you dropped all to read every word, the tears in your eyes and the warmth in your heart when you shared with me how it lived in you, and your ecstatic pride when we found a publisher are diamond sparkles in the radiant jewel of our union. You are love. You are my love. And your love is what Dante knew. It moves the sun and the stars. And any orb that eclipses them.

And Justin, my son. For many years, it was you and me. And through most of them, we were accompanied by this phantom third person—the novel your dad was ever working on. You were there for it all—the night it came to me in a dream, the hours I spent at the desk upstairs with you in the Lego room on your corner perch, the afternoon I wrote the last word and we danced and howled in the living room then went to Heroes for dinner. Thank you for always believing in it, for indulging me ruminating on it while driving to and from school, for beaming with pride when you told your friends your dad was writing a novel, for losing a weekend when you read it in a near single sitting, and for sensing in ways beyond words that writing this story was somehow restoring my life. My love for you is as limitless as the horizon from our Malibu promontory, as is my joy for the last twenty years—every second of it—with such a remarkable son.

And one last thing. Thank you for the Tic Tacs. Both when you were four and you dispensed them to sick stuffed animals as if they were medicine. And twelve years later, when you knew—it had to be Tic Tacs. And they had to be orange. This is the novel's hope—the simple acts of Shekinah kindness that defy even suffering's horror. That kindness lies within you. It has fed my hope. It always has. And for that, from the beginning, this novel is for you.

Midway on our life's journey, I found myself
    In dark woods, the right road lost. To tell
    About those woods is hard—so tangled and rough

And savage that thinking of it now, I feel
    The old fear stirring: death is hardly less bitter.
    And yet, to treat the good I found there as well

I'll tell what I saw.

    —DANTE ALGHIERI

May every statement uttered—
    be it theological or otherwise—
    be credible within the sight
    of burning children.

    —RABBI IRVING GREENBERG

The way to God is not up, but down.

    —PARKER PALMER

Prologue

Mother's Day 1999

"OPEN YOUR EYES FOR Chrissake! That's how kids get killed!"

I was as shocked as the flattened toddler blinking wildly towards his mother.

"You *slammed* right into him," the dad went on. "That's *concrete* right there."

It was true. I slammed right into his boy. I was racing through the crowded grounds like a stalked man whose airlift was leaving without him; I dodged kids with walkmen, sidestepped strolling couples, barreled around garbage bins, and Bam! I smacked the boy in the chest with my knee. He went down as if sucker-punched—straight onto his diapered bottom then backward.

Maternal instinct kicked in within a heartbeat. His mother plunged to her knees, whisked the boy into her arms, and stroked the back of his head as he dissolved into tears.

"It's okay, baby. Mommy's got you. Oh, honey, it's okay." She clutched him tight and rocked him from her knees.

"I'm sorry," I said, feeling as careless as the dad accused. "I didn't see him. Honest to God."

"Yeah, well," the father grunted, not nearly satisfied. "That's how kids get hurt."

I inventoried the boy's condition. No blood dripped from his head. And his body sobbed freely. He was stunned and scared to death; but thank God, he wasn't hurt.

"I *am* sorry," I repeated, knowing nothing else to say. I spotted a stuffed monkey on the grass, retrieved it, and held it out for the boy. The mother clutched it and snuggled it close to his cheek. Wrapped in maternal warmth and nuzzled by a knowing companion, the boy's sob simmered into a whimper.

"It's okay, honey," the mother soothed as she kissed him on the forehead and stood him up. Sniffling, the boy held out the monkey for care as well. The mom kissed it on the forehead, too. Then the boy, cradling his doll, snuggled back into her arms.

The boy fine, I felt the tug to get on my way. But I hesitated. I looked into the mother's face and noticed her eyes. A film of tears, a reservoir's rim of compassion, glistened like sunlight on a pond.

The tears are what hit me. Cold-cocked me, really. They stabbed into my belly with a self-loathing so biting I turned my head to fix on something—anything—to erase their searing sight. I should have recognized the omen. I should have scurried to my truck, driven home, and gone to bed. But I didn't. I lidded the tremors of my self-recrimination and worked to reclaim my composure.

When I was steady enough, I stole another glance at the mother and her child. I cast a look at the seething father. Then back, for a last look at the boy. And edged with the leaking remnants of my guilt, I apologized again. To the boy and his monkey. To the mother and the father. To everybody. To nobody.

"I'm sorry," I said. "I didn't see him." Then I walked away.

I told them the truth. I did not see him.

But I did not tell them why.

I did not see the boy because I was lost. Not in the woods. Not in a maze. And surely not in the crowd. I was lost in my single-minded tear to find an answer to my question. And I could not see a thing but that my one chance for a personal epiphany was quickly slipping away. The loudspeaker announcing my tour time's final call had startled me awake. I opened my eyes still weary from my nightshift and caught the distant sight of an usher securing the doors behind the patrons he had herded into the lobby. I leapt from my bench, dashed out the pavilion, and rushed through the crowd between the museum and me. That's when I hit the boy.

The truth is, I did not see him because I was in too much of a panic to see a painting.

"Open your eyes for Chrissake. That's how kids get killed." Even with the spectacle I made once I got inside, this sorry story starts with those words. From a father defending his son from a driven pilgrim on an ill-fated quest.

Unfortunately, the words came seven years too late.

For the truth is, my eyes *were* closed.

And that's how kids get killed.

———

Of course, that's not the worst of it. Not by a long shot. The real truth is, I did not cry. Not then. Not since. To this day, not one tear. Seven God-forsaken years of wandering through institutions, court proceedings, and wonder-drug treatment programs. Seven years of observing my life's work deteriorate into the pathetic station I occupy now—I used to heal troubled children, a narrative psychotherapist specializing in the regenerative powers of soul stories for depressed teenagers. Now I sit shipwrecked in a box, a security guard for Paramount Pictures, watching the backs of Hollywood players as they produce the movies-of-the-week that anesthetize the American masses. And through it all, my eyes have stayed as dried as stones.

Don't get me wrong. I never did cry much. I can chart my life by the tragedies I stared through dry-eyed.

I never cried during my mother's spells of silent sorrow, and certainly not during my father's raging assaults. I did not cry when my sister ran away from home, the darts of my dad's obscenities hurled at her back as she receded into the distance. Nor later, when she finally disappeared altogether, swallowed by the Berkeley drug culture like a pebble in a pond. Hell, I didn't even cry at my own divorce. A woman who loved me more than I deserved too. We even lost a baby together. And there Jennie stood in her navy suit, sobbing on the courthouse steps, searching me with those tear-soaked eyes, wondering without words how it ever came to all this and where did the tender guy she knew go and why couldn't we just hold each other until we got through all the pain. And all I could do was stare at her unmoved like I was locked away in a soundproof booth that no amount of pleading could penetrate. I tried. God, I tried.

Why is life so filled with pain? I don't know. I only watch it through plexiglass.

But even that was years ago. God, a lifetime ago. That was before I went back to school and studied with Woody, before I discovered the healing power of stories and lit up like a convert, before my invigorating work at San Francisco, and Munich, São Paulo, Crossroads, for Christ's sake. That was before . . .

That was before the last time I cried.

And the last time I didn't.

Seven years, and not a single tear. No sniffling during a sentimental song. No whimpering after a hammer to a thumb. Not even the whisper of a wail at my mentor's wake. They say that even Satan weeps, that though his eyes are frozen with fury in the icy depths of hell, a cold trickle of tears flows from his paralyzed stare. Not me. My fury has remained frozen without tears, my eyes a waterless wasteland. I simply have not cried.

And then this morning happened.

———

I have staked seven years of my life on the conviction that if I stared too long into the face of evil, I would go blind. After all, that's what happens if you gaze into the face of God. Jews have always known that. An Icarian absorption into God's flaming splendor would obliterate all moorings in the creaturely realm as certainly as the blindness that would follow an extended stare into the noonday sun. Hell, Moses saw but the backside of God and his face so shined in the aftermath he had to veil it for its glare. I have clung to the belief that the same is true with evil. If I stared into the searing cold blackness of evil's void, that realm where malignance is so palpable God's presence is utterly and repulsively absent, I would go just as blind. Be it an abyss of cynicism or despondency's black hole, a pull of despair would swallow me into a core so dark I would never see light again.

I am stupefied, then, at the stories of people who not only delve into the sordid sources of their suffering, they emerge from that encounter with their spirit intact. These are people who know the deepest of wounds. They hunger for healing and purpose in life. And they look for it in the most unlikely of places. Not in drugs or alcohol, not TV or the magazine rack, not the office or shopping or trimming their handicap or any of our other cultural diversions. No. They plunge into the pit of suffering itself. And somewhere in the midnight belly of their pain's tomb they find, or are found by, a womb of grace and a heartbeat of hope that births them back into the world with pathos and sober gratitude. Some even transform the filth of their suffering into something sublimely beautiful, as if to reveal not that evil is any less repugnant, but that even in the midst of perversity most vile a creative life-force beats that can never be extinguished.

That astounds me. How does Elie Wiesel endure the nightmares of a Nazi concentration camp and emerge with the tenderness of spirit and tenacity of purpose to write a novel? How does Maya Angelou, sucked into the seedy underworld where children are used sexually then disposed of like rags, rise up and write poetry? How does B. B. King, pounded by the relentless blows of pernicious poverty and ubiquitous racism resist the dopey drag of drugging out and play the blues? I can barely fold bread around cheese for lunch. These folks make music.

And frankly, I find it difficult to swallow. Here I sit, so repulsed by the stench of my stewing memories it's all I can do to keep from shooting myself, and they suggest that wallowing in depravity's depths not only eludes the abdication of despair, it leads to the very source of life. Come on. I don't like being teased by that which mere mortals can never attain. So I want to know for myself. I want to meet up with one of these guys and ask them directly. No bullshit now. I've got a gun to my head and you've got to tell me. You plumbed those depths. Is it really true? If you open the Pandoran hatch and descend into the pit of your pain, would an average Joe like me really find a life-force at the cold dead center of evil? Tell me. I've got to know. Because I swear to God, I'm going to shoot. Please.

This morning, I had my chance.

———

Vincent van Gogh knew those depths.

A person who stared more fully into abject misery would be hard to find. Throughout his life, he dwelt in the Dickensian squalor of city slums, the Appalachian poverty of backwoods mining country, the barbaric severity of fanatical households, and the Dark Age terrors of primitive insane asylums. Through it all, he slummed about in the ripping torments of the underworld within the soul. Depressions crippled him, his family's ridicule ravaged him, his lovers' rejections impaled him, and society's ceaseless scorn tortured him. Vincent van Gogh more than plumbed the depths of suffering. He slopped and splashed and gurgled and thrashed through every stench-filled pool within the decaying sewers of suffering's depths.

And within them, he did the most extraordinary thing. He painted. He found and found again, in whatever cesspool he was soaking in, some creative spark buried in the muck that rippled up through him with such fierce urgency he was compelled to swipe a canvas with color in a half-crazed drive to bring beauty into being. He created art. And his art was a raging howl of expression from a man but one step from madness holding on for dear life to the only current of life-giving spirit he knew.

Sometimes his art ached with poignancy. Like his painting, 'Sorrow.' Here he drew, in melancholic charcoal, the prostitute he loved and lived with, the woman he forfeited his father's blessing to share destitution with, before she abandoned him for one of her tricks who no longer felt like paying. A naked solitary figure sits on the floor. Her used-up body is slumped over in raw despair. Her legs are tucked up like a fetus. Her arms, too tired to hold herself, too tired to comfort herself, too tired to clothe herself, sag on her knees, strong enough only to hold her hanging head. Buried in her caved-in crouch is her face, hidden in shame at the hell her life has become. And yet, in Vincent's tender portrait, she is held by compassion, a compassion that holds all people busted up by life's brutality.

Other times his art soars in an explosion of life-affirming ecstasy. Like 'Starry Night.' My God, what a breathtaking connection he must have felt with the pulsating, copulating vitality of the night sky where sun and moon, man and woman, flowing rivers of cloud and still starry centers are all held together in the one great dance of life. And how does one taste such mystical union with the heaven's dazzling spheres? Not through the church. The tall spire of a cathedral's reach up from the town below barely tweaks the bottom edge of the cosmic dance in the sky like a toddler's timid toe dipping but the tip of the vast sea's surf. No, organized religion stands aside while unleashed artistic passion sails into and mingles with the musicality of the stars. A blazing, bursting cypress tree erupts from the fiery bowels of the earth and penetrates into the deep reaches of the receptive night in a climax of transcendent vitality. God, what I would give to feel what he felt then, to know even a spark of the life-force that cascaded through him in the ecstasy of painting that painting. For that, I would journey into the depths of hell and brush shoulders with the devil himself. Yes. For that, I would.

But of course, this current of life did not carry van Gogh to his natural end. At some point, his sojourn through misery turned too dark, the spark that births life became too well hidden. At the age of thirty-seven, having sold but one painting and that to his brother, Vincent packed his supplies one last time.

He stationed himself at the corner of a farm. Across the dirt road a field of wheat tossed in the wind. A distant storm rumbled. An ominous flock of crows, ancient heralds of death, hovered over the grain. In a frenzied rush, Vincent painted. A whirlwind of jabbing stabs and sweeping slaps. Through the morning. Through lunch. Into the afternoon, the sun drooping toward the horizon when he swatted the last swipe of paint onto the canvas. Then, he set down his palette, stepped into the field, and withdrew a gun from his trousers' pocket. Amidst the creature's cawing, Vincent scattered the flock of crows. With a bullet blast into his belly.

For some time he lay in the field, his blood leaking into the soil. Then he gathered his depleting strength, grabbed the painting, and crept back to his bedroom. He died three days later.

His last painting held vigil on an easel by his deathbed. It bore the wheatfield in which van Gogh shot himself. With the bullet that was killing him still lodged in his gut, Vincent took the time to reach over and touch up the crows in the painting. The bullet came from a gun owned by a farmer. The farmer used the gun in the very wheatfield Vincent painted. He used it to kill crows. On the final canvas he brushed, Vincent van Gogh painted his death site. And in the crows, he painted himself.

The anguish of his last days reverberates throughout this obviously symbolic and cryptically self-revealing final message. The hauntingly troubled sky is thrashed with chaotic strokes of midnight blue and slapped-about black, a foreboding storm poised on the horizon. In counterpoint to the ominous tempest, a vast pregnant field ripples with golden waves of ripening wheat. Three earthen paths slice the center and either side of the field, trails of green grass and dirt streaked with the red of blood and wine, each leading nowhere but towards its own abrupt ending. And crows are descending, black and forlorn, sweeping in to gather a few strays then sweeping out again to escape the thunderous threat. But one crow is off to itself. It flies away from the flock. It soars lonesomely to the side, lost within a once-swirling disc of light now tiredly being swallowed by the melancholic sky.

This painting is Vincent's final testament. More than the act of self-immolation itself, the painting is the final statement from a man who wrestled the demons of darkness to the bottom of the pit and stood toe to toe with the face of suffering. He left no other note. And his last words are lost to us, hidden in the riddle of two competing stories. They both have his brother Theo, who hurried from Paris to share his last hours, as their recipient. One story has Vincent gazing into his brother's eyes and whispering the despairingly capitulative words, "Saving me would be pointless . . . as the sadness will last forever." The other story has Vincent, flush with a final infusion of life, offering words apocalyptically hopeful with their reach for food and their promise of Eucharistic consummation, "I am hungry, Theo. Please, get me some bread." No, we do not know the words on his last breath. We only know the work from his last brush. Regarding the question, 'Is life worth living?,' the painting itself is Vincent's final word.

This piece has taken on the status of a sacred text for me, a scroll as reliable as that from Mt. Sinai in revealing the secret about the possibilities of life within the crucible of suffering.

But exactly what it reveals is difficult to discern. Take the perpetual counterpoint between storm and wheat. Which one is ultimately victorious? Is Vincent saying that, in the end, the wheat is always pelted by the fury of nature's storm, that all of our stabbing attempts to stake claim to life are inevitably consumed by the debilitating tempest of despair? Or is he saying that the wheat holds sway through the storm, that even in the midst of wave after wave of brutal pounding the roots of the stalks reach deep, the field's harvest flowers, and a regenerative life-force fuses with the soil's body and blood to birth grain from the ripening seed?

And what about the crow, the single soul separated from the rest of the flock? Is it flying *into* the impending storm, its flight the lonely and resigned escape of one whose grasp after an elusive peace proved futile and now sails helplessly into certain destruction? Or is it flying *out of* the storm, its flight the soaring and determined return of one once lost, now winging his way back to field and flock?

Or the paths, splayed in three crooked directions. Are they capricious crossroads at the intersection of life and death, each one but a separate path to the same dead end—finding oneself lost and isolated in the sea of stormy chaos? Or are all of the paths coming home, each crooked road gathered here at the center where earthen arms stretch wide to embrace every raging storm, every promise of life, every lonely flyer no matter how forlorn in the boundary-less expanse of the earth's bosom?

In essence, is his painting a melancholic warning, a poignant exhortation from one who has been mortally wounded in the journey, to avoid the life-sucking chaos of suffering's abyss? Or is it a hopeful affirmation, a burned-out thumbs-up from a battle weary scout pointing the way to a Promised Land on the other side of the valley?

That's what I had to know. From one who made the gutsy journey to one who's hugging the edge and terrified to let go. Vincent, in the murky muck of it all, did you discover an eternal pulse that ever pumps life and hope and peace into the depleted souls of the world? Or did you discover that the relentless barrage of tragedy and sorrow thrash with such savage fury, even the fiery force you once soared upon gets pummeled into the flicker that is snuffed out altogether? You were there, Vincent. What were you saying in your final painting? God knows the pilot light of my own life is barely sputtering. Please, Vincent. Tell me. Did your journey into suffering blind you, or did you see the face of God?

That was the question that burned within me. That was the question I planned to pose to the source itself with the passion of a religious seeker on pilgrimage. I wanted to stare into the actual painting and catch, through the strokes and colors that came from Vincent's very hand, my own glimpse of that life-giving pulse if it was truly there to be found. I wanted to meditate on the icon itself until the canvas slipped away and I was face to face with either the sacred, or the eternal emptiness. I went to the museum seeking nothing short of the first-hand epiphany Moses found from a burning bush in a desert.

I was not disappointed.

———

I drove to the museum from work. On a weekend morning, it's a quick shot from Paramount. Straight down Melrose then south on Fairfax. I knew that the van Gogh exhibit was a hot-ticket event. The Los Angeles County Museum of Art only had the Amsterdam paintings on loan for several months. Which is why I chose mid-morning on Mother's Day. Everybody would be at church. Or standing in line for the breakfast buffet at some trendy cafe. I wanted to view the painting with as few people as possible. The last thing I needed was a crowd of socialites from Westwood, silver-haired couples in Pierre Cardin and pearls, sipping chardonnay and having a tasteful orgasm over the 'bold interplay of form and theme.' That stuff makes me nauseous. Or want to take the GQ pair to the burn unit at the children's hospital to comment on the interplay of form and theme there. No, I wanted Vincent to myself.

The second I scampered around the corner I could see that it wasn't to be. The place looked like a revival had sprung up. Huge circus tents were pitched, colorful balloons bobbed in the wind, and people were camped out everywhere—huddled around plastic tables, clumped on blankets on the grass, swarming around the snack carts and souvenir stands proliferating the premises. All kinds of people too. College kids with knapsacks, children chasing balloons, retirees who could have just left their Winnebagos at the beach, Korean youth trying on t-shirts, black couples pondering programs, Mexican families waiting in line—the parents yelling at their kids in Spanish to stop playing on the ropes. A vast and vibrant congregation, as diverse as LA itself, packed the grounds in an expectant buzz, the whole lot of them, for today at least, choosing the flames of art over the pinprick of church for their brush against the starry skies of the spiritual mysteries. Vincent would have been pleased, I suppose. I was pissed.

I picked up my tickets at Will Call and, with some time to kill, scouted out a free end of park bench. Already frustrated, I was not about to make small talk with a tourist so I folded my arms and feigned to nod off. The next thing I knew the loudspeaker startled me awake announcing my tour time with the preface, "Last call." I couldn't believe it, I actually fell asleep. Now I was not only swarmed, I was late. And I was damned if I was going to miss this. I bolted into action and hustled through the crowd like I had a plane to catch. That's when I bumped into the boy. I tell you, I could have exploded. This was *not* how I envisioned the morning unfolding. Which is the problem with pilgrimages. They always play better in your imagination. No crowds, no noise, no hucksters hawking holy water at a buck a bottle. And you never know when a boy's going to pop up to stumble over. Or the face of God for that matter. Fortunately, this one at least, bounced back quick enough and I was on my way with the quest at hand.

I missed my final call, but the usher nodded knowingly at my security uniform. Figuring we were professional allies, he waved me into the building with a toss of his head and a conspiratorial smile. In the lobby I paid the extra five bucks to get a pair of headphones, more to protect my solitude than to be briefed on the exhibit. To be honest, I wasn't interested in the rest of the show. I had purity of heart, and I willed one thing. I wanted to see Vincent's final painting. And I hunted for it like a lover searching for his beloved in a crowded train station.

The exhibit was more teasing than impetuous. Its layout was labyrinthine, a twisting array of rooms and hallways meandering through sketches and studies and less significant oils spanning the artist's entire career. I started in an antechamber where a few early drawings hung on the walls and recessed alcoves. I glanced at the pieces then moved through a door in the corner. It opened into a huge reception hall bisected by a vast partition and sliced by dozens of panels randomly skewed throughout. An overwhelming number of paintings were scattered as scores of clumped people snaked their way up, down, and around the self-portraits and Japanese prints strewn throughout the room. I brushed by the milling bundles of people and scanned about in vain for both Vincent's final painting and the way out of the convoluted array of artwork. Finally, I found another corner doorway, this one funneling the flow of traffic from the entire auditorium through a single opening big enough for but two people at a time. A mass of bodies crowded the corner like cattle shoving through to a single trough on the other side. So much for solitude.

I joined the herd and jostled through. The door siphoned us into a transitional room not much broader than a hallway. The jam-packed bottleneck of people strained over and around each other to peek at pictures of sunflowers and irises. Still, no sign of my sought-after painting. Which was just as well. In that streaming horde I'd be lucky to stand still in front of it let alone study it a while. Straining on tiptoes, I saw the far end of the hallway. The exhibit made a sharp left. I ignored the paintings and shouldered my way through the crowd. At the end of the hallway, I turned and faced the final leg of the exhibit.

Several identical rooms, wide enough to disperse the crowd, reached one after another in a single line, each room connected to the next by an identical square archway. Looking through the row of them was like looking at a descending series of funhouse doorways each one smaller than the last, extending dizzyingly forward and converging at a distant disorienting center. And there, in that distant center, some five or six rooms away, framed perfectly by that room's remote square archway, van Gogh's final painting hung like an illuminated treasure tucked snugly at the deepest reach of a cave.

Even from the distance, I could feel the violent power of those black-blue skies boldly reverberating toward me through the tunnel of archways. Clearly the exhibitors knew the compelling power of this piece and staged it as the show's climax. A group of admirers surrounded it.

The heady realization that I was actually in line of sight with the very canvas that rested by Vincent's deathbed transformed my smoldering frustration into an adrenaline rush of anticipation. I took a moment to collect myself. Then, with heightened breath and a faint rumble in my empty stomach, I slowly meandered through the first of the interceding rooms. As I had yet to do all morning, I paused before the various paintings adorning the walls. I had not developed a sudden interest in these other pieces. I barely looked at them, really. I was savoring the moment. Vincent's 'Wheatfield with Crows' at the far but throbbing end of the series of rooms was drawing me toward it. And I rested in its tow, drifting through the interceding rooms like a tiny river twisting through swampy deltas but being pulled all the same by the inescapable lure of the depthless sea. Perhaps I refrained from a mad sprint to the end because I instinctively knew that something powerful was brewing. Perhaps my body knew, even before my mind, that I needed to secure my bearings before I risked being swept away by the awesome fury of that piece.

What I did not know was that 'Wheatfield with Crows' was not the force for which I should have been on guard.

I circled patiently through one room, then another, scanning the various works, pausing here, lingering there, then moving through the next boxed archway. Though I dawdled, the hair on my skin tingled and my heart beat in pounding syncopation with my breath. Each deliberate step brought me closer to Vincent's last painting. It radiated heat from the final room as sure as if it were an eternal inferno feeding off the never-ending but ever-evolving flock of followers transfixed before it. Though I felt its fieriness, I refused to steal even a glance. When I finally faced the purifying furnace of Vincent's final word, I wanted to leap headlong.

I entered the second to last room of the exhibit, a mere archway away from the scorching power of Vincent's final painting. From the center of this penultimate chamber I scanned the works to my right, peering through the heads and shoulders at some sketches from St. Remy. Then I turned to the left. A flock of eight or ten people gathered around a painting in the corner behind me. From over the tops of their torsos I could only glimpse a fraction of the piece. A head twisted sideways, draped in blue linen, was held in the drift of a blue-river sky paled with the light of an anemic sun. From the crooked head, a pair of eyes stared.

The eyes, angled down, were hollow. Past crying, past caring, they were tired. A drained stare of resigned vacancy. I was more intrigued than moved. What were the cold, crooked eyes looking at?

I took a step toward them. Like a veil tearing in two and slipping away, the crowd separating me from the painting parted. I found myself face to face before the Virgin Mary, and the broken body of Christ.

It was a Pietá.

I had no idea van Gogh painted a Pietá. I knew that other artists had. Michelangelo sculpted the classic version sitting at St. Peter's Cathedral in Rome. I saw it once. It was encased because some asshole beat it with a hammer but even under glass, its graceful stillness radiated. Mary, her young face gently bowed in depthless sorrow, holds her son after he's been lowered from the cross. Jesus' dead body is but a moment away from being buried in the tomb. And yet, it rests with rock-solid security in his mother's lap. In this moment, Mary reveals herself to be the Madonna, the archetype of maternal presence and compassion, the comforting model and mending comrade for all the mothers who mourn the crucified children of the world. Mary holds Jesus with a mother's pity. She also holds Jesus with *divine* pity. For in this moment, Mary reveals herself to be, the maternal face of God.

And here Vincent, this sad painter resting out a tempest in an insane asylum, took the time to paint his own Pietá.

But his was different. I could see that in an instant. It was different in two striking ways. First, the man held in Mary's arms was not Jesus. He had red hair, a rust-colored beard, that familiar tight-lipped scowl, and those classic triangulated cheekbones. It was the artist himself. Vincent painted his own face on the face of Jesus.

The beauty and genius struck me at once. What a poignant sight to behold. To see our own weathered face on the face of Christ, our own beaten body within the broken body of God, our own dead spirit poised to descend into the abysmal tomb held by the Mother of us all, the womb-like grace that holds this whole wounded world of ours. Yes, Vincent. You're right. It is your face on the face of Jesus.

But van Gogh's Pietá was different in a second way. He was not cradled by Mary's compassionate arms. Vincent was falling out of her lap. His body was twisted and bent as if a spasm shot through him, jerking him clean out of Mary's grasp. Or no. Worse. Mary's hands were agape, not enclosed. Her arms pushed outward, they did not draw inward. Mary was dropping him. No, she was *thrusting* him. She was actually *shoving* him into death's shadowy pit.

And now that I looked back, Mary's face was not grieving. It was not pained. It was not filled with sorrow. It was blank. A mask. The faint trace of a smirk at being done with this distasteful business held in check by the callous resignation from one who, quite frankly, did not care anymore, if she ever did in the first place.

And you could see it in her eyes. They weren't even looking at Vincent. They stared away in indifferent preoccupation. I mean, my God, her own son has been tortured and killed. Thugs have beaten him. Mobs have spit at him. Spears have split him open. And for the last few hours he's been hanging off a crossbeam by spikes in his hands and feet bleeding to death in the desert sun. And his own mother could not deign to give him her attention.

But more, her eyes were cold. Unfeeling. Pitiless. Remorseless. Her eyes had no tears. They had nothing in them. They were as dry as the pathetic eyes of Pontius Pilate himself. And I swear to God. I wanted to grab the closest stick, the nearest board, the length of post from the Goddamned cross if I could find it, and pound those eyes until they bled with tears. I mean, why the hell are you not crying? The bones you are holding are crushed. The flesh you disdain to touch is sliced open. The blood from the blood-let body in your lap is insufficient to even stain your virgin cloak. And now you're dumping the defiled corpse of your own son into his grave. Don't you care? Don't you see his pain? Don't you feel anything? Why in the middle of this Goddamned hellhole are you not crying?

Then it hit me. The absolute horror of it. Like a sucker punch to the groin. The Virgin Mary, the Holy Mother of God, is not crying because, quite simply, she does not give a flying fuck.

That's when it came. From the bottom of my being. From the bottom of the sea. Like a vast tidal wave, it receded into the deepest cavern of my soul, curled up in raging power, then crashed through the tiny cork of my resistance in an unstoppable explosion of hopeless defiance. At the top of my lungs, from the depth of my bowels, I leaned back and howled, "*NOOOOOOOOOOOO . . .*" I howled it and howled it in a single sustained pitch of revulsion for as long as I could hold on, until the scream died out and I doubled over, my stomach in contractions with gust after gust of disgorging bawling anguish.

I wept.

In waves of sobbing convulsions I wept. In gasping, full-belly wails I wept. Snot drained from my nose, tears dripped from my chin, moans gutted through my raw throat as I curled in on myself, cradled my arms around my stomach, and rocked on the floor in writhing, agonizing spasms. I wept. And I kept weeping. As embarrassed tourists skirted away. As awkward patrons placed tissues in my hand. As a security guard, unsure what to do, came to the cause of one of his own and backed people out of the room. And still I wept, catching my sobs in choking sniffles, then looking back up at Vincent's anti-Pietá and losing it all over again.

I didn't even know why I was weeping.

Maybe I wept for Vincent, that lonely, haunted man whose only asylum solace in this madhouse world was a God who could not care less.

Maybe I wept for myself, seeing my own face in the face of Vincent, seeing for myself God's dry eyes looking away from the imploring look in my own.

Or maybe I wept for all the faceless, suffering peoples of the world held in the single, all-inclusive face of Jesus, all the motherless children who have no one to weep for them, no one to hold them, no one to soothe their pain in the cradle of compassion.

Like I say, I did not know why I was weeping. I simply wept. And I wept until I knew. Then I wept some more. Because somehow I realized, I knew all along.

I wept for him.

Seven God-forsaken years I have kept my eyes closed. Now, in the middle of a county art museum, hoping for nothing short of a glimpse into the face of God, my eyes were opened. I saw a face all right. It just wasn't God's face. And it wasn't Vincent's, and it wasn't my own, and it sure as hell was not all of broken humanity's.

I saw your face, Carey. I saw your body being dropped into the darkness. I saw your haunted eyes pleading in vain for a tear.

That's why I wept.

And that's how I knew.

It's time to paint a Pietá.

It's time to brush some crows in a wheatfield.

It is time to stare into the face of evil and finally tell your story, Carey. All of it. Good news and bad.

Only this time, I'm keeping my eyes open.

Even if it kills me.

PART ONE

Ash Wednesday

1992

1

THE NIGHT CAREY WAS raced to the hospital, surrounded by medics in an ambulance, I was surrounded by medics as well, racing up a fire-road to rescue a client.

Carey was eleven years old, and his wrists were sliced so savagely it took a grown man on either side, each squeezing gauze with two-fisted grips, to slow the flow of his depleting blood. I was thirty-three. And if blood was depleting in the boy we sought, I was the one responsible.

Carey was sinking, descending ever deeper into the drift of despair. I was climbing, pushing through a midnight forest to find a mountain cliff.

We met at the bottom.

———

"The dragon warriors are following us."

I glanced in the rear-view mirror. The only one behind us was a housewife in a mini-van. I was tired of this, like an exhausted parent in the middle of the night pleading with a toddler to go back to bed. When would Hannibal's meds kick in and the dragon warriors disappear?

"There's nothing back there," I assured. "We left them all at Crossroads."

Hannibal, twisted around in the passenger seat, scanned the horizon with paranoiac intensity, darting about like prey certain that snipers had him scoped.

"No," he panted. "They're following us. I can feel 'em."

"Fine," I conceded. "They're following us. But we're in a truck. They'll never catch up."

"They've got wings," he rebutted. "They're faster than us." Realizing the full sweep of the danger, he spun around, grabbed the dash, and searched the skies through the windshield. I looked out my own window and sighed. I didn't have the energy for this.

"I'm telling you, Hannibal. There aren't any dragon warriors."

He knew better. "Oh, there are dragon warriors," he insisted. "And they're coming after us."

"Of course, they are," I muttered.

"We've got to get to a church. Only God can save us."

"Sure, Hannibal. Whatever you say."

———

Hannibal saw demons all day. To a teenage schizophrenic, they can be tenacious. They stalked the grounds, leered through the windows, then finally invaded our facility's living quarters. I gave him what I could. I tried talking him through the episode, distracting him with schoolwork, enticing him into shooting some hoops all while checking and rechecking his dosages. But to be honest, my efforts were half-hearted. The truth is, I was mired in my own madness.

For months, a squall of depression blustered through me. With disarming regularity, it followed a predictable weather pattern. When I woke, it lingered close, a wearying marine layer dampening the monotony of the day. Once I dragged my body out of bed, it receded a bit. An automatic pilot kicked in as I stepped through the motions of my routine—make the coffee, scan the paper, shave and shower, and off to work. Through the morning it kept its distance, though its lurking presence hovered like a fog bank on the horizon. As the day wore on, it floated back. By work's end, its sapping gray rolled in and wrapped me in its thickness. It was all I could do to crawl back home in my truck, haul my body through the door, and drop it onto my bed. Too tired to cook, too tired to read, too tired to turn on the God-forsaken light, I lay wasted like a body tossed at sea.

Lately however, the fog refused to recede. I drifted through the gray contours of my day in some netherworld between wakefulness and slumber. Sucking up the energy to attend to twelve boys in a group home was becoming near impossible. Especially on a day when our high-maintenance Hannibal was having another spell. I was actually relieved when I blurted out, "Isn't there anyplace safe from these infernal warriors?" and Hannibal blurted right back, "These are nasty. Only a church can protect us."

I hadn't been to a church since my son had died, hadn't been to Mass since I was thirteen. God and I had long since parted ways. But the demons of a church beat the dragons at Crossroads.

"Fine," I told Hannibal. "Let's go for a drive."

St. Mark's off Highway 12 was tucked at the base of the Sonoma Mountains. But for a few cars close to the sanctuary, the parking lot was vacant. Hannibal swept the skies for dragons until I pulled into a parking space. Before I could kill the ignition, he leapt from the truck and raced toward the open church doors, his hands waving to ward off an attack from behind. I cut the engine and hustled after him, hoping to catch him before he burst in on a prayer service. I didn't have to worry. When he reached the doors, he stopped short, turned to gauge the danger behind him, then eased his head through the doorway to determine the shelter's safety.

"What's the matter?" I asked as I caught up.

He shook his head still scoping it out. "No . . . This isn't right."

I looked in. Though it was too dark to see clearly, the place seemed empty. "Hannibal," I reminded, unable to come up with something else to appease him, "you said yourself a church would be safe."

"Not this church," he resolved. "They're in here too."

"Well, we're not looking for another one." I refused to church hop through Sonoma County to find one devoid of non-existent dragon warriors. "Come on. Let's just check it out."

Against his better judgment, he let me lead him by the arm into the narthex. Two steps in, he stopped dead and wiggled free from my grasp.

"What's wrong?" I asked. He didn't answer, too absorbed in scouring the foyer's shadows.

To prove the place was safe, I stepped toward the sanctuary and peeked in. It was disarmingly similar to the Catholic church of my childhood. I could almost make out my last time there. My mother's funeral Mass. Her picture on an easel, wrapped in white roses. Me at thirteen, staring dry-eyed from the pew. My sister to my right, clutching my hand. My father to my left, seething at the secrets that caused him to loathe the woman we gathered to celebrate; the white rose in his lap was so strangled with contempt he was oblivious to the thorn stabbing his thumb.

"It's not safe here." Hannibal exclaimed.

"It's just a church," I bemoaned. "There's nothing here."

Hannibal wasn't buying it. He twitched as if sure this was the dragon warriors' stronghold. "No. It isn't safe."

"Then where is?" I implored as I turned to him.

"I don't know," he said. "But not here."

"Look," I said, "I'm not hauling you all over creation to hide from dragons that don't exist." As if to refute me, Hannibal leapt around at some people who suddenly shadowed the door. They weren't demons, only churchgoers, early for a late afternoon Ash Wednesday service. I nodded at them politely—a couple of college students, a mother with a toddler son—then whispered at Hannibal hoping to avoid a scene. "Let's just sit down for a couple of minutes." I started back toward the sanctuary. "Come on," I coaxed. Hannibal trembled as if I mocked mortal danger. "It's fine," I said.

Then he saw them. Over my shoulder. Making their way right for us. Without concern for the volume of his voice, he shattered the cathedral quiet.

"*They're coming, Dr. T. Right behind you.*"

I turned. An altar boy, maybe ten years old, paced up the aisle with a long poled crucifix to be used in the opening processional.

"It's just an altar boy," I said. "They're getting ready for Mass."

Hannibal panicked like he was the one they were on their way to crucify. He lunged for my sleeve, tugged toward the door, then cowered as several more churchgoers slipped in for Mass. Not knowing which way to turn, he begged for help. "We've got to get out of here," he pleaded as strangers filed in from the front and the crucifix advanced from behind.

"Okay, Hannibal," I soothed, smiling weakly to reassure the crowd. "We're leaving."

"But *now*," he insisted. "It's not safe here."

"Okay," I said.

But now!" he yelled.

"I'm coming."

But before I could move, their leader attacked from the shadows. A hand reached out from behind Hannibal's back and touched him on the shoulder.

"Is everything okay?" asked a priest clad in vestments. Hannibal spun around, took one look at the cleric, and screamed,

"*AHHHHH!! Run Dr. T.!!*"

But he didn't wait for me. He bolted. Right out the door, through the trickle of churchgoers, and off across the parking lot. The startled priest, a saintly older man, peered at me. I must have looked like an intern in over his head.

"Don't worry," I said, my embarrassment compelling me to flee too. "He's having a reaction to his meds."

"Will he be okay?" the priest asked with genuine concern.

"He'll be fine," I assured, hustling toward the door. "But I need to attend to him." I glanced around at the gawking crowd. Then I turned and took off after Hannibal.

—————

With the determination of one fleeing the mouth of Hell, Hannibal made for the foothills. I yelled his name but I might as well have been one of the dragon warriors. Without slowing a beat, Hannibal tore across the lot, leapt a waist-high security gate, then disappeared up a fire-road within a wooded ravine. I chased as fast as I could but I was no match for a frenzied schizophrenic half my age. By the time I hit the fire-road, I was both winded and so far outpaced all sight and sound of him were gone. After scanning the mouth of the path in vain, I was certain he had followed the road. Castigating myself for taking him out in the first place, I dismissed the idea of getting help and jogged up the road to catch him.

The woods were savage and dense, the cliffs on either side too steep to be quickly scaled. I scrutinized them anyway, along with the brush and branches. He had to be up the road. And he couldn't have gotten far. I sustained my jog until the road's steady climb reduced me to a labored walk. I expected to glimpse him around every bend, each turn dangling another as I wound more deeply into the hills. I hiked, and called. But it was futile. I was a voice crying in the wilderness, without a soul listening. Where in the hell could he be?

As the afternoon sun slid toward the horizon, the forest shadows deepened. My fears deepened with them. I was scanning every crevice of the tree-soaked cliffs around me, but what if I somehow passed him? What if he had scurried up a hillside, or buried himself in a darkened hideaway? I toyed with going back, perhaps securing a search party. But it would be dark before we returned. He'd never last 'til morning. Jesus, where is he? Hoping to God I was still on his trail, and determined not to abandon him to a night in the wild, I kept hiking. And calling. And despairing at every turn that found him nowhere to be seen.

My panic spiked when I reached the top.

The fire-road finally crested over a ridge then sloped down the far side. From that vantage point, I had a view of the wilderness we were wandering in. In all directions, the foothills stretched for miles, the sinking sun casting the expanse in shadows. Spanning the horizon of canyons and hilltops, I spied an enormous rock to my left, maybe a quarter mile away, protruding up out of the hills some fifty or sixty feet. The eruptive iceberg of stone, its flat-top bathed in sunlight, taunted with cliffs so steep vegetation had yet to find a toehold to cling to. Halfway up the near face's craggy surface, oblivious to the sheer drop below him, Hannibal clambered with the swift dexterity of a rock climber out for a record. Foreboding snuffed any flicker of relief that flared at having found him. What in God's name was he doing? And how was I going to get him down?

"Hannibal!" I yelled. He was too far and too driven to hear me. I hurried through the grassy hillside, but by the time I reached the cliff he was scaling he had disappeared over the top. I started to climb a pull or two, then stared up at the tidal wave of rock wall. Terror unnerved me, a fanged beastly growl of dread that drove me down before the mammoth momentum thrust me in a backward plunge. It was suicide to scale that rock.

"*Hannibal!*" I bellowed. Only silence bellowed back. If my shout could scale that precipitous height, it failed to rouse the boy perched somewhere on top.

Desperate to find a better way up, I hiked toward the back of the rock. Halfway there, I could tell. Quite simply, the backside cliff was impossible to climb. Sheer and violent, it rose straight up from the drifting dunes of eroded shale heaped against the base. I imagined myself, midway up, clinging to splinters of slate as the chips flaked free and I fell away plunging into the rockslide of shards below. I was still pondering my plunge when Hannibal stepped into view. Gazing at some invisible phantom, he perched himself at the edge of the cliff and faced off with the sky, his head jerking from side to side, his arms poised like a ninja.

As if from a dream, I suddenly woke up. I saw the true danger. Not me falling off a cliff. Hannibal. Jumping. And in his state, he wouldn't even know he was doing it.

"*Hannibal!*" I screamed. I was out of earshot, or too superfluous to his fantasy to puncture it. I yelled again anyway. "*Don't move!*"

Adrenaline chasing my fear away, I raced around to the cliffside he scaled. Without thinking about the danger, nor how in the hell I'd ever get down, I climbed. I clawed after every nub of a handle and knob of a toehold and scampered up the craggy face hoping to God that Hannibal stayed where he was. When I dragged myself over the top, I had to crouch at the vertigo. Sheer drops fell from all sides as I clutched a plateau barely large enough to support a picnic. Ten steps away, still perched on the far cliff, Hannibal held off his nemesis. His ninja stance stood dead ahead while his head jerked between the army of warriors that pinned him from both sides and their chieftain mounted for attack in front of him.

"Hannibal." I spoke softly not to startle him. He didn't respond. I crouched a step closer.

"Hannibal!"

He bolted around to check his back then bolted back to contain the chieftain.

"It's okay," I said. "It's me. Dr. T."

I inched closer. He checked his back again then flinched forward more furiously. The army was approaching from all sides. I was but their ambush. I held my position, my mind reeling for a way to talk him back from the cliff.

"Hannibal," I said. "I see them. There's too many to take alone." My words penetrated his world. His flinch from side to side grew frantic. The army was huge. "I've got a plan." I risked a step forward. He jolted around in terror. I stepped back. Any closer would drive him to jump.

"We can take them together," I said. "I have an idea. Step back from the cliff and I'll tell you." He wasn't sure if I was friend or foe and he wasn't about to relinquish position. He faced the chieftain down and held the encroaching troops in check.

"Hannibal," I tried again. "I know who they are. They don't mean you any harm. They think you're armed, and you want to hurt them." He threatened them with his hands to confirm that he was lethal. At least my words were registering. "Your power scares them, Hannibal. They don't want to attack. They just want to know that you won't hurt them." He jerked from side to side taking it in, a spin that hadn't occurred to him.

"They're your friends," I urged. "They only want to help you. I can prove it. Just slowly drop your hands. You'll see. They won't charge. They just want to know you won't hurt them." He glanced at both flanks then studied the chieftain to ascertain his colors.

"Really, Hannibal. Try it. Real slow. Just bring your arms to your sides." Hannibal glanced around again, then cautiously gave it a try. One degree at a time, confirming that they were staying put through every step of the way, he lowered his hands. Nothing happened. The dragon warriors stayed where they were.

"Excellent," I encouraged. "See. They're not attacking. They're just watching. They're not here to hurt you." He kept studying them to confirm their goodwill. "Now let them know that you're not here to hurt them. Step back. Just a step. You'll see. They won't attack." Carefully, he grabbed the buoy I threw him. He took a step back.

"See," I said, "they're not attacking. Just keep coming back." He took another step, and another, then stopped, and slowly turned around.

He looked straight at me. We had contact. A shade of coherence dimmed the fever in his eyes. He eased toward me, each step a step back into sanity. I held his gaze as if my eyes were the lifeline reeling him back to reality. He held mine as if ready to be so reeled. He took another step. Then I saw it. His eyes were not coherent. They were resolved. He had a plan of his own. And I was merely the ruse.

"No, Hannibal," I begged. "They're not here to hurt you."

But the madness in his eyes knew better. He gave a slight nod like our ploy had worked. Then before I could lunge and hold him back, his face twisted into a warring scowl and, with the battle-cry shriek of a banshee, he turned once more, sprinted full gallop, and leapt right off the cliff. His arms flailed; his feet kicked; he crested in attack; then he dropped completely out of view. I dashed to the edge and watched as he landed in the drifts of shale some fifty feet below then tumbled end over end like a cascading skier in an avalanching snowbank before sliding to an unconscious stop in an ominous cloud of dust.

All my previous vertigo vanished. I scurried back across the plateau and scrambled down the cliff face fearing not my own falling but of finding Hannibal no longer alive. Once down, I raced around the backside and came upon him nestled in the drift. Though covered with dust and surface abrasions, he breathed and his pulse, though fast, was steady.

I was afraid to move him. But for the first time that day, I was not afraid to see him. His eyes closed, his head cradled in shards of rock, he looked as calm as a child sleeping in its mother's lap. All he wanted was rest from his demons. And the attentive care of those who tamed them.

Seeing the scratches on that beaten face, I swore to Hannibal, myself, and any God still listening.

I'm getting this boy to safety.

Then I'm getting some help for myself.

———

Hannibal was not the only one fighting off demons that night. Down in the valley, an eleven year-old boy was having his wrists prepped for surgery. Peering through the masked faces and fluorescent glare, his eyes were fixed on a random crack in the ceiling.

Hannibal battled under the guise of sleep. Carey did not. In fact, Carey refused to close his eyes at all. In fierce, defiant silence, he fought like a devil to keep those eyes open.

He fought as if his life depended upon it.

Later, I saw the truth.

It did.

2

"*Dare you defy me . . . ?*" The storyteller cackled like an evil witch, each staccato syllable enunciated with venomous precision. "*Choose now, you impudent urchin. **Which bowl of porridge will you eat?**"

As the elevator doors parted, I found myself in the middle of a story. The waiting room was packed. Children, parents, and siblings were poised on the floor and Naugahyde sofas, the arms of couches and ends of tables, on window ledges and heating units and leaning against the muraled walls. Even the hospital staff paused from the day's labor. Nurses, orderlies, a doctor or two, a uniformed custodian anchored to a mop handle were clustered in the corridor and peeking over counters. Some of them smiled in amusement; others widened their eyes in suspense. To a person, however, they were all held captive— by the gesticulating wizard telling a tale up front.

I had not seen Woody for nearly two years. And given the mess I had become, I had second thoughts about popping in then. I was scared. Pit in the belly scared. My stomach festered the whole drive over and swelled into an eruptive fury as the elevator rose toward his ward. But as the doors opened and he appeared in a larger than life flurry, I was washed with a wave of affection. I was home.

Like a ship navigating a marina, I spied a space in the hallway to slip in unnoticed. I tacked through the crowd and tied up against a wall. Woody was full sail in the open waters of the story. Something about choosing between bowls of porridge, one leading to everlasting sleep, the other promising the power to face a hideous witch. He was magic. He could unfold a story like a fine chef unveiling courses in a banquet. He whet your appetite with a dramatic opening, teased your palate with suspenseful pacing, tantalized your taste buds with tense pauses, then made you cry out loud with the *pièce de resistance*, a rushing climax to cap the satiating feast.

I settled in and watched him work. I could not help but admire him. He was the object of my secret paternal crush. I wished he was my father.

I took second best.: he was my mentor.

Dr. Woodrow Wainwright Woodruff, Woody to all who knew him, was the chief resident and supervising doctor at the university hospital where I was trained. For four years, at once grueling and exhilarating, he was my on-site professor, my clinical supervisor, my unfailing patron, and my unapologetic, teen-age idol icon of all a child psychologist is supposed to be.

Woody defied all medical caricatures. His wrinkled doctor's smock draped his faded blue jeans and Hawaiian shirts. His jet-black mane and Mark Twain mustache flared from his head with the wildness of Einstein's hair on the wrong end of a windstorm. And he bounced about amongst the kids with such elfish abandon and pixie curiosity it was hard to tell adult from child. He looked more suited for a Marx Brothers movie than a hospital ward for disturbed children. Groucho with a stethoscope. Crossed with Columbo in a lab coat.

Woody's extra-curricular pursuits were equally antithetical. He was at once a devotee of Dostoevsky novels and a fanatic for Pink Panther movies, savoring *Brothers Karamazov* every winter break and playing Peter Sellers videos whenever he wrote reports. He loved poker but was addicted to baseball, limiting a fix for the former every Friday afternoon with custodians in the cafeteria, while still humping doubles into triples each summer in the Orinda slow-pitch softball league. He made a bandanna-clad pilgrimage to a Grateful Dead concert every year, and played trombone in the Fourth of July parade with the Berkeley Band for Brotherhood. He grew hemp but never smoked it; brewed beer but never drank it; rode Harleys but never raced them; and was both a pilot and a parachutist, but never at the same time. Yet.

And through it all, like the ever-present bass note that accompanies the lines of melody, Woody was a storyteller. Funny stories, scary stories, true stories, outlandish stories, stories with animals, stories with people, stories of creatures with body parts of each. But always, his stories were captivating. And always, his stories were healing.

Literally. Woody pioneered a therapy centered around story. He argued that children, like us all, live by stories. To be human is to be an actor within a narrative. Too often however, people compose life stories that are self-defeating, or worse, self-destructive. These need to be exposed and transformed into stories that nurture hope and personal power. The central therapeutic task for becoming whole, the central spiritual task for becoming human for that matter, is to learn how to narrate our lives with stories that give rise to life's fullness.

Healing stories was his passion. And he was a master.

I remember a young Pakistani girl, eight or nine years old, brought to us after she simply shut down at school. Tahira was her name, a spindly stick figure of a child with the wide dark eyes of the traumatized. She barely spoke, and when she did, she refused to open her mouth. Her words whispered surrealistically through the paper-thin slit between her unmoving lips. She was a girl with a secret. And the terror to keep it quiet.

True to his technique, Woody invited her to tell a story. She declined. After a few days of hearing his and the other kids' however, she wrote one. A village was terrorized by a monster hidden in the deepest part of a cave in the deepest part of the jungle. A young girl innocently wandered into the cave. Inside, something unspeakable happened. When she returned, she couldn't talk. The monster wrapped an invisible bandage around her mouth and vowed to kill her if she ever removed it. The girl never did. For the rest of her life, she remained mute.

Woody told Tahira a story in return, transforming her immobilized character into a heroine with power. A girl rendered mute by a monster in a cave recovers her voice, then spearheads an elaborate plot to forge through the jungle, stalk the monster, and restore the beast to penitent civility. The story kindled something in Tahira. She fused it with her own, then allowed Woody to share it at the celebrated storytelling session he held each afternoon in the waiting-room lounge. The story kindled something in the rest of the kids as well. They converted it into a play. The youngsters, now an acting troupe, designed scenery, created props, crafted costumes, and adapted dialogue for the various characters.

Energy swelled throughout the building. Woody's kids were staging a production. The waiting room was too small for the anticipated crowd, so the children converted the cafeteria into a makeshift theater, then sold out two benefit performances for the hospital staff, patients from various wards, the children from the daycare program, and a boatload of beaming family members. And who was at the center of it all, the sustaining passion and star performer? Tahira. The once-mute Tahira now cast in the lead role as the wounded child who discovers a warrior's courage within and a voice of thunder without.

It was incredible. To see that young girl hitting her notes through two standing-ovation performances was to know the power of story. From out of nowhere, Tahira discovered an instinctive stage presence that would have made Meryl Streep proud. She opened the play cowering in intimidated terror, barely risking a peek from behind the layers of scarves wrapping her face. With crowd-hushing trepidation, she opened a slim space within her mask and drank from the stirring waters of the wise woman's well. She held the moment as the drink washed through the winding canals of her body. Every person in the audience held their breath as she slowly unwrapped the swirl of scarves. Cautious in her fresh exposure, she glanced from face to face.

Then the waters took hold. Her tiny frame rose full stature. A tigerish determination gripped her face. She flung the scarves aside, faced down the fear in each skeptical villager, and with all the ferocity of a field marshal emboldening the troops for battle, she took charge of the pint-sized battalion. By the time her General Patton speech reached its climax, the healing waters bubbling within her rushed into a roaring stream for justice.

"No! We're not going to let some measly monster beat us." (Her upraised fists pounded the air.)

"*We are going into that jungle . . .*" (She gathered in every last skeptic.)

"**We are marching into that cave . . .**" (She held a dramatic pause.)

"AND WE ARE DEFEATING THAT FEROCIOUS MONSTER!"

A battle cry of conviction erupted; the villagers became freedom fighters; their fear transformed, they would follow their leader into the very cave of evil. I tell you, that battle cry reverberated through every heart poised on a plastic chair in that cafeteria. We were *all* prepared to follow that leader, *all* prepared to storm the cave, *all* inspired to tame the monsters that threatened our children's spirit. For we knew. We could feel it in the place where our own courage is kindled. Tahira was no longer acting a story. She became the story for real. The tiniest tot in the lot transfigured into a conquering captain. Her gag *had* torn free. A voice of thunder *did* crackle through her. A warrior did *indeed* rage before us. And no secret-bearing, voice-destroying abuser of a beast would ever be safe again.

And leaning against the coke machine in the shadows in the back of the room, smiling a knowing smile as if sensing all along Tahira's true power, was Woody. The storyteller. Receding into the background. Letting the story heal on its own.

Woody was brilliant. His stories transformed lives. I give him that.

Too bad the story he gave me proved to be so destructive.

———

With the porridge story over and the witch subdued, the crowd dispersed, their faces glowing as if the cells in their souls had been restored by a shot of spiritual penicillin. A gaggle of children flocked around Woody, pumping him with follow-up questions like reporters mobbing a presidential candidate. Woody, ever the sidestepping politician, puzzled over each query then, stumped but curious, turned the question back to the child. "I don't know. Why do *you* think the witch was so mean?"

I walked over and sat in a chair about a stone's toss from Woody crouching before his entourage. He made no indication that he noticed me, his attention taken over by the kids lit up like fireflies in his circle.

Being that close to him sent my stomach into a spastic tailspin. Two years and I hadn't stopped by once, hadn't taken the time to write a short note, couldn't be bothered to leave a greeting on his voicemail. And now I wander back, the one-time bonus baby up all night after nearly costing a patient's life. What was I thinking? I should have gotten up and left.

A nurse pulled the last of the children away and Woody stood up. Without hesitation, he turned his head toward me and smiled.

"Well, look at what the wind blew in." He shuffled over and sat in the chair cornering mine. "It's good to see you, Tony." He passed no judgment on my appearance, acting as naturally as if I had popped in to borrow a book after class. That was all the warmth it took to disarm me.

I wanted to say something but I couldn't. I couldn't even smile my pleasure at seeing him again. It was all I could do to keep the knot in my chest in check. God, I wanted to crawl up into his grandfatherly lap and sob my eyes out. But I wasn't about to. No way.

I looked at the floor and hardened myself to keep from breaking down. When I could finally risk words, I whispered through a granite hold on composure. My mouth barely moved.

"Woody. I need your help."

For several heartbeats, his moist eyes held me. Then he leaned over, squeezed my shoulder, and nudged his head toward more confidential quarters.

"Follow me," he said.

As in everything else, I did.

———

His body wrapped in but a white sheet, Carey slept in an elevated hospital bed. Though it was late morning, the room was dark, the sun veiled by the drawn curtains. A skeletal stand stood beside the bed. The plastic bag dripped plasma through tubes into his veins.

A concealing stillness shrouded everything about him. His blank face masked his nightmarish slumber. His mouth remained gently shut. His chest scarcely rose with each soundless breath. Only one thing interrupted his napping-child repose. His finger.

Almost imperceptively, the middle finger of Carey's right hand twitched. Robotically, the finger curled in, cocked itself on the inside of his thumb, then gently flicked outward.

Every few seconds. Curl, cock, flick. Like the steady tracking signal of a downed aircraft's black box. Curl, cock, flick.

The nurse on suicide watch got up, routinely checked the plasma level, and studied his wounds. The underbelly of his wrists exposed stained bandages from the bend in his elbow to the base of his hands. 'What could possibly make a boy do such a thing to himself?' she pondered. Unable to discern an answer, she stretched the sheet to his chin, grabbed the tray of uneaten breakfast, and momentarily left.

As the door closed behind her, the silent shadows wrapped the boy once more.

The room was still.

Except for the finger.

Curl, cock, flick, the homing device called.

Curl, cock, flick.

3

NAVIGATING THE CHILDREN'S WARD was like negotiating a labyrinth. The ward was hexagonal, six self-contained units forming a perimeter around a central locked cell for the suicidal. Each unit circled its own nursing station and harbored an array of hospital rooms and examination cubicles. Walking through the honeycombed hallways, I had time to pull myself back together. Hell, I pulled myself back through the years. I followed Woody to a room that at one time was more home for me than my own bed.

Woody's office was the educational and administrative nerve-center that coordinated all the treatment programs for the children and all the training procedures for the interns. Those four walls housed more action than many entire campuses. Passing through its door, I could hear the echoes of erudite lectures, rousing pep talks, intimate counseling sessions, confrontive conferences, spirited symposia, and light-hearted jam sessions—of both the colloquial and musical varieties—still reverberating off the walls. I longed to be a grad student again, with nothing more than a philosophical insight to bounce off my professor.

I sat in a sofa that was more suited for a mountain cabin than a doctor's office. Apparently, a colloquy had recently taken place. Psychiatric journals were scattered about the coffee table, as were several partially-filled styrofoam cups, splayed napkins collecting the wrinkled remnants of sweetener packages, an opened book of Japanese folktales, and a second-hand, paperback copy of *Healing Stories: Narrative Therapeutic Interventions with Traumatized Children*. Author: Dr. Woodrow W. Woodruff.

I picked up the scholarly text that definitively described Woody's groundbreaking approach to narrative therapy. With my thumb, I pulled the curling cover closed and stared at the block letters hovering over a picture of a grandmother reading to a child in her lap. I always liked the double entendre of the title but the jacket design was sappier than a Norman Rockwell painting. I turned grandma over and glimpsed the bright yellow sticker on the spine. The black letters spelled 'USED.' A grad student's cheap acquisition from the university bookstore.

Woody took his customary position in the recliner, feet firm on the floor, arms resting on the sides, ready to receive whatever might come.

"You're not exactly getting rich off these used copies are you?" I jockeyed more than joked. I wasn't ready to bare my soul quite yet. Wasn't sure I could at all.

Woody chuckled in stride. "You know, I think I only sold one copy of that book. It just recycles through different students' hands."

"Yeah, I recognize the underlining. I dumped this off to a freshman when I left."
God, I loved the way Woody and I could play off each other.

"Well, not to worry," he came back. "I'm soon to be an international author. A clini-
cian in Frankfurt is translating it into German."

"That's quite a compliment."

"Yeah," he said with amused perspective. "I told my Dad about it. He looked at me
and said, 'So your book's in German now. What *I* want to know is . . . when's it gonna be
translated into *English*.' I said, 'Pop, just read the stories, they're not technical.' And he
says, like I've offended him, 'I spend a small fortune on a Harvard education so I can read
my son's *stories*? Oy!'"

Smiling, I set the book down. Uneasy with the conversational ball back in my court,
I stalled by glancing across his office. As usual, a cyclone of medical charts and legal
pads overwhelmed his desk. They seemed strewn at random but they bore a logic hidden
from mere mortal eyes. Within the mess, Woody could locate anything he needed in an
instant.

I noticed the picture frame placed prominently next to the window. Three large panels
displayed a vintage photo of his wife in the center and elegant pictures of his two daughters
in evening gowns on either side. Several wallet-sized pictures were tucked into various
corners on each of the panels. I couldn't make out the smaller photos, but a couple of them
I could see by memory. One bore an ecstatic college-aged girl, in a floral skirt and white
linen top, being pummeled by a Hawaiian waterfall, her slick wet blouse transparent to the
enticing bikini top pressed against it. The other bore a younger version of the same girl,
all of five years old, in a pilot's cap and pig tails, two fists to the steering stick in the open
cockpit of a Cessna, her schoolgirl grin and frolicsome eyes a free-spirited promise of the
life-guzzling woman to come. How many times I wished she guzzled me. She was the first
woman to awaken my libido after several years divorced from Jen.

"How's Deirdre?" I asked, daring to crack a container sealed for some time.

"Deirdre?" Woody smiled with pure paternal pride. "Deirdre's excelling at being
Deirdre."

"She's painting then? Or did she pursue that newscaster gig?" It was an amazing story
really. Deirdre was sitting in a Starbuck's when a complete stranger came up and asked
her if she had ever considered television reporting. Turned out he was a producer for the
local NBC affiliate and thought she had the presence for being on screen. There are people
busting their butts and bank accounts whose idea of a big break would be a head shot as
far as the desktop pile this guy's going to toss in the trash, and here's Deirdre, doodling
on a napkin and sipping espresso, and he wants to make her the next Barbara Walters.
That's Deirdre. To see her was to be smitten by her glow. And want to be as close to it as
possible.

"No, no," Woody snickered. "She's painting. She had fun with the screen tests, but it
wasn't her. No, she moved to Half Moon Bay and lives with three other artists. All week
long they paint themselves silly. Then on weekends, they fill their vans and travel to every
art show, craft fair, and folk festival they can find. Monterey, Mendocino, Grass Valley. If
two kids set up a lemonade stand in Yreka they'd drive through the night to show their

work right next to the box of Dixie cups. She's poor, underfed, and overworked. But she's following the star that makes her shine."

"Sounds like Deirdre. A lot more than schlepping drinks for Tom Brokaw." I imagined her—hair disheveled, paint splotched around her nose, eyes narrowed as she dabbed at the canvas in front of her. Then I popped out with one of my secrets before I could think to stop it. "You know, I once had a big-time crush on her."

Woody smiled slyly. "I know," he confessed. Then he added his own secret. "She liked you, too. She said you had the eyes a painter lives for—soulful, with belly laughter hidden behind unshed tears. She always wanted to paint them." He sighed. "You know, she always wondered why you never asked her out."

I had to shake my head at that. I used to drive reports over to Woody's house just so I could run into her. And when I did, I was so tongue-tied I acted like an attaché on an emergency errand to see the general. Not that it would have mattered. I had a crush on her. But Jen was always the one.

"You could have said something," I replied mostly to keep the volley alive.

"Nah, it was none of my business," he dismissed.

"What?" I put on. "Didn't want me for a son-in-law?"

He searched me to see if my throw-away remark masked something serious. It didn't. Not really. I knew of Woody's respect for me. And his affection. We all did. I was the favored apprentice, the one he recommended to Crossroads, the one he sent off choking back a tear when he told me how proud of me he was. God, I lived off that for months. But still, that glow had long since dimmed. And a familiar chill returned. What father would ever warm at my homecoming? Let alone my coming home with his daughter?

Woody saw enough. "The truth is," he revealed, "I didn't say anything because I wanted it too much." I rolled my eyes at that one. "No, really," he said. "You know Katy and Deirdre. They're as different as a banker from a beatnik, and I love them both, don't get me wrong. But neither one of them cares about their ol' man's work more than a 'How's things at the hospital, Dad?' over Thanksgiving dinner. There's a large part of me that would love to have a son-in-law to take over the family business—someone living in my backyard, loving my daughter, raising my grandkids, and stopping by to talk shop while I'm rocking on the back porch. It's patriarchal bullshit, I know. But it's pretty sweet bullshit."

"I don't know," I toyed. "Sounds pretty good to me."

"No," he nixed in no uncertain terms. "You can't turn people into pawns in your own dream."

"What if the person's willing?"

He shook his head. "It's the difference between killing their spirit or setting it free. You know that. It's the difference between life and death."

I didn't know it well enough. "I guess there's no coming back as a hired hand then," I said, edging toward the reason I came.

He studied me like he'd seen this before—a recent grad wanting back in after a bad spell in the field. "Things not going well at Crossroads?" he asked.

I winced and looked at the ground. "I just wonder if the kids might be better off with somebody else."

He waited for more. When it didn't come, he redirected. "You know how eagles teach their young to fly?" I shrugged at the non sequitur. "The mother grabs the eaglet with her claws and carries it over a canyon precipice. Then she drops it. The eaglet plummets to the ground, thrashing its wings wildly. Either the wings catch hold and take flight, or just before the eaglet hits the ground, the mother sweeps down and catches it. Only to fly back into the sky and drop the eaglet again. Eventually, the wings take hold, and the eaglet flies. It's the most terrifying thing in the world, I suppose. And that mother must wish to hell she could stop the eaglet midway in its fall. But the only way the eaglet will fly is to hold its wings steady as it falls through the air."

The transparent parable was apropos. I was plummeting. Only I was too tired to hold out a wing as I sped toward the ground.

"What's going on, Tony?" he asked.

I answered, my head still hanging. "I'm falling, Woody. And the current's not taking hold."

"How so?"

I sighed and looked around the room where I once commanded the skies as Woody's right-hand man. "I've lost it. I just don't give a damn anymore. And I don't know how it happened. I mean, you know me. I gave everything to healing kids. Every time I saw one in pain it did something to me. I couldn't rest until I helped them—no matter how many journals I had to read or interventions I had to come up with. I fought for them. Nobody cared like I did. Nobody."

Like a sputtering flame in a dying fire, the memory of my zeal stirred a flicker of my former passion. But the hearth was too cold. And the memory of zeal was insufficient to kindle coals that close to death. As fast as it flared, it faded again.

"Now I look at them and I just see another screwed-up kid taking the place of the last one. It's like a shooting gallery at a carnival—one goes down and another pops up. Only I've got nothing left to shoot anymore. I'm dialing it in, Woody. I scribble out my treatment plans, fake my way through a story, wing it through groups, then call it a day. I've become their worst nightmare. Another callous asshole who doesn't give a damn. I hate myself for it, but it's the truth. I just don't care anymore."

I avoided his eyes as if his stare would burn me. To my surprise, he did not scold me. Nor did he come over and comfort me. He just took it in. Or let it sit. Which is its own consolation, I guess. But I still couldn't face him when I begged for relief.

"It's to the point where I can hardly get out of bed anymore. I'm depressed, Woody. And I need some help. Prozac, Haldol, whatever you think. Just something to take the edge off, and get me back to where I was."

That was my last stab. I was ready for meds. And Woody was the guy who could get them. All he had to do was dial the hospital pharmacy. Or pick up a pen and fill out a prescription. That was all.

But he didn't do it.

When he spoke, he was the epitome of paternal tenderness. "I always knew that one day you'd be a great therapist. And you're well on your way."

"C'mon, Woody," I said. "I don't need a pep talk. I'm desperate. I'm over the edge."

"I know it's hard, Tony. It's the hardest thing in the world. But you're right where you need to be. You don't need something to take the edge off. And you surely don't need to get back to where you were. The edge is the way."

I shook my head, wishing it didn't have to come to this. Then I looked him straight in the eyes like a prosecutor springing a surprise eyewitness. "The edge is the way, you say? I almost killed a kid yesterday, Woody."

My revelation hit. Concern washed over his face. "What happened?"

"A boy in my care jumped off a cliff. I was so zoned out I didn't take him seriously until he ran away, climbed a cliff, and jumped off. That's the edge we're talking about."

Woody was still concerned. "Is he okay?"

"Thank God he hit a drift of shale that softened the fall. He just got scraped up pretty bad." I fast-forwarded it all in my mind—me racing down the fire-road and hailing the priest for a phone, speeding back up with the paramedics and strapping Hannibal to a trauma board, rushing him to the emergency room then shuttling him to a psychiatric facility. I didn't believe he was really okay until he was stabilized in the hours before dawn. "He'll be fine," I continued. "But that's not the point. He just as easily could've died."

Satisfied about Hannibal, Woody tended to me. "So what were you feeling—when you were with him before he ran away?"

"That's just it. I wasn't feeling anything. I was exhausted. It was all I could do to crawl into work let alone deal with him all day."

"You know, it's no accident that you've been so tired. Your body's trying to tell you something."

This was exactly what I was afraid I would get. "Woody, please," I groaned. "Don't start in with mental illness being the soul's grasp for healing." I dismissed his book on the table with a backhand to the air. "I know the drill. 'Don't fight the disease, befriend it.' 'All symptoms tell a story—listen to their logic and let it unfold.' Or my personal favorite, 'Holding the wound precedes healing the wound.'" I rattled off his maxims like a disgusted adolescent. "It's bullshit, Woody. I'm sorry. But I'm depressed. And the slogans don't mean a thing."

Anyone else would have checked my insolence. But anyone else was not Woody. He always wanted us to be completely candid about our feelings. Demanded it really. And he always did what he was doing right then. He sat there, unruffled, and waited for the storm to pass.

"It's not a textbook anymore," I said more calmly. "Or some case study. It's me. I'm depressed. And I just want it to go away."

"Tony." He was all understanding. The bastard. "The most difficult journey in life is facing our own shit."

"Yeah," I countered. "The whole 'Physician, heal thyself' thing."

"No," he smiled tentatively. "Physician, *hold* thyself. Holding the shit precedes healing the shit."

I snorted at that one. A new Woodyism to add to the list. But I was still in the dark. "And what does that mean exactly? In real life."

"That's what depression is. It's digging a ditch in your psyche where we stuff all the *shit* that slides out our backside. All the feelings we can't accept—our rages, our attractions, our wounds, whatever. And they simmer and stew until they sap all the energy out of us. Depression is the body's way of saying, 'Stop stuffing it all down. It's time to deal with it.'"

"I'm so depressed I can hardly get out of bed and you're telling me that's a good thing? My shit's wanting some attention? I don't buy it. I want my life back. I don't want to wallow around in that muck."

"I know," he conceded, "it sounds crazy. But I've been there too. And it's the only way home I know."

I didn't know anything at that point. Except the knowing look in his eye. And the desperation of having tried everything else I could think of.

"And what way is that, Woody?"

"It's the way of stories. The stories we guide our lives by."

"Okay. You got me. What stories are you talking about?"

"You know the routine. If your depression could speak, what story would it tell?"

"That's easy. 'Boy Wonder crashes and burns. News at Eleven.'"

"That's the story your *ego* is telling, not your depression. Relax a minute. Take a deep breath. If you could create an image, what would your depression look like?"

I closed my eyes and tried to picture this suffocating feeling. What did it look like? It was dark is what it was. A cold, slimy cave of darkness.

No. It was more. Something lingered in the darkness. Something that wanted to slither around me like a snake, squeeze all the life blood out of me, then sink with me into some netherworld where my corpse would be swallowed in an eternal swamp of sludge.

"Okay. Yeah. It's got a story to tell." I had him now. "It's saying, 'Come here, pretty boy. Come down into our depths so we can crucify your ass and bury you forever.' That's its story. That's why any person with a pittance of sanity would race to the Prozac Express and ride the hell out of there. Because it's true. It means business. It will destroy me then deposit my body someplace where the light of day is a Goddamned joke."

I stared him right in the face. I knew my truth, too. And I dared him to tell me my story was wrong.

He stared right back. Then slowly, he nodded his head. "Depression is one nasty bastard."

"I'm right, you're saying."

"Yes. You are."

"That's the story of my depression."

"It rings true to me."

"Then you agree."

"Yes."

"That it's evil."

"Yes."

"And dangerous."

"Absolutely."

"And it wants to kill me."

A pause. "Yes. It does."

"And I should get some meds and run like hell."

"No."

I looked at him with total exasperation.

"Then what, Woody?"

"You don't need drugs, Tony." He got up and reached for a book from his shelf. "What you need is a good Greek myth."

"*Jesus, Woody!*" I screamed. "I've *got* a story. Get the hell out of Dodge. Anything else is psychotic."

"There is another story, Tony. I'm not being flippant. Not by a long shot. There *is* another story to live by."

"I DON'T WANT ANOTHER STORY!" I was enraged. "Don't you see? It's ripping me apart. There's like . . . a demon inside of me. It lies in the darkness and waits to erupt right through me. Rage, Woody. Raw fucking rage. I swear to God, I could kill somebody. Or myself. I can't take it anymore. Damn it! I need some help." I reeled myself in before someone called for a straight jacket. "This isn't a game, Woody. Something really bad is inside of me. I don't see how a stupid story's going to help me deal with it."

He took me in, measured my seriousness, and matched it with his own. "The story will tell you that you're not alone. Others have gone before you. And yes, they're going to say that it's as scary as hell itself, that it's a place of beasts and ghosts, of torments and tyrants. But they're also going to tell you, when you're lost at sea, and Poseidon's got you squalled in a tempest of Biblical proportions, and you want to get home, the only way is through the Underworld. The demons. The darkness. They really are the way home."

"Why? Why do you have to go through the Underworld to get home?"

"I don't know why. I only know that it's the way."

"To face my depression. To face the shit I'm stuffing into my depression."

"To trust what your body's telling you. Something wants you to stop fighting the sinking sand. I don't know what's down there. I don't know what ghosts you'll meet or what demons you'll face. But one thing I do know. And of that I'm certain. It's the path you're being invited to take. This story will show you the way."

I let the echo of Woody's truth resonate with a deep truth within me. I knew he was right. But I knew something else as well. And it scared me into absolute seriousness.

"Woody." I held his eyes like I never held them before. "It's evil down there. There really is such a thing as pure, spirit-killing evil."

"Yes, Tony. I know."

"And what do you do when you come face to face with *that*?" I hoped to God he could answer me.

"I don't know. I only know that the truth is in the story."

"And what does the story say, Woody? What does the story say?"

"The story says . . ."

Yes, Woody, what does the story say?

"It's time to dine with the demons."

It's time to dine with the demons. That's what he said. I swear to God. Those were the very words that came out of his mouth.

Well, this time, Woody, you really blew it. Because it wasn't time to dine with the demons. It wasn't. You had no idea where that story would take me.

Or Jesus, maybe you did. Which is worse. Because of all that you *didn't* say about the journey into hell.

You didn't say that the rivers of rage and sorrow and icy treachery are devoid of markings, that you thrash in conflicting currents with nothing but your own terrified vertigo to navigate between the way of death and the way of life.

You didn't say that the savages in those pitch-black depths, the snarling dog with blood-stained teeth, the raging bull with raping testicles, the phantom prophets who seep with deceit, that they have faces that ice you stone cold—not from ugliness, but from familiarity.

And you sure as hell didn't say that some of the heroes who dared enter that foul world never found their way out—that Hercules himself ventured to Hell's core to save two warriors imprisoned behind a veil of forgetfulness but he only came back with one. Such is the price you pay for descending into the Underworld. Somebody always gets killed. And whoever lives ends up as good as dead anyway. No, you didn't say that. I read the book. I read it all right. And you didn't mention that part. You just sat there, with your book of stories, as cool as if you were talking about the latest ride at Universal Studios instead of a descent into an abyss from which none return unscathed.

Shame on you, Woody. Shame on you.

But what was I to do? He was Woody. The great Dr. Woodrow Wheelwright 'Take-two-stories-and-call-me-in-the-morning' Woodruff.

And Woody was telling me to dine with the demons. To descend into the Underworld. To follow the story home.

Well, look at where it got me.

I finished up the session. I told him I'd see him again the next week. Then I took the book he handed me.

I promised him I would read it.

If you can believe it, I even thanked him for it.

The doctor calling on Carey had no stories to tell. That was fine. Carey wasn't listening. He stared at the draped window with such blank stillness, he could have been a sentry keeping silent post at a military compound.

"You're a lucky young man," said the surgeon, the trace of a scolding lacing his words. "You cut yourself so deep I was called out of a good night's sleep to check the damage you did. Good news for you is, you missed your nerves, though you did scratch a bit of muscle. That's some pretty severe whittling, son."

The doctor paused. The boy did not. Not even a ripple in the steady beam of his night watch.

"Son, I know this isn't any fun, but you're going to have to talk to us."

The boy said nothing.

"Can you at least move your fingers for me?"

Still nothing.

"Then how about letting me know if you can feel me squeezing your thumb?"

Still, absolutely nothing.

The doctor pulled a steel prick out of his lab coat pocket and poked each of the fingers along the boy's left hand. He reached over the boy's body, and did the same to the right. Involuntarily, each finger twitched in response.

"Well, your hands are going to be okay. But it's not your hands I'm worried about. We need to get to the bottom of what's wrong with you."

The surgeon paused, then sighed. "Okay. I'm going to send you upstairs overnight. You don't need to be in intensive care anymore. I'm going to ask another doctor to come see you. A psychiatric doctor. He'll talk to you in the morning and determine where we should go from here. We'll get to the bottom of this."

The boy remained silent. As silent as a sentinel sculpted in granite stillness.

The doctor hesitated, gave up, and left.

Still, the silence screamed from the boy. Not a word. Not a twitch. Not a blink.

Only silence.

4

"LAY-NA, PLEASE. WHAT DO I have to do? Just tell me."

My father's pleading echoes from the end of an endless tunnel. I am six or seven years old. The tunnel is dark—a midnight passageway between my and my parents' bedrooms. I walk toward his distant entreaties.

"It's going to kill me, I swear. Please. I beg you to stay away from him."

I am naked, but for my briefs. Draped across my outstretched arms, I carry my pajamas like an acolyte processing with priestly vestments. I'm cold. And I want my mom to clothe me.

"I swear," my father's agony continues, "if you kiss him again, if you so much as touch him . . ."

His anguish trails off. My mom does not answer. As I approach their bedroom doorway, I see why. She is dressed for death. Seated in front of her coffin, she wears the gown she will be buried in. My father, kneeling, begs to her back. She is as still as stone, deaf to his pleas, the accusations themselves beneath her.

"Lena, please. Give me your word. Never do it again."

I have never seen my father like this. Usually his jealous rants are rabid. Now he is bent and broken. I stand until they sense my presence. My mother turns first. Her eyes are proud but pained. She looks straight at me. Though she does not talk, her gaze beseeches my allegiance.

"Tony. Believe me. I would never do anything like that."

My father turns next. Seeing me, his tear-streaked face hardens. He is wordless as well. He matter-of-factly rises from his knees, paces toward me, then slams the bedroom door in my face.

I stand in the cold. Still naked but for my briefs. I gaze at the garments in my arms. They are no longer my pajamas. They are death-camp clothes from Dachau. My mother's crimson patch stares boldly from the sleeve.

———

I woke up to my bedroom gloomily lit. A drizzly day. Both inside and out. Right on schedule, my morning marine layer of melancholy wrapped me in its dismal haze. Though I had slept for twelve hours, I was still bone-tired. My mind felt drugged, my body made of lead. Lacking the will to heave myself out of bed and into the day's overwhelming tedium, I lingered in my covers' warmth. My nightmare lingered with me.

Though my father routinely berated my mother for her alleged promiscuity, I could not remember a single episode where he broke down and begged, let alone me stealing up on one in the middle of the night. I could, on the other hand, remember quite well my mother's Dachau patch. And the middle of the night on which she bestowed it upon me.

I was thirteen. We had celebrated Passover before my father turned sinister. Later that night, I laid in bed as he assaulted my mother. Screaming that she was a whore and fuming just short of hitting her, he forbad any further trysts with her unnamed lover. Though I couldn't see her from my bedroom, I could picture her all too well. To my knowledge, she never slept with another man, nor was rumored around town to have done so. Nevertheless, she endured my father's verbal pummelings with penitent submission. She sat on the edge of her bed and held her head in her hands until my father's rage expired and he stormed to his perch in our living room. I longed to go and comfort her. But I didn't dare. My father never hit me; but his rage always paralyzed me. So I stayed in bed. And as the house settled into an uneasy détente, I stared at a St. Christopher statue and prayed for my father's death.

I awoke in the dead of night, the house eerily still. My mother knelt beside my bed in her white cotton nightgown. She had already peeled my covers to my waist and unbuttoned my pajama top. Now, as reverently as a priest unsealing the oils for last rites, she was opening an aged military envelope, the kind a commander would use to conceal a classified document. I knew the envelope well. But I had never seen its contents.

My father prohibited all relics from the war. He did however, indulge my mother this single item. She kept it, hidden within the envelope, tucked inside the pages of her Catholic missal. Though she never received Eucharist, my mother attended Mass religiously. And though she never read the prayers, she spent hours on end with the Missal in her lap, staring out her bedroom window as she fingered the envelope's edges like one would beads in a rosary.

My mother seemed unaware that I awakened. She carefully unlooped the elastic band that clasped the envelope closed. My shirt splayed open, I laid frozen, like the drugged scapegoat in a macabre sacrifice. My mother turned the envelope over and lifted the back flap. She paused, as if gathering the strength to proceed. Then she slid her fingers inside and slipped out a tattered triangle of fabric. A patch, once boldly scarlet, now faded to a bloody red, was stitched to the remnant of a black and white prison uniform. She held the fabric in her open palm, careful not to touch the badge. A childish sensation shot through me. Like the red-hot end of a branding iron, the patch would scald at the touch. My mother reached down. I braced for pain. And onto my bare chest, she set the patch, stared at it, then held it in place with one hand over the other.

Only then did she look at me. She knew I was awake. Her eyes were moist with murky emotion. I searched them, trying to understand. And though I was too young to consciously form them, questions burned into me with the press of the fabric.

What are you doing? With this death-camp badge a symbol, are you recognizing our solidarity in this camp we call a home? Or are you passing on your burden to a son who will ease your load? Or is it perhaps your talisman, bequeathed to me for protection through an ill-omened future without you? Why, mom? Why are you emblazoning my soul with the crest of your Dachau secrets?

With the wraithlike force of her weight, the questions seared into my skin. Still a boy, freshly surfaced from the deeps of sleep, I craved to know the reason for this bizarre observance. And yet, she remained quiet. As quiet as the screams silenced in death-camp smoke. Until she lifted one hand, stroked my cheek, and leaned in.

"My, Antony," she whispered. But she explained no more. Before she could, *he* showed up, filling my doorway with menace. Though she did not turn, she felt him. Like a runaway spirit tracked by the Reaper, she knew she had to go. Her hand on my cheek, she held my gaze, her eyes filled with indecipherable tenderness. Then she stood up, walked from my side, and into the mysteries of the night.

But she left the patch.

And the questions scorching my chest.

Though that was all.

The next day, she was dead.

How could I have been so blind?

I glanced at the clock. 9:40. The last thing I wanted was to haul off to work. I had skipped the day before to see Woody in the city. I was tempted to skip another day as well. In hindsight, I should have. But I didn't. I called up Crossroads and told them I'd be in by noon. I shaved and showered and looked for something to eat. Without food in the fridge, nor the spark to cook what I had in the cupboard, I decided on coffee and a bagel at Caty's. I grabbed my wallet, and I grabbed my keys.

It was only to kill time that I also grabbed something to read. The book on my kitchen counter.

Woody's collection of classical myths.

While I lay in bed pondering nightmare phantoms, Carey lay in bed oblivious to bedside doctors. The psychiatrist beside him wore a brown suit with a beige blouse. She held a medical chart at her side. Carey stared past her at the drizzle out the window.

"Hi, Carey," she greeted. "I'm Dr. Carter. Dreary day, isn't it?"

Carey did not answer.

"I understand things aren't going too well."

Not a word.

"I've got some good news. Dr. Olson's discharging you. He says your arms will be fine."

Nothing.

"Okay. I understand you don't want to talk. That's fine. But I don't think you're ready to go home. I'm sending you to another kind of hospital, a psychiatric hospital, for children who feel just like you do. They'll take good care of you there. Do you have any questions? . . . Okay . . . I hope you feel better real soon."

The doctor opened the chart and wrote, 'Patient is dissociative, uncommunicative, and self-destructive. Section 10—Involuntary admittance to psychiatric facility. Recommend intensive anti-depressant therapy and suicide watch level one.'

She folded the chart, looked at the boy, then left.

Carey didn't blink. His arms lay with his bandaged wrists in full view. The finger on his right hand curled, cocked, and flicked.

All symptoms tell a story, Woody insisted. The whole story was right there. Uncommunicative? The boy was all but shouting it out.

If only one's eyes were open.

5

Santa Rosa's downtown was a study in contrast. A million-dollar renovation project restored the municipal district into a shopper's paradise aimed at attracting consumers from all of Sonoma County. Trendy boutiques and flagship bookstores, chic delicatessens and a requisite Starbuck's lined the manicured park and bordered a state-of-the-art shopping mall. Behind the mall, across the freeway that sliced an economic chasm through the city, Santa Rosa's Historic Railroad Square sat as a forgotten and decaying counterpart to the fiscal recovery but a quarter's heave away. There, a tired collection of dilapidated buildings bordered an abandoned train depot plopped in the weedy patch of dirt that passed for Railroad Park. On the far side, a swath of rusted railroad tracks cut through the ground like a stitched wound. They broke off before a beaten down telegraph warehouse that harbored the only life-giving spring in that ghost town of a square. Not a Starbuck's. A funky underground hangout known as Caty's Coffee Cavern.

With its dark interior and thrift store furnishings, it was the perfect refuge for tortured artists, bearded radicals, and angst-ridden adolescents with hair spiked and noses studded. The black ceiling held neon stars aligned in astrological precision. The step-high stage sported a stand-up mike and stool. And the walls were filled with avant-garde paintings, shelves of ceramic pieces, and bulletin boards bulging with flyers, index cards, and half-sheets torn from spiral notebooks pitching everything from acupuncture and candle-making classes to tarot readings and poetry nights. If a haven for the troubled souls of the world, it was also a home for the local potters and sculptors, painters and poets, singer songwriters and spiritual seekers of all kinds in search of a place to nest.

And Earth mother and hippie comrade to them all was Caty.

Caty was a work of art herself. With her tie-dyed smock and unshaven legs, her braid of smoky gray hair and yellow octagonal sunglasses, her floppy motorcycle cap bulging with buttons and peace signs—'Flower Power' in rainbow colors, 'Groovy' in green, John Lennon's head in a chopped up blur worthy of Warhol—she looked like she fell asleep during Woodstock and woke up somewhere in the middle of the Bush administration. I always imagined her shacked out in a Russian River commune, smoking grass and singing Joan Baez while baking her baked goods barefoot and braless.

But whether they were made braless, topless, or completely in the nude, Caty's baked goods were otherworldly. Vegetarian quiches, multi-grain breads, and mushrooming muffins stuffed with fresh berries crowded her counter in mouth-watering abundance. All of it as organic as Caty herself. All of it so good young professionals, neat and trim in business suits, wandered down from the courthouse or on a break from Nieman Marcus looking as out of place as tourists from North Dakota taking a wrong turn and finding themselves in the middle of Harlem. But the resuscitative powers of Caty's food made a foray into her cavern entirely worth the dislocation.

When I arrived, Caty was stooped on the sidewalk out front, a yellow raincoat protecting her from the drizzle. She nudged a bowl of milk, soy I'm sure, toward a three-legged mutt the size of a chihuahua but yelping with the ferocity of a pit bull. The dog, a companion of a homeless man sleeping one off on the strip of dry pavement at the building's base, was unappeased by the milk. It nipped in such high-pitched defiance, Caty could have been a dogcatcher hell-bent on euthanizing the creature.

"Oh . . . it's okay . . ." Caty purred, oblivious to the junkyard venom. "You're just a little puppy-dog, you are." She pulled out a hunk of whole-wheat biscotti and dangled it inches from the dog's snapping teeth. I was prepared to punt the creature should it come after me. Caty just cooed as if it were a giggling infant. "Here you are, little puppy-dog." To my astonishment, the dog hobbled forward, quieted to a throaty growl, yelped a final impotent yelp, then snatched the biscotti from Caty's fingers and attacked it like a lion after raw meat. Caty caressed the munching dog, each stroke visibly calming it. It finished the biscotti, lapped a little milk, then made a three-legged limp to the sleeping man and curled into a ball like a golden retriever lazing an evening away by the fire.

"What did you put in that?" I joked as I held the door.

"Just a little lovin'," she said sprightly, skipping into the cavern like a nymph dancing across a field of flowers. I followed her in and smelled the usual assortment of baked delectables spread across the saloon-style counter. Caty lifted up a hinged section, slid inside, and hung up her slicker. Still basking in contentment, some mix between the satisfaction of a job well done and the flightiness of one having smoked too much reefer, she sauntered over.

"Do you hear it?" she enticed. "The one calling your name?" Pure Caty. A seer in touch with mysteries unknown to the rest of us. Or a quack one snakeskin short of a potion.

"Why?" I played along. "You put some spell on these to lure your customers?"

"Oh, you'd be surprised what I sprinkle into these goodies." Not me. Stardust or weed either one, I wouldn't be surprised.

"I hear the oatmeal bagel calling me. And it'd like to be toasted, with a touch of butter. And a cup of French roast, please."

"In a twinkle," she bubbled.

As she prepared the bagel, I wandered toward the register. A macramé basket hung from the ceiling cradling an assortment of fresh fruit. I grabbed a banana.

"I see I should've sprinkled something extra into these," Caty said setting down a mug of coffee.

"How's that?"

She motioned toward my book on the counter. The cover displayed Theseus slaying the Minotaur. "That's some world you're playing around in."

"Not to worry." I held my banana like a pistol. "I'm armed."

"*Put it away, cowboy!*" she snapped. I was taken aback. "Violence only kills. Never heals. Only kills." Her eyes held my own, then darted down to the coffee. In her glance, I saw a flash of fear. Or an old wound resurfacing. "Trust me," she said as if asking a favor. She looked at me again. Then rang me up for two ninety-nine.

I parked at a seat by the window and nibbled my bagel. Though I hadn't eaten well for weeks, a few bites left me full. I pushed my plate aside, cupped my coffee with both hands, and stared out the window. The rusty railroad tracks, once a major artery in northern California freight, now held but a single fading freight car so old and tired in the dripping rain it was as if, weary of moving, weary of hauling, weary of the very act of turning its wheels, it simply rolled to a stop and expired. I knew how it felt. And yet somehow I needed to suck up the steam to roll back to Crossroads and deal with ten boys. Strike that. Nine boys. One had fallen off the end of the ever-revolving conveyer belt of troubled children to tend. Not to worry. Surely another would appear to take Hannibal's place. How will I keep from nearly killing that one?

My only clue lay back on the table. I looked at Woody's book. Theseus held his sword within the chest of a beast boasting a man's body and a bull's head. 'What you need is another story,' Woody prescribed. And here it was. A collection of ancient myths describing the journey through the Underworld. Whatever this had to do with dining with one's demons, I had no idea. But Caty was right. This was some world to be entering. Theseus—his face chiseled in confidence and power. The Minotaur—its raging head gasping out a final defiant cry. From the cover, it looked so easy.

I hesitated as if unseen dangers spat and spewed within the book's pages. Once I cracked the cover, I'd dive headlong into the monster's lair. So this was the story that would show me the way. God, I was plenty lost. But the question hung. Was I ready to journey home?

I took a deep breath.

Then peeled the veil open.

———

"No room at the inn," Dr. Carter repeated as she hung up the phone. "Their very words. That's nothing in Marin, Vallejo, or San Francisco. What are we supposed to do with him until a bed opens up?"

"What about Norton?" the nurse volunteered.

"They don't take children."

"What about St. Jude's?"

"They don't take psychiatric kids." The doctor sighed. "Where's the directory of local facilities? Somebody's got to have a secured unit he can stay in."

She skimmed through the Santa Rosa treatment centers. "Here's one, Willow Creek. They've got a locked unit."

"What about Crossroads?" the nurse suggested.

"Is that the place out by the detention facility?"

"Yeah. We sent a boy there a few years ago. They're small but they have a secured bed."

Dr. Carter finished the list. "So that's it. Willow Creek or Crossroads." She dialed Willow Creek. While the phone rang, she twisted the cord around her finger like Minos twining his tail to consign a sinner to a circle in hell. The phone kept ringing.

"Jesus," she bristled, looking at her watch. "Why don't they pick up?" The phone rang on. "Forget it." She hung up. "I'll try Crossroads. It's only for a couple of days."

Such were the whims that determined Carey's fate.

Somebody at Crossroads answered the phone.

6

W OODY'S BOOK WAS A veritable who's who of heroes who journeyed through the Underworld and lived on to tell about it.

It was supposed to show me the way home.

Not seal my fate.

The Lord of the Underworld was Pluto, his bride, Persephone. Pluto's abduction of the earthly maiden was a story in itself. Persephone was Pluto's niece. He lusted for her from afar and plotted for a way to take her. One day, while picking flowers with her friends, she wandered off alone when a chasm erupted from the earth and Pluto, standing tall on his stallion-borne chariot, emerged in rapacious majesty. With his reins in his teeth, he snatched the maiden with one arm, speared a protesting nymph with the other, then captained the steed back into the chasm. The ground snapped shut and Persephone was locked in a bridal vault where Pluto commenced to woo her. Despite his persistence, Persephone resisted.

Persephone's mother, Demeter, was the goddess of all vegetation. When she heard of her daughter's abduction, she was outraged. Before Zeus, she demanded Persephone's return. To leverage him, she held the earth hostage. Crops dried up in the field, trees stood leafless in the wind, no seed sprouted, no plant bore fruit—the entire land withered in an agricultural holocaust.

With famine threatening, Zeus interceded. He sent Hermes to retrieve Persephone. With one caveat. The maiden was to be freed only if she had refrained from eating even a single morsel during her captivity. Zeus knew. A person's ties to a place are forged through the foods they feed by.

Persephone had refused both her captor's advances and his food. So Hermes escorted her to a carriage bound for home. Before it departed, however, Persephone glimpsed a pomegranate tucked in the backseat, a luscious fruit planted by the seductive Pluto. Persephone's hunger was aroused. She handled the fruit, and mouthed a single seed. With her tongue, she stroked the silky shell, savoring the promise of juice within. She poised the seed in the soft bite of her teeth. Her belly screamed for a taste of the nectar. Her teeth pressed more firmly. Just a taste. She bit. The juice squirted into her mouth in a sensual burst and soaked her tongue in pleasure. Then she swallowed.

By divine law, Pluto now had rights to Persephone. Satisfied and secure, he granted her a brief visit to her mother. Demeter, however, was unappeased. Claiming that Persephone had been deceived, she refused to relinquish her back to Pluto. Pluto was outraged, claiming that Persephone wanted him all along. A deadlock gripped the gods, with Persephone's fate and food for the planet hanging in the balance.

Finally, a compromise was brokered. Demeter would both restore fruitfulness to the earth and release Persephone to be Pluto's bride. But not at the same time. Persephone could stay in Hades for but one fourth of the year. The other nine months she would spend with her mother. While mother and daughter were together, the earth would flourish. But when they were apart, as a protest against Pluto's rapacious ways, the earth would lay indignantly fallow. Those three months comprise the season of winter.

———

Few people dared sojourn into the foul kingdom of death. For good reason. A host of demons and beasts abided there rivaling the horrors of the most psychologically disturbed. Three-headed dogs tore intruder's flesh, snake-haired women turned people to stone, shrieking spirits incited insanity, all within an abyss coiled by four oozing rivers—one of raging fire, another of stagnant stench, one spiked with stupefying waters, the last with the saltless tears of the damned. At its best, a mournful monotony of languishing ghouls, at its worst, a perverted chamber of retributive torture, Hades was the land of nightmares. Literally. Nightmarish to endure. And the origin of all nightmares that haunt the sleeping. From the Greeks, little else is known about Hades' geography. The lack of detail itself is foreboding testimony to the place's terror. Only if you had to did you travel to Hell. And if you did, you did your business, then got the hell out.

———

I turned the page and was surprised to find that the mighty Hercules had made the journey. Apparently, Hercules was prone to fits of violence, a trait neglected in the Disney version of the story. In one such rage, he mistook his wife and three toddler sons for enemies, beat them into bloody oblivion, then threw their pummeled bodies, unconscious but still writhing, into a bonfire. When he recovered his senses, he nearly killed himself with grief. His hand stayed by his friend Theseus, Hercules sought penance instead.

The priestly oracle at Delphi instructed him to see a certain King Eurystheus and perform whatever tasks the king dictated. With the delight of a sadistic prison warden and a palette full of the most monstrous creatures in all of mythology, Eurystheus gave new meaning to the term taskmaster by devising the grotesquely dangerous and ridiculously impossible feats known as the twelve labors of Hercules. After such stunts as cleaning 3000 cattle's thirty years of crap and killing a serpent with multiplying heads, Hercules had to foray into Hell and capture Cerberus, the savage three-headed guard-dog with a tail of snakes. Such was Hercules' twelfth labor, his last and most dangerous—unless you count his mythic thirteenth in which he, in a single night, conjugally slept with forty-nine out of fifty sisters, sired fifty-one children (two sets of twins) and single-handedly colonized the island of Sardinia, a labor that many consider not only his true last labor but his most dangerous one as well.

With the cocksure confidence of a varsity-lettered jock taking on a grade school wimp, Hercules swaggered right through Hades' front door. He sent the ferryman Charon scurrying away on a raft. He scattered the wraiths with a bogeyman scream. He intimidated the stone-chilling Medusa with a flash of his sword. Then he had the balls to march right up to Pluto and parley for the rights to Cerberus. Pluto was in a gaming mood and surrendered the surly sentry, as long as Hercules overcame the beast without the use of weapons. Hercules agreed and stalked the brute.

He found Cerberus keeping watch by the river Acheron. A mythic battle ensued—the snarling scourge of the Underworld against the strongest hero the Earth had ever seen. Hercules grabbed a throat, then another, and throttled the dog. Cerberus whipped its serpentine tail around Hercules' neck. Locked in a writhing, pummeling hold, they rolled and rumbled throughout the Netherworld until Hercules finally subdued the dog with a strangulating surge, Cerberus landing but a single serpentine bite before submitting.

Hercules emerged from Hades and brought the hound to Eurystheus. Some say the animal was slaughtered as a sacrifice then devoured in a celebratory feast. Others say that Eurystheus was scared to death of the beast and made Hercules take it back where it belonged. Either way, Hercules' penance was complete (with the exception, of course, of the alleged one-night stand of heroic debauchery). He fulfilled each mythic feat with the self-confident bravado of an Olympic shotputter heaving tennis balls and was none the worse for wear. Damn, he tramped all the way to Hades' center and took on the Hound of Hell with no more than a bee-sting serpent's prick to scathe him along the way. Such was the only price he paid to battle the beast in the belly of the planet and wipe clean the stain of killing his loved ones. A bee sting. What a hero.

To be honest, I didn't get it. I gnawed a bit of bagel as I chewed over the myth. *This* was a story to live by? A narrative that leads to healing? What in God's name does the Greek Paul Bunyon have to do with engaging your depression? All I could get from it was that going into the Underworld wasn't that difficult—you rustle up a ghost or two, wrestle a few monsters, and come away with the confidence that there's nothing you can't overcome. Was that what Woody was trying to tell me—suck it up Hercules-style and Rambo your way through any inferno thrown at you? I'd do that. If the penance really took. No problem.

Like I said, I didn't get it.

I sipped my coffee, and kept reading.

My cockiness about Hercules quickly faded. The next story was more poignant. And more disturbing.

Orpheus was a musician renowned for the healing melodies he played on his lyre. To linger in his music even a moment was like soaking in sacred springs. Laborers rested from their toil when his music filled the land; warriors cocked an eye from the fronts; the gods turned an ear from the heavens; animals stopped their preying; storms settled into breezes; wounds were soothed; nature, renewed; the pulse of life was resuscitated.

Love should only have augmented a song so restorative. But such was not to be. Orpheus became enraptured with a young maiden, Eurydice. They married. While honeymooning, Eurydice frolicked one morning through a flowered meadow. She was followed by a man whose unrequited lust would take by force what would not come with delight. The stalker attacked. Eurydice fled. In her panic, she stumbled and a poisonous viper bit her. Before her beloved could race from their bridal quarters and hold her to his sobbing chest, Eurydice died.

Sorrow threatened to silence Orpheus' music forever. For months he wandered, his lyre strapped noiselessly to his back, his hands too crestfallen to finger his instrument. He wanted to kill himself, wanted to join his lover in death. Instead, he resolved to do the unthinkable. He would journey into the Underworld and, appealing to Pluto's own love for Persephone, would petition the god to release Eurydice back to the land of the living.

Armed only with voice and lyre, Orpheus descended into Hades. As he stepped through the stagnant darkness, he sang. He sang a song unlike any he had ever sung before, one unlike any ever heard before within that vast shrieking wasteland. The crisp clear note of its pain, its raw and irremediable pining, reverberated throughout the inferno, piercing through all the brutality and torment to touch a soulful chord in that most unsoulful of places. Everyone was moved—beasts and ghouls, torturers and victims—each one melting as they remembered a long forgotten place of primal compassion, the womb in which the soothing, steady, life-sustaining rhythm of their mother's heartbeat held and lullabied them well before the poverties and poundings that corrupt the innocence of infancy into the cold calcification of evil.

For several moments, Orpheus' song was heard. For several moments, all of Hell went still.

Cerberus, the snarling watchdog, was lulled to a puppy-dog sleep, and Hydra, the fifty-mouthed monster, swallowed chokes of homesick longing. Medusa, the hideous Gorgon who turned faces into stone, found her own stony face thawing into momentary tenderness, and the Furies, those cold-hearted bitches who sucked sanity dry, cried their first tears since the crib.

In that crack of time when the tortures of Hell were eased, the mournful troubadour wound his way in song to the very heart of Hades. There he found Pluto and Persephone. Likewise vulnerable to the wounded lover's melody, their malicious eyes gave way to pity's tears, their fingers reaching out and finding each other, laced together in their own love's reminiscence.

Orpheus made his appeal. In their transient soft-heartedness, Death's King and Queen could not help but grant his wish. They would allow his bride to return to the land of the living. On one condition. As Orpheus led her through the dark pitch of the Underworld, and passed through the gray Valley of Shadows, he must refrain from looking back at her.

Not until they both emerged fully into the living light of day could he turn and reunite with his beloved.

Orpheus agreed, and made for home.

With mounting expectation, Orpheus climbed out of Hell's abyss. He resisted the impulse to swirl around and wrap Eurydice in his arms, or even to simply twist his head for a glancing sip of her beauty. On he walked, straining to hear the patter of her step, to feel her breath on his neck. Yet all he had was Pluto's promise to stay his head and trust her presence behind him.

Finally, he saw it. A dim light emerged in the distance. His pace quickened. His heart pounded. The black of night eased into a misty gray, then thinned into a cloudy brightness. Hades' edge was but a stone's throw away. The desire in his belly screamed. But a moment more. The edge was just yards away, steps away, feet away, until finally, unable to resist any longer, he leapt into the light of day and swung around to welcome his beloved back to life.

But he turned too soon. Just a second too soon. And in that second, eternity gaped. For though Orpheus had entered the land of the living, Eurydice had not. She was a single step away from life. But before she could take that step, the darkness behind her yawned like a poised prowler and swallowed her back into night. Orpheus, horrified, watched his bride drop into the pit of nothingness, a single wail of farewell rising from her plummeting spirit and echoing without end through the stunned silence of Orpheus' heart.

For many years thereafter he wandered the world, songless and alone. Over time, he unstrapped his lyre and played again. But his music had lost something. No longer did it sparkle with spring's rejuvenation. No longer did it haunt with pain's sorrow. The sun did not stand still. The gods did not stop their play. Orpheus simply sang by himself, getting on with life. Until years later, he wandered into a wooded orgy. The drunken partiers goaded Orpheus for a song. Then they humiliated him. Then they raped him. Then they dismembered him. And Orpheus' music was silenced forever.

———

I looked up from the book and gazed out the window. The drizzle had turned into an all-out rain. But I was not checking the weather. I could not shake the story. Here was a guy whose foray into Hell teased him with then deprived him of that for which he longed. How do you go on after losing your beloved? How do you risk hope again after being so close to reunion only to watch it dissolve like a fading phantom? No wonder his song went silent. And with it, the music that plays through the abyss restoring the song of life.

Caty came by and warmed my coffee. I sipped it absently. Mulling over this kingdom of failed quests and lost love.

And as I mulled, I heard nothing. Not a whisper. Not an echo. Not a single note from life's song that supposedly pulsates at the center of creation. I heard only silence. And rain. I may have been distant. But I was listening. God, was I listening.

The trace of coffee at the bottom of my mug was cold by the time I returned to the book.

The next hero to soil his feet in Hades' sleaze did not go to retrieve a lost loved one, nor to test his strength in penitential obligation. He was trying to get back home.

Odysseus, King of Ithaca, spent twenty years in exile—twenty years separated from the son he had never seen, the wife and father who pined for him, and the mother whose broken heart led to her death of which Odysseus was entirely unaware.

He spent ten years in the Trojan War, the skirmish that ended with Odysseus' assault through the infamous wooden horse. He spent the next ten years on the high seas trying to sail back to his homeland. The latter battle pitted Odysseus against Poseidon who battered the hero with a string of storms each one stranding him on an island more perilous than the last. On one, Odysseus fought off the Lotus-eaters whose drugged petals stupefied his crew with amnesia. On another, he took on a one-eyed giant. On yet another, he outsmarted cannibals. Each escape led back to the sea, where another of Poseidon's storms swamped the crew on another precarious island.

After years of such pummeling, Odysseus and his crew washed ashore on the island of an enchantress. Circe turned the crewmen into pigs, then seduced Odysseus. But his unwavering drive to return to his loved ones worked on her. Eventually, Circe released him from her charms and gave him the elusive help he needed. She financed the repair of his ships; she supplied him with provisions; she restored his crew.

And she told him what he had to do.

To the men's horror, the only way back was by way of the land of the dead. At the mouth of Hades, Odysseus was to prepare a sacrificial meal that must remain untouched. The ghost of a dead seer would come, feast, and advise the hero how to get home.

Odysseus followed Circe's instructions and sailed through the night. Beyond the ocean's end, he beached his boat at the city of the Cimmerians, those melancholy men whose shadowed land never sees the light of day. In the pitch darkness, Odysseus hiked through the barren trees of Persephone's forest to the mouth of Hades. Odysseus dug a pit. Within it, he prepared the meal that would entice the dead out of Hell's stench. Milk and honey. Wine and meal. The blood of a lamb.

Baited by the banquet's aroma, a crowd of ghosts emerged from the grave-like cave and scratched toward the food. Odysseus fended them off with a drawn sword. One of the ghosts was a young sailor in Odysseus' crew who had recently died. He pleaded with his captain for a proper burial so he could be released from his ceaseless wandering. Odysseus promised to comply. But he did not let the unburied boy near the alluring meal. Other spirits surged in hunger—anemic children and emaciated elders, young brides still clad in wedding dress and bloodstained soldiers still geared for battle—all writhing and moaning in a mass push for a taste of the lifeless food. Odysseus fought each one back.

Then a sight pierced him through.

He saw his mother.

Alive when he left home twenty years earlier, she now haunted Hell's doorway. Demented by grief, she had no clue that the personage before her was her son. She was one of the pack, mindlessly pushing forward in a mad crush to quench the unbearable hunger of death. Odysseus ached to appease her. But the way home was clear. He held tight his sword. And refused her near the meal.

Finally, Tiresias emerged from the mob of spirits. Odysseus laid down his sword and the blind seer partook of the bloody dinner. Once he dined, Tiresias spoke. He told Odysseus the sacrifice that would appease Poseidon, the route that led home, and the nature of the enemies he would need to vanquish. He warned of betrayal, predicted bloodshed, but foresaw victory. With that, Tiresias returned to the shadows and disappeared into the Underworld.

Now that the prophet had claimed his portion of the meal, Odysseus was free to appease any hunger that so moved him. The deranged spirit of his mother approached once more. This time, Odysseus allowed her to eat. At once, she returned to her senses and recognized her son. Odysseus begged to hear the details of her death. She told him. She did not die from an arrow's shaft. Nor from a fatal sickness. Nor from a tyrant's beating. She died from sorrow, the unendurable agony of missing her homeless son. For years she stared, silent and stoic, from the perch of a palace balcony. She ate little and conversed less. She gazed at the empty horizon, longing for a single sail to surface at the ocean's edge, but seeing only the undisturbed slate-gray of the sea.

Against the hypnotic backdrop, memories materialized like ghosts. Walks on the beach holding her toddler son's hand, then releasing him to flirt with the waves. Private chats over afternoon refreshment with a son now grown, confiding in her about the intricacies of love and palace politics, consummating their daily communion with a wine-whispered kiss on her cheek. The temple visit on the day he set sail, resting in the pre-dawn hush to pay homage to the gods for safe and swift passage.

And the pledge her son sealed in that sacred moment. He lit a lamp for the gods, placed her hand on his chest, and held her eyes with rock-hard certainty. He swore that the flame of her maternal love would ever burn within his breast, that this flame would swell with a warrior's courage and it would simmer with a sea captain's intensity. But it would always glow, day and night, until he came home a hero, his triumphant arms wide, and he swept her up in the undying love that would cradle her for the rest of her days.

On the same strand as all mothers who have held vigil for their children fighting distant wars, Odysseus' mother sat on her balcony and fingered her string of memories as if each were a prayer bead uniting her both with her faraway son and the sacred presence that might bring him home.

But over time, the beads were rubbed beyond recognition, and the strand began to unravel. The details of her mental pictures faded away—what he looked like, where they walked. And her resolve to hold them with precision slipped away as well. Her memories mingled indiscriminately with one another then degenerated, with her sanity, into a single fog of vacant longing. Still she sat and stared. But there was nothing to stare at. Nothing on the horizon. And nothing in the burned-out regions of her lost mind. Until even sitting and staring required a hope she did not have. And she wasted away.

Odysseus was so moved he tried to hold her to his chest. But his arms drew air, slipping through her smoky spirit. Defeat crept into her eyes. Even this long-sought reunion was powerless to comfort her. She was alone. Forever.

Odysseus' heart broke further. He reached out again and grabbed after her drifting presence. But his arms passed through her like a sword through vapor. She closed her eyes, sealing her lonely suffering within herself, slipping away from him, from any human contact, from any spark of sanity, back into that feeble-minded region where eyes are too tired to open and hope too overwhelming to hold. Frantic now, Odysseus clutched after her a third time, flailing in his attempt to hold her in the moment, to hold her in the haven of sanity. But once again, his arms sliced through her.

Unmoved by his thrashing arms, Odysseus' mother opened her dull eyes. She recognized the man before her as someone she once knew, but she couldn't fit him into the soupy fog of her memory. She blinked confusedly, but still could not place him. So she turned and made for Hades. With each step away from her son, her dementia further reclaimed her. By the time she disappeared into the mouth of Hell, she completely forgot about the crestfallen man reaching out behind her.

Odysseus lingered. He allowed a few others to feast—a fallen comrade, an old friend. Words were exchanged, tears were shed. But he had already received enough. From a prophet, directions and hope. From his mother, a phantom goodbye. These lodged in his soul, he trekked back to the beach, mounted his ship, and sailed for home.

Though it was late morning, the Santa Rosa sky was dark and menacing. Charcoal clouds, a womb for thunder, portended a storm. Poseidon thrusting a last lick from the coast. Slapping down another wanderer hell-bent on getting home.

Woody scored again. Here was another story I could buy. I wasn't sure about the prophet part, that a wise seer pops up and leads you out of depression's squalls. But I bought the rest of it. It didn't take a PhD in psychology to get it. In Hell, you meet the ghost of your dead mother. You make peace with her. Then you say goodbye.

God, what I would have given for that to be true. To see her face again, her coal black hair, her own slate-gray stare, and feel my arms around even the misty wisp of her ghost.

And tell her I'm sorry.

I'm sorry I let that bastard kill you. He may not have been at the wheel, but he killed you all the same. Just as sure as the death you lived long before you died. And Mom, I swear to God. If I thought I could find whatever Hell the dead inhabit, and I could smoke out your spirit hidden within the shadows, and I could turn your head and catch your eye and spark even a flicker of recognition from your face, I would get on the next boat, hoist the mainsail, and exile myself for every second of twenty years, and twenty more after that, until I found you.

And Mom, I would save you. This time, your rescue would be sure. I would not let you slip back into the cave. I would not let the monsters get you. I swear to God. I wouldn't let it happen again.

Yes. I was the promising hero ready to rescue my mom from Hades. I sure as hell was.

Except like Odysseus, I wasn't ready for the mom I would find there.

The last story of a hero voyaging into Hades did not amuse me. It did not move me. And it sure as hell did not open up a soft spot of maternal sorrow.

It flat out pissed me off.

It's the story of Aeneas, the legendary discoverer of Italy, founder of the Roman Empire.

The rags-to-riches storyline starts with Aeneas on the losing end of the Trojan War. His homeland literally reduced to ashes, he barely escapes with his son, his father, and a handful of compatriots in a skimpy fleet of crippled ships. With only fate to guide him, Aeneas seeks his destiny—finding a new land on which to birth a nation.

Fate does not let him down. With impeccable timing, the gods intervene each step of the way with enough guidance to keep Gilligan and the Skipper out of trouble. Neptune starts off and stills the storms stirred by a jealous goddess. Aeneas limps into shore and begins to build a city. But a murderous mob is on the make, so Jupiter sends the ghost of a comrade with a warning to get out of town. Aeneas flees, and finds another island on which to settle. Another danger emerges, an approaching plague, so another god appears with shipping orders. So they sail. And find another island. And start to settle. But this one lacks fertile promise. How does Aeneas know? Another god tells him, in a vision this time. So back to the sea they go.

From island to island, Aeneas and his crew connect the dots across the Mediterranean. They party and play sports at some. They tussle with bird-women at others. At one, Aeneas' father dies of travel weariness and is buried. But all along the way they are advised through every nasty spot of sea and coached through every threatening encounter by a prophet or a guide or a ghost or whoever else happens to be available to keep our hero on the straight and narrow. At one point, even a former enemy pops up, a sailor stranded by Odysseus, who's only too happy to warn Aeneas of the Cyclopes inhabiting their latest stopping point. So they set sail yet again. With all the help he got, Aeneas was never really lost at sea, never really crippled by tornadoes, never rendered clueless about how to stay afloat let alone find the way to the Promised Land. For him it was as simple as navigating a maze with instructions at every turn. Like that really mirrors life.

On one island, the gods even bail him out of a romantic entanglement. The beautiful queen Dido falls for Aeneas, though he plays it coy until a rainstorm ruins a country excursion and the two seek refuge in a cave. Soaking wet, they get out of their clothes and give in to their passion. Their love consummated, Dido considers them married. But Aeneas is just waxing his sword on the way to his destiny—a destiny in jeopardy if he doesn't zip up that sword pretty quick. So the gods send Mercury, who snaps our horny hero to attention with the cold-shower reminder of his pre-ordained mission. Aeneas reorients his rudder and bails, leaving Dido to burn herself with his picture stabbed to her breast.

Eventually, the anointed one sails to the boot-shaped land he is destined to conquer. He makes camp, then hankers for a heart to heart with his Dad about how to tame the hostile territory. A Sibyl appears and reveals the way to the Underworld. Aeneas must first bury a recently killed boy from his company, then find the passkey to Hades, the legendary golden bough. He buries the boy then ponders the passkey's location. Straight from his dead mother's spirit, white doves appear and lead him both to the golden branch from Persephone's tree and to the stagnant swamp that marks the cave to Hades. Aeneas prepares a sacrificial meal then enters the cave with the latest guide in the tag-team plot to secure his destiny.

The cave is three times darker than a moonless night but not so dark that Aeneas can't see the phantom forms of hundred-handed giants, maidens fused to the bodies of boars, the usual assortment of Centaurs and Gorgons, and enough evil spirits to debauch orgies and incite violence throughout the ancient world. And with his sword serving as a dapper cane, Aeneas saunters through it all with the cool savoir-faire of a James Bond in black tie. He sidesteps the wailing infants weeping at their premature deaths, he skirts by the bitter grief of those wrongfully executed, and he ignores the victims of abuse who took their own lives. His high-society debonair isn't ruffled at all until he pauses at the holding pen for those who died for jealous love. Spying Dido wandering in the woods, he feigns sorrow with B-movie theatrics while blaming it all on the gods. She looks at him with disgust then turns away. Aeneas shrugs it off and carries on.

And he comes to the most outrageous feature in the whole geography of the Underworld, the eternal crossroads, the fabled 'Y' in the road that divides the paths of the wicked and the just. One side passes through a wall of fire and into the mouth of Hydra, the humongous serpent who swallows all reprobates into the intestinal abyss of Hell. The other side leads to the Elysian Fields, a brook-fed meadowland in which the cultured and virtuous engage in sport, feast on fine food, sit in the shade and tell war stories or lie by the pool and write poetry, all to the airy backdrop of a string symphony that ever plays.

It's infuriating how ridiculous the whole scene is. As if you ever find yourself standing in such stark clarity before the paths of good and evil, as if Hell and Utopia exist with such unambiguous purity in the first place. I swear, if such a thing as the crystal-clear eternal crossroads exists in this world then I'm Hercules with only a bee-sting prick cramping my style. But there it is. Two paths. Sheep to the right, goats to the left. And the jackass making up his mind in the middle is our hero, pondering the paths laid out so distinctly he might as well be God sitting on a cloud with twenty-twenty vision into the whole cosmic order. Of course, his destination's not in doubt. He's as clean as the guide nudging him along into the Holy Land of caviar and sweet berry liqueur. So in he strolls and stumbles upon that ancient precursor to Ward Cleaver with all but a cardigan and pipe—good ol' Dad.

Of course, there are teary greetings—oh I'm so proud of you Son, oh how I missed you Dad, oh isn't it great how the gods granted us this Kodak moment together. Then offering the ultimate in unfair advantages, Dad walks Aeneas through the future. He forewarns of betrayers and plots battle plans and pinpoints the location for the Roman Empire's capital. Warned of every forthcoming danger and cribbed on the way to beat it, who couldn't be a conquering hero?

Once armed with this Imperial cheat-sheet for life, it's time for Aeneas to go. Dad escorts his boy by the cozy picnic spot where the two of them will spend eternity together then drops him off at the ivory gate through which dreams float back into the world. Stuffing a final win-one-for-the-Gipper homily into the pads of his son's spirit, Dad exhorts Aeneas to victory and shoves him back into the game of life. Aeneas charges through the gate as if he was busting through a butcher paper cheer at a high school pep rally and finds himself right back at his ship where his crew remains worried about this land they've discovered. But it's okay. Aeneas is back. With Ronald Reagan optimism and the confidence of a gambler who already knows the outcome of the game he's betting on, the valiant hero takes charge. He gathers his army, prepares for glory, then slaughters the Italian natives and founds himself an empire.

And off in the corner of paradise, viewing it all from a front-row seat, Dad watches with pure paternal pride. His boy's a hero. Hell, he's gone one better. He's the Chosen One. Look for his sun-tanned mug at the right hand of God. He'll be the one you're supposed to toast your champagne to. If you can keep it down without retching, that is. Jesus Christ, give me a break.

Damn, that story pissed me off. Like all you got to do is seek your destiny and the gods will fall all over themselves to make sure you find it. And the happy reward at the end of the voyage is a Leave-it-to-Beaver reunion with your father. I needed Woody's stories like I needed a death sentence. I had already been down that road. And the gods were nowhere to be found.

I closed my book and glared at the window. Against the dark, stormy background, my face stared back. Its eyes seethed as I swore. If Woody wanted to ride into Hell, so be it. But I'd be damned if I was going with him. Someone would go down before I took the time to make those stories my own.

So imagine the crow I eat now. The stories became mine anyway, the entire batch of them. As sure as the script for a movie in which I was fated to star, these four stories charted the whole sordid affair right down to the last mythological detail.

But I learned something along the way. Woody promised the stories would heal. The stories led me home. But they did not heal. I wish I had never found that out. I wish I had left Caty's Cavern and capsized my life in the rocks.

But I didn't.

I turned from my reflection in the window, grabbed my things, and hit the high seas for work. Inadvertently, sailing right into my new stories.

Somebody went down all right.

And I took my crew with me.

The ambulance bore no siren and flashed no lights. As slow and sullen as a funeral procession, it left the hospital, meandered by the high school, and merged onto Highway 12. A sign declared the road a scenic drive. The only scenery the boy at the window noticed was the rain-beaten foothills. And the gigantic stone cross that scarred their face.

The ambulance followed the highway just past the juvenile detention facility, then turned onto an access road separating the facility from a vineyard. Traversing soil on which both blood and wine had been spilled, it crossed an irrigation ditch then drove past jailyard and field alike until it reached the compound of cottages at the base of the foothills.

The Chinook camper following the ambulance passed the access road and parked behind an abandoned gas station up and off the highway. Across the crimson-soaked fields, the driver had a clear view of the residential treatment center behind the reformatory. From his stakeout, he peered through field glasses.

He saw Carey step from the ambulance.

An attendant escorted him to the middle cottage of three.

The cottage door opened.

Carey disappeared into Crossroads.

7

"Well, look who decided to make an appearance." Fast Eddie leapt off the sofa and strutted towards me like a used-car salesman working a prospect. "Where were you yesterday?" He slapped me some skin like a homie from the 'hood. "A little late-night action with one of those honeys you been hiding?"

I smiled to keep him guessing. I didn't care how burnt-out I was. No sweet-talking con-artist would get the better of me, even if he was Fast Eddie Firelli, the master manipulator with enough moves to get him his own casino in Vegas—if he wasn't elected to Congress first.

"No can do, Eddie. I'm sticking to my story. I was too sick to get outa bed."

"I got you covered, boss," he winked. "No need for details. We'll just keep this between you and me."

I nodded like I wouldn't have it any other way. Then it hit me. "What're you doing here anyway?"

Crossroads was small-scale. Not counting the two in the locked unit, we only had beds for twelve. Our entire grounds consisted of a ragged rec area in front, a small garden out back, two cottages for sleeping, and the main building which housed the large common room, the nurse's quarters, a director's office, a kitchen, and the locked ward the boys called 'The Box.' Within the cabin-fever conditions of such cozy quarters, a dozen charges slept, ate, shot hoops, struggled over homework, staked out turf on the sofas, fought for control of the TV, scrimmaged over checkers, postured over ping pong, moped through chores, honed dance moves, and participated in the battery of workshops, group sessions, and consultations that constituted the Crossroads treatment program. But they did not school there. Without funds for teachers or curriculum, we bussed the squirrelly residents to the vocational school in Sonoma. Which was just as well with the staff. In the battlefield bedlam of housing a dozen troubled boys in foxhole proximity to one another, weekday mornings were the sole cease-fire reprieve.

So here it was not yet noon, the premises steeped in the hot-spring soak of a morning without kids, and Fast Eddie's lounging around like a moneyed man on holiday. "What gives?" I asked.

Instantly, Eddie slumped over, pounded his chest, and hacked with a sudden attack of bronchitis, emphysema, and tuberculosis all at once. "I got it bad, Dr. T." he wheezed. "I think I got what you had. You know how nasty this stuff is."

"Okay, you got me. What's the deal?"

Miraculously cured, he straightened up and flashed me a crocodile smile. "Man, you know those guys at Vo-Tech. They got no sense of romance like you and me."

"What did you do this time, Eddie?"

"Look, all I did was give Miss Simmons some flowers for teaching us so good and looking so fine everyday."

"Flowers."

"Yeah."

"And?"

"Okay. So they were tulips from the school's garden. Where else am I supposed to get flowers for my lady?"

"Keep going."

"Of course, they had this dirty root bulb hanging off the bottom. I'm not gonna give her something that's not classy."

"Of course not."

"Right. So I broke the bulb off and replanted it." He smiled. "Someplace where there's lots of fertilizer so it can grow real good."

"Like where?"

"Through Mr. Anderson's window."

"You threw a tulip bulb through the principal's window?"

"Well the window was open, Dr. T. I got respect for public property. And you gotta admit, there's enough bullshit in that office to grow a whole field of tulips."

I shook my head. "So he expelled you."

"Not for that."

"For what?"

"I told him how he could use that bulb to stop his shit problem." He smiled again. "You know, Dr. T., they just don't have a sense of humor over there."

"Eddie, you gotta watch that mouth of yours. You can't just say everything that pops into your head."

"I know." He worked me like a con man in confession. "I don't mean to. It just comes out before I can stop it."

"Well, you gotta work on that."

"I hear ya, boss." He was as interested as a pickpocket in the priesthood.

"I'm gonna put some things down, then we'll talk." I wasn't two steps to the nurse's office before he stopped me.

"Hey, Dr. T." I turned. "Did you get some?"

"Get some what?"

"You know." He humped the air with his pelvis. "Did you do some planting of your own?"

"Watch it, Eddie, or *I'm* gonna expel you."

"I'm with ya. We'll keep it on the Q.T. Just let me know if you need some flowers to help grease the way."

"Like tulips with the root bulbs are gonna be much help."

"Come on, Dr. T. I'd treat you right. I'll give the bulbs to Mr. Anderson. I'll say they're from you."

"Eddie."

"Just watching your back, boss."

"We'll talk in a while." I was halfway this time before he stopped me again.

"Dr. T." I looked back. "It's you and me, right?" He smiled as if he was still jiving. But his eyes told otherwise. Eddie had the moves to fast-talk the stash away from an addict. He came by it honestly. His father was a heroine user who pimped Eddie for drugs. Eddie had to give himself to the pleasures of the doped-up depraved or sweet-talk his way out of it. He came to us when his dad went into a cardiac arrest while shooting-up. Eddie drove him across town to the emergency room. He was thirteen years old, and nearly as high as his father.

He sized me up with the same searching eyes as when he first came to Crossroads. He wanted to make sure he hadn't offended me. And that I really was back at work. He didn't need to worry.

"Yeah, Fast Eddie." I said. "It's you and me."

Fast Eddie got me with a single look. Of course it was him and me. If not me, who else would he have?

In ancient days, the emotionally tormented were housed in colonies far outside the town gates. Downstream, downwind, down beyond earshot of the city wall's backside, the lepers and demoniacs, the maimed and insane, the tortured souls who slashed their own bodies and the disfigured bodies who cursed their own souls, rotted away amidst the grave-pits for the unmourned dead and the dumping grounds for the village waste. One step deeper into the sewer of social hierarchy than even the prostitutes and tax collectors, these cultically unclean and culturally cast-out were considered condemned by God. They endured an earthly hell of forgotten squalor—out of sight, and out of their minds.

Not much had changed in two thousand years.

Crossroads Residential Facility was ditched at the extreme rural edge of Santa Rosa's borders. Even the juvenile detention facility sequestering the felonious adolescents whose social deviance found more criminal outlets had greater geographical prominence than us. Albeit in decaying condition, the reformatory was perched within sight of the high-way leading out of town. Crossroads was hidden behind, wedged between the jailyard's last layer of barbed wire and the spooky wilds of the Mayacamus Mountains. Concealed from the sun let alone society, we were home to the youthful strays who wandered the world unwanted. Foster kids who couldn't adjust to their placements and orphans whose edginess deterred their adoption, delinquents who graduated from their stretches in Juvey, and schizophrenics fresh from commitments at the hospital—these were the kids with whom I ate and to whom I told stories. I soothed the demons that ravaged them, and I taught them the ways of life within the prescriptions of civilized humanity. For twelve teenage outcasts in need of shepherding toward mental soundness and social inclusion, I was all they had.

Fast Eddie reminded me of that. These boys needed more than the Trojan horse persona of an affable doctor hiding the burnt-out melancholic who'd rather be home in bed. They needed *me*. From demons well buried beneath bravado and banter, they looked to me to save them. I suppose they even loved me. After all, it was them and me.

Lucky for them, so I thought at the time, I had decided to make an appearance at work.

8

THE NURSE'S STATION AT the far end of the Commons served as operational nerve center, medical supply house, and firewall for the locked ward behind it. It could also have been a temple for an ancient goddess religion. The three women within it personified the matriarchal trinity.

Jody was the maiden. A social work major at Sonoma State, she was satisfying her senior year internship with us. Jody had the brains of a bookworm, the idealism of a Peace Corps volunteer, and the gung-ho readiness of a rookie phenom called up to pitch in a pennant race. Refusing to enflame adolescent libido, she dressed as promiscuously as an Eskimo in January. Her baggy slacks and oversized sweaters disguised every feminine curve of her figure; and the arid tundra of her face was so void of make-up that lip balm would have been a capitulation to the trade winds of sensuality. Nevertheless, every kid at Crossroads had a crush on her.

Irene, a psychiatric nurse in a life before marriage and grandkids, was the mother. After her children moved east and her husband passed away, she dusted off her credentials and returned to the profession. What she lacked in familiarity with the field's modernization she more than made up for with maternal charm. She knew all the boys' birthdays and decorated their cakes. She even baked cookies on rainy days.

Rose was the crone. A wrinkled hag of an RN, she seemed to dislike caring for kids as much as she disliked changing bedpans. Perhaps the beauty of her youth belied the irony surrounding her name, but in old age, the only rose she resembled was one that had long since withered on the vine. If Ebenezer Scrooge ever liquidated his accounting firm to work in a boy's home, donned the dour formality of a stiff white uniform, and traded his banker's visor for a nurse's cap, you'd be hard pressed to tell one curmudgeon from the other. Then again, in a medical emergency, I'd take on the terror of Christmas future to have Rose there to take charge. When a life was at stake, her stern manner transformed into an unflustered medical efficiency that was as awe-inspiring in its efficacy as it was eerie in its prescience.

A few months earlier, Hannibal suffered another psychotic reaction to his meds. In the middle of a basketball game, he spotted an army of ninjas advancing upon him from all sides. He fought them off with frantic kung fu moves, swirling in increasingly erratic circles, until he launched off on their dragon-mounted general only to smash full speed into the cast-iron basketball post. He was knocked unconscious but his body convulsed as if Beelzebub was busting to break out of his skin.

Out of nowhere, Rose materialized at his side, slipped a rubber guard into his mouth, and jabbed his thigh with a shot of Dopamine. His body went still. So did his heart. The boys, sure he was dead, gaped from the sidelines as Rose pounded Hannibal's chest and administered mouth-to-mouth. Finally, like a drowning swimmer coughing up water, Hannibal choked air back into his lungs. His eyes shot open and fixed on Rose. He was so terrified he could have been staring at the angel of death. His voice cackled like he was possessed.

"Please don't kill me."

Rose cupped her bony hands around his head and responded with absolute authority. "Nobody's going to kill you, son. I promise."

The boys were blown away beyond reason. They talked about it for days. No psychotic stupor diminished their capacities. They saw it in their right minds and with their own eyes. The enigmatic ogress smocked in perpetual white had the power to bestow life or death at will. Just as surely as she brought Hannibal back from the dead.

I'm not entirely sure they were wrong.

"Good morning, gals." I walked in without a clue about the bombshell awaiting me. Only Irene looked up. Jody pored through a feminist volume critiquing Freud. Rose scowled at a medical chart.

"There's not much good about it." Vintage Rose. Her perennial grumpiness could dampen any greeting. I let it pass.

"Everything go okay yesterday?"

Rose came back. "Two takedowns, one AWOL, a fist fight over a game of checkers, a flat tire on the bus, one parental no-show, three boxes of confiscated matches, and the little stunt Edward pulled at school." She recited the litany like we were lucky to still be licensed.

"Is that all?" I said. "For a second there I thought the kids took over Alcatraz." Sometimes I could coax from her an exasperated smirk. Not this time. She ignored me as if my cluelessness rendered a response superfluous.

"Everything was fine," Irene reassured. "Nothing we couldn't handle. You should have seen Jody with the groups."

Jody popped up from her text. "We had some real breakthroughs, I think," she relayed proudly. "I wrote it all up in the charts."

I smiled at my first years with Woody when I was certain every session I soloed would restore a child's health with a single strategic intervention. "There you go, Rose. The boys were in great hands." Jody nodded as if it were all in a day's work then returned to her studying. Rose grunted at the folder.

"How was your day away?" Irene inquired.

"Not bad," I downplayed. "I saw an old friend. He gave me an interesting story. Maybe I'll use it next week with the boys."

"Can it keep a kid from killing himself?" Rose could be as curt as cold-water, but this came out of nowhere. When she wasn't forthcoming, I looked to Irene for help.

"We have a new guest," Irene explained. "Sent over from Sutter until there's a free bed in a psych unit."

"He's a cutter." Rose spat out the epithet like it was a gang affiliation. "Meant it too. Both wrists lengthwise. Near down to the bone." Most kids cut their wrists horizontally, a relatively minor wound as the blood can coagulate before much is lost. A serious suicide attempt is when the veins are sliced up the arm so the blood can flow fast and free. Apparently, this kid knew what he was doing.

"How long's he gonna be here?" I asked.

"Two, three days," Irene answered. "Just until something opens up."

"He shouldn't be here at all." Rose sounded like a forewarning oracle. "There's not much in this file but there's enough. This kid's in trouble. He belongs in a hospital."

"What's the problem?" I asked. "We can keep him safe for a few days. It's not like he's the first cutter we've ever had."

"He's a good kid," Irene offered. "Came right in and just sat in a chair."

"Look," I continued, "after what we've been through with Hannibal and Blade this'll be like pasturing a sheep. I'll talk with him, help him feel settled."

"Good luck," Rose shot.

I looked to Irene for exposition.

"He's not talking. Hasn't said a word for days."

I wasn't deterred. I'd seen kids shut down before. "That's okay. We'll keep an eye on him then. This is no big deal."

Rose was not deterred either. She snapped the file shut and glared at me. "I'm telling you. He shouldn't be here." She tomahawked the file into my hand, pushed by me, and made for the door. Before she opened it, she turned. I couldn't tell if her eyes were pleading or forbidding. "The boy's in trouble," she repeated. "He belongs in a hospital." Then she left the station to scold Eddie into doing his schoolwork.

I raised my eyebrows at Irene to ask what that was all about. She smiled and repeated the assessment with which she sized up every boy that came through Crossroads. "He's a good kid."

I shook it off and stepped toward my office. A simple curiosity came over me. "Where's he from, anyway?"

"A boy's home up north." I didn't see it coming.

"Yeah, which one?"

"Salve Regina."

I froze. Rose's foreboding finally hit its mark. What were the odds? I hadn't been back for ten minutes and, of all places, a boy shows up from Salve Regina.

I feigned composure and reached for my door. My over-the-shoulder response seemed nonchalant. My words, however, betrayed a tremble. And they lacked Rose's prophetic insight.

"Yeah, well. He's just gonna be here a couple o' days."

9

THE CLOSED MANILA FOLDER had an innocent face. But the pages within were serpentine. They enticed me to step from my cliff-side perch into the black-hole plunge of professional impropriety. Never had I been so tempted to compromise my standards. I always met a new patient face-to-face before prejudicing my observations with the prior histories and clinical diagnoses that filled their medical files. This boy's file implored me for a premature glance. I might have taken it too—had I not been whipped back by the scourging reminder that in the end I'd only be using the boy. For the moment, professionalism won out. I set the folder aside and tried to focus on the day's tasks.

I pulled out a notepad and composed a to-do list. I had to call the hospital in Marin and check on Hannibal's condition. The boys should rehearse for their Friday night performance of the stories they wrote during the week. A group required facilitation. Charts needed updating. And Fast Eddie had to come up with an accountability plan to make restitution at his school. The day's agenda plenty full, I studied the list for the drive to begin.

The medical file would not let it come. From the corner of my desk, the folder tingled with intrigue. 'Foster, Carey,' the label read. One of Schuyler Peckham's boys. I could not help but wonder. Who else did he know at the Catholic boy's home?

I could have left the kid alone, let the nurses take care of him until he was transferred. But Jesus, a boy from Salve Regina was right in the room behind me. I resisted the urge to thumb through his file. But I stepped off the cliff all the same. With my clipboard in hand and a fresh intake form attached, I decided to pay Carey a visit.

I fell as far as the doorway that separated us.

———

At the back of my office, a metal door led directly to the locked unit. Head-high within it, an observation window was set. A web of fine wire, cut in intersecting slashes, was embedded within the glass. Before entering the ward, I peered through the meshed pane. That's how I saw him. Through the crosscutting latticework that sliced him, I first laid eyes on Carey Foster.

I had worked with troubled children for six years. I had seen kids wail in courtrooms while pulled from intoxicated parents. I had seen kids spit obscenities at guardians driving away without them. I had seen kids stew in silent defiance after taking on death with pills and turpentine. But never had I seen a child gutted by such naked despair.

He sat on the floor against the far corner wall wearing play-clothes that mocked the broken body they draped. His bombed-out eyes stared vacantly at the ground's blur before him. His wrists, wrapped from elbow to hand in snow-white gauze, laid limply at his side. His legs splayed-out, his head fallen forward, his mouth hanging open in traumatized submission, he looked like a rag-doll of a kid, too tired to stand, too tired to move, too tired to resist the train of degenerates taking their turn to assault him before discarding and forsaking him in the dark deserted corner of an asylum.

He looked like he had seen it all. And the all he had seen could kill him.

I was stunned by pity. His sorrow slayed me more than beauty or splendor ever could. I had no idea what had defiled that boy, but I ached for the suffering that disfigured him. Something in me wanted to cry. Something in me couldn't. And as my pity settled into belly depths, it stalled and transposed then came roaring back—cresting, curling, and crashing in an all-consuming resolve. No matter what else was to happen, I would never bring harm to that boy. He was entangled in a web of despair as sure as the lattice that sliced him through my window. And Goddamn it. From that labyrinth. He would be delivered.

To this day, that is how I see him. I only see Carey through the crossed mesh of a wired window. And wonder what went wrong.

———

I eased the door open and slipped into the ward. It was as quiet as a stockade on reckoning day. The boy did not move at the intrusion upon his solitude. He stared into the floor with such absorbed dejection he could have been the scapegoat for whom the gallows was prepared. I walked to the wall that was corner to his own and sat on the floor against it. His surrender to defeat seemed complete. Without a word that could stand against the weight of his sorrow, I set the clipboard aside and settled into the sea of his isolation.

We sat as the ripples of my entrance stilled once more to a dead-calm quiet. Then neither of us moving, neither of us speaking, we soaked the silence with our sadness like blood from a wound seeping into the waters that embrace it. I had no idea of the source of his pain. I barely knew the source of my own—Dachau patches, my dad's slammed doors, the long-buried ghosts at Salve Regina floated past me like oracles I learned to ignore. But sadness I knew. And I knew when silence was its only container.

The minutes drifted by without notice. The lunch hour came then waned. Irene slipped in with a meal for Carey. The spaghetti cooled. The ice cream melted. And still we sat. Until Irene returned to a meal long spoiled and silently signaled that the boys were soon to be back from school.

A rapport with Carey was still far away. He had yet to even register my presence. But for a spell, our sorrow shared that ocean of silence. When I needed to leave, I troubled the waters with as gentle a whisper as I could mouth.

"Sometimes silence is all one can say," I spoke to the floor between us. "I know. The silence speaks for me as well."

I lingered a moment longer. Then I left. He didn't move. His sorrow had much more silence to speak.

I did not return to my office and pore over Carey's file. And I did not stay for the boys' return. I made the excuse that Hannibal needed a visit and passed the rest off to Jody. I knew I had nothing to give them. As I knew what I had for Carey was more about me than him. Before I'd be good for anyone, I needed a handle on all these shadows that kept intimating their presence.

I needed to dine with some demons. Whatever that was supposed to mean.

10

I N THE YEARS SINCE my divorce from Jen, the sum total of my romantic entanglements
was limited to a single proposition at a holiday party the preceding December. I didn't
come on to her. She did me. Though she quickly found her charms powerless before the
frigid firmness of my unavailability.

I was only at the hospital in the first place to drop off some gear for a charge from
Crossroads when the festivities began in the staff room and a social worker insisted I stay
for a drink. Monica, a cute psychiatric nurse emboldened by a few sips of bubbly and the
prodding from a gaggle of co-workers, wandered my way with two paper-plates of sheet-
cake. Submerged in my usual sexual apathy, I thought nothing of it, thanked her for the
cake, and returned her Merry Christmas. As if she needed to ride her nerve before it faded
altogether, she popped right out with her proposal while stabbing at her plate.

"I was thinking, Tony, maybe, you'd like to get some dinner once the party is over."

Terror cold-cocked me, like a post-traumatic stress survivor returning to the battlefield that scarred him. "I'm sorry, Monica," was all I could think to say. "I'm not really
available."

She paled with apology. "I'm sorry. I didn't know you were married."

"I'm not," I replied. "It's just . . . I'm not over my divorce yet."

She regrouped with the sympathy that might ease a guy back into the game. "Oh . . .
how long's it been?"

"Seven years," I said.

She looked at me to be sure I wasn't lying just to ditch her. I wasn't. "That's a long
time," she offered.

"What can I say," I answered. "From the second I saw her I lost my heart."

The sentiment touched her. She continued with genuine concern. "What happened?"

I happened, I thought to myself. And I haven't been right ever since. "It's a long story,"
I brushed off.

She wasn't so easily brushed. "I'd like to hear it sometime."

She had no clue about the story for which she was asking. Nor the guy she was asking
to share it. Both are the cradle of nightmares. "Thanks a lot," I said. "But some stories are
better left untold."

She nodded like she knew. "Okay," she said. "But let me know if you change your
mind."

I assured her I would.

Then I excused myself, and got the hell out of there.

———

It was testimony to my distress that I walked into the psychiatric hospital without a way to forestall Monica should I happen to run into her. Seeing me from across the lobby, she intuited why I was there, picked up a chart off her desk, then drifted over with the warmth to remind me that her holiday offer still stood.

"Hi, Tony," she greeted. "You must be worried sick about Hannibal."

"I am," I answered. "How's he doing?"

"His injuries are healing fine. But he's still very agitated, and hallucinating. We're trying to find the right combination of meds." I nodded, expecting to hear as much. "Boy, it sure sounds awful," she continued, "what you two went through."

"Yeah," I admitted. "It was pretty scary."

"It's amazing you were able to get him to safety."

"Well," I dismissed, "I shouldn't have had him out there in the first place."

"You couldn't know he would break like that."

"I don't know," I said, knowing full well. Then before the spotlight got much hotter, I bolted. "Say, is it alright if I see him?"

She looked at me like I was a mystery she couldn't decipher. "Of course," she said. "Do you want a consultation room?"

"No, I just want to peek in on him."

"Sure." She led me to the locked ward, unlocked the door, and let me in. "If you need anything, I'll be right out here."

While various troubled young people crowded the sofas and chairs, Hannibal paced the back wall alone. Dragon warriors were poised on all fronts. He was so lost in his world he was beyond the ability to recognize me. It broke my heart. The poor guy was in for a several week stay before he'd be stabilized enough to come back. Knowing my approach would provoke him, I watched from the door. Though assailed from all sides, he stalked the room with the ferocity of one who would take down a battalion before going down himself. I admired his tenacity. I was so worn-down I would have let them have me. Resistance takes energy I no longer had. I wished him strength for the fight. Then I sucked up enough to leave.

Monica was busy with a nurse near the office. Seeing my chance for an easy escape, I made for the exit. I mouthed my thanks and waved, letting her know I knew she was busy. She waved back, letting me know she was only too glad to help. I felt bad for hurting her. Kind and attractive, she was plenty desirable. She couldn't help it that she lacked one thing. And everything. She wasn't Jen.

I found my truck and fought the Friday rush hour traffic back up the 101. When I reached Rohnert Park it hit me. I did not know if I was ready to face my ex-wife in person, but I knew the site which held her ghost, along with a host of others. I pulled off the freeway, toward one of our haunts—the pond at Sonoma State.

I met Jen the night I was saved. More accurately, I was saved the night I met Jen. For the truth is, I found Christ hoping to get a phone number.

I was a senior at Sonoma State looking to kill time on Halloween. I hated the holiday; I even spat at my roommates about it. Six of us lived in a Victorian house custom-built to be a haunted mansion. My roommates decorated it with such ghoulishness Bela Lugosi would have been spooked. I dropped by for a quick bite before leaving them to scare the bejesus out of every kid in the neighborhood.

"Come on, Tony," Jake pleaded while face-painting stitches at the kitchen table. "You'll miss out on all the fun."

"I told you, I got things to do."

"Do them later."

"They can't wait."

His vampire fangs flashed a diabolical smile. "Think of all those kids screaming."

"I've heard it before." I stung my fingers on a cheese melt as I pulled it out of the toaster oven.

"Look, you don't have to dress up. Just slip on some shades and play some scary music from the steps." Back then, I played a mean blues harmonica.

"You look," I came back. "It's not about dressing up. I just don't like Halloween."

"Aww, wut's da madder, Tony?" the hulking Kirk walked in, blood dripping from the axe lodged in his head. "Afwaid of a few mon . . . sters?"

"No, Kirk. I have a mid-term. Leave it at that."

But he didn't. He grabbed my neck with crimson-soaked hands. "Ooooh," he teased. "Tony's scared of a liddle moooon . . . sterrr."

"*Look!*" I shoved Kirk away. "*I don't care about dressing up, and I'm not afraid of any monsters.*" My quivering voice rose. "*I don't. Do. Hallo. Ween! Got it?*" I grabbed my backpack and left.

Of course, I lied. I detested dressing up. And I was only too afraid of the monsters unleashed on that night when demons roam free.

⸺

I was twelve the last time I costumed for Halloween. I didn't do it for the candy. Nor to hang out with my friends.

I dressed up with my mom.

Like the night sky, my mom had two sides—impenetrable darkness, and starry brilliance. Most of the time, she hovered between melancholic distractedness and outright dementia. She either sleep-walked through cooking dinner and making small talk, or she lay hidden in her darkened bedroom for days at a time. During such spells, my father forbad entrance into her room. We crept around the house as if sound would slay her, listening for a toilet's flush to divulge she was still alive, or a bathrobe's rustle that she was ready to return from the sullen land within which she was lost. Even after she died, my first impulse upon coming home was to check the most accurate barometer for her mood—her bedroom door. A closed door silenced all play.

But once in a while, her door swung open and she emerged in full flourish. She could snap out of a stupor straight into the gaiety of a Hollywood starlet ready for a night on the strip. Trained as an actress before the war, she had an entire stage show of personalities available to her. She sizzled in the sequin-gown flare of Fanny Brice, played coy in the come-hither coquetry of Raquel Welch, melted into the schoolgirl sensuality of Marilyn Monroe, then turned with the stiff-shoulder brashness of Mae West.

And such a Godiva demanded an audience. With Petaluma as her stage and shopping as a pretense, my mom promenaded and sashayed, teased and winked her way through grocery stores and bank lobbies, doctor's offices and five-and-dimes, mail rooms and retail outlets more focused on getting a rise from her fans than getting the business at hand completed. My mom did not run errands; she made appearances. Security guards, bank VPs, grocery store clerks, postal supervisors, it mattered not. She smooched cheeks and squeezed love handles, patted backsides and squealed at pinches, feigned helplessness and gushed over assistance, all while complimenting hairstyles and extolling tie selections, fussing over disheveled shirts and smirking over lipstick stains, admiring shapely builds and fanning her dress around her own, then locking an elbow and strolling through the establishment like Vivian Leigh crashing a ball on the arm of Clark Gable. People went out of their way for a charge of the free-spirited juice that flooded out of her. Managers opened checkout stands. Doctors jostled appointments. The mayor canceled a city hall hearing to help her fill out a voter registration card. I swear to God, she would have got the Royal Guard at Buckingham Palace to break rank and give her directions to a telly—then she'd plant him a big wet one for his courtesy.

My mom was great.

Halloween was one time each year her Hello Dolly exuberance faithfully showed up. When I was twelve, *Butch Cassidy and the Sundance Kid* had just come out. Like everybody else, I fell hard for the affable head of the Hole in the Wall Gang, so for the big night I dressed up like Butch. I found a derby like the one Paul Newman wore, cowboy boots, and a frilly white shirt at a thrift store. My mom converted a plaid tablecloth into pleated pants and a matching vest, then snagged a tie from my dad's dresser. To complete the illusion, I snatched a family heirloom passed down through the men of the clan for three generations, my dad's pocket watch. I snuck it from his closet, tucked it into my vest pocket, then sagged the chain through a buttonhole. The gold gleamed so brightly I felt ready to duel with my timepiece alone any lawman who interfered with my rapscallion ways.

My mom followed suit with the theme. She disappeared into her bedroom then reemerged as the sexiest saloon singer west of the Mississippi. Her spaghetti-strap dress of deep purple silk barely slipped past her petite bottom. A lilac garter belt hung teasingly high on her black-nyloned thigh. Violet heels adorned her feet as matching silk wrapped her head and hung to the side like a drunk wearing his necktie as a headband. And entwined around her shoulders like a snake around an Egyptian dancer, she flaunted a lavender feathered boa, more roaring '20s than gay '90s, but it didn't matter. She could wrap a man with that plaything as easily as wrapping thread around her finger.

I was no taller than her shoulders but I was her escort. I looked like a tenderfoot going to his first barn dance with a Vegas showgirl. And I had the perfect affair at which to cut my courting teeth—the annual Halloween party at the Petaluma Fire Department.

My sister's friend dropped us off at the corner and we made a proper entrance. With my mom's arm slipped through mine, we sashayed toward the middle-aged firefighter gathering tickets at the station door. The second he saw us he put two fingers to his mouth and jumpstarted my mom with a piercing whistle.

"Lay-na Backman, you are a feast for my eyes."

"Oh, look at you," my mom retorted, her German accent all but worn away after twenty years in the States. "You're just a boy." Then she winked and cast her boa over his shoulder. "Come see me when you're all growned up."

"I already am," the firefighter backed off. "And you're still too hot for me."

"Such is the cross I bear," my mom lamented. "You have no idea." Then she snapped the boa back, turned toward the party, and pranced straight onto center stage.

Mr. Petrocelli, my school principal, sat precariously perched over a dunking tank pool. My mom dallied her way to the front of the line, grabbed three balls, and smiled at Mr. P. as if she had the power to wet him down or hang him out to dry at will.

"Vell, vell, Jimmy," she toyed with a Lady Dracula accent straight from Transylvania. "Should I or shoun't I?" She fingered the balls teasingly.

"You're killing me, Lena. Throw the balls already."

She played with him a moment longer, then threw the balls in wild disregard for the target. One hit the tank, the other two smacked the adjacent booth. Mr. P. heckled, "Come on. You can't steam a guy up without cooling him down."

My mom was unperturbed. She waltzed right up to the bull's eye, slapped it with her hand, then sauntered off, pleased as a princess disposing of recalcitrant peasants. Everybody clapped as Mr. P. good-naturedly protested the assault but my mom had other scenes to play.

She sweet-talked the mayor into bobbing an apple for her, and playfully held his head as he pretended to drown. She coaxed a firefighter into letting her sit behind the wheel of a hook and ladder, and squealed when she inadvertently set off the siren. She declined an invitation to judge the pumpkin-carving contest, mere vegetative beings not worth the effort, but headed a charge through the haunted maze, leading a parade of costumed kids and outfitted fire officials all holding hands to take on the ghouls together.

By the time the hoopla was over she formed a chorus line with the firefighters, herself at the center, posed for pictures from an engine, her leg held high through a fireman's coat, and cooled off the crowd with a mock spraying, clenching a humongous hose to her chest before its bulk and her exhaustion brought the manic run to an end. To the disappointment of the hardcore partiers, but the relief of the worn-out, it was time to go. She bid her farewells, then shagged a ride home with the chief of police.

We sat three abreast in the squad car, my mom in the middle wearing the captain's hat. When we pulled up to the dark house, she returned the cap to the officer's head, pecked his cheek, and thanked him with the nobility of a grande dame.

"You are such a darling, Captain." She wrapped her boa around his neck as a gratuity then slipped into an immigrant fresh from the Fatherland. "Danke for ze rite."

The cop turned to me. "You're a lucky boy, Tony. Your mom knows how to have a good time." He let us out and drove off.

My mom took the derby off my head, placed it askance on her own, then slipped her arm through mine. She was as content as an actress returning from the Academy Awards with an Oscar in hand. And as tired as if she celebrated until dawn.

"My lucky boy," she purred leaning into me as we swayed up the unlit walk. She had not been drinking, she *never* drank, but her steps became increasingly unsteady as we neared the porch.

"Sshhh," she whispered loudly like a tipsy teenager coming in after curfew. Her voice slurred to reinforce the drunken charade. "Don't . . . want . . . to waken . . . any . . . body . . . up."

By the time we got to the door she was too wasted to think clearly. She patted random parts of her body trying to remember where she hid the house key. Groggily, it came to her. She pulled up the side of her dress, then fumbled inside her panty hose. As she pulled it out, it dropped to the concrete. "Ooopsie-Daycee," she stammered, her alcoholic act accelerating by the second. She was too tanked to stand on her own. I leaned her against the house, retrieved the key, and unlocked the door.

"SSSHHH!" she bellowed unaware of her volume. Barely staying upright, she pivoted around the doorjamb and slammed against the inside wall of the house. She closed her eyes and puffed from the exertion. She looked ready to slide onto the floor. I feared I'd have to carry her to bed, or drag her trying.

"My lucky boy. Ve had a yummy time, no?"

"That we did, Mom."

"Do you tink ze fireboys, dey like me?"

"Sure they do. Everybody likes you."

"Such goot boys dey are."

She half-opened her eyes. A misty amorousness clouded them. She could have been seeing one of the firemen for all I knew. "And you are such a goot boy, too. My Antony." She placed her hand on my cheek. "Do you love your mother?"

"Sure, Mom."

"Of course you do. You're my number vun."

She closed her eyes and dropped like a puppet whose strings were snipped. I caught her and pulled her up, draping her arm over my shoulder. "Be my number vun," she slurred. "Take your mother to bed." I held her hip to my side. My hand slid on her silky dress. She pressed close. I turned toward the hallway.

That's when we saw him. He sat in the far corner of the living room. In the darkness, we would not have seen his sinister silhouette. But he took a slow drag from a cigarette. The rusty glow of the ash swelled. We couldn't see his eyes. But their searing stare reached across the room and filled us both with dread.

Without severing his gaze he stood, fingered the cigarette, and flicked it at the wall. Then, as unhurried as a hunter approaching trapped prey, he stepped toward us. I did not know the source of my father's malevolence. But I could feel it. My mother felt it too.

"No, Yakov. Please. No." Her voice was scared-straight sober.

He said nothing. He stared with cold disgust as he paced toward us and stopped so close I could smell his smoker's breath. He cocked his head and eyed me from head to toe to head. I was dressed like an outlaw, but I was even too scared to flee. He dismissed me with a grunt and turned back to my mom.

"So," he savored maliciously. "Our boy's a man now."

"No, Yakov," my mom pleaded. "Don't do this. I beg you."

"Don't you think it's time he sees you for what you really are?"

She shook her head, staring with terror. "Please, no."

"Eine ganz . . . normale . . . Fotze," he spewed with guttural venom.

Her eyes fell to the floor. "Please, no." She knew it was useless.

My father gritted his teeth and spit each word again.

"Eine ganz." He grabbed my mother's dress above her chest.

"Normale." He cinched the dress in his fist.

"*Fotze!*" He puked the word out as he forced his hand down. The spaghetti straps snapped. The stitches on the side tore. The dress ripped down my mother's front and dangled from her waist.

I flinched as if afraid his hand would come after me. But she stood utterly still. Her arms lay lifeless by her side. From her hips up, she was naked. With the exception of the ridiculous derby atop her head.

"Get a good look at your mother, Tony." His contempt was depthless. He pressed his middle finger into the hollow of her neck. He slid the finger down her skin, between her modest breasts, and along her bare belly.

"It's time you know who she really is."

The finger slid past the fabric at her pelvis. It stopped underneath her crotch. He toyed with the sagging silk. "A whore." He turned his palm up. The erect middle finger pointed between her legs. He deliberated. Then snorted as if it wasn't worth the effort. He lifted the finger towards himself. The snagged dress rose with the pull. When it reached breast high, the dress snapped free and returned to its exposing sag.

"Your mother's a whore, Tony. A *Fotze*." The last word he spit into her face. "Nothing but a common *cunt*." Then he turned his back and returned to the dark.

No. I don't do Halloween.

My senior year in college, I sat the holiday out against a tree in a moonlit meadow. I had wandered to campus after storming out on my roommates and passed on hitting the books at the library. The Commons rocked with a costume ball so I passed by that as well. I rambled into Commencement Park and stumbled on a giant blue spruce set back from the path. Its lower branches drooped to the ground to create a secluded grotto within. I ducked through the limbs, leaned against the trunk, and pulled out my harmonica. The fir-thatched pocket was thick enough to shelter one from a storm but sparse enough to peek both at the Commons to my right and the pond dead ahead.

Commencement Lake held a crescent moon on its still surface. The night was quiet, except for the occasional swell of music that puffed from the Commons like intermittent smoke signals as people slipped into the party. Until something better came up, I cupped my harp and played.

I didn't pay attention to what flowed from my instrument. The riffs rippled freely as I mused about where to go once the night chill discouraged my musical interlude. A billow of music escaped from the Commons. Count Dracula and June Cleaver, equally scary monsters in my book, checked out the bash. 'I could start on my psych report,' I considered. A fresh swell of music—two jocks violated the spirit of things by simply wearing their football pads. 'Maybe I'll take in a movie.' More noise slipped free—Richard Nixon in prison garb and Dorothy straight from Oz breezed in. 'I could sneak over to the lounge and watch TV.' My options grew but none took hold. I was slack at sea without as much as a whisper of wind to inspire a course to sail on.

A wind came soon enough.

Another gust of music escaped from the Commons. Freddy Kruegger with knived fingers held the door for Madonna, the latter in lingerie with funnels for breasts. They entered. The door narrowed, the music faded. But not completely. It swelled again as the door swung out. The party's glow washed over the porch. And into its brightness stepped the woman I still believe was more source than reflection of light.

She wore faded denim and downy flannel but shown with an angel's nobility, a country girl used to homemade bread and feather beds, with a tickle for Waterford crystal and champagne. She wore hiking boots but eased with buoyant grace, a sleeveless vest but radiated warmth through smiling eyes. And flowing in wind-tousled, shoulder-length waves, her strawberry-blonde hair sparkled as if knit by the rays of the early morning sun. In a moment, the axis around which my life was lived shifted. I should have leapt up and danced. And I should have broken down and wept. For from that point on, all bliss would be measured by the ambrosial sweetness of consummating my love with that earthen apparition. And every sting that sorrow might bring would pale before the anguish at missing her by my side. A new god ruled in my life. And the god of love is both bountiful and bitter.

She was with a young lady I vaguely recognized from a Western Civ. class I took the year before. She glanced at a watch then strolled around the far side of the pond. I watched the light bounce in her step, the sway in her perky bottom, the faint firefly flicker of her hair in the moonlight. I still played, but not any melody I ever played before. My improvised licks bubbled up like spontaneous poetry serving the single desire quickening within me. I wanted to brush close to the featherbed flannel of her sleeve, brighten in the hearth of her smiling eyes, lay beside the embers of her fireside hair, and come home to the warmth of holding her in my arms.

She looped the pond and made for a gazebo some fifty yards to my left. She paused before the pond's stillness, my serenade but a murmur if she heard it at all. I ached to amble down the path to meet her. But I was paralyzed to the spot. She turned with her friend and resumed the path in my direction. My heart pounded as she neared me. I kept playing. She was well within earshot of my music. Did she know that the melodies coming out of the shadows were melodies composed for her, a love song hoping to kindle a love song in return? If she did, she gave no indication. She glided along the path as if the music was as natural as the hum of the crickets. Until she passed the break of branches directly before me. She did not break stride. She did not say a word. She did not make a gesture. As she passed, she simply turned her head, caught my eye, and smiled.

I will suck the milk from the plump breast of that smile for as long as I am able to breathe.

I did not smile in return, nor even nod my head. I kept playing as she turned back and walked on with her friend. I hungered to hurry after her, but I hesitated. I was not playing it cool. I was scared stiff. Women have always terrified me. The only date I had in high school came when my English teacher arranged one after hearing I wasn't going to the Christmas formal. My only college romance had been a near platonic fling that ended after I froze up after our first French kiss. I kept the Pandoran box of sexuality locked shut. God only knew the plagues that were suppressed within it.

But that smile worked on me. And finally it kindled a fragile resolve. After the two women gamboled around the student union, I gathered my pack and set out. Keeping to the shadows like a stalker on the make, I watched them drop a volume in a library book-slot, meander around some classroom buildings, cross a quad, then bounce up the steps into Ives Hall. Every light in the building was muted save one, the first floor amphitheater that served as a lecture hall.

I lingered in the shade and sweated over a plan. How did guys do this? I'd have ten seconds max to come off charming enough or cultured enough or studly enough to keep her from taking a good look at me and laughing in my face. Do I make like it was Orientation Day and ask her where she came from, pretend to recognize her from a ficti-tious Arthurian legends class, or just come clean with my desire to lay by her side for the rest of my life? Get real. A junior-high geek had a better chance getting a date with the high-school homecoming queen.

Time wasted away as I agonized. Streams of people shuffled up the steps and into the hall. Whatever was going on in there, it attracted quite a crowd. I limply plotted to inquire about her taste for harmonica music, make a quick bid for a phone number, then get the hell out of there before I hurt myself. Still I waited, until well after the last of the stragglers hastened up the steps as if late for a final exam. I didn't want anybody to see if I lost nerve and beat a hasty retreat.

The lure for the crowd was unmistakable. The building throbbed as I scaled the steps. And as I opened the door a gale-force blast of noise hit me with enough impact to sweep a small child off its feet. A rush of music blared from the lecture hall off the foyer with the volume of a rock concert and the spirit of a square dance. Inside, a swarm of revelers were wrapped up in a whirlwind of singing and clapping, toe-tapping and swinging. I edged forward and found a poster-board sign propped on a chair in front of the door. In bright orange letters it declared, 'GLORY GATHERING HERE.' A stack of flyers lay beside it.

> Looking for an alternative to Halloween?
> Come to the Glory Gathering.
> We don't wear costumes. We don't praise demons.

But we have plenty of spirit.

Ives Hall
7:00 p.m. October 31
Sponsored by Campus Crusade for Christ
(Dedicated to bringing you a scare-free environment!)

All are welcome.

I didn't know what a Glory Gathering was, didn't know if I was ready to be swept up into the hurricane contagion driving every spirit in that room. But the object of my nascent lust was in its midst, so I stepped through the wide-open door.

The amphitheater was packed. Two hundred people were carried away on the musical current, each one standing as they grooved with the enthusiasm of a pep rally. Dancing Hasids could not have been more ecstatic, Pentecostals no more energetic. They faced a projection screen at the sunken stage displaying the song's words. To the side, a small ensemble was assembled—keyboards, bass, drums, a gal with a flute, another with a tambourine. And at the center, leading the singing before a stand-up mike, strumming a guitar like a folk musician, stood the most joy-filled human being I had ever seen. As I was to learn, Danny was his name—the man destined to be my big brother and spiritual father, my mentor in romance, and my partner in song. The man who would stand by my side at my wedding. The man we would name our first-born son after.

"*Glad you're here.*" The music swallowed the shouting voice at my shoulder. "*My name's Matt.*" He shook my hand and smiled with such warmth I could have been the honored guest at the party. "*Follow me.*"

He clapped along the amphitheater rim then down the aisle to a couple of free spaces at the end of a row. As he stepped in, he was flooded with spontaneous affection. The guy next to him widened with glee and wrapped him in a bear hug, a guy in front turned and did the same, a guy behind massaged his shoulders, folks all around shook his hand, patted his back, high-fived him, and flashed him winks as if he just walked in after being lost at sea. They loved this guy, and he glowed in their embrace. Matt nodded toward me like I was his long-lost brother and the circle of folks showered me as well. They shook my hand, patted my back, and beamed me grins, all while clapping and singing as if their delight flowed straight from the music. They loved me too, like I was one of their kin who brought them joy by simply showing up to the shindig. I was so overwhelmed I almost forgot why I was there. Then I saw her, halfway across the room, a bit further down. She was taken up into the same musical whirlwind. And it only magnified her beauty. Lightly clapping and swaying as she sang, her radiant face lit up like an apricot rose in full beaming bloom.

I gave in to the contagion and clapped with the revelers, stumbling through the words on the screen. It was a foot-stomping, barn-raising, hoedown of a tune with enough juice to electrify a county fair.

Give me wax for my board, I'll go surfin' for the Lord
Give me wax for my board, I pray,
Give me wax for my board, I'll go surfin' for the Lord
I'll go surfin' 'til the break of day.

A chorus of hosannas to the King of Kings interspersed the verse then we swept around for another ride.

> Give me umption for my gumption and I'll praise him through consumption,
> Give me umption for my gumption I pray,
> Give me umption for my gumption and I'll praise him through consumption,
> I will praise Him 'til the break of day.

The tune was so catchy and the lyrics so snappy, by the time we docey-doed to the last verse I was swinging like a card carrying member of the heavenly choir. I didn't understand the words, but I sang like a cherub.

> Give me hot sauce for my taco and I'll witness in Morocco,
> Give me hot sauce for my taco, I pray, Hallelujah,
> Give me hot sauce for my taco and I'll witness in Morocco,
> I will witness 'til the break of day.

It was as invigorating as hell—like currents of fresh air lifting me up into the thrills of good humor. I sailed along, feeling right at home with the mock blues beat of the next tune.

> Jesus is the rock 'n' he rolls my blues away.
> When you wake up in the mornin' and the sky ain't bright 'n blue,
> When you wake up in the mornin' and the big world's after you,
> When you wake up in the mornin' Jesus gonna pull you through,
> Why? . . . 'Cuz . . .
> Jesus is the rock 'n he rolls my blues away.

These people were a blast. Of course they could use a little harmonica, but they were flying high without it, taking me right up with them. The next song, I even knew—a bee-bopping hop with Simon and Garfunkel romping down the cobblestones, loving life, looking for fun, and through it all, feeling groovy. The tunes kept coming and we kept soaring, each song lifting me higher and gliding me freer through the boundless sky of elation. I didn't know what we were drinking, but I was guzzling. We were sailing on the currents that eagles soar on, that clouds float upon, that mountaintops cool to. I wanted to break free and fly to the sun but I stayed with the others as we glided like a broad dense flock of starlings, sweeping far and arcing near, circling high and swirling low, now here, now there, now up, now down, carried by the fresh sweet breath of life blowing through the music.

"I just want to praise the Lord," we sang, borne by God's unfathomable goodness. "Father, I adore you," we cooed, sustained by God's awesome power. "Love Him in the morning," we hailed, uplifted by God's unquestionable faithfulness. And "Love Him in the evening," we answered, held aloft by His promise to be there through happiness and hardship alike. This was nothing like the God I knew, but I sang to Him anyway. And His music kept me in flight through the atmospheric heights of a spiritual euphoria I had never experienced before.

Then something happened. The songs slowed in tempo and mellowed in mood. We eased through a slow descent, not back to the lecture hall, but to some hushed world pregnant with the sacred. We sang softly through a mountain pass portal, over evergreen forests, across trickling streams, and down into an alpine valley of reverent stillness. We set foot on a grassy meadow. A gentle breeze breathed through the trees. The sun's warmth bathed us from above. A pond lay still at our side. We rested on holy ground.

Our singing grew whispered with reverence. We closed our eyes. We held out our hands. We rocked in peace. Our choruses became chant-like, repeating lines soaking more deeply with each caressing pass.

"Oh how He loves you and me . . ."

"God is so good . . ."

"Holy is His name . . ."

"Alleluia, Alleluia, Alleluia . . ."

As I sank into the sacred center of the music, I sensed a Presence, fatherly and benevolent, fill the meadow from behind. Like the sun sweeping over a shadow, warmth intensified as it neared. It bid me to turn into Him. I ached to. I ached to feel His touch on my shoulder. I ached for His arms to wrap me. It swelled around me like a blanket. I turned. And was swallowed into the numinous like a star dissolving into the bright sky of daylight.

I didn't sing. I didn't speak. I didn't exist at all. Or maybe I existed for the first time. But for a timeless moment, I found myself in my Father's arms. And for once, this Father held me close.

When words finally came, they came from our leader. He gave language to my feelings.

"Praise you," Danny whispered. "Praise you, Heavenly Father. ('Praise you.' I echoed at the edge of my consciousness.) You are here, and we adore you. ('Yes, you are here.') You keep us safe. ('I am safe.') You hold us in your mercy. ('I am held.') We are yours forever, shielded from evil in your everlasting love. ('I am shielded from evil; don't ever take this love away.')

"But Father-God, the powers of darkness threaten to steal us. ('No, don't let them near.') Tonight, we are reminded that demons prowl the earth. ('Don't let them prowl.') All over the land, people wear costumes like people of old mocking these demons, hoping to scare them back into darkness. ('Scare them away forever.') But we know better; the Devil himself is a master of disguise. ('A master.') And it takes more than a Halloween mask to scare him from his wicked designs. ('More than a mask.')

"You have given us more. ('What more?') A true costume to protect us from all evil. ('What costume?') Your Word provides the belt of truth and the breastplate of righteousness. ('A belt and a breastplate.') Shoes of steadfastness with which to stand firm and a shield of faith to fight off the arrows. ('Shoes and a shield.') The helmet of salvation and the sword of the Spirit, the sword of life, the sword of God's Word to wield in our enemy's face. ('A helmet and a sword.')

"We want to be costumed in the armor of Christ. ('Yes.') We want to hide behind the shield of your love. ('I do.') We want to live in your Presence forever. ('Please.') So we open our hearts to receive you. ('I open.') We entrust to you the throne of our being. ('I entrust.')

We accept you as Lord, as Savior, as Armor against Satan. (I accept.') And we raise to You our hands as a pledge as we claim your Lordship in our lives."

I had no idea what I signed on for, but I didn't care. I wanted to hide in the costume of Christ. I wanted to flee from the Devil. I wanted to soak in that moment forever. And I would have followed anyone who promised to sustain my bliss.

"Praise Jesus," Danny swooned. "Praise Jesus," murmured the crowd. "Praise Jesus," I joined in. Sure I did. I raised my hands and praised Lord Jesus. And Jesus came into my life.

Softly, within the mountain meadow of our communion with God, the music returned. It lifted us into a last soaring circle of praise and carried me along the final glides of my maiden flight through the heavens of God's faithfulness.

Then it brought me back to earth.

Some say that on the day we are born into Jesus, the mask of sin falls away and our true face shines in fresh innocence. I don't buy that anymore. But for a night, it was true. I felt so clean, so alive, so *right*, I bubbled with goodwill and self-assurance. Free and emboldened, I did things that quite simply were not me. Or if they were me, they were a me I had never been before. I hugged a bevy of total strangers, embracing Matt and all the people around him, saying 'God bless you' to each one with the giddy abandon of Scrooge on Christmas morning. I dashed onstage and begged to try-out for the band with the unapologetic adoration of a groupie tickled to share floor space with his musical idols. I held a man's gaze as Danny welcomed me to the fold with a lingering smile, one hand on my shoulder, the other cradling my cheek, both of us looking into each other with the unashamed affection of two guys destined to be soul brothers.

I even introduced myself to a girl.

As I turned to leave the stage, I spied across the room the young lady with hair the color of an autumn sunrise. She perused a leaflet while her friend chatted off to the side. Without hesitation, I walked over as if it would be the most natural thing in the world for her to find me as attractive as I found her.

"Hi," I said as I walked up. "My name's Tony."

I thought I had already flown rather high. But when she looked up, her eyes sparkled like sunlight on the sea. I swear, I sailed as close to that fiery disc in the sky as any man has dared before. If I was going to fall, it would be right into those waters.

From that height, I could almost intuit it all—the first date giggles and the harvest moon smooches, the Bible study fellowships and the coed softball leagues, the sunny afternoons of playing my harp in her lap and the starry nights of interlaced ecstasy. It was poised like a vision awaiting an incantation to set it all into consummating motion. The incantation came. With magic to spare. Right in her very first words to me.

"Hi," she smiled back. "I'm Jennie."

The incantation seemed to hold those many years later as I wandered the pond where I first laid eyes on her. The memory of that initial sighting swelled with such force Jen could have been strolling beside me as I looped the water, lingered at the gazebo, then approached the blue spruce shelter where I once was hiding a Halloween away.

It had not changed in all those years. The tree towered. The limbs flared. The fir-thatched grotto received me as I nestled within its shadows and sat against the trunk that once supported my music. The only difference was, I did not have my harmonica. My music died when Daniel did. That was the flaw in the Glory Gatherings, and the choruses that sustained them. They could not hold a baby's death. Nor the parent responsible.

Sitting in the dark beside Commencement Pond, the night's silence was appropriate. I had yet to find a song that could.

11

I DROPPED BY CROSSROADS Saturday morning to catch up on some paperwork. The boys were away on a day-trip to Clear Lake—the place was productively quiet. When I entered the nurse's station, I ran into Irene. We exchanged greetings. Then I inquired after Carey.

"How's our boy in the Box?"

Our enduring optimist furrowed with concern. "Not too good," she admitted. "He tossed in his bed until the night nurse gave him a sedative. This morning, he hasn't eaten or spoken. He won't even look at anybody. I'm worried about him, Tony."

I was too. But I was worried about getting involved as well. "Any word about a bed opening up?"

"Nothing. Then again, they thought it wouldn't be until the beginning of the week."

"Well, all we can do is keep him safe," I offered. "And get him to a hospital."

I slipped into my office, set down my backpack, then observed him through my door's wired window. He sat on a Naugahyde sofa as if careful not to soil it. A jean jacket covered his previous day's clothing, the collar turned up but for a single flap that sagged like a bird's broken wing. I thought about sharing his silence for a while. But I knew he didn't need it. What he really needed was a therapeutic alliance with a doctor who would see him through the long haul. Connecting with me would bring another loss when his permanent placement came through. I let him be, and turned to updating the files on my desk.

I was still detailing the incident with Hannibal when Irene peeked into my office.

"Someone from Salve Regina's here," she announced.

My heart-rate skyrocketed. I feigned nonchalance by continuing to write. "You're kidding."

"I'm sure they're worried sick about him," she explained.

I kept writing as I braced myself. "Who is it?"

"A Father Ichabod Eichler." Irene sensed nothing. "Father Ike. He's one of Carey's teachers."

I was both relieved and disappointed.

"Good," I replied instinctively. "Tell him I'll be out in a minute."

Irene left. I stopped writing. 'Come on,' I said to myself. 'This is not that big of a deal.' I stared at my notes. They trailed into scribble. I set my pen down, and sought out our visitor.

———

Ichabod Eichler was not the tall gaunt scarecrow his name connoted. To the contrary, he was short, plump, and bald with the nervousness of a chauffeur who had just dinged a Ferrari. He sat on a chair's edge in wrinkled clerics, fingering his tweed sporting-cap as if rushing through the rosary before the oncoming confrontation. I was the same way when I first worked with Woody. I had so many demons besetting my own psyche, I entered the mental health facility certain I'd be the first one restrained. There are two kinds of people in the world I've found—those that visit an asylum like voyeurs at a brothel and those that walk the wards watching out for their backs. I was the latter. Apparently, Father Eichler was too.

"I'm Dr. Backman," I greeted. "It was nice of you to come."

"Oh, Monsignor insisted on it." He fidgeted off the chair and shook my hand with a grip as limp as a child's. "He's very worried about Carey. We all are." He sat back down and hastened the prayer around his cap's lining. "How is he?"

"He's pretty shook up," I reported. "Hasn't said a word since he's been here."

"Not a word? My." He frowned at the floor as if his worst fears were confirmed.

"I understand you're one of his teachers." My words took a moment to reach him.

"What's that?" he fluttered back. "Oh, yes. I am."

"What subject?"

He blinked in time with his fidget. "Music," he said, glancing my way between beats. "I conduct the boy's choir."

"And Carey's in it?"

"Oh," his cap stopped, as did his blink. He brightened toward me, then down at the floor savoring a memory like a maestro would a symphony. His transformation reminded me of my high-school drama teacher. In the real world, he stuttered to the point of unintelligibility. But when he acted onstage, the stutter disappeared as his love for the theater inspired a flawless performance. Clearly music inspired Eichler. Along with Carey's apparent talent. "Carey's in it," he assured. "He has a voice that could make the Virgin weep. The purist soprano Monsignor's ever heard. Me too." The shadow returned to his face, as did his finger's fidgeting. "That's what makes this so strange. He should be elated right now."

"Why's that?" I asked.

He shook his head with bewilderment. "We're finalists in the Association of Boys' Choirs' national competition. They're sending a jury to our Easter recital. This has never happened to us before. It's a dream, really. And it's all because of Carey. He's our lead soloist."

"Does he know about it?" I was bewildered as well. The mute boy in lockup bore no resemblance to this lead soloist in a choir on the verge of national recognition.

"Of course. We found out the very day . . . I just don't get it. He was so excited. Everybody was cheering and slapping him on the back. He positively glowed. Then later that night, he's . . . he's done that to himself."

It wasn't adding up. "You're telling me he got this news the very day he cut himself?"

"Exactly."

"And he was ecstatic?"

"You should have seen him."

"So what happened?"

"That's just it. Nobody knows." He frowned as he fought through the extremes of that day. "Monsignor figured something must've happened in the dorm that evening, but nobody noticed a thing. Now he thinks Carey just snapped."

"Was he feeling that much pressure?"

"Not exactly," he revealed. "I've never seen Carey anxious about singing. He's soft-spoken to be sure. And when he first came to us he was so self-conscious he hardly said a word. But whenever he sings, something happens. It's like he loses himself in the music so completely he forgets where he is. I'm not sure he knows anybody else is listening. It's amazing. It's the one place in the world where he's not self-conscious."

"Well, he's not singing right now," I said. "He's traumatized beyond words. Something literally unspeakable must have happened."

Eichler shook his head with genuine anguish. "I wish I knew what it was." The horror of Carey's secret rendered us mute as well. Until Fr. Ike shuddered back. "Well, do you think it would be alright if I see him? Monsignor wants me to tell him we're all looking out for him."

To be honest I wasn't sure. I couldn't imagine Carey wanting to see anybody, but maybe greetings from his choir director would comfort him. "He may be resting," I covered. "I'll check."

———

Carey had not moved from the Naugahyde sofa. And he did not stir as I sat in the chair beside him.

"I hear you had a hard time sleeping," I opened. He did not respond one way or the other. He wasn't being rude. He was beat. "I want you to know," I assured, "that you are completely safe here. You don't have to see a soul you don't want to. And you don't have to talk until you're absolutely ready to." He took me at my word—remaining as mute as a corpse.

"Carey, Father Ike's here." He jolted back to life. He shot me a look of such terror and pleading I regretted having brought it up at all. "Don't worry," I insisted. "Like I said—you don't have to see him. I just wondered if you needed anything from school."

He looked back at the floor, craving to trust me. I assured him he could, and returned to Fr. Ike.

Eichler understood that it wasn't a good time. He almost looked relieved. He retrieved an envelope tucked at his side.

"Would you be so kind as to give him this, then," he asked. "I think it might console him."

"Sure," I said. "What is it?"

"It's a bit unusual," he confessed. "Monsignor would be furious if he knew that I did this." He paused to explain. "Carey has a peculiar fascination."

He opened the envelope and slipped out a card. The cover was an icon. Mary was framed against a barbed-wire backdrop—her yellow Star of David patched to a Jewish prayer shawl. The picture pierced me. It never occurred to me that, at the hands of the Nazis, Mary would suffer a Jewish fate. Dachau—a death-camp for mothers. "It's uncanny," I said.

"Yeah. No one thinks of the Virgin that way."

"No, it's . . . My mother was a Dachau survivor."

"Oh, I'm sorry." He feared he upset me.

"No," I reassured, "it's dead and buried. I've just, I've never seen a depiction like this." I was about to evade it by opening the card when I asked, "Where did you get it?"

"His religion teacher found it. We had the whole choir sign it."

To my credit, I did not crack the card. I ached to. But my demons were too dangerously poised already. I handed it back as if it enclosed the devil's temptress. "Of course, I'll see that he gets it," I said. "I'm sure he'll find it comforting."

I found it anything but. When I left for the day, I spied through my office window once more. Carey remained on the couch. But he no longer stared at the floor. He gazed at the icon of Mary. Perched on the coffee table, it was splayed open so it could stand. Demons indeed. They hovered within as sure as a crypt with the door already ajar. Would Mary be there when they came out to dine? I thought it best not to find out. I grabbed my things and went home.

12

$\mathbf{F}$ACING A SATURDAY EVENING alone, I stopped by Biaggio's for a pizza to go. I didn't have it in me to cook anything, and I certainly wasn't up for a night on the town. Besides, during my debacle of a year at seminary, it was Jen's and my Saturday night tradition. Friday evenings our fellowship group met, Sunday evenings had youth groups. The night in between was ours. We'd grab a pizza at Picardy's—half pepperoni and sausage, half olives and tomatoes, anchovies on the side for Jen—then picnicked by candlelight on the living room floor watching videos until *M*A*S*H* reran at eleven. Seven years of single life later, I no longer ordered a half-and-half pizza. But in a moment of nostalgia, I asked for a side of anchovies. The entire drive home, their briny smell stirred whispers of Jen's scent—I pondered the aperitif that followed the reruns.

As I pulled into the driveway, I noticed a package on my porch. I parked in my back-yard carport, brought my dinner in through the kitchen door, then walked through the house to see what it was. A brown paper-bag with its top crumpled closed had two dozen oranges inside. The note on top was written in the shaky scrawl of an old-timer who never much used a pencil. 'They make good juice. Harry.'

Harry was my next-door neighbor—a retired telephone repairman who lost his wife some ten years earlier. Without any family of his own, he devoted his time to his backyard garden. It was a pocket of paradise—fruit trees, grape arbors, vegetable plots, flowers enough for an arboretum, lawns you could putt on, and two fountains. The harvest far surpassed a single-man's needs, so he hauled his bounty to a hospice for cancer patients. Occasionally, he dropped by with something for me.

I put the oranges in the fridge then, inspired by the anchovies, I dug out my candle-sticks after grabbing a plate. Woody's prescription was somewhat a mystery, but I was aware enough to know that engaging my depression at least involved coming to terms with my ex-wife's ghost. If I prepared the meal, she was sure to come. Though I hadn't a clue how to begin to make peace.

I took the pizza and dinnerware to the living room floor. I didn't have videos, so I turned on a cassette—a tape I made and labeled 'Moody Music' for those times when a sweet melancholia overtook me so completely I could not help but settle into its intro-spective sadness. With Barbra Streisand grieving "The Way We Were," I lit the candles and sat against the sofa. The scene was set—mood light, a meal heaped with memories, a torch-song serenade, the salty essence of Jen's aroma.

But if Jen came, I wasn't receptive. Suddenly annoyed at the contrivance, I lost my appetite. I turned off the music and blew out the candles. I boxed the pizza and was about to toss it when a better idea occurred to me. I'd give it to Harry in thanks for the oranges. The anchovies I'd throw in for free.

As soon as I knocked on Harry's door, I wished a mist would render me invisible. A pizza still warm from the oven seemed a silly gesture for a bag-full of oranges. I just about dropped it on the porch—an anonymous quick-strike act of kindness without the awkward explications.

Then Harry opened the door.

His eyes, wrinkled at the edges, seemed to laugh and cry at the same time. His thinning white hair was greased back in crisp combed streaks. His hunched head nodded in a barely perceptible palsy.

And he smiled. So pleased and unsurprised to see me it could have been our Saturday night routine to cough back a cold one while catching the fights on TV.

"Please," he said, nudging the screen-door open. "Come in."

I held the door and hesitated. Harry was dressed for a special night out—a well-worn tweed jacket, a tie clipped tight to a pressed dress shirt, creased slacks extending to spit-polished shoes. A whiff of aftershave hinted of romance.

"I was just going to drop this by," I said, "to thank you for the oranges."

"No, no," he insisted. "Come in for a minute." I got the impression Harry didn't get much company. I stepped in as far as the entryway.

"So you got a big date?" I cracked.

"Oh, no." He chuckled as if his courting days were long since over. "I'm going to Mass."

That cut me short. "Hey, I'll let you go. I just thought you might like this."

"That's okay. I've got lots of time. And coffee in the pot. I'll get you some." Before I could decline, he shuffled off with the pizza. "Do you want a slice?" he called from the kitchen.

"Thanks," I answered, "but I already ate." I walked into a living room as immaculate as the gardens he kept outside. A museum-like untouchablility pervaded, circa the post-war era. The afghan draped over the couch was meticulously stretched. A Glenn Miller tune boogied out of an antique console. Framed embroidery worthy of exhibition decorated the walls. The fireplace, cold and immaculate, hadn't felt heat for years. Activity seemed restricted between a well-worn recliner and a Sony TV in the corner. I bypassed the chair and sat on the sofa.

I knew Harry lived alone, but evidence of his marriage was abundant. A waist-high bureau draped with a white lace cloth held a number of photographs scattered around a large wedding-portrait. The centerpiece displayed a much younger Harry, decked out in a suit and tie, standing next to a bride who looked like an angelic Lana Turner. The shrine of pictures, conspicuously absent of children, paid solemn tribute to a couple going through life as two.

"Looks like good pizza," Harry said, scuffling back with two mugs of coffee. He handed me one then set the other on a TV Guide next to his recliner. The chair conformed to his body as he sat.

"Boy, those oranges sure look juicy," I said.

He smiled his pride. "Those trees do put out, don't they?"

"I'll say. I've never seen a garden like yours. Every time I look something new is blooming. You keep it up all by yourself?"

"Forty-two years," he beamed. "Never missed a week of mowing."

"Well, you sure have the touch."

Our chat proceeded pleasantly enough. Harry was as charming as a small town barber. We sipped coffee and talked about baseball as politely as if enjoying an English High Tea. Until I inadvertently asked about his evening plans. "So, where do you go to church?"

"St. Eugene's. Father O'Brien says a good Mass."

"Is there a reason you go on Saturdays?"

"I don't know," he said. "Just got in the habit. Martha liked to sleep in on Sundays then have strawberry waffles in the backyard. Been doing it ever since. You prefer Sunday," he asked, "for church?"

"Oh, no." I shivered at the thought. "I don't go at all. God and I are not exactly on speaking terms."

"No? Why's that?"

I shook my head as I considered how much to say. Harry's mild manner pulled more than I was prepared for. "It's a long story, really. I lost a baby and I lost a wife. I cussed God out so bad He turned His back and hasn't shown His face since."

"Yeah," he said like he knew. "Our prayers can really get heated sometimes."

I smirked at that one. My display of profanity on the bluff was as close to prayer as Harry was to a psychopath. And I could picture him getting heated about as much as I could picture the Pope flipping off the Virgin Mary.

"Well, the way I've heard it," I said, "telling off the guy who's running everything is the way you get yourself burned—forever."

Harry smiled like a saintly grandpa who didn't know all the fine points of theology but had prayed his way through a few long nights. "I don't know. Maybe God takes our prayers however they come."

"Yeah, well . . ." This had already gone further than I ever wanted and I suddenly craved to be the hell out of there. The last thing I needed was a theological debate with a retired telephone repairman. No, I evened the scales of good mannerliness. I'd leave it to him to ruminate about the prayer habits of the criminally enraged. I drained my mug and composed a goodbye.

That's when I saw that Harry wasn't debating. He was looking across the room, lost in some region our exchange had surfaced. I followed his gaze. He stared at the shrine of photographs, pictures that spanned some fifty years. Black and white snapshots from the 40s depicted a G.I. smooching the cheek of a coy young lady in a shipyard, and a young couple setting out—standing on the porch of the house I was sitting in—the yard unlandscaped and the windows without curtains. Kodak prints from the 60s rendered a vacationing middle-aged pair with matching Sea World ball-caps ducking the spray of a splashing Shamu, and the profile of a woman in a bouffant hairdo at the rim of a canyon sunrise. More recent photographs radiated from the 70s and 80s, an older woman with hair primped in a gray bun deep in concentration with her embroidery, and an elderly couple dressed to the nines, flanking a man in a tuxedo, all arms draped in effervescent affection. Fifty years of life and love were religiously laid out in an archipelago of memories, each picture but an island tip intimating depthless fathoms of underwater topography.

Harry was submerged deep within those waters.

When he finally surfaced to speak, he began with his eyes fixed on the pictures. As if he was telling the story to them as much as he was to me.

I was thinking about Martha the other day. Of course, that's not news. She passed twelve years ago and I still pat for her backside when I wake up.

She was a real looker. Could've had her pick of the litter, and she picked me. I wasn't much of a catch—fresh out of high school and waiting for a war to give me something to do. But she waited for me. Three years, two months. And when I came off the ship and saw those rascally eyes, I popped the question right there. I wanted nothing more in this world than to marry her, and I promised I'd do anything to make her happy.

We never did have kids. I always felt real bad about that. Martha said she didn't want kids anyway, that I was all the kids she could handle. But I knew better. She was great with the youngsters. She baked cookies, and knit caps. And that crepe myrtle out front, that was her holiday tree. Every month she hung ornaments on it—valentines in February, shamrocks in March, flags for the Fourth-of-July. All the neighborhood kids came by just to see her holiday tree. Yeah, she would've been a great mother. And when we couldn't have kids of our own, well I was just all the more determined to give her whatever else I could.

The thing Martha loved most was to travel. Now I was just a telephone man and couldn't afford any fancy trips. But we'd go one place every summer. Not far, mind you. But always someplace we never been before—Yosemite, Disneyland, one year we went all the way up to Seattle, climbed up in that space needle. I tell you what, that was something. She looked forward to those trips all year. No sooner than we got back from one and she'd start planning the next. "What d'ya think, Poppy?" she'd ask. "How does Palm Springs sound? Or that Grand Canyon? I'd sure love to see that just once." And I always told her, "Mama, wherever you want to go, I'll go. As long as I don't have to fly in no airplane or step on no ship." I'd had enough of both.

We only made it back east once. Denver. But New York City was where her heart was set. She always dreamed that one time she'd stay at the Plaza, eat at The Russian Tea Room, go to a Broadway show—it didn't matter what show but it had to be Broadway—then ride on one of those buggies through Central Park. Just once she said, she wanted a night on the town like the rich folk do it.

So I got an idea. I was staring down retirement and I thought, why don't we rent one of them motor homes and take a trip all the way across America, be gone two months if we had to, but don't come back until we seen all there is to see?

Well, you would've thought we won the lottery the way she lit up. She bought one of those maps of the United States, hung it in the dining room, and planned the whole thing with thumbtacks and yarn. She had us going to Yellowstone and Mt. Rushmore, Niagara Falls and New Orleans. But the place with the gold star was New York City. I never saw anybody so excited in all my life.

Well, about six months before my last day at Ma Bell, Martha fell and broke her foot carrying clothes in from the backyard. We figured she was just being clumsy. About a month later, she broke her arm on the counter reaching for a cup she dropped. We figured she was being unlucky. But about a month after that, she broke a rib rolling over in bed. That's when we knew something was wrong. Turned out she had cancer of the bones. Multiple myeloma they called it. Doctors said there was nothing to be done. Just gave her some pain pills and told her to stay down.

We both knew we weren't going on our trip no more, but you couldn't tell it by Martha. She kept talking about getting better so we could go to New York City and have our night on the town. And I played along. I even found this scarf at Rosenberg's saying 'I heart New York,' you know, 'I love New York.' Martha was always particular about her hair, and now that she couldn't go to the beauty parlor she kept a scarf on during the day. So when I saw it, I had to get it.

She loved it. Every morning she'd say "Poppy, where's my scarf?" Sometimes I'd get out a different one, or put a dishtowel over my head, and she'd say, "No Poppy, I want my New York City scarf." Then she'd put it on, and smile, and say, "I gotta stay pretty for our night in New York City." You know, once I got it for her, she wore that scarf every day of her life.

Well, things weren't going too good. I knew we weren't ever going to no New York City. And it just broke me up.

Until I got this great idea.

I read in the paper how they were bringing this show about a chorus line from New York to the city. And I thought, here's our chance. Broadway's in our own hometown.

So I talked to the doctor and the day nurse and rented a van where she could lay down in the back and where the nurse could sit too. I got reservations at a fancy restaurant in the Wharf and three tickets for the show in a special row for wheelchairs. I even had a hairdresser coming over to doll her all up. I had it all covered.

You should have seen the look in her eyes when I told her about it. She could have been eighteen again she looked so young and happy, that scarf wrapped around her hair. Yeah, she was going to look real pretty for our night on the town.

But we never went. The night before, she sneezed and broke a bone in her back. I was laying right there. It sounded like a twig snapping in two. I don't know if she cried from the pain or from knowing she'd never have her night on the town.

We put her in the hospital. They said she wouldn't come home. Her bones ached from the weight of her skin pressing down on them. Her teeth chipped if she bit into a banana.

She lasted two weeks. They gave her so much medicine she could hardly stay awake. Her skin got so yellow I could hardly recognize her. But she still wore that scarf. Everyday. And even when she couldn't talk, I could see it in her eyes. What she was trying to say to me when I tied it around her head. 'Don't worry, Poppy. I'm going to be real pretty for our night on the town.'

She died ten days after my retirement date. Not four months from when we first heard of the cancer. I was sitting by the bed when she passed. She hadn't wakened up in two days. Then her heart just stopped. And she was gone.

I looked at her. Forty-four years we were married. And I still loved her as much as the day I first saw her coming out of the Mission High swimming pool. She was the prettiest woman I ever knew. Even in that scarf. I kissed her for the last time. Then I thought of what I wished I would have said to her before. 'You don't need that scarf. You're beautiful without it.' I took it off her head. And left.

I went to this chapel down the hall from Martha's room where I sat sometimes when she was sleeping. It was late at night, the place was empty, practically dark except for the candles. I sat in a pew and looked up at Jesus. I figured I ought to say a prayer so I started a Hail Mary. But it wouldn't come out. So I just sat there.

After a while, I heard something rip behind me. I turned and saw a young Mexican girl, maybe eighteen years old, sitting in the corner. She was all broke up inside. And she had this baby blanket in her hands, all tattered up and thin looking. She tore a little piece off it, then walked to a statue of the Blessed Mother. She laid the rest of the blanket in front of Mary's feet, real particular, like someone laying out a carpet across the mud for a princess. Then she wiped her eyes, kissed her fingers, made a sign of the cross on the blanket, and left.

After a while, I went to the statue myself. There was Mary, standing so pretty, with that blanket spread out real nice to keep her feet from getting dirty. And I don't know . . . it just did something to me. Now I've been a good Catholic ever since the church took me in. And I ain't never once questioned God's ways. But sometimes, it's just a lot to hold on to. And standing there in front of Mary, it just didn't seem fair. And I thought, well, if you're going to walk all over people's things to keep from getting dirty you might as well walk all over this too. And I took Martha's scarf and threw it on the floor right there where Mary's feet touched that baby's blanket.

And I walked out.

Well, I tossed and turned all night. It was no way to treat Martha's scarf. And it was no way to talk to the Blessed Mother either. So the next morning, I went straight to the priest. Told him I needed confession, first thing. Told him everything—about the girl, the blanket, the scarf, what I said to Mary. I knew it was ugly, but I left nothing out. When I was done he sat there for a long time. Then he said, "I see why you're troubled. That's no way to treat the Virgin Mary, nor Martha's memory neither. God's ways are a mystery—it's ours to trust. But Mary forgives you. And Martha does too."

Then he gave me the strangest penance I ever got. I had to say ten Hail Mary's and ten Acts of Contrition. But I had to say them in that hospital chapel. And while I was there, I had to get Martha's scarf back, and keep it real respectful.

So I went to the chapel right away, I wanted to get the scarf before someone took it. I rode the elevator to Martha's floor, walked past her old room, and straight to the chapel. The second I opened the door, I saw it. It was not at Mary's feet. It was on the cross. The baby's blanket was there too. They were wrapped around Jesus' hands like bandages right where they nailed him to the cross.

I don't know. I looked at Martha's scarf, and that blanket, and Jesus' hands. And I guess it's like, God sees it all you know, the good and the bad. And maybe, well maybe He can take a whole lot more than we think He can.

I do know one thing though. It was the first time in my life I ever disobeyed a priest.

───

My plate for pizza was still in my living room. A candle wrapped it in a womb of light. Moody music played from the stereo. Wrapping me in a womb of mournfulness. Though I left Harry an hour earlier, he still remained with me. Martha too. And the simple love that held them. I wished I had known them together—wished I could've seen Martha bringing Harry some iced tea in the garden, Harry holding the ladder as Martha hung jack-o-lanterns in her tree, both of them sitting on the porch-swing at sunset, she crocheting an afghan, he tuned into a ball game.

And I wished my family had known them too. For that's how it should have been. Harry and Martha should be sitting on our couch. Jen should be on the floor next to me. Daniel, all of seven with dirty shoes from playing in the yard, is snuggling tight between us. All of us holding slices of pizza as we settle in for a vacation video of Harry and Martha's trip to New York.

But none of them were there. My family disintegrated like tissue in a fire. And God denied Martha her night in New York with the man whose only joy in life was to make her happy, then take her picture. Now Harry was dining at the Communion table with that capricious God. I didn't know how he did it. I knew I couldn't. I ate at that table before. But things turned nasty and God denied us. I haven't been back since. Then again, neither has He.

That was where Harry and I were different. Harry's idea of rage was tossing a scarf on the floor. My rage took a hammer to the whole hollow mask. I didn't wrap a blanket around Jesus' hands. I pounded in the nails. God died. Without rebirth.

The problem is, what do you do afterwards—when the stories about God you once staked your life on shatter like a toothpick tiller in a monsoon?

Find a new story, Woody advised. And dine with the demons. Well, the demons are edging toward empty plates. And the story's unclear how to navigate a lonely Saturday night let alone a world that God has forsaken. What in the hell do you do when it's only you to appease their insatiable appetite?

The answer came from an unlikely source.

My tape player.

───

If I believed in patron saints, people who have stumbled upon the sacred and could point the way for the rest of us, my pantheon of the pious would have but one to marbleize. Not the nature-loving St. Francis of Assisi. Not the nurse to lepers Mother Teresa. Not the soaring mystic St. John of the Cross. I'd tune my life to the man whose pilgrimage literally sings with divine sublimity. James Taylor.

JT's epiphany into my life came my last year in high school—I've been a believer ever since.

I was ditching school with my buddy, Lew, on a spring day so lazy it could have inspired an epidemic of senioritis. Lew and I had been friends since fifth-grade Little League. His dad, the high school vice-principal, was coach. His mother, into everything from Cub Scouts to the PTA, was team mom. And I was second base to Lew's shortstop. As quick as the pivot of a double-play throw to first, I grafted to Lew's side as his inseparable best friend and into his family like an adopted son. Afternoons, we practiced our timing in his front yard so late I'd be invited to dinner. Weekends we went to the Carmichael's cabin on Clear Lake—aping Huck Finn and Tom Sawyer by day, devouring barbecued burgers for dinner, and stretched out by the fire at night nibbling Mrs. C's Rice Krispy treats while playing Yahtzee with Coach Car and Lew's little sister, Lisa. With perfect parents and postcard kids, the Carmichaels wrapped me in the cozy covers of familial affection, covers that kept me warm at night when I lay in bed at home longing to escape the chill of my own family's depravity.

Lew and I saw less of each other in high school. I spent the evenings walking the fields to avoid my father's smoldering sneers. Lew flipped pizzas at Shakey's when he wasn't fly-fishing in the hills. We were still friends, but the streams of adolescence had us eddied in two different pools.

So when I ran into Lew in the hallway and he broke into a grin then dusted off the first toss of our standard banter, I caught the ball and shot it right back.

"It's an awfully pretty day," he started.

"About the prettiest day we've had all year."

"It'd be a shame to see it go to waste."

"Too bad we don't have connections."

"Who says we don't?"

"I'll get my things."

"I'll talk to dad."

Just like that, we had two excused passes and were off to the cabin.

We spent the day soaking up rays on the deck with an occasional dip to cool off. Lew's banter stayed as light as the cool breeze off the beach—what girl he should ask to the prom, all the anatomically-detailed reasons I should get over my phobias and ask out Nina Rosen, what fun it would be to double-date then drive to the beach for some midnight nookie. We steered clear of deeper waters—how I was putting up with my dad, if I had any more clues about my mother's death, what either one of us would do when the buoyed boundary of high school slipped free and we faced the open seas of adulthood. I simply munched on chips, let Lew talk about sex, and luxuriated in the mellow and time-less high that only a snuck six-pack and the sun's heat can induce.

Creedence Clearwater Revival finished a set from two speakers we positioned at the sliding glass door. Lew got up to take a leak and change the record. For several moments, the day was still. I closed my eyes and basked in my toasty buzz. A distant toilet flushed. It subsided. Once more, it grew quiet. Still quiet. Too quiet. A second toilet flushed, to muffle a hurried phone call. Lew was at the breaking point.

". . . *Yes!* Her bra! Right on the towel bar . . . *No!* Mom's bringing Lisa's den here tomorrow. What if *she* finds it? Or one of the girl scouts? Can you imagine? . . . No, Dad, I'm not . . . Why do *I* have to carry it around? *She* left it . . . Fine. . . *Fine!* . . . I'll put it in my trunk. But you get it out tonight. If my friends . . . Right . . . Sure . . ."

The silence returned. Soft steps crept on the gravel out front. A car trunk closed gingerly. More steps. Silence.

Then Lew bounced onto the deck with a couple of cold ones as chipper as a cocker spaniel puppy.

"Here you go, Tone." He tossed me a can.

"Is everything all right?" I asked.

"Sure. Why?" His eyes hoped to God I hadn't heard a thing.

"Nothing. I . . ."

"Hey, I forgot about the tunes." He returned to the family room. "How about James Taylor?" he yelled.

"Who's that?"

"You've never heard of James Taylor? You gotta hear this. Hold on."

I held. But I was already slipping. At the first plaintive note I lost all bearings of where I was. Everything receded—the sunny day and cool breeze, the erotic banter and baby oil bouquet, the tipsy giggles and insufferable secrets. It was as dark as a mesa at midnight. And I was in the cold. With only a drifter's easy-going pluck to fight off the chill. His fingers rambled across steel strings until they stumbled on a tumbleweed of a melody rolling across the desert as it uncoiled into a song. He sang of longing—longing for a mother who didn't have to die and a father who didn't have to punish, longing for a family that didn't have to shatter and a hero who didn't have to break faith, longing for someone to share a life with and a friend who doesn't need to hide his own. Longing for home. For hope. For something more than a song on which to lay one's head.

But only the song was there.

> "I've been wandering early and late," he sang . . . and "it don't look like I'll ever stop my wanderin.'"

My wandering wasn't stopping soon either.

By the time I came back to Lew's cabin, I knew I had found both a comrade and guide. I pumped Lew for biography and begged for more songs with the thirst of a convert pressing a Zen master for handfuls of koans to gulp down. Lew indulged me like a seasoned monk eager to initiate a novice into the spiritual mysteries hidden within the music. Eyeballing the needle between different selections, he illuminated JT's story— the depressive adolescence within mental institutions, his soul-mate's suicide to pills, his fledgling band going down in pieces as he battled the stranglehold of drugs. And through it all—the music he made. A music that healed as it kept him alive.

Lew never referred that afternoon to his father's affair and the secrets he had to finesse. I never mentioned the obliteration of my fixed star illusion of the perfect family. The terrifying truth went unspoken. No home holds you through life. They take different forms. Some shriek with death and rage. Others bubble in surreptitious malignance. But none keep you warm through the cold for long.

There is, however, music. That holds the longing and holds the hope and trickles from the waters that are the source for both. That afternoon, I was baptized in those waters. Lew was the attendant. JT was the priest. And for several hours we soaked like scorched nomads holing up in an oasis.

The sun was setting when Lew dropped me off. He stopped across the street as if my house was haunted. The place was dark—but my dad was home. I walked around the car, paused at Lew's window, and reprised one of our old lines.

"It was a nasty job but somebody had to do it."

"Yeah," he picked up. "A job worth doing's a job worth doing right."

I smiled. "Thanks." And started across the street.

Within a few strides, Lew stopped me. "Hey." He reached into his glove compartment, located an object, and tossed it through the window. Then he made his only allusion to our troubled times.

"I hope it helps."

I had nothing to toss back. Lew was left on his own.

I didn't see him much after that. I skipped the prom and the midnight nookie. He kept to the hills when not flipping pizzas. We slung our hats at graduation, then made good on our vows to leave home. I enrolled at Sonoma State. Lew fled to U.C. Santa Cruz.

I saw him only once after that. About two years later. I heard that his parents split up and I dropped by his house on spring break. It looked like an opium den. Lew was crashed out in a beanbag chair surrounded by college cronies in various degrees of dress. He was so stoned he didn't recognize me standing before him.

I had nothing to toss him then, either. I wish I did. Within a year, his car was found at the bottom of a coastal cliff near Santa Cruz. Where the car hit the rail, the road bore no skid marks.

But that senior year evening, he still had hope to toss. And I was smart enough to catch it. With the instinct honed from a thousand such tosses from his hand. Lew drove off leaving me halfway to my house. I looked at what my hand held. A face stared back. With brown hair down to its shoulders and eyes of defiant desolation. It was James Taylor. On a well-worn cassette. "Sweet Baby James," it read.

And it helped.

———

Ever since that afternoon apprenticeship, James Taylor has been my spiritual companion. To be sure, his wistful ballads and sorrowful songs gave me verse and melody for the elegies that haunted my soul. But his music did more. It set free the music within me. For it was not enough to simply listen to his melodies. I had to make music with him.

So I took up the harmonica.

For years after that senior year epiphany, I either had a blues harp in my mouth or within a shirt pocket of its pucker. Sitting in my bedroom, riding shotgun in the car, up against a tree at the park, wherever I was I rocked and rolled and riffed and rippled with the ten-holed instrument cupped in my hands. I communicated with the outside world more through notes than words. I got good enough to jam with blues bands on campus and even considered playing the wheel of my own career in music. I might have done it too. If I hadn't gotten saved.

And I owed it all to James Taylor. My entire novitiate came under his tutelage—I taught myself to play by accompanying the songs on his records. And the first one I learned on the harp, the song that sparked my twenty-year down-for-the-count love affair with his music, was "Wandering."

It was also the 'Moody Music' song that filtered into the dining room as I sat in my living room's candlelight. It was a reprise epiphany. Like the first, its haunting melody gave voice to my melancholic mood; and it kindled the musical spark within me. For the first time in years, I felt like jamming.

Like a lonely young adult on a Saturday night with a sudden invitation to a party, I rushed to the bottom shelf of my bookcase and retrieved my cigar box of harmonicas. Then I sat on the couch and pulled out my E-harp. I stroked its silver plate like it was the key to the kingdom. The only heaven I ever knew came when I played a harmonica. I pulled it to my mouth to see if I could still make it sing. I could. Bluesy riffs cascaded like undammed waters through deeply carved canyons. I rode the wave in a tumbling stream of playful wailing. God it felt good. Then I flowed into my standard, "Wandering," sustaining the first notes in plaintive tension then resolving into bluesy depths. I remembered why I took it up in the first place. Playing didn't take the sadness away. But it got you through the night.

I eased into a couple of classics—"Shenandoah" and "Road to Laredo"—deep river songs that course along drooping willows and grassy graveyards. Then I hastened back to my master. Years earlier, I made a tape of all my favorite JT songs strung one after another to blow to in a single sitting. I rifled through my cassettes and tucked it into the stereo. The songs were in different keys so I placed my box of harps within easy reach. Then I settled into a long-overdue jam session with the man from Martha's Vineyard.

The set began with the nostalgic standard, "Fire and Rain." I grabbed my F-harp and wailed with James about the pieces of our dreams on the ground and the loved ones who were now long gone. We looked to Jesus to see us through another day, but we played on in his absence—through the fire and rain, the days and nights, the heat and the cold, hanging onto the slipping hope that we'd see love's rise again. Our hope died with the fade to silence. But another song promised to take its place.

I hadn't played the tape for so long I couldn't remember what came next. The instant I heard the aching steel string I recognized "Rainy Day Man" and snatched my G-harp. James wondered about the worth of a happy lie when all you wanted to do was cry. I backed him up knowing just how he felt. It's another fall, and your friends don't call, and your feeling small, and a happy song can't hide the truth—simple pleasures all evade you, store-bought treasures none can save you, the only face whose eyes can aid you is the man who's bleeding the rain. Our prayer fades, with my final bent draw. And I wait.

I hear it. He sings. And I back him up, through one sad song then another. "Something in the Way She Moves," my F-harp wailing through those times when the things we lean on lose their meaning and we find ourselves careening into places where we shouldn't be. "Long Ago and Far Away," my E-harp grieving that love is but a word we've heard when things are being said, and the stories our poor heads were told no longer wake the dead. "Nobody but You," my A-harp coming clean that we're just a couple of Joes who like to hang around, talking about our problems, bringing other people down. But we can't help it. It's our song. And my throat is scratchy from all the notes I've bent in playing it.

But something changes. I vaguely remember. Like a performer who knows he'll lose the crowd if he doesn't lighten things up, I pulled the taping out of its melancholic tailspin by adding a set of upbeat tunes. "Country Road" opened up and down it they waltzed—JT with his guitar's pluck, Carole King and a keyboard tinkle, Russ Kunkel with a snare drum roll, and me, running to catch up with my G-harp blowing. I'm coming too y'all, I'm lending my name. Your way and my way are one and the same. We're on a road so bright we hear the band-full of angels. We know nothing 'bout the why or when but we can tell you that they're setting us free, 'cause we can feel it, boogieing down our country road.

I'm one of the band now, and I'm flying with James. We're "Up on the Roof," that trouble-proof paradise for when you're feeling beat, a haven from the world where the air is fresh and sweet; the rat-race noise is down in the street, and the stars put on a show for free. I'm moving with those stars, dancing on that terrace, making another pass by that starry-sky chorus. I slide a trill up the harp and change octaves on James. The high-pitched notes tingle with elation. We're not just playing in my living room. We're stoking 12,000 at the Concord Pavilion. They're jiving in front of the stage. They're rocking on top of their seats. They're singing out on the grass. And I'm grooving on stage with the main man himself. Where're we going next, JT? That's right. "I Will Follow." My G-harp's out and off we go. I chug and growl, tongue-block and slide-roll, shake, slap, and wah-wah with the maestro. We climb every mountain, cross every river, ride every cloud across the sun-drenched sky to follow love, to fall in love, to flow in love anywhere it leads us. Come on up and join the song. Screw the Concord Pavilion. We're blowing the top off of Carnegie Hall. We're inciting hysteria at the LA Coliseum. We're bringing the house down at St. Peter's Square. John Paul's cutting a rug. Heads of state are doing a jig. The gods on Olympus two-step it in the clouds. All of creation beats as one—following the love that moves the earth.

I'm sweating now but I'm not stopping. I swap harps with one hand as James plans his encore. We "Shower the People" we love with love, and rain it on the whole human race. He flashes "Your Smiling Face" my way, and I thank the stars for how we feel today. He calls out my name with "You've Got A Friend," and brightens my darkest nights; he pledges to come whenever I call—winter, spring, summer, or fall; he knocks at my door when people are cold and I'm losin' my hold 'cause they're takin' my soul. The man is *there* for me, in my home, playing my music to keep me going. I am here to testify, he quickened me back to life.

Then he kicked me right in the balls.

He looked back too soon.

The ground ripped open.

And I slipped through the chasm to the core of hell.

I had not heard the song in seven years. I forgot it even existed. As James sang, my harp stopped stone-cold.

"Close your eyes . . . It's all right." James couldn't sing love songs. He couldn't sing the blues. But for his child, he could sing this song. And his child could sing it too. Even after he was gone.

This was the lullaby James sang for his children. And the one I played for mine. Every night of our pregnancy, I played that song to Jen's womb. It was my prayer. And my pledge. I wanted the song of the sacred to hold Daniel throughout his life. And I vowed that the song of my love would hold him throughout my own. Every night of his three-and-a-half month life, I reprised the prayer. I sat by his crib on an antique rocker. I cupped a harp to my mouth. I played soothingly soft. And through song, I invited Daniel to settle into the sleep that would bring him into morning. Close your eyes, Daniel. It's all right. Because I can sing you this song. And I'll keep singing it. Until I'm gone.

Daniel closed his eyes. He just didn't open them again.

Hearing James sing, my harp laying mute in my hand, it hit me. I never did my penance. I had a demon with whom to dine. I had a ghost to bury. Maybe a couple of them.

And I knew just how to do it.

———

The caretaker at Crossroads took out the trash. In the dark, he didn't notice the footprints along the locked ward's back wall. The boy in the Box wasn't aware of them either. But his finger flicked all the same. He had some demons to dine with too. One of them had scoped the grounds and was now staked out in his camper.

Carey needed a protector. The promise of it being me was unclear. It depended upon one thing.

How well I dined with the demons within me.

All of them.

PART TWO

Lent

13

For miles, trust in the road's name is based on faith, not sight. River Road reveals no river. Fields bleed grapes for local wineries. Grazing cattle await slaughterhouse knives. Distant hilltops lined with fir portend the ocean deep beyond.

But no waterway toward it can be seen.

The fields give way to a forest so thick sunlight pierces but in scarce streaks. The road coils through thick coastal hills. Shadows of redwood swell. The darkness deepens. Then, with sunny brilliance, a two-lane suspension bridge explodes into view. Twenty feet below, a stream trickles out to sea.

The bridge was deserted. No white-haired captain waited to ferry me. No hordes of pilgrims mobbed to pass. No well-traveled guide appeared to chaperone. I was alone. And I crossed the river as uneventfully as an autumn leaf drifting to the ground from a backwoods tree.

The brightness was fleeting. Fresh shadows swallowed my truck in groves so dim the sun's direction was lost. Though dark, the forest was not ominous. Not until I came upon the sign. Still spiked to a tree, the fading shingle foretold the ghosts' arrival. Camp Maranatha. As I passed the abandoned grounds, buried memories of my romance with Jen and evangelicalism appeared so powerfully it could have been the winter of 1984 again when both enchantments climaxed into an exultant height. Though paint peeled from the cabins and weeds assaulted the paths, the Siren's song of high-school squeals rose from the decaying camp. And Jen's presence was so real sitting next to me in my truck, I could have reached over and stroked her strawberry-blonde hair. It was appropriate that Jen should materialize with the phantom echoes of Christian merrymaking.

The time I spent in each of their spells coincided precisely.

I kept driving, deeper into the woods a few miles. When I reached the town of Russian River, I pulled into a Safeway parking lot. I stepped out of my truck and made for the market. The store's glass doors mirrored my anxious approach. I trembled like a boy about to bluff a strip-club bouncer on a dare that promised to bestow manhood. A step through those doors would be a step into another world. A world whose spell once looped me high—before it dropped me flat.

Like a triggered dungeon passageway, the glass doors opened before me. I passed through. I did not parley with gatekeepers.

I bought picnic supplies.

Exactly as I had done eight years before.

I spent three years beached on the tropical island paradise of life with Jen and the hand-ful of Christians who became my closest friends. Like the legendary eaters of the lotus flower, the sweet fruit was so enticing I lost interest in all else but savoring their intoxi-cating delights. My final semester of college, I practically ignored my academic work in an all-consuming thirst to see Jen, study the Bible, hail Christ at Glory Gatherings, and be discipled in His ways by Danny. I filled out every new believer's workbook I could get my born-again fingers on, pumped Danny with queries about theology and morality, spiritual living and Christian dating, and put it all to the test with a by-the-Book romance with Jen. I also became a full-fledged member of the band. My harmonica, infused with a convert's enthusiasm, was perfect accompaniment at our musical praise sessions. In fact, I harmonized so well with Danny's lead we became something of an evangelical folk duo—a sanctified Simon and Garfunkel who made good music while sharing the gospel.

We even took the show on the road. The year after we graduated, Danny and I vol-unteered for Young Life, an association that shared Christ with high-school kids. The program we ran at Montgomery High was so successful we expanded the operation the following year, coordinating three separate high-school programs between Santa Rosa and Petaluma with the iniquity-fighting dexterity of the dynamic duo. We led weekly gatherings for each school, taught early morning Bible studies at local restaurants, and made as many on-site visits to cafeterias and football games as we could manage with the other labors of love and work in our lives. But the programmatic capstone in our evangelistic crusade occurred once each season—a multi-school retreat in some wilder-ness setting where we overwhelmed the teens with the fun, fellowship, and faith-filled euphoria endemic to a life lived with Jesus.

Our strategy was simple—'Hook 'em, Cook 'em, and Book 'em.' Through festive games and Christian fellowship at the weekly gatherings and on-site social calls, we lured the kids to our retreats where we sautéed them on a veritable fish fry of a weekend. We tenderized them with limit-stretching athletic contests and community-building obstacle courses. We seasoned them with camp-style skits and fireside songfests. We marinated them in intense encounter-group rap-sessions and strategically-themed devotions, and fattened them up with junk food and a sugar-high adventure of river rafting or snow-skiing, scaling a mountain peak or sailing on a schooner. Finally, when they were exhausted and commu-nally bound, we sealed the meal with an intense revival style campfire complete with teary personal testimonies, inspiring faith stories, uplifting praise songs, and fervent appeals for decision. It was a brilliant game-plan. By Sunday night, more young people made crying-eyed commitments to Christ than all the high steeple altar calls in California.

In the winter of 1984, two years after my Halloween conversion, Danny and I orches-trated what turned out to be our largest ever weekend retreat—a whale-watching beach trip on the Russian River. The plan was fine-tuned. Friday night we'd stay up late play-ing games and singing songs. Saturday morning we'd navigate the ropes course at Camp Maranatha followed by an afternoon van-ride to the beach for volleyball and devotions. Saturday evening we'd be back at the camp for barbecued burgers and a talent show culminating with a moonlit praise service by the campfire. Then we'd cap the weekend off with a charter boat trip from Bodega Bay to watch for whales and worship God on the open seas. The sighting of whales on Sunday in all their spouting glory was to be the crowning confirmation of the Christ-intoxicated conversions we'd secure the night before.

As it turned out, spouting whales were sighted, and commitments were secured. But not only by the high-school youth.

I had a few plans of my own.

———

Jennie and I moved as fast in our courtship as I had as a believer. For all the things we had in common, our first dates felt like old friends catching up. We grew up an hour apart—Ukiah a quick shot up the 101 from Petaluma—and camped out at the same lake during our adolescence. Neither of us had much of a father—Jen's chased skirts as much as his dream to be a bass player and followed both to LA with a local bank teller the day Jen started high school. Like mine, Jen's mom had an artistic flair—crafting earrings out of feathers and thrift store salvage and hawking them at the back of a New Age bookstore. We both longed for large families, revered folk music, had a Catholic parent, and floated joyfully in the eddies of evangelicalism. We couldn't identify all the invisible lassoes tossed to secure our coupling—the unconscious strands that loop and snag, circle and knot, in weaving the tangled latticework of love. We credited God. And hormones.

We were as hot for each other as caged tigers in heat.

By Thanksgiving we were inseparable, by Christmas we talked marriage. The attraction was palpable. The only doubt we harbored about our romantic future was not if our desire could endure the monogamous demands of matrimony, but how long we could go without kissing before blowing up in a masturbatory explosion. We were Christians. And we believed it was the way of Jesus to stifle, swallow, smother, and otherwise sublimate by all means possible, one's sexual passions until that two-ton detonation of a wedding day.

Our boundaries were set by our third date. After two consecutive evenings at a Christian coffeehouse, we went to an Andre Crouch concert then walked the campus in the November moonlight. Lost in our chummy intimacy, we circled the campus so many times security simply smiled and waved at our every pass by the guard-booth. I was terrified to walk her to her dorm, terrified that my mounting desire would make a move and kiss her, and terrified at the guilt I would feel if I crossed the boundary to attempt it. Each lap of conversation only intensified the attraction. At one point, though I kept my arms rigidly at my sides, our hands accidentally brushed. They brushed again. And yet a third time. Before, aghast at the turn-on of her touch, I pocketed my hands for the rest of the stroll. It was just as well. The other manifestation of my libido also needed concealing.

Sometime near dawn, we found ourselves in front of her dorm. I swear I saw desire in her eyes as we hemmed and hawed at the pleasantness of the evening. But within the mandates of Christian propriety, we did not kiss. We embraced. I trembled with arousal, careful to maintain a genital distance. Jen must have sensed my temptation. She affectionately squeezed, then politely withdrew herself. She took a breath for strength, and laid it all out.

"I really like you, Tony," she said. "But I must tell you about the vow I made when my father left my mother. Before we knew he was leaving, we ran into him at the gas station. We stopped after school and there he was—filling the tank, his van all packed, Miss Senter sitting in the passenger seat. My mother pumped gas as if he wasn't there. He stumbled around—didn't know what to do. Wouldn't even look at us—until he got in the van, started it up, then glanced at me for just a second before he drove away. My mother finished pumping, got in, and made it as far as the stoplight before she broke down and sobbed.

"I would never survive if I got hurt like that. So I promised. I would never get physically involved with a man, I wouldn't even kiss him, until I knew he would be with me the rest of my life."

She stared at me, hoping I wasn't put off. I wasn't.

"I couldn't agree more," I gushed with relief. "And one thing I promise. Married or not, I'll never do to you what your father did to your mother."

Jen sized me up. Then trusting me, she grabbed my fingers and squeezed. Apparently, holding hands was admissible. Thank God. In the months ahead, I went after hers like a puppy would a nipple.

For nearly two years, we confined our physicality to appropriate erotic discretion. To be sure, as our courtship flared then blazed, our appetites flamed in tandem. Beneath Jen's conservatism, a nookie-loving farm girl burned in wait. But we petted within respectable boundaries until the winter of our whale-watching beach trip when we fortified our self-restraint with the specific goal of a wedding date. Our game-plan was as well intentioned as it was desperate. We would spoon and cold shower our way to the first Saturday of spring break for both the Montessori Christian School at which Jen taught and the high schools at which I evangelized.

We discovered that the game-plan was flawed.

Due to scheduling restrictions dictated by school holidays and Super Bowl Sunday, the whale-watching beach trip was booked for the last weekend in January—five weeks before our sexual purgatory would peak on the mountaintop of marriage. Unfortunately, that Saturday happened to be Jen's birthday. She was happy to forego a lavish celebration in service of the spiritual cause and appreciated the quaint one we had the Thursday before the trip. I was not so content. For if there was one person for whom an abridged party was not appropriate, it was Jen.

One of Jen's most conspicuous and endearing characteristics was soon revealed to all who met her. Jennie loved birthdays. She loved everything about birthdays—cakes, candles, balloons, presents, birth flowers, gemstones, she even hallowed horoscopes, although astrology was considered demonic by our Christian friends. Birthdays, she believed, were sacred events—the one day a year when a person is celebrated for simply being born into this world.

Jen lived as true to her credo as any saint to the gospel. She kept a prayer journal—a bound diary with a silk ribbon—that doubled as a portrait portfolio for every one of her loved ones. With two interfacing pages per person, she kept notes of everything particular about you—your favorite foods, musical tastes, reading pleasures, travel fantasies, treasured memories, clothing sizes, decorating patterns, car preferences, the color scheme of your complexion. Make an off-the-cuff remark about your love for cheesecake and it'll show up on your page. Say it twice and she'll star it. Then for bedtime devotions, she dwelt with different people—filling out the details, reverencing their uniqueness, and divining through the runes the longings and pleasures, the untapped talents and emerging triumphs that constitute their soulful essence. And when your birthday rolled around, she crafted a celebration that so attended to your particularity you could not help but feel that God Himself delights in your beauty.

For Jen, celebrating a birthday was a form of prayer. And she made praying an art.

Our first kiss came after a party she threw.

I never saw anything like it.

She celebrated me.

———

Jen and I had been dating just over a year. On the Saturday morning before my mid-week birthday, I dashed out of the house late for work to a truck that wouldn't start. Danny had moved in after Kirk moved out, so I woke him up for a ride. He hustled me over to UPS and swore he'd be there when I finished at three. Jen had bought tickets for a B. J. Thomas concert, and I promised to pick her up by six.

When Danny arrived at twenty after three, he came with apologies. And a van full of teens. He met some Young Life faithful at a water polo game and promised them all rides home. After shooting the breeze at Baskin & Robbins we dropped off each one. Of course, their homes were spread out across the city's four quadrants with two rural route deliveries in opposite directions. I was antsy to be sure, but we were building relationships.

Vince was the last one dropped off, a junior emerging as a teenage leader. Unfortunately, he had a question of faith that bled into an impromptu Bible study on his driveway. By the time we blessed him on his way, it was 5:40. I begged Danny to bolt for home. He did, after a frantic stop for three dollars of gas. We pulled in at six o'clock straight up.

The house was dark, as dark as Jennie's mood would be by the time I shaved, showered, and dashed to her place. Before Danny could turn off the ignition, I sprinted out the van, leapt up the steps, and raced through the door where I had the devil scared straight out of me. From the pitch-black dining room, 35 people screamed 'Surprise' so startlingly I nearly screamed something surprising back. All the kids we dropped off were there except Vince, who straggled in behind me with Danny. As Danny walked in, he caught Jen's eye. They smiled like cat burglars having just jacked the crown jewels.

And what a con job they pulled off. In the twelve hours I had been away, not only was the dining room decorated for a party with blue and purple balloons and streamers, a table full of Buffalo wings, and a giant centerpiece carrot cake sculpted like a harmonica; the living room was downright remodeled. With mood lighting hanging from the beams, and cocktail tables draped with white cloths and candles, a blues club had been constructed. Photos of blues giants and homemade playbills peppered the walls, while a makeshift stage at the room's far end sported the spotlight and sound equipment from our Campus Crusade gospel ensemble. Two posters flanked the mics. One resembled a marquee:

> For one night only,
> appearing exclusively at the Icthous Club
> —the singing duo sweeping the charts—
> James Taylor on guitar
> and
> Tony Backman
> on blues harp.

The other was an enlarged photo of James Taylor performing live on stage with a superimposed shot of me playing harmonica at his shoulder. I stared at my dream. I was jamming with the main man himself.

And that was just the decoration. Jennie and Danny choreographed a stage-show tribute and good-humored roast to my blues musician soul. A dozen friends from our Christian fellowship dressed up like John Belushi and Dan Ackroyd and performed a campy medley of JT tunes with rewritten lyrics. Their swan song was a bastardized rendition of 'Fire and Rain' with the chorus,

> I've played harp and I've raised Cain,
> I've seen softball games that I thought would never end,
> I've seen lonely times when I could not find my Jen,
> But I always knew that I'd see the light again.

They saw the light too—a spotlight flash on the poster of James before which they swooned like ecstatic groupies.

The high-school kids performed a skit entitled 'Name that James Taylor Tune' in which Vince impersonated me as a game-show contestant. I obliterated every opponent by naming obscure songs in as few as three notes, two notes, one note, then crescendoed with a burst of bravado, "I don't need *any* notes, James and I are in such perfect sync. I know *exactly* what's coming next." I rattled off an insufferable number of songs proclaiming for each the date it was released, the album it appeared on, and the key it was performed in until I ranted out of control, claimed to *be* James Taylor, and was carried off by two orderlies.

But these were merely the warm-up acts. The main event was an appearance by the melancholic melody maker himself. Danny walked out the spitting image of JT on his Mud Slide Slim album. With shoulder length hair and mustachioed smirk, he ambled up to the microphone and soliloquized about his artistic dissatisfaction after years of acclaim and his schoolgirl giddiness at the upcoming performance that would culminate his singing career. He was going to play with that blues harp virtuoso, Tony Backman. He turned stage left. The spotlight shone. And I made my appearance. Who else? Jen, dressed in one of my flannel shirts and trademark jeans, sauntered onstage holding one of my harps. And God bless her, she played with James Taylor. She actually learned a song on the harmonica. As Danny strummed and sang, she riffed. 'Whenever I see your smiling face, I have to smile myself, because I love you . . . Yes, I do.'

More than the gifts she hunted down for me, the cake she baked, the skits she directed, the surprise she orchestrated, it was that sight that cinched it for me. Jen as me, eyes glistening, hands fluttering, head nodding, as she eased into our song and let herself swell in musical tandem with my hero.

If she couldn't tell by looking at me then, she knew it by the end of the night. I drove her home in my mysteriously restored truck. On the way, we stopped behind the football field. Though careful not to transgress our boundaries, she snuggled close to my side. As she savored the party, my heart pounded. Not out of desire. Out of fear. But with her gift, the words fought through the fear.

"I love you, Jen." I knew as I said it I need not have worried. She turned to me and smiled as if she had been waiting for the words. Then before my propriety could check my desire, I sealed my first declaration of love with my first sexually aggressive act. I kissed her.

The second I did, I felt the guilt. She sensed it. She leaned back and studied my eyes. Love sparred with the fear of abandonment.

"Do you really?" she asked like a plea.

I did. I swear. "Of course I do, Jen."

She saw. And smiled. Then keeping her eyes open, she kissed me back.

Of course I loved her. How could I not?

How could I not love her still?

So when Jen's birthday fell on the Saturday of our whale-watching beach trip, I could hardly let it slip unnoticed into the swift streams of senior-high evangelizing. Besides, I had everything in place for a jewel heist surprise of my own. I had the opportunity. I had motive. I had an accomplice.

But most importantly, I had the weapon.

When Jen and I became engaged, I proposed without a diamond. It was not for want of trying. Like a seeker after the Holy Grail, I scoured jewelry stores and catalogues, studied gemstone meanings and wedding band symbology, sought counsel from learned specialists and cautions from longwearing bearers, ever in search of the perfect ring. Jen was not much help. She conceded but the scantiest of parameters. She preferred simple settings to ornate ones, modest diamonds to knuckle-sized rocks, and yellow gold to platinum silver. Beyond that, I was on my own.

"Tony," she said as I teased out her tastes and antipathies. "The ring that comes from your heart is the only ring I want."

Like that was a lot of help. A single band and stone had to embody both our abiding commitment and Jen's unique beauty. And what was most unique about Jen was the way she reflected light in such antithetical directions. She was evangelical, but drank alcohol and shunned the church. She dressed conservatively but often went inconspicuously braless. She voted Republican in one election and endorsed rights for children in another. She seldom wore make-up but polished her toenails, loved to wear jeans but slept in silk, was as gentle as a kitten but totemized a lion. She wiggled through labels like Houdini through knots—not out of defiance, but out of a feline instinct to follow her own star. How could a single ring capture Jennie Gallagher's simple eccentricity?

My long-awaited inspiration came in early October.

I knew I was proposing on Halloween night. I even knew where. But autumn was upon us and I still had no vision for the ring. Under the pretense of stopping for harp reeds at the folk music store, we dropped by downtown Petaluma. Jen obliged me with a third stroll through Steiner's Jewelry Store. Mr. Steiner was as patient as a fisherman while Jen nibbled at various settings. But she did not take the bait.

"I don't know, Tony. I just want it to come from you."

Empty-handed, we left the store and stopped for cherry cokes at Elroy's Soda Fountain. On our way out, I ran to the restroom. When I returned, Jennie was on a park bench out front, sitting on the far side of an adorable blonde-headed girl whose five-year-old eyes were wide as she listened to Jennie gush.

"That's what's so great about carnations. They come in all kinds of colors—white, orange, yellow. I bet they even come in your favorite."

"Red?" she asked as if such a dream was too wild to conceive.

"That's perfect," Jen exclaimed. "Not only is red a beautiful color for a carnation, red is the color of your gemstone."

"Really?" The girl could scarcely believe the magic of the universe.

"Oh, yes," assured Jen, that magic's fairy godmother. "They're called garnets. And they are *so* pretty. Oh, Tony. This is Natalie. And guess what. Natalie has a birthday the same month I do—January. It's only six days before mine."

Natalie blushed as if sharing a birthday with Jen was as special as sharing one with a princess. I blushed too. My vision had appeared.

I returned to Petaluma the next day and shared it with the jeweler. I imagined a round diamond centerpiece with a birthstone on either side representing the months in which Jen and I were born. I hoped for a garnet that matched Jen's hair, more orangish-gold than red. Such a color in a garnet was rare, but Mr. Steiner went on the hunt. My gemstone was easier. Topaz were found in a gold-hued amber, closer to my own dirty blond hair and one that harmonized well with the garnet I imagined for Jen.

Mr. Steiner was amazing. He found a reddish-orange garnet and fashioned the ring exactly as I had envisioned. The two gemstones were cut in triangles and set in a gold band on either side of the diamond. The effect was stunning. The three jewels shined with their own unique glory yet blended into an artistic unity. The white diamond sparkled through the orange and amber stones to resemble a lion's eye flaring to life as it flickered with light. The symbolism was perfect. Our two birthdays were distinct yet held together by the diamond purity of Christ's brilliance shining through us. With Him at the center, Jen and I were united into a new creation, a trinity of radiant jewels—three in one, one in three, a mandalic integration of disparate spirits harmonized to bring beauty into the world. I could not wait to slip it onto Jen's finger. It was more than a ring. It was my yearning, my commitment, my prayer.

Unfortunately, it was not to be.

The ring was not ready by Halloween. I proposed anyway, using a stand-in. With a dollar fifty in nickels, I fished out of a gumball machine a plastic ring with a carrot-colored crystal on top. I released it from its plastic bubble and placed it in a jewelry box.

Halloween was cloudy that year; the moon did not float on Commencement Lake. I was not deterred. I walked Jen to the blue spruce and sat her in the very place from which I first spied her two years earlier. I showed her the break in the branches through which I glimpsed her stepping into the doorway's light. She smiled as I told her how I lost track of what I was playing but was certain that the melody was an echo of the music she awakened within me. I smiled as she told me how beautiful my harp sounded, and how tickled she was when I decided to follow her with decidedly clumsy stealth. I played her a song that I composed for the night—not the same melody from that first Halloween, but one inspired by the same source.

Then I knelt before her and slipped the box from my pocket. Her eyes widened with comprehension.

"Jen," I quivered. "I tried hard to find the jewel I would have you wear for the rest of our lives. I found it, but it won't be ready for a while. So I have only a cheap substitute. Which strikes me as only appropriate. Because even the real jewel I'm having made is but a cheap memento compared to the love I feel for you. *You* are my jewel, Jen. You are the sparkle that brings beauty into my life. And I want to be with you forever. Will you marry me? . . . Please."

By then Jen was crying. I slipped the plastic ring onto her finger. She chuckled through her tears as she admired it. Then she wrapped her arms around me.

"Of course I'll marry you. It's beautiful. It's all the ring I need."

I lingered in her response. But I had to reassure her. "I'm serious, Jen. I *do* have a real ring for you. It's just not ready yet."

She released her embrace and held my face in her hands. "I'm serious, too. What ring could be more precious than this? It comes from your heart. And it's your heart I love." She squeezed me again. "Oh, Tony, isn't God awesome? We're going to have such a great life together."

Then in the shadows of where our love was birthed, we kissed again. Not our first kiss since my birthday a year before. Far from it. Though we hadn't actually made love yet, in the interceding months, our bodies' unique beauties were becoming well acquainted.

How awesome would God find that?

———

For all my words about the pale splendor of the real ring, I was busting to give it to her. And for all her words about not needing a real ring at all, Jen was busting to receive it. As the weeks passed, her curiosity intensified. She never brought it up, but she suspected an unveiling at every occasion. Her eyes twinkled at Thanksgiving when I hinted of an after-dinner surprise, but I only had her favorite chocolate-covered strawberries. She sized up my pile of presents on Christmas but didn't find it among them either. Her anticipation flared at my New Year's Eve toast when I fingered her plastic ring and told her I couldn't wait until we were married. But I followed that with a sumptuous kiss. No ring. And her suspiciousness passed as we tasted each other's champagne long into the night.

I wasn't toying with her. The ring wasn't ready. Not until mid-January, two weeks before Jen's birthday. By then, her eagerness grew weary. Especially after she opened my gifts at the early birthday party the day before the whale-watching trip. I gave her a sweater and earrings, an apricot rose and chocolates, a stuffed lion to hang from her rear-view mirror and a Narnia poster to pin in her classroom. But I didn't give her the ring. With yet one more no-show, she figured all bets were off. The way things were unfolding, she'd end up getting married before she was officially engaged.

She had no idea the surprise that awaited her.

———

Seven vans drove the sixty kids and twelve chaperones to Camp Maranatha. I followed in my Datsun pickup, ostensibly to haul gear in my camper shell. On Friday night we stayed up late with songs and games. We hit the ropes course first thing Saturday. After a hearty lunch, everyone took advantage of some downtime before the afternoon trip to the beach. While the others curled up in the lodge, I sprang into action. On the pretense of foraging for forgotten hamburger buns, I drove to the Russian River Safeway. Though I had started planning it as soon as the ring was ready, my birthday surprise required some finishing touches.

I prepared a picnic for the two of us on some secluded beach. While the diamond ring was the meal's crown jewel as it were, the whole affair, down to its most trivial of details, prefigured the ring's unveiling. I bought a white Christmas rose and bordered it with our birthday flowers—a rust-colored carnation on one side, an amber chrysanthemum on the other. I straddled a large white balloon with slightly smaller orange and yellow counterparts. I baked a carrot cake, designed cryptic lion's eyes out of candy corn on the sour cream frosting, and brought a tall white candle for the center with orange and yellow votives for the sides.

All of the accessories followed the same color-coordinated pattern. One blanket was wheat-colored, the other off-white terry cloth. The utensils were yellow, the paper plates orange. The champagne flutes were yellow as well, the cutting board white plastic. The cloth napkins were checkered in amber and orange, and a yellow vase held the flowers. The entire ensemble was a patchwork of color in which the ring's hues, in shaded variations, were blended together.

Even the food got into the mix. Tangerines and golden delicious apples, orange cheddar cheese and milky Monterey Jack, were heaped in a basket of lemon drops and butterscotch balls. From the Safeway, I added a fresh loaf of French bread swaddled in white wrapper and a cold bottle of crystal bubbly. Every dimension of our feast foreshadowed the ring and embodied the theme. I wanted to celebrate Jen's birthday. I wanted to celebrate the union of our two births. And I wanted to celebrate the new birth that would emerge as the two of us became one in the life-giving love of Christ.

I was so pleased I was positively giddy.

The chaperones were herding high-schoolers into vans when I drove back into camp. Jen chatted with Danny on the lodge's steps. I grabbed a bag of buns and ambled over.

"You know, Tony," Danny opened, in on the charade from the beginning. "Somebody needs to come back early and get the barbecue going for dinner. Would you mind volunteering? Maybe Jen'll help you."

"We can do that." My voice was well oiled. Jen nodded she was game.

"Great. Why don't you two drive over in the truck then, and come back when you need to."

A few minutes later, Jen and I tailed the caravan of kids onto River Road and west toward the coast. I glanced at her so excited I could scream. But I played it cool.

"This worked out great, didn't it?" Jen sat modestly on the far end of the cab. I wanted to reach over and hold her hand but we were still within eyeshot of the teens.

"Yeah," she smiled. "It's nice to have a few minutes alone." Her hands set a platonic example on her lap.

"What a day for the beach," I observed. And it was. Though late January, the sun was warm and the sky cloudless.

"Maybe we'll see some whales from the shore," Jen mused.

"May-be," I bit the inside of my cheek to check my broadening grin.

"What are you all smiley about?"

"Nothing. It's just . . . you look great that's all." I wasn't lying. She was dressed for a campout—a flannel dress with a pullover sweater and jean jacket, flowered long-john bottoms and hiking boots—but she couldn't have been sexier if she were wearing satin lingerie. Her hands squeezed her legs in restraint.

"So do you." I wanted to pull over right there and make out on the side of the road. But those damn kids were right in front of us. My knuckles grew white as I clutched the wheel.

The road meandered alongside the river toward the sea and neared the juncture of Highway 1. Danny must have said something because all the kids turned around and waved. Jen assumed they were just having fun. Until we hit the highway. The vans pulled into the left turn lane. I passed by on the right. The kids and chaperones waved widely and smiled brightly. I waved back through the driver's window and eased to a stop at the sign. As the lead van turned left and trailed south, I turned right.

"Tony?" Jen's suspicion rose. "Where're we going?"

"You don't expect me to work all day on your birthday, do you?"

"So what're we doing?"

"We're going on a picnic. Just you and me."

"What about the kids?"

"The others can handle things."

"They don't mind?"

"They're all for it. It was Danny's idea to bring along the truck so we could use it to get away."

"You mean . . . you've been planning this?"

"Guilty as charged."

"Oh, Tony," she squealed. She glanced behind us. Unshackled from our responsibility to be paragons of sexual uprightness, she scooted over on the seat and kissed me hard on the cheek. "This is so romantic. How long do we have?"

"As long as we want. Though we might get teased if we're out too late."

"Well, let them think what they want. This is *exactly* what I want to do on my birthday." She put her hand on my thigh. With her touch, I sped faster. "So where's the picnic going to be?"

"I don't know. There's got to be a secluded cove somewhere around here."

"Yes, let's find someplace where we can be absolutely alone." She squeezed my leg and scouted. I placed my hand on her leg and stroked the textured cotton of her long-johns. Touching her again was like a sip of wine after Prohibition.

We came into sight of the ocean where the river fanned out and met the sea in a wide sandy delta. The beach was exposed to both the highway and cliffside dwellings so we drove on. We curved past some Cape Cod bungalows then up a craggy bluff. Soon, layers of switchbacks climbed hundreds of feet above the water. The only snatches of beach we glimpsed were at the feet of eroding cliffs. My hopes for a secluded dune deteriorated with each curve of the climbing road. I refused to give up, though. Surely on the other side of the promontory the road would descend back to the sea.

The road curled over the hump of bluff, and Jen and I gasped in wonder. We crossed into a sanctuary of early springtime wilderness. A series of rounded verdant hills reached up the coast for miles. They looked like the derrieres of a dozen giant Earth maidens sunning their backsides with legs in the water where the waves could lap at the rise of their rear ends. Scattered across the emerald slopes, clumps of yellow poppies and spears of purple lupine grew in fertile pockets. Here and there, spiked pines stood erect, multiplying as they moved northward until they splurged forth in a thick forest consuming the hills from water's edge to Eastern ridges for as far as the eye could see. It was as beautiful as the pregnant meadow of a garden goddess poised at the edge of spring's nativity. Unfortunately, it birthed no beach.

I checked my disappointment and kept driving, hoping something would turn up by sheer force of will. But nothing did. The road rambled up, down, and around the sloping hills bordered by occasional cliffsides. There was no trail to hike, no turnout to park in, no widening of road to even turn around. Besides, we were hundreds of feet above sea level.

"There's gotta be a way down to the beach somewhere," I persisted.

"It's okay," Jen said. "What a beautiful day for a drive. I'm just happy to be with you."

I wasn't happy, though. I had a surprise poised to burst right out of my truck.

Then I saw it. As the highway arced over a hillock then curved toward the coast, an aberrant lane angled, parallel to the shoreline. It ascended in a near straight line onto a distant bluff then disappeared over the top. On an impulse I followed it.

"Where are we going?" Jen wondered, knowing that any hope of a beach lay in a road that went down, not up.

"I don't know exactly. Maybe we can find something up here."

The road rose through fields bordered by barbed wire on either side. An occasional gravel driveway teed into the lane but we saw no homesteads. About a mile up we leveled off and drove through a wooded ridge interrupted by periodic pasture. Though we couldn't see it, the ocean laid somewhere off to our left.

"I think we're in the middle of nowhere," Jen observed.

"Maybe so, but I have an idea . . ." I followed the road, then spotted a turnout. "Here we go."

"Honey, where are we?"

"I don't know. Let's explore. Hold on a second while I get some things from the back." Jen skeptically scanned the landscape while I gathered the goodies. When I came around with the balloons bobbing from my bundles she leapt out of the truck and rushed over.

"What have you got there?"

"Happy Birthday, Babe."

"Oh my God, let me help." She took the blankets and balloons and left me with my softball duffel bag and picnic basket. She looked around nervously. "Now what do we do?"

"Follow me." A barbed wire fence dotted with 'No Trespassing' signs lined the road along an empty pasture. Across the field, maybe a hundred yards, a patch of woods reached westward. "Let's make for those trees. Maybe we can see the ocean on the other side."

"But Tony, it says 'No Trespassing.'"

"It's okay. There's nobody around for miles. This is just grazing land."

"What if something's grazing out there right now, like a bull?"

I smiled. "Trust me. The place is deserted. The only bull you've got to worry about is the one standing right here." I leaned over and kissed her. "It's gonna be great, I promise."

I stretched the barbed wire for Jen to slip through, then handed her the supplies over the fence. She widened an opening for me, then we crossed the forbidden field. Apart from the cow pies we sidestepped, the pasture was uninhabited. We reached the grotto of trees undetected and peeked in. A canopy of alders, poplars, and fragrant cypress matted with ferns and mulberry bushes stretched before us so thick we couldn't tell how far the grove reached. The brush was so inviolate we could have been standing at the edge of a virgin wild. Hoping the payoff was worth the effort, we penetrated the lush tangle and trudged toward the ocean. Within a quarter of a mile we made out the vast airy openness beyond the final rim of trees. We trekked toward it.

At its edge, we were spellbound.

The woods ended on top of a rugged cliff so high we looked down upon the hawks soaring on the ocean's breeze. The shore was less than a mile away, but so far below us we could not hear the waves as they crashed against the protruding rocks. From that craggy height, we could see forever—to the south, past the cove at Duncan's Landing, beyond the head of Bodega Bay, all the way to Point Reyes a full morning's seagull flight downwind—to the north, over the jagged wooded shoreline, across acres of evergreen, clear to the far-off threshold of Fort Ross. And before us, the ocean spanned the full breadth of the horizon with such vastness it could have been the infinite watery void out of which creation was first fashioned.

We stepped onto a small grassy bluff no larger than a backyard lawn. I set down the supplies, pulled Jen in front of me, and cradled her with my arms as we took in the panorama. Standing in utter isolation on that majestic last ledge of the known world, we could have been humanity's first-born at the boundary of terra firma, the primordial pair appointed to populate this vestal planet, the commissioned seed-bearers poised in amorous contentment before taking up the Maker's call to play in the garden's fields with abandon.

Or we could have been two kids in love, looking for a little seclusion and landing upon the location of a lifetime.

I nibbled Jen's neck. She scrunched at the tingle and leaned in for more.

"What d'ya think? Will this do for a birthday picnic?"

"It's spectacular." She squeezed my arms. "You think it's all right we're here?"

"Trust me, Babe. It'd be a sin to waste such a beautiful place." I patted her hips then turned to the supplies. Time to get to work. I laid out the blankets, one on top of the other in case the ground was damp. I need not have worried. The afternoon sun toasted us, the cool breeze a welcome antidote. I unzipped my duffel bag and laid out the plates and napkins, utensils and cutting board. Jen took off her jacket and kneeled down.

"Anything I can do to help?" she asked.

"You can find a place for these." I eased out the flowers, already vased.

"Tony, they're beautiful." As she took them, she leaned in for a kiss.

"Hold on, Babe. We're just getting started." I unpacked the bread and candies, the fruit and cheese, and sliced while Jen deciphered the flowers. With her birthday prowess, she was quick.

"A carnation and a chrysanthemum . . . these must be you and me. So the white rose is . . . Jesus?"

"You're good."

"How thoughtful." She set them down then nibbled my ear from behind. I brushed her off with a slice of apple.

"Now be patient, Jen. I'm not done." As she munched the fruit, the mystery of the balloons dawned on her.

"The balloons . . . They're just like the flowers—you, me and Jesus."

"You *are* good." I checked my grin but was pleased she figured it out. She studied the unusual collage of food. The conspicuous absence of any color save orange, yellow, and white worked on her.

"Tony, did you pick out the food to match the flowers and balloons?"

"Guilty again." My smile came clean. "As far as I'm concerned, these colors go good together."

"You are so adorable. Come here." She pulled me on top of herself as she leaned backward on the blanket. My knife fell as I followed her down. I let her pepper me with kisses then pulled myself up.

"You're gonna have to wait," I teased. "There's more." I appeased her with another slice of apple then pulled out the cake. Through the cellophane wrap she discerned the colors.

"You are too much," she bubbled. "What will you think of next?" I took off the wrap and set the candles—white in the center, orange and yellow on either side.

"Let's see, what else do we have? Oh, yeah . . ." I pulled out the champagne.

"*Whaaaat have you got there?*" She sounded like a child enticed by a snuck cookie from the jar. "Is that real?"

"Of course it's real. We can't have a birthday toast without some champagne."

"What about the kids. If their parents found out we were drinking . . ."

"It's okay, Babe. Really." I unraveled the wrapper. "There's not much alcohol in champagne. Besides, it's your birthday." I popped the cork and took in the bouquet snaking out of the bottle. Then I poured.

"Happy Birthday." We clinked our plastic flutes and sipped.

"This is delicious." She took another mouthful. I did too. Then I kissed her, savoring the sparkling aftertaste in her mouth.

"I love you, Tony." The wine flushed her cheeks.

"I do too, Jen. Oh, and I have a toast. I wrote it down."

I retrieved the card from my bag as Jen, warmed by the wine, lifted off her sweater.

"Happy Birthday, Babe." I handed her the card and grabbed my own apple slice to ease my sudden self-consciousness.

Jen lifted the homemade card from the envelope and studied it like a mother would a picture of her infant. On the cover, I drew the head of a lion in charcoal, copied from a picture of Aslan in one of Jen's Narnia books. The only color was in the eyes. The pupils were white centers, but the triangulated irises were shaded—orange on the outside, yellow on the inside. Jen and me. She was sure to get it. Each eye of the Messianic lion was a union of the two of us joined at the center of Christ's stare. Simultaneously, we were held in the eyes of God and the lenses through which God looks into the world. My birthday toast was written within.

"May our love ever be held in the loving gaze of Christ. And may it ever be an instrument through which Christ brings love to the world."

Jen read the words. She contemplated the cover. She read the words again. When she looked at me, her eyes shimmered.

"I could never love you more than I do this very minute." She eased me down, laid on top of me, and kissed me, her tongue reaching as if to my center. Through her dress's sag I glimpsed her bare breasts hanging freely like two pears in a plump ripe dangle before falling from the tree. Jen lifted her head. "This is the most beautiful birthday surprise I have ever had."

I corralled my desire to caress her. "I do have one more thing," I shared. "I haven't given you your birthday present." I rolled away and pulled the jewelry box out from my duffel bag. There was no mistaking it. Her eyes grew as she sat up on her knees.

"I know we're in the middle of making plans to this effect. But Jen, I can't wait to marry you. I wish it were today. I am totally ready to make my vows and love you for the rest of my life."

Her eyes moistened as I slipped the ribbon off. When I opened the case, she gasped. She opened her mouth, held her hands to her lips like she was praying, and gasped. I knew. She not only recognized its meaning. It outshined the phantom sparkles of every wedding ring fantasy she had conceived since girlhood.

"It's unbelievable." She pulled my hand to see it more closely. But she did not touch the ring, not even the box. She studied it, cupped in my hand, then looked up and whispered. "Tony, would you do it? Would you place it on my finger?"

I took the ring from the box as she removed the plastic one she was already wearing. I poised it at the end of her finger and looked into her eyes.

"Jennifer Gallagher, will you marry me?" Then I slipped it into place.

It was some time before I realized that, judging by the letter of the law and not the spirit, she never answered me. Her response though, was unequivocal. I've relived it a thousand times. Holding her hand with the other, she eyed the ring. She turned her hand around and studied it from the front. She lifted it into the air and watched the jewels sparkle in the sunlight.

Then she looked at me. She placed her hands on my chest and eased me onto my back. She hiked her dress and straddled my waist. She held my face and kissed one eye, then the other, the middle of my forehead, the end of my chin. Then she blessed my mouth. I received her response. Our tongues sealed it.

Though I fought to resist the temptation, I slipped my hands under her dress and caressed the silky skin of her back. The delicious absence of a bra strap emboldened me. I slid my hands around and dared approach her dangling breasts. Jen moaned to my touch, unashamedly rubbing her hips on my jeans until I bulged to the breaking point. I slid my hands down and fingered the elastic band of her long-johns, then slipped them into the forbidden territory of her backside. Jen withdrew her tongue and nuzzled her cheek against mine. Her sigh carried her whisper.

"I want you inside of me." Her lips brushed my cheek like a courtesan's veil. "Do you think it's all right?"

Did I think it was all right? *Did I think it was all right*! Jesus Christ! For two years I was tormented by that question. The Bible was clear—fornication's a sin. But my passions pounded like a tidal wave against a cardboard dike. I tried not to feed them. I fought like hell every impure fantasy that lap danced through my imagination. I distracted myself with Bible reading. I busied my hands on the harmonica. I even became an exercise fiend, dashing out for a run every time I felt the pull of my member. But my sexual impulses were all-consuming. And they consumed me to the point of depravity. For the secret shame of our Christian relationship was that Jen and I could not wait until our wedding day before succumbing to our carnal desires. We opened the Aeolian bag of sexuality and their winds blew us all over the sea.

Within weeks of our first birthday kiss, our making out in the back of the football field turned into heavy petting in my truck's camper shell. The previous summer we discovered how to make each other come through our clothes. By Thanksgiving we graduated to coming without clothes. We were literally inches away from all-out intercourse, and narrowing the gap with dangerous persistence. Finally, the magnetic pull of our bodies won out. We crossed the line. Twice. The first time barely counted. At Christmas, I entered Jen with merely my tip while we rubbed each other to climax. I felt like we barely dodged the trespass. For about two days. Then I figured that technically we'd done it already anyway, so what the hell.

Throughout our whirlwind tour of the body's pleasures, my mind scrambled to keep pace with my loins. I rationalized our erotic romping according to every Christian principle I could cleave to—that in the eyes of God we were spiritually married even if we were not legally so, that God desired relational harmony to which a healthy sex life uniquely contributed, that God designed our bodies such that unreleased sexual energy would surely drive us insane. I even took the total depravity way out figuring I was damned no matter what. I already lusted after Jen enough to warrant an eternity of hurricanes tossing me in hell. Masturbation was a decided religious abomination. Which only left intercourse. Didn't Luther say if you're going to sin anyway, sin boldly?

But for all my theological contortions, I felt as guilty as a child sex-offender. After each erotic foray, my blissful cry of climax became a groan of self-castigation before I could catch my breath. After our last violation, I vowed that I would remain genitally pure until that mysteriously transforming ceremony would turn our moral libidinal limbo into unadulterated carnal freedom. But time was passing so slowly. And my thirsty scepter, once dipped in sacred waters, ached for another lusty splash.

Of course I didn't think it was all right. But I wasn't about to tell her. Not that close to the satisfaction of that for which my every pumping blood cell craved. I should have said no. I also should have had my Bible ready for us to read our way back to the ways of righteousness. But I didn't. When it came to the Good Book's guidance, Jen and I read no more that day.

I resisted my super-ego's assault and bluffed my way through. "Sure it's all right, Babe. We're practically married as it is."

"No," she smiled, having long since outgrown my puritanical hypocrisy. "That's not what I mean. We don't have any protection. What if I get pregnant?"

Even though we were suspended on the exasperating knife's edge of 'should we or shouldn't we,' the reality of the situation had not changed. My hands were down her pants, her legs were spread over my crotch, and my rod was ready to rip through my trousers and strike pure gold in the deep mother lode. I did not care if I was consigned to the lowest circles of hell, I wasn't about to let a condom's absence get in our way now.

"Babe, we're getting married in five weeks. Even if we got pregnant, it's so close, who'll know?" She searched my eyes then kissed me again. I waited for an indication of which way she was leaning. She entered my mouth with a sweeping spiral. That was all the indication I needed. I slipped my hands between her legs. They parted to receive me.

"If you think it's okay," she whispered with lips still pressed against mine.

"It couldn't be any more okay." She kissed me again, then sat up and pulled my shirt over my head. The outdoor air against my skin tickled with a seductive delight. The rest of my body screamed to be free of clothes as well. Jen swiveled off me, unlaced her boots, and slipped them off with her socks and long-johns. Then she caressed my chest, tongued my breast, and slid her hands down to my waist. She unbuttoned my jeans, flayed my pants open, slid her hand through my boxers, and gently squeezed. I thought I would burst. I tingled in her touch until I couldn't take it anymore. I grabbed my jeans and shorts and pushed them down as Jen slid them off my feet.

The breeze blew whispers across my bare phallic skin sending shivers of delirium through my body. As Jen straddled me, I reached under her dress and massaged her tush, the inside of her thighs, the moist crevice between her legs. Her hips stroked, her wetness sliding the length of me. In undulating passes, she pushed, and pulled, and panted.

Then she stopped. She looked at me with eyes both hungry and vulnerable. She glanced around to be sure we were alone. Then she did something that will fondle my libidinal fantasies for as long as I can tease up a sexual desire. She stood up. She glanced around again as her bashfulness returned. Satisfied enough, she looked back. She crinkled her nose like she couldn't believe her boldness. Then she crossed her arms, grabbed the hem of her smock, and in a silky sensuous rise, she pulled the dress right over her head.

She had nothing on, save the ring upon her finger. And she shined. The golden rays of the afternoon sun wrapped her in a radiance of erotic glory. She could have been an angel of light, the maiden guardian of morning, the living daughter of the sun god himself arrayed in transparent threads of sunshine. Her breasts were perched in delicate attention, the nipples pink and hard. Her hips curved, the pale skin bright with fresh exposure. Her legs spread slightly, the blue sky peeking between them in furtive flashes. And between those naked limbs, a patch of pubic beauty boiled my desire into a bubbling lust.

Her hair matched that on her head, an orange misty mound the color of molten lava. Her smell, carried on the breeze that passed between her legs, watered my mouth. I wanted to hold my arms around her waist and bury my face in that feathery tangle of strawberry-blond gossamer. I wanted to fill my lungs in the apple cider musk of her scent. I wanted to spread her legs and lose myself in the taste of her juice, that intoxicating concoction of Muscat sweetness and salty brine. A nymph need look no further to keep me at the table. I was ready to drain the keg, lick the barrel, then smack my lips for another go. I didn't know where to start. But I wanted that goddess in any way she would have me.

Jen stood a moment longer. I don't know why she hesitated. Perhaps she held the moment in sensuous suspense. Perhaps she took tipsy pleasure at the risqué display of her bare-skinned beauty on a bluff. Perhaps she reveled in her womanhood, propped up by my unabashed desire for her. I don't know. But she lingered. Or she lingers now in my mind. She stood there, sparkled in naked brilliance, poised to step boldly into the skin of her sexuality. Then without caring on whose bluff she stood or whose eyes were watching, she kneeled back down and came on top of me.

———

The sun was much lower in the sky when the perfect climax of our afternoon spewed forth as a satiated exclamation point. The remnants of our birthday feast lay scattered around us—tangerine peels and candy wrappers, bread crumbs and paper plates, toppled plastic glasses dappled with warm droplets of champagne. We sat undressed, gazing at the sea with a blanket wrapped around us. Jen was in front enfolded in my arms. My characteristic self-castigation miraculously held at bay, we sat as cozy as bundled-up newlyweds cuddled by the fire in our honeymoon cabin.

"I'll be so happy when we're married, Jen. Then we can do this all the time."

"What?" she answered. "Have sex? Or sit around naked all day?"

I laughed as if she caught me. "Both."

"Just think, Tony. We get to enjoy each other forever."

"Well, at least until we're eighty or so."

"Why only eighty?"

"Well the sitting together is fine but there won't be any sex in heaven."

"Sure there will be." She said it like she'd been there and was reporting back. "Heaven's filled with all the good things in life. Including sex."

"I think you've drunk a bit too much champagne."

"I'm serious." Moonshine or not, she was having fun with her bold swim through the seas of theology. "God made us to enjoy sex just like He made us to enjoy food. There's going to be food in heaven, why not sex?"

I was tipsy enough to swim along. "I can see it now. We're going to finish the heavenly banquet then just push the plates aside and have at it on the tables?"

"Maybe not on the tables," she teased like a call girl with standards. "There's discretion in heaven too." She was priceless.

"Wherever then—in the bushes, by the still waters, in the mansion's bedrooms. My point is, I can't imagine sex *anywhere* in heaven. You'd have people going at it all over kingdom come."

She turned with a coquettish grin. "Why do you think they call it kingdom come?"

"Jen! I can't believe you said that."

She turned back toward the sea. "What's the big deal? It's going to be like the Garden of Eden. You don't think Adam and Eve explored a few bluffs?"

"Maybe so. But there were animals in the garden too. *They're* not going to heaven."

"Who says?"

"Okay, I get it. You're yanking my chain." She was. And enjoying it. But she was serious too.

"Why? God loves animals too."

"Jen, they don't have souls. They don't have feelings. They certainly can't praise God."

She shrugged suggestively. "There's *lots* of ways praising God."

I chortled at the insinuation. "So sex is praising God now?"

"Sure it is," she glanced back again. "Why do you think people say 'Oh God' when they come."

"Jennifer Gallagher, what has happened to you?"

"Nothing. I'm just celebrating our great prayer life."

"You and the rest of God's creatures."

"Exactly."

"Who can't enjoy this great prayer life, but they're up in heaven doing it."

"Oh, they enjoy it all right." She squeezed me tight as if channeling just how much joy they actually did feel. "They find a secluded bluff. They drink a little champagne. They snuggle up with their sweetheart. And they say, '*Ohhhh . . . God.*'"

That's when we saw it. Both of us. Two darkened humps just off the coast. Even from a distance, seeing a live whale is breathtaking. And as if on cue, as if it had been listening all along and wanted to underscore the precise accuracy of Jen's speculations, one of the whales erupted with a geyser of a blowhole spray.

Jen bolted around to make sure I saw it. Without saying a word, we read each other's minds to a tee. It's funny really. We didn't have the slightest idea what those whales were doing. They could have been lost and signaling for help for all we knew. They could have been celebrating a kill. They could have been grim harbingers of the deep warning us of troubled waters ahead. But in the know-it-all bliss that all lovers share, we knew exactly what shenanigans those creatures were up to. And we knew exactly how they felt about it.

And we laughed. We laughed so hard my sides ached. We laughed so hard my jaw hurt. We laughed so hard tears came to my eyes.

Who needs heaven when such bliss is known on earth?

———

Our afterglow shined all evening at camp. Its tingle was so pleasurable we couldn't keep focused on the night's agenda. We toasted from afar over barbecued burgers and flashed back to the bubbly we tasted interlaced. We passed smiles at the talent show when I caught Jen eyeing her ring during a teenage love song. We stole a kiss in the kitchen when we collected supplies for s'mores. Our bodies were in a camp full of sleep-deprived teenagers. But our spirits were still on a seaside bluff.

Even the midnight service, crafted to convert the crowd to Christ, could not hold my concentration. Personal testimonies were shared, petitionary prayers were lifted, praise choruses were sung. But each word declared my love for Jen as much as my faith in Jesus.

When Young Life's signature song capped the evening off, it summed up all that I was feeling. It was the standard crescendo in our emotional appeal to the kids. I played it on the harmonica behind Danny's guitar as the whole company huddled in a campfire love-fest. While various teens closed their eyes to make personal commitments to Christ, I kept mine open. I watched Jen across the circle and played my harp as I kindled with flames of love. The song was 'Pass It On.' I played it for my fiancée.

Jen hugged a young lady who wept in rapture, sharing her happiness like a mother would a daughter who had just received her first kiss. I still felt Jen's kisses quickening me as the music crackled through my harp. Jen kept rocking the girl, on through the second verse. But she lifted her eyes to me. She sparkled with affection. My eyes grinned in return. In our silent lover's shorthand, we beheld the whole glimmering jewel of our afternoon feast—the champagne's popping, the ring's unveiling, the naked playful romping—all of it elevated before us like a host awaiting consecration. The song climaxed with the last lines' reprise. Danny and the kids were intoxicated with Jesus. Jennie and I anointed our day. As I played, my eyes never left hers.

> "I'll shout it from the mountaintop,"
>   (Jen and I were still on the mountain,)
> "I want my world to know,"
>   (And we didn't care who knew,)
> "The Lord of Love,"
>   (Truly a sacred love,)

"Has come to me,"
   (Had come to us,)
"I want,"
   (Yes, we want,)
"To pass,"
   (To dwell,)
"It on."
   (In us.)

We held our gaze. Jen's eyes twinkled in the twilight flicker of the fire. In that moment, all fear and shame had fled to the shadows. Only love remained. As true as the unblinking stare that held us.

Could she have known that the seeds of our lovemaking were conspiring even then to plant a child within her womb? Could I have known that I would return to that bluff the following spring to face off with the God to whom we sang so triumphantly? Could either of us have known that even as we stood on a mountaintop of joy, our love was slipping away as surely as an eroding coastal cliff pounded by a relentless sea?

No. In that moment, lover's bliss was all we knew. And the song that promised to sustain us. I'll shout it from the mountaintop. I want my world to know. The Lord of Love has come to me. I want to pass it on.

As it turned out, I could have done without the Lord of Love coming.

And *that*, I'm passing on.

14

Y THE TIME I passed them with my reprise picnic supplies, eight summers had blistered the shingles siding the Cape Cod bungalows; eight autumns stripped the madrone trees clawing the craggy rise; eight winters battered the switchbacks clinging to the cliff like barnacles on a barge. I scaled the snaking road on the eighth Lenten slumber since I searched with Jen for a place to picnic. Any promise of spring within the pregnant brush was lost on me. I nursed from the bosom of my memories with Jen.

Even after the milk had long since run dry.

In January of 1985, I started my second semester at Gospel Light Seminary. With Danny and the battalion of other first-year plebes beginning their tour through the mission fields of ministry, I enrolled in the 'Introduction to Theology' course. 'God 101' we called it. In his opening lecture, Professor MacIntyre argued that the question of theodicy was the ultimate furnace through which any theological orientation could be tested.

"Shallow conceptions of God burn away like chaff within the flames of senseless suffering," he expounded. "Only the precious metal that withstands such a crucible is worth devoting one's life to."

His final exam was a paper. After analyzing Christian thinkers throughout history, we were to articulate our own perspective on the decisive question, 'How can a good God allow suffering and evil in the world?'

I did not pass the course.

In fact, I never finished the paper.

Daniel Joshua Backman was born on November 1st, 1984. He missed his due date. Both of them. He came six days after the one Jennie's doctor set, three weeks before the one we shared with our friends. He weighed six pounds, twelve ounces—a tad small for a term pregnancy, rather healthy for a baby born three weeks premature. The precise due date should have been easy to figure out. You could set the lunar calendar by Jen's cycle. But then again, you'd need to know the true date of conception.

When we announced our pregnancy to our friends, we surmised that conception must have occurred close to our wedding night. They were unsurprised. God is an awesome God. Blake, the scholar of our group, recalled that in biblical cultures a child conceived on a king's wedding night was considered ordained for greatness. Awesome indeed.

Daniel was not so lucky. He lived three months, eighteen days. He died on a Monday. That afternoon an autopsy was performed. As was a death scene investigation. On Tuesday, a detective from the homicide division questioned us. The hospital's public health officer followed him. On Wednesday, we met with the social worker from Child Protective Services, then the psychologist chairing the review board. We buried Daniel on Thursday. The hearing was on Friday. Finally, the case was closed.

———

"They thought we were child abusers for God's sake." For the life of me, I could not contain my rage. *"Can you believe it? They thought we actually killed him."*

Our friends were speechless. They stared into their mugs' cold dregs as if comforting words would appear if only they waited. Jen was curled on the couch. She covered her mouth with a wadded tissue while I fumed around our living room. Danny was the only one from our Friday night fellowship that dared a consoling response.

"They didn't think you abused Daniel. It was all routine. Wasn't it Jen?" Jennie nodded, her face crinkling up as tears returned to her eyes. Ruth, Jen's closest friend, reached over and squeezed the free hand in Jennie's lap.

"I don't think so," I came back. "You should have heard what they kept asking. 'How much conflict was in the home? How many other children have died in your care? Did you ever give him cocaine?' Can you imagine? I even asked her, 'Are you *serious*?' 'You'd be surprised at how many children die from occult cocaine exposure,' she tells me. My God, they put us in the same league as *Satan* worshippers!"

"They were just covering all the bases. Nobody thinks you're a child abuser." Danny's words paled before the fury pounding in my temples. "Come on. Sit down. Tell us what happened from the beginning."

I glanced at Jen to see if she was up for this. Her eyes were filled with sorrow—and a longing for comfort from any source that could give it. Danny led me to the stuffed chair that cornered the couch. Kathy, Blake's wife, went to the kitchen with Jen's untouched teacup and my half-empty mug. The others let the heaviness hang as I put the wretched pieces of the investigation together. Kathy reappeared with both drinks refreshed.

"The point of the review hearing," I began, "was to determine the official cause of death."

"Tony," Blake timidly interrupted. "Can you start with Sunday night? Some of us don't really know anything about what happened."

"Sunday night . . ." I closed my eyes as images from the onset of the nightmare flashed. As if needing the distraction, Jen leaned forward and grabbed a pitcher. Powered more by habit than volition, she poured milk into her cup then leaned toward mine. I opened my eyes to the white creamy liquid trickling towards my mug.

"*No!*" My shout startled us all. "I'm sorry. I just don't want any milk in my coffee, Jen."
She looked at me bewildered. "Since when do . . ."

"I *hate* milk in my coffee," I interrupted. "Just don't. Please." She looked at me like a
mother examining her child for signs of a fever. I reached for my drink, thought better of
it, and left it. Jen leaned back, abandoning hers as well. Blake cut the budding tension.

"So, what happened Sunday night?"

I looked at the floor as the swirl of memories resurfaced.

"That's just it. *Nothing* happened Sunday night. We had dinner, we . . . oh, that's right."
Daniel's face materialized. "He smiled for the first time." I looked at Jen. She pressed tissue
to her nose with the fresh flow of tears. I should have held her hand. But I continued with
the same statement I gave to the investigators. "Anyway, he was fine. Better than fine. We
played, dressed him for bed, and put him down. It was probably 8:00. I had that Church
History paper due the next morning so I went out to study. I got home about 11:30. Jen
was asleep in our bed and Daniel was sleeping next to her. I picked him up and put him
back into his crib. He stirred a bit, but didn't wake up. I covered him like I always do. Then
I went to bed. When Jen woke up the next morning, she found him exactly as I had left
him. Only he was dead. He simply stopped breathing. I'm telling you, absolutely nothing
happened that was out of the ordinary."

"Except I was late." Jen whispered through her balled Kleenex.

"What?" said Ruth.

"I was late." The tears gushed forth with her words. "I woke up too late. He's always
up by six. It was past seven before I got up. I was an hour too late." She sobbed into Ruth's
arms.

"Jennie," she consoled, crying as well. "He was already dead. That's why he didn't wake
you up."

"You don't know that." Jen whimpered into Ruth's shoulder. "He might have been
alive still. He might have needed me. I should have woken up on time."

"My God," Ruth pleaded. "You hadn't slept a full night since he was born. Of course
you would sleep in if he didn't wake you. *Anybody* would."

But Jen was inconsolable. As she was all week. She was convinced that her prompt rising would have kept him alive. We sat as her tears rolled down ravines already well worn.

As her sobs subsided, Sandy became indignant. "And they made you go through a
hearing for *that*?"

"It's routine," Danny reiterated. "I even asked the officer."

"You talked to the officer?"

"Yes. They question everybody who's watched the parents with their child. They talked
with Ruth too. Everything they did was completely routine. They would have investigated
President Reagan the same way."

"So what all did they do?" Blake asked.

"They did an autopsy," I said.

"They gave Daniel an autopsy?" Sandy was horrified.

"Yes," I said. "They had to check him for bruises, strangulation, poisoning. It makes
you sick what some parents do to their kids."

"My God," Sandy was sickened too.

"They also tested him for diseases like meningitis . . . pneumonia . . ." Danny added.

"Like we wouldn't know he was sick," I defended. "Come on. We doted on that boy."

"Which is the point," Danny argued. "He simply died on his own."

"Anyway," I continued. "They taped off his bedroom and investigated his bedding, his clothes, his blankets, anything we could have suffocated him with."

"Again, routine."

"Then we were questioned by a child maltreatment specialist, a social worker, two police officers, one detective, a public health official, and the child psychologist who chaired the review process."

"And what did they determine?" Sandy asked.

"Crib death," I answered.

"Tony," Ruth revolted.

"That's what it is. Sudden Infant Death Syndrome."

"Do they know what causes that?" Sandy asked.

"They have no idea," I said. "All they know is that he stopped breathing and died in his sleep."

"I can't believe what you've had to go through," Kathy said, holding her arms around her stomach as if protecting a child she had yet to bear.

"I'll say," Sandy added. "The whole thing's just tragic beyond words." As if that said it all, everyone grew quiet.

I glanced at Jen's hands folded in her lap. I didn't have it in me to look her in the eye. She didn't know everything that I left out of the story. But she knew enough.

The psychologist warned us that a child's death could precipitate alienation in a marriage.

She was off base.

Daniel's *death* didn't separate us. His *birth* did.

The evening before Daniel died foreshadowed no hints of the tragedy but hours away. Quite the contrary. It was the brightest moment the three of us ever shared.

Jen and I ate dinner across from each other at our kitchen table. Daniel, well-fed and wiggly, cooed in his Baby Bouncer propped on the floor angled towards Jen. His infant eyes unable to focus, he nodded about in dopey abstraction, fascinated by the deluge of colors in his blurry world. He still recognized us more by sound than sight.

"How's your paper coming?" Jen asked. She knew I was stressed out about it. Dr. Nesbith, the Church History professor, was the toughest grader on campus. By the grace of God and an inspired all-nighter, I aced the first assignment. But this one, like the final paper, was worth forty percent of our grade. I wanted to impress him again but still struggled with my argument. It was due in the morning.

"Pretty slow," I replied. "Looks like a late night."

"Anything I can do to help?"

"No."

She twirled her spaghetti in silence.

"You don't feel like talking?" Jen asked.

"Not really. I'm working this out in my head."

"Okay."

Her disappointment hovered like an unacknowledged rain cloud. I hoped it would pass as I stumbled over Luther's critique of the Catholic theology of Eucharist. How was Christ *really* present within the elements but not *substantially* so? As Jen nibbled her garlic bread, something came to her. She started to speak, then caught herself, swallowing her desire to talk with a sip of milk. I knew she just wanted to connect for a minute. And it wouldn't have incapacitated my paper to take the time. But I couldn't come through. Jen let it slide and amused herself. She was getting used to it.

Daniel continued his distracted flight through the murky collage of light and shade around him. Jen looked down at him. Her discouragement softened at the sight of his contented curiosity. Daniel sensed it. His random looking about stilled and fixed in her direction. He stared at her with puzzled inquisitiveness, as if this blur held a special fascination for him. Slowly, the blur came into focus. For the first time, Daniel saw a distinct shape, a human face. He gazed, captivated, as if trying to place this new presence before him.

Then he recognized her. The face was his mom. And he did the most incredible thing. He smiled. That was all—a simple smile. But with it shimmered a ray of sunshine so bright it washed away Jen's discouragement and kindled her into a beacon of delight. She broke into a grin, sprang to her knees, and squealed like a tourist sighting the queen.

"Did you see that? He smiled at me." Her face fluttered as she swooned at her boy. "Yes you did. You smiled at your mommy, didn't you? Yes you sure did." How could I not see it? Daniel beamed with joy, giggling and cooing with Jen's gush of baby talk. And Jen beamed back. Their joy bounced back and forth like mirrors reverberating sparkles of light until they dazzled in an all-out blaze of bliss.

"Tony," Jen bubbled, her countenance as radiant as that of Moses before the burning bush. "You gotta see this." She grabbed my hand and pulled me down, holding me from behind as I looked into Daniel's face. Like a cloud passing over the sun, his smile dimmed as his gaze shifted from Jen to me. He took in the features of this strange new face. Then he recognized who it was—his daddy—and once again he flickered into a glorious grin.

It was magical, like peering into a looking glass of gladness. I could not help but smile. Daniel gazed at my grumpy mug with such unconditional delight I bubbled over in waves of purifying playfulness. He giggled and gurgled and bounced in buoyant rapture, I tickled and snickered and kootchee-kootchee-kooed in childlike abandon the two of us sparkling into an explosion of happiness.

Jen nuzzled my cheek to bask in the joy, creating a visual feast for Daniel. He bounced between us, first giggling at one, arms flailing, feet kicking, then wiggling back to the other, the three of us laughing ourselves into a mystical moment of effervescent union. We wanted to soak in that glory forever. Our knees got sore, our cheeks grew cramped, our dinner got cold, yet still we sloshed in the enchanted waters that washed us into our truest selves until a surfeited exhaustion overcame us and we sighed to a blissful stop. Jen turned to me still dripping with joy.

"Isn't he just the most beautiful thing?"

My grin still sparkled. But as I looked into her eyes, I saw hope lacing her happiness.

"He is, Babe." I kissed her forehead and turned away.

I already knew what was coming.

And I dreaded it.

———

When we finished dinner, Jen did the dishes while I readied Daniel for bed. Exhausted by all the excitement, he declined Jen's nipple for his evening feeding so we slipped right into our bedtime routine. We read a story from his children's Bible, bade goodnight to the critters on his dresser, and prayed to the painted Jesus overlooking his crib for protection throughout the night. Jen laid him into bed and covered him with a blanket. I pulled out my harmonica and played him a lullaby. To the sounds of my harp and his mother's hum, he closed his eyes and faded to sleep. We lingered before his belly-borne rest, his fists pressed to the mattress breaking his fall into slumber's hold. Then we turned out the light and left.

I returned to my card table in the living room corner and continued to wrestle with Reformation treatises on Communion. Jen retired to the back of the apartment and prepared for bed.

Before long, I felt the sensuous brush of Jen's lips on my neck. Her hand slipped between my shirt buttons and caressed my chest. "The baby's asleep," she whispered. "Can you take a little break?" Her other hand fingered the beltline of my pants.

"Not now, Jen. I'm right in the middle of this."

"Are you sure?" Her fingers brushed my crotch.

"Jen!" I jerked. "Cut it out!"

My snap cut through her amorous mood like a slap on the face. She withdrew her hands and slouched on the sofa-arm behind me. She was more than hurt. She was dejected.

"Tony, what's wrong?"

"Nothing's wrong. I just have to finish this paper." I knew this was coming.

"It's not the paper. You haven't touched me in months."

"I've touched you." I felt the trap poised to spring.

"You don't hold me. You don't kiss me. We haven't made love since early last summer."

I heard the panic in her voice. "Seminary's hard, Jen." She didn't buy it.

"What is it? Don't you find me attractive anymore?"

"That's not it."

"Then tell me. Why don't you want me?"

I held my head and sighed. I didn't want to face her, didn't want to face myself. It stung like hell to admit. But she was right. I had stopped wanting her. As soon as she became a mother.

When Jen started to show, I shuddered at the way her underwear stretched with her mildly bloating body. As her belly swelled with new life, my sexual desire dwindled. By the time she matured to maternity smocks, I shivered at her touch. We didn't talk about it. We diverted our energies into Daniel's arrival. I hoped my drive would return once the baby was born. But it didn't. And Jen knew it. As my excuses wore thin, her doubts took hold. Her sexual frustration turned into terror. She feared she was no longer desirable to the man she loved. It killed me to see it. And I hated myself for it. But it was true. My shame lies in the dark fact that, even as I sensed the pain I caused her, something about my son's mother quite simply repulsed me.

"Tony," she finally offered. "Why don't you talk to someone? Like Danny." At that I turned around. I hesitated when I saw her. She was dolled up in the black negligee she wore on our wedding night. She retained none of that evening's sensuous boldness however. She was slumped over, all played out. I cocked my head forward then back halfway and talked over my shoulder.

"And tell him what, Jen?"

"Tell him the truth about when we got pregnant."

I nearly snorted. "What's *that* got to do with anything?"

"I just think . . . I don't know. Something's eating you, Tony. And if you talk to somebody, maybe you'll feel better."

"It's not going to happen, Jen."

"Why not?"

"I'm studying to be a youth minister for God's sake. Christians don't get their girlfriends pregnant. Especially ministers."

"It's not that big of a deal. Danny knows we're all human."

"Sin is sin, Jen. Danny knows *that* too."

"He also knows Daniel. And you can't look at that beautiful boy and think it was a sin to bring him into the world."

"Not everybody knows Daniel. They *do* know right from wrong, though. If word got out . . ." I let it hang.

"I think you'll be surprised at how understanding people'll be."

"How can you be so sure?"

"I just am, Tony."

Something in the way she said it made me shoot around to look at her. "You didn't tell Ruth did you?" She didn't answer. "*Did you*?!"

"Tony, the baby."

"**Did you!!?**" I didn't care about the baby, or the people downstairs, or the people across the Goddamned street. If she betrayed me, God help me, I'd come uncorked. Her defeated eyes made a denial futile.

"*How could you, Jen? Goddamn it*!" I leapt out of my chair and fumed around the room. "How am I supposed to face her now?"

"It's not like that. She thinks you're wonderful."

"It doesn't matter, Jen. You should *never* have told her, Goddamn it. Who else have you told?"

"Nobody."

My pencil snapped in my hand and I threw it on the floor. "Why did you do it? Goddamn it."

"Do you have to keep swearing, Tony?"

"I'll talk the way I want to talk," I dared. "Do you have a problem with that?"

"No, it's just . . . you're scaring me."

"*What do you think I'm going to do? I'm mad, that's all.*" Her insinuation made me all the madder. I was red with rage and ready to punch my fist through a wall.

"I know, but look at you."

I glared at her and saw what she saw. A rabid pig. I detested him. And I detested her for seeing him.

"Look at what, Jen?" I spit. "You did this. You should *never* have told Ruth."

"She's my friend, Tony."

"*I* decide what people know about me. Not you."

She stared, scared and confused. She had never seen me like this before, had never seen anybody like this before.

"What are you looking at, Jen? Stop looking at me!" Her shock immobilized her. "*STOP IT!*"

It was like I flashed a knife at her. She twitched her head then looked down. I knew she was cut to the bone. But I wasn't taking the heat for it. "You *did this, Jen. Goddamn you. Goddamn you to fucking hell.*"

She did not say a word. Nor did she look at me. She rose from the sofa-arm, walked by me like I wasn't there, and closed the bedroom door behind her.

I was a whirlwind of conflicting passions. I was so enraged I could have shattered glass, so self-loathing I could have sliced myself with it. I wanted to walk out the front door and never come back—fuck Jen, fuck Ruth, fuck the whole lot of unforgiving accusers. And I wanted to go into her and take it all back, bury forever the bastard I had become. But I hadn't done anything wrong. And she was the one who should apologize to me. I must have paced for fifteen minutes before I knew what I had to do. I needed to calm down, then rationally convince Jen of just how wrong she had been.

I drank some water and organized my thoughts. My case was self-evident. I didn't need to yell. I needed only to be clear. And clear I was. She should never have shared our secrets without my permission. I marshaled my arguments, confirmed my resolve, and walked down the hall. I paused at the knob, affirmed my rightfulness, then opened the door.

The second I saw her, my rightfulness left me.

Jen sat in our bed, her back to the headboard. She wore her customary silk pajamas and held her prayer journal in her lap opened to the page marked by the satin tassel. She hadn't been reading it. She'd been gazing at the curtained window. When I opened the door, she turned. A single tear slid down her cheek. With eyes holding no malice, only frightened yearning, she stared at me. And in that moment, all of my angers and indignities, my arguments and anxieties, dissipated like fog before the noonday sun.

I *saw* the person sitting in our bed.

She was not the betrayer who divulged our shame to her friend, nor the adversary who recoiled before my rage. She was not my son's mother, not my own wife, not even my furtive lover. She was simply Jen—a beautiful young woman who loved to wear silk and pray for her friends, smile with her boy, and picnic with her husband—a simple, kindhearted person who wanted no more from life than to love and be loved, to hold and be held, to touch and be touched. I saw the Jen I fell in love with. I saw the Jen that Daniel had seen when his face broke out into unrestrained delight. I saw the Jen that God must see when He pauses from His midnight labors, steals up on her while she is sleeping, and casts a tender gaze at the daughter He fashioned with such care.

For several moments, we looked at each other. I longed to walk over, kiss away her tear, then hold her in my arms. I wanted to. I really did.

But something held me back. I was paralyzed by a coldness no determination could break. I could only look at her. Her stare held me like a lifeline reaching from a rescuer to a drowning swimmer at sea. The rope was all we had left. For that moment, we both held tight.

Then I let go.

"I'm going out to study," I said. I glanced at the journal on her lap. A harmonica sketch headed the page. I glanced back up. Then I walked down the hall, grabbed my books, and left.

The next morning, Daniel was dead.

———

After our Friday night fellowship group bemoaned the loss with us, after they prayed for our sorrow and shared reassurances, they washed the evening's dishes, embraced our broken spirits at the door, then left for home.

Silently, Jen and I put away our clothes and went to bed. I laid on my side and faced the wall. Jen slipped into her side and turned off the light.

In the five days since Daniel's death, neither of us had mentioned our fight. From the moment Jen found him, we were caught up in the macabre roller-coaster ride through crisis interventions and criminal investigations, burial decisions and funeral arrangements. Lying in bed with the house now empty, the surreal ride came to a stop. We were left alone to face the wasteland of life after the loss of a child.

For several moments, we laid in our mute, private vigils. I sensed a stir. Almost apologetically, Jen turned towards me. Her body was but inches away. Tenderly, as if to say that all wrongdoing was forgotten, as if to ask if we might face this horror together, she placed her hand on my shoulder. Instinctively, my body cringed. Jen withdrew her hand, hesitated, then turned back to her own side of the bed.

She never reached out to touch me again.

———

Time flowed through the coming weeks like an eroding river widening the chasm between us. The currents eddied Jen in a depressive grief. I raged on rapids of an inexhaustible fury. By the time we touched our respective shores, the canyon between us was all but unbridgeable.

While Jen mourned in our apartment's shadows or sobbed into the shoulders of friends, I stormed the streets and pounded my rage through fuming midnight drives.

My face went unshaved and my hair grew wild as I checked out of my classes, Friday night fellowship, weekly Bible studies, and Young Life meetings at the high school to spew through the darkened streets. My misanthropic excursions had a single purpose. I searched for a suitable target on which to vent my rage. Red lights and snarling dogs, gawking pedestrians and dawdling motorists, I did not care. If you were on my path or in my face I spat and swore not giving a damn who was within earshot.

By Easter, my rage focused onto one all-consuming transcendent target. Though I was flunking out of the rest of my classes, I reattended Professor MacIntyre's. I sat in the back and refused to take notes. But I caught every detail. We had a paper to write. On a topic in which I had a sudden vested interest. 'Why did a good God allow suffering in the world?' Or as I was tackling the subject, 'Why does the suffering in the world annihilate any notion of a good God?' For the first time since Daniel's death, I had a project that captured my imagination. I attacked it like a pit bull going after a mail carrier.

In mid-April, I took a late-afternoon break from studying. Shadows deepened over my corner desk as dusk's shroud covered the apartment. I needed air before I resumed my scholarly assault well into the night. As I walked down the hall, I noticed Jen sitting on a rocker in Daniel's darkened bedroom. It had been six weeks since he died, yet his room retained the firstborn anticipation of the day we brought him home.

Jen stared at the frozen mobile suspended over the crib. On the chest beside her, several books lay by the unlit Noah's ark nightlight—Daniel's children's book of Bible stories, Jen's prayer journal, a friend's copy of *A Severe Mercy*. The whole scene incensed me.

"Wallowing in it won't bring him back, Jen." My words didn't touch her.

"He'd be five and a half months old by now. He'd be rolling himself over and reaching for his mobile." Like others who have lost a young child, Jen was doomed to mark time by the phantom growth of her absent son.

"How's this making things better?"

She looked at me, life drained from her face. "We need help, Tony."

"If you mean counseling, I've told you. I'm not letting some stranger mess around with my head."

She looked back at the mobile Daniel couldn't reach. "I know God doesn't give us more than we can endure. But I don't see how this is bringing us closer to Him."

"Is that what you think? That God killed Daniel so we would love Him more?" I wanted to throw the book at her side through a Goddamned window.

"Maybe we loved each other too much," Jen wondered, "put each other first instead of God."

"So He killed our three-month-old baby? And we're supposed to fall on our knees and tell Him we're sorry and promise to put Him first from now on? Fuck a God like that, Jen."

She stared at me like she couldn't distinguish me from the devil. I glared back, defying her to defend her God. She didn't. She only looked bewildered. And alone.

A knock at the door interrupted us. Danny dropped by with his backpack.

"Hey, Tony. Can I come in?"

"Sure," I said like a child declaring it was a free country. Jennie came out to the hall.

"Hey, Jennie," Danny said. "You look good. You holding up?" She looked like shit. And she wasn't holding up well enough to feed herself.

"Hi, Danny." She returned his hug with relief in her eyes. Then more from habit than hospitality, she prepared some coffee. Danny sat on the couch.

"The kids keep asking about you," he said. "They made you this."

He held out a card. A sketch of Jesus holding a baby graced the cover. Jesus had angel wings opened wide to embrace the entire unseen world below Him. The inscription was inside. 'The same hands that now hold Daniel, hold you during this time of grief.' Signatures and scratchy notes flooded the page in various colors and handwriting styles. 'Hurry Back!!', 'We Miss You!!', 'Keep the Faith!!'

I scanned the card. "Sweet kids."

"They care about you, Tony."

"Yeah." I was noncommittal. "Tell 'em thanks . . . But don't tell them I'm coming back soon. I don't know when I'm coming back."

"Take as much time as you need. Sandy's helping out until you're back to yourself."

I should have been grateful, but I was pissed at how quickly I was replaced. Danny frowned with concern. He knew it went a lot deeper than not feeling up for the drive to the high school.

"Maybe you should take a break for the rest of the year, start up again in the fall."

"Yeah well, we'll see . . ."

I tossed the card onto the table. Jen interrupted the awkward silence with two mugs of coffee. The caramel color betrayed the milk stirred into mine. I didn't know if she was deliberately defying my desire for black coffee or if some unconscious rebellion warred within her. Either way, I was sick of it. I did not say a word. I did not shift my posture. I merely turned my head and looked at her as cold as a dagger of ice. She looked perplexed, then remembered, closing her eyes like a servant berating herself for repeatedly forgetting this one simple thing. Such was the state into which our marriage had degenerated. Simple domestic rituals became the symbolic battlefields on which our hostilities were waged.

Danny broke the tension.

"Tony, I've been thinking. Maybe you ought to take a break from school, too. You know, a leave of absence. It'll do you good."

I had already been through this with Jen. They could kick me out but I wasn't just crawling away. "We can't. We've already paid for the apartment with the scholarship money."

"They'll work something out with you. I'm sure of it."

"I'm not taking a leave, Danny." Danny should have heard it. The discussion was over. He paused, then boldly trod on.

"Professor Nesbith asked me to talk with you. As your friend. You're flunking out. You haven't handed anything in since . . . since before Daniel died. It's too late to withdraw, but Nesbith says the school will give you a leave. I think you should consider it."

"Why don't you, Tony?" Jen supported. "It could take some of the pressure off."

"What do you know about it, Jen? You don't have the slightest idea . . ." She looked at Danny and I saw it in an instant. "You knew about this? You two have been talking about me behind my back? I can't believe this. My best friend and my wife." Jennie looked down disheartened.

"We're just trying to help you, Tony," Danny consoled. "We care about you."

"This is a great way of showing it—ganging up on me behind my back."

"We're not ganging up on you," Danny pleaded.

"No. You're just trying to run my life for me. And gossiping about my dark little secrets."

"We weren't gossiping about any dark secrets," Jennie said, as if tired of reasoning with a recalcitrant child. "There *are* no dark secrets."

"Yeah. Whatever."

"Look," Danny stepped in. "We have to come up with a way out of this. If you flunk all your classes, you'll lose all your aid, if they don't kick you out altogether. It's either take a leave or you've got to pass two of your three courses."

"The last thing in the world I'm doing is writing some stupid Church History paper just to keep my scholarship money."

"Well." Danny played his trump card. "There is a way out of that class. If you aced the first two papers and you show up the rest of the semester, Nesbith'll pass you even if you don't do the final paper. He's willing to buy you time until next fall. He thinks you're sharp, Tony."

"There it is then." The subject was closed.

"Well, except for one thing."

"What?"

"He needs the second paper—the one due the day Daniel died. You said you did it, right? But in the confusion of it all, you never handed it in."

I looked at Danny. He was just trying to help. I looked at Jen. She was just trying to get through. In that moment, I wanted to kill them both.

"I'm not handing in any Goddamned paper."

"But Tony, it'll make this go away for now." Danny begged to let him help me.

"Don't you fucking hear me?"

"Tony," Jen scolded as Danny winced from the attack.

"*Listen! I'm not. Turning. In. The god. Damned. Paper!*" I glared at them both to make sure my words landed. "*Got it*?" Then I grabbed my coat and left.

I didn't tell them that I didn't have a paper to turn in. I never wrote it. In fact, the night I left Jen sitting in our bed, I never got to the library. I went to see someone. The devil showed up too. It was the night I conceded him my soul.

15

CURLING OVER THE SWITCHBACKED cliff, I came upon the coastal paradise Jen and I had eight years earlier. The emerald hills, though lush with springtime promise, were pricked with pine. Statued evergreen speared the fields like memorials to the fallen dead in a skirmish fought long ago—lone casualties here and there, clumps of groved fatalities further on, an entire forest commemorating the massacre up north. If indeed a former battlefield, the screams that protested the spilt blood had long since gone silent. It was as tranquil as a cemetery on a sunny afternoon.

The highway ambled across the hills, then curved toward the sea. I recognized the lane at once. It angled off and shot up the rise, disappearing atop the ridge where a family graveyard of pines overlooked the combat zone below from the comfort of its perched height. As I climbed, I recalled the night of Daniel's death, the night I fought with Jen, and left her to her prayers.

That night, I had visited another family graveyard.

When I walked out on Jen in bed, I didn't know where to go. I only knew I'd be damned if I was working on that paper. I got in my truck and drove up the 101. I was halfway to Petaluma before my destination dawned on me.

At 9:30 Sunday night, the cemetery gates were locked. I was not deterred. I parked on a side street and stalked the adjoining woods to the graveyard's back fence. The twelve-foot pillared cornerstone had several bricks jimmied loose. I knew they would be. I had done it myself.

With grace honed from countless adolescent incursions, I scaled the column, then leapt over. Moon shadows of tombstone silhouettes stretched toward a small rise with three large trees atop it. Ignoring the statues of Mary and the plaster crucifixes in between, I made for the mound. On the far side, within reach of the final tree's shade on a clear summer's day, a row of modest headstones rested. I stopped before the last one on the left. I did not need the moonlight to read it. Its inscription was to the point.

Magdalena Haecker Backman
1926–1972

My mom died when I was thirteen, the age most Jewish boys celebrate their bar mitzvah. My father would have rather I'd joined a cult. The Torah commands Jewish fathers to nurture within their children a passionate attachment to the Lord. My father complied. He sought to make us hate his Jewish God as much as he did. He boycotted synagogue, banned Jewish scriptures in the house, and religiously ate pork every Sabbath at sundown. On Yom Kippur, he read Marx at the bus stop in front of the temple with his back turned to the atoning liturgy. During Purim, he butchered a chicken in the park across the street, the fowl's squawks drowning out the names of Haman and the Lord alike. On Hanukkah, he placed candles in the mantle menorah and each window of the house, the wicks defiantly resisting the night *unlit*. He was as devout in his blasphemy as any Hasid in their obedience.

And yet, for some cryptic reason that resonated with his diabolical sacrilege, my dad's jihad against the Hebrew God observed an annual reprieve. Every spring, he celebrated Passover.

It was my favorite night of the year.

Like my mother, my father trained as an actor in prewar Munich. Unlike her, he lidded his theatrical panache as if it bore the Sitra Achra's stain. He condescended himself to his craft but one night a year—the night he unleashed his showman's charisma, fused it with a pittance of paternal charm, and gifted his family with an inspired reenactment of the Hebrews' liberation from Egypt.

The stage was always propped and a captive audience in place. The table was set with china, the food covered with cloth, the candles lit, the wine uncorked, my mom, my sister, and I in pillowed seats anticipating his arrival as if the prophet Elijah were appearing in our dining room.

He held us in suspense, thespian that he was, then entered with a priest's reverence, donning the kittel as if it ordained him with sacred powers. Solemnly, he poured the wine, unveiled the food, and invoked a blessing from the Master of the Universe. We sipped the wine, washed our hands, and dipped parsley into salt water. He broke the unleavened bread, set aside a portion, and removed the egg and shank-bone. Then, with the majesty of Melchizedek, he lifted the platter with two hands and ceremoniously intoned, "This is the bread of affliction which our ancestors ate in Egypt. Let all who are hungry enter and eat; let all who are nearby come to our Passover feast. This year we are here; next year may we be in Israel. This year we are slaves; next year may we be free."

I tingled with anticipation. Not for our freedom. For the show that was seconds away. And I got to launch it.

My dad set the plate down and poured more wine. With closed eyes, he breathed in the bouquet as if it fueled the performance to follow. We waited. Then he opened an eye and gazed my way. It was the one time a year when we were a team, the one look a year I savored in my sleep, the one sweet spot of the year that made bearable the twelve months of bitterness.

"Is there something you want to ask me?" he queried with his conspiratorial single-eyed stare.

"Yes, Papa."

"You may ask."

In concert with every other youngest child spread throughout the Diaspora or settled in the land of Zion, I asked the four questions—why on this one night did we eat unleavened bread, why did we eat bitter herbs, why did we dip the herbs twice, why did we eat while reclining on pillows? Indeed, I wanted to know. Why was this one night different from all other nights of the year?

My father pondered the questions, closing his eyes as if traveling back through his ancient memory to the time when he was a slave in Egypt calling upon God to hear His people's cries. A smile traced his face. He reopened his eyes and looked at me.

"Son, let me tell you."

And tell us he did.

He did not recite the Haggadah; he enacted it. With the inspired mania of Danny Kaye switching hats through a one-man tour de force, my dad relived the story right before our eyes. *We* were the embattled Israelites. *He* was Moses. And, with the room as his stage and our silver as his props, he led us to the Promised Land all over again.

"You recall," he began, bent over in hunger and shame, "that famine drove us to Egypt in the first place." Slowly he rose, grabbing the hardboiled egg. "But we grew strong." Single-handedly, he flipped the egg and caught it, standing taller with each continuous throw. "We multiplied." He gripped the lamb-shank by the bone with his free hand and lobbed it end over end catching it in between tosses of the egg. "We prospered." He snagged a crystal wine glass and juggled all three items still rising in stature. "And we got dangerous." He seized a carving knife, threw it into the air and deftly handled the four spinning objects with the boldness of a professional at the height of his powers.

Then he caught the egg, shank, and wineglass in one hand while snatching the knife with the other, shaking the blade menacingly.

"But Pharaoh hated us." He drew the knife to my throat. "He slaughtered our first-born sons." He caressed my mom's neck." He raped our handsome women." He dangled bitter herbs in Catherine's face. "He turned our daughters into concubines. And the rest," he slammed the herbs on a cutting board and hatcheted them with the knife, "he forced into slavery, beating our backs as we built the buildings that bore our oppressor's glory." He stabbed the knife through the butchered parsley. "As a people, we were debased."

He eyed us each one. "But God did not abandon us. He called forth a leader." A raised candlestick became my father's staff. "A man who approached Pharaoh and spoke with the voice of God. *'Let my people go.'*" The plates rattled at my father's bellow. "'*Or the wrath of God shall fall upon you.*'"

"Pharaoh called God's bluff and refused. So Moses unleashed his fury." Like Zeus hurling thunderbolts from his throne in the sky, my father flung afflictions to force Pharaoh's hand. "Rivers—turn into blood. Frogs—fall from the sky. Boils—ravage Egyptian flesh. Lice—infest their scalps. Locusts and hail, blight and darkness—pelt our captors until they plead for my mercy.

"And still, Pharaoh refused our freedom." With sadistic deliberateness, the knife was back at my throat. "So Moses grew more lethal. He deposed God's servants of death to murder every first-born son throughout the land of Egypt." The blade grazed my skin. "Every child. Even our own.

"But wait. Moses devised a plan to elude the bloodthirsty avengers. We butchered our lambs, marked our doorposts, and huddled in our homes. That night, they came. No mansion was too majestic, no tent too destitute, to escape the claws of death. Except for the homes of the Jews. God's massacring ambassadors passed over the bloodied Hebrew households. At daybreak, cries of anguish pierced the streets, none louder than those from Pharaoh's palace. Only with his own son's death did he let our people go.

"Knowing his heart would soon harden again, we gathered our belongings before our morning bread could rise, and we fled. Our dust still clouded the horizon when Pharaoh recanted his pardon. He deployed an army of chariots to hunt us down on the open road. We raced as fast as the aged can hobble. They chased at the speed of stallions. We felt the ground tremble; we heard their war cries; we saw their swords flash. Through the stumbling, we dashed. Dragging the children, we scurried. Snatching the fallen, we staggered, pushing fiercely toward the dream of freedom that refused to die within us.

"Then we dead-ended—before a blockade that promised to seal our death. Not a canyon cliff, nor a mountain wall. We were trapped by a sea whose waters stretched past the horizon. Moses however, refused to go down. Lifting his staff, he bellowed,

"'For the sake of justice, I command these waters to part for my people.' The sea did not stir. He marshaled his rage and yelled once more. 'By the power of the Almighty Lord of Creation, make way for us to pass.' The sea remained calm. Moses did not. '*By the power of a defiled humanity whose vengeance will terrorize this world until every creature within it shares our suffering, open a path for my people. OPEN, I say.* OPEN!'

"Only then did the sea separate. A mountain of waves rose up on either side of a path that plunged headlong into the watery crypt at the ocean's bottom. Into the pit we raced, across the carcasses of sharks and through the skeletons of whales, over the planks of shipwrecked boats and around the sockets of drowned sailor's skulls. On either side, cold-blooded scavengers waited to feed like piranha should the walls give way and the avalanche of surf crash down upon us. But still we lunged forward, through the darkness, straining toward the promise of dry land rising somewhere on the far side of the sea's cemetery.

"Finally, the path sloped toward light. We scrambled for fresh air. The mob of marauding forces, now on foot with their chariots mired in the mud, was but minutes behind us. Moses waited for the last Jewish soul to rise from the ocean's depths. Then, with his staff outstretched, he defied nature once more. His authority over the earth now rivaled that of God's. As did his wrath at those who oppose God's will. He voiced his command but once, and his shout thundered all the way back to Pharaoh's throne.

"'*Let all who oppress God's people be swallowed into the bowels of the sea . . . NOW I TELL YOU. NOW!*' The ocean obeyed our liberator's command. The wall of waters crashed down. The creatures of the deep feasted. Our tyrants disappeared into a cursed tomb whose seal remains unbroken to this day. Moses spit on their memory. Then he turned his back, and led our people to the Promised Land."

Without fail, my father's performance left us awestruck. He brought the story home with such force it could have narrated our personal family saga. A post-show afterglow lingered through the rest of the meal. We replayed highlights while dining on lamb and bread, bitter herbs and adobe paste. We clinked glasses as we drank our wine, four goblets full. Catherine and I stole the leftover matzah and dad chortled at our demands for a chocolate ransom. We thanked God through psalms. We shouted wrath on His enemies.

And we voiced our benediction. We hoped to spend next year in Jerusalem. But not really. I yearned for another Passover right in our own home. I do so still. After all, my father liberated us. For a night, we were freed from our family's bondage. We wandered as one. We escaped the wilderness. We glimpsed the Promised Land.

It's a place where fathers are ravaged by stories, not rage.

I know. I was there.

———

On the Pesach of my thirteenth year, my father put a malicious spin on Passover that haunts me still. I sensed something wrong the second he entered the dining room, a brown paper-bag crumpled in his fist. He donned the white coat like a demented scientist prepping for a sinister medical experiment. His face bore the exhaustion of a lifetime of sleepless nights battling off the devil. His crazed stare suggested he had just lost the war. He started with unusual directness.

"Today is Pesach." He spit out the words like an infuriated headmaster before obtuse school children. "This is the day we tell the story of how God's people were liberated from the flesh camps of oppression. Why do we tell this story? Not because it matters what may or may not have happened 5000 years ago. But because it matters what happens in the Egypts of today. This story reminds us of who we are. We are the people who refuse to debase ourselves in the face of oppression, who resist the temptations of our captor's ways, who wait in faith for the One who promises to rescue us. Isn't that right, Lena?"

My mom stared at him as alert to danger as a mouse before a poised cobra. My dad unveiled the food. The plate was set as my mom prepared it—three pieces of matzah, parsley and horseradish for bitter herbs, an apple and nut paste for brick mortar, a shank of lamb whose blood adorned our doorpost, and a hardboiled egg for our commitment to freedom within oppression's heat. My father did not consecrate the meal. Nor did he wash his hands. With two fingers, he lifted a matzah by the corner and scowled as if he held dung.

"Lena, this is not how we remember the story." He searched to dispose of it. Spreading open a napkin, he dropped the bread upon it, scraped the plate clean, wadded the cloth up, and set it onto the floor. Then he opened the bag and gazed inside. "Yes, this is better." He pulled out and placed onto the plate a Catholic communion wafer.

My mother gasped. "Where did you get that?"

"Where is your faith, Lena? It is Passover. The Master of the Universe provides."

"Don't do this, Jakov." My father ignored her. As methodically as a medieval prison warden placing instruments of torture beside a bound victim, he placed onto the plate one by one five more wafers, six blades of grass, and a single potato.

My mom squirmed as if nailed to the spot of her execution. "My God, Jakov. I will not do this. I can not."

"Oh, you will, Lena. It is your *penance* as I recall. You will satisfy your penance or this time you will not be passed over."

My mother looked like she was slapped. "I was not passed over, Jakov." She held his stare, pleading for mercy, then dropped her eyes. "I wasn't."

"But you were. You were one of the Chosen. For whom tonight we give God thanks." He turned to me. In his malevolence, I recognized my true father. "Is there not something you want to ask me?" I did not know what to say. I was terrified to be a party to his abuse and terrified not to. "Ask me, Tony. Don't you want to know something?"

"Father," I trembled, unsure if being disobedient or complicitous. "Why do we have hosts tonight instead of matzah?"

"Good, son." He glared back at my mother. "That is exactly the right question."

"Don't, Jakov," she whispered to her empty plate.

"And I will tell you."

"Please, don't. I beg you."

"It is because God always provides. Let me tell you a story."

"NO!" My mother shot up crazed with defiance. "*You will not tell that story!*"

My father savored the malignant effect. "But Lena, it is Passover. God commands me to tell this story." He turned to me then my sister. "We eat wafers tonight because devils once brutalized our people. One person arose to appeal for mercy. But they would not listen. So God brought death. Many were killed. But not all. The Chosen Ones, they were passed over."

My mother slumped into her chair as my father began. By the end, she sobbed like Rachel before gutted children. "I am sorry, Jakov. I am so sorry." She rocked in tortured waves as if berating herself for a distant crime from which she could never be redeemed.

My father glared at her. Then something melted. He dropped into his chair wincing as one who loathes his own sadism but remembers no other way to be. When he finally spoke, he voiced despair.

"Ours is a God who kills the many to save the few. How do we live with a God like that?"

My mother whimpered through her sobs. "God did not save me, Jakov. He did not free me like the others."

"But He did, Lena. And for what? For what I ask you?"

My father was right. The Passover story is definitive. Meditating on its mysteries reminds us of who we are.

I remain defined by the mysteries of that evening.

And they were just beginning.

I awoke the following morning with my pajama-top splayed open. On the mattress beside me, my mother's blood-red Dachau patch stared with foreboding mystery. If not for the evidence, I would have written off the night's cryptic act as a bad dream. My mother exposing my prepubescent chest, her pressing the patch to my skin, my father's presence forbidding from the doorway, even the muffled shouts of 'whore' from their bedroom—all of it would have wisped away within the underworld shadows where nightmares are buried.

But the patch was there. And stayed there. Until I flicked it with a ruler, like I would a dead spider, and hid it in a shoebox under my bed.

The rest of the house seemed routine. My parent's bedroom door was closed and my father's car was gone. I readied for school, boarded the bus, and lost myself in the muddy current that coursed through junior high. I pushed the riddles from my mind, until I returned to the house. The place was as quiet as a tomb. The living room was void of signs from my father's nightly vigils—no ash on the floor, no butts in the tray. The kitchen was untouched since I left it—cereal bowls in the sink, toast crumbs on the counter. With trepidation, I checked my mother's bedroom. The door was open, but her bed had not been slept in. Her Seder dress lay spread over the covers as if it had slept in her place. Her nightgown was folded on the bureau. Unable to decipher the mystery of her absence, I retired to the family room and sat it out before a murmuring TV.

By dinnertime, neither parent had called nor made it back. I baked frozen chicken and tater tots. Catherine came home and asked where mom and dad were. I told her I didn't know. She shrugged it off, declined any food, and shut herself inside her room. At 10:00, I went to bed.

Sometime after midnight, my father shook me awake. His hand was so cold he could have been handling ice. Wearing his leather flight jacket, he led me into the living room and sat me on the couch next to Catherine. He retrieved a dining room chair and squared off before us. He stared at the floor as if eye contact would scald him.

"I'm only going to say this once." He grunted like one who never coddled to children and was damned if he would start now. "Your mother's dead. She drove off a cliff near Highway 128. They only found her body a couple of hours ago, but she'd been dead since morning. The last person who saw her was the priest she talked to before dawn. He won't say where she was going. Well, there it is."

The news was so overwhelming my mind had yet to form the questions that would henceforth torment me. Like, where in the world was she going—running away, joyriding with death, or clearing her head before coming back home? Like, why was a woman who didn't know how to drive handling a car in the first place? Like, what was she doing with the priest—seeking domestic advice, securing a blessing to start anew elsewhere, or cleansing her soul before kissing us and this sorry world goodbye?

I wasn't yet asking. I could only stare at my father. He wasn't answering. He could only stare at the floor. Catherine started to cry. My father winced. Then he snapped a look at me, another at my sister, and bolted out of the house, the sliding back door slamming behind him. For but a few seconds, I gazed at his empty chair. Then, afraid he was leaving us too, I ran after him as far as the backyard. "Dad," I called from the dewy edge of lawn. He stopped, almost to the woods behind our house, then turned to look. I didn't have words. He didn't either. We stared across the darkness. Then he brushed me off with his hand, turned away, and disappeared into the trees.

I stared at the forest shadows not knowing what to do, not knowing how to feel, as disoriented as a sole survivor in the bomb-field obliteration of his township. I waited for something to surface in the night, some signal from the universe prompting me towards life within the wreckage of a devastated world. But the night was indifferent, my backyard desolate. In the wake of death, the universe was silent.

Until the silence gave way to a scream. It ruptured forth from the forest darkness and ripped through the quiet like a knife in the night's gut—guilty and grieving, as desperate as the blade of despair. My father, the man who concealed pain behind brutality, shrieked into the night like a lover stumbling upon the butchered remains of his bride. His howl sliced through the darkness in agony then disfigured into an unrelenting rage. Smack after screaming smack cracked through the night while he pummeled with a club every tree and rock around him as if ripping away the façade of creation and laying bare the abyss over which the planet is pitilessly and precariously poised. Only when the chasm was complete did the beating stop, a final spasm of grief straining forth from the ditch and echoing out into the cosmic night.

The silence that followed was unlike any silence I had ever heard before. I slipped over the edge myself and fell through the pitch-black pit rent open by my mother's death and my father's despair. In that abyss, all was dark. The stars had disappeared. My backyard had disappeared. The woods consuming my father had disappeared. I sank in a weightless freefall, stunned and staring, receding ever deeper toward the sterile, still center of absolute aloneness, the midnight nothingness into which every scream descends and dissolves. Maybe I fell for a minute. Maybe I fell for eternity. Unable or unwilling to resist the sucking drift, I simply fell.

Then something pulled me back. A hand touched my shoulder. I was too far down to respond. The hand gently shook. The features of my backyard murkily materialized. The hand squeezed. I turned around. I saw Catherine, my sister, all of fourteen years old and clad in a Led Zeppelin t-shirt for a nightgown, her cheeks streaked with tears.

"Tony," she whispered. "You can't keep it all in. You have to cry. You have to let it out." I stared frozen. "Really Tony, you have to cry."

Then I did. I placed my head on her chest and heaved with gasping sobs. She held me close and cried along with me. But even as she rocked me, I heard the voice. It spoke with absolute resolve from the bottomless pit within me. 'I will shoot myself dead before I ever feel this depth of pain again.'

Sixteen years had gone by since I cried with Catherine in our backyard. I was now 28 years old. I had lived through my mother's funeral, my sister's disappearance, my father's checked-out misanthropy, and I was on the verge of confronting my own son's death.

So far, I had kept my promise.

I felt no pain.

Through it all, I had yet to cry a single tear.

———

The cadaver coldness of my mother's chiseled name brought back memories of her burial. Catherine and I begged our father to purchase an ornate marble plaque to testify to the loving memory with which our mother was held. He refused. A gray slab with name and dates was all the marker she got.

The Saturday after the funeral, Catherine and I bike-hiked to Mt. Tamalpais. From her bedroom window, our mom had gazed at that peak for hours. It was not snow-capped. Nor did it boast stunning granite ridges. But to her, it recalled Alpine vistas in Bavaria. And childhood memories of the few moments of happiness in her otherwise horrifying life. We combed the woods for rocks reminiscent of those nostalgic peaks and came across the perfect token in a brick-sized boulder with white marble veins crossing the smooth gray face. We loaded it and some fifty pounds of smaller stones into our packs and pedaled home. The next day we hauled them to our mom's grave. Digging out the grass lining the headstone, we ringed the marker with rocks and placed the crossed boulder at the center like a medallion adorning a necklace. We hoped the circle of stones would comfort her as her childhood memories had, separated from her life as it were by more than an ocean and a continent.

In the dim moonlight, I recognized the circle of rocks. I also noticed, lying across the tombstone base, a white rose still virgin fresh. I missed my father by but a few hours.

A year had passed since I had last been there. I came with Jen on our wedding day. We were heading to our honeymoon cabin on the coast when Jen insisted we stop by. We arrived at dusk. Jen had never been there before. The first thing she saw was the white rose at the base. Its edges were wilted in week-old decay.

"Look, there's a rose," she said. "Is it from you?"

"No," I said curtly. "My dad." I wasn't about to let him infect our day. "He leaves one every Sunday."

"I didn't realize your dad had a romantic side."

"I doubt it's romance. Penance probably."

"Why a white rose?"

"I don't know. Something between him and my mom before the war. They didn't talk about it much."

Jen knelt down on the grass and studied the headstone. "I wish I could have known her."

"She would've loved you."

"She seems so sad."

I smiled, kneeling beside Jen. "You say that like you can see her."

"No, it's just . . . I imagine her free-spirited and vivacious, colorful. This is so stark. Maybe the starkness is more true."

"What can I say? She lived a brutal life."

Jen slipped her fingers through mine. "I hope she's finally happy."

"She deserves it. She's already put in her time in hell."

Jen peered at the headstone like it was a veil through which she could see her resting place. Then she addressed her as naturally as if we just dropped by for tea. "I wish you could have been there today, Mrs. Backman. You would have loved how happy Tony looked when I first walked into the church. He was as happy as I was when I pledged a lifetime of loving him. Please bless our marriage. Watch over us. Hold us in a mother's love. And just as you did for Tony and Catherine as well as you were able, protect us from all that would rob us of our happiness. For as long as we are wrapped in love, no evil can ever prevail."

Then Jen lifted the crossed stone centerpiece from the ring of rocks and lifted out of her blazer pocket the plastic ring—the gumball trinket with the carrot-colored top I had not seen since our day on the bluff. She planted it deep within the damp soil and replaced the stone upon it. With the ring secure, she turned toward me, held both my hands, and stared into me as if reciting her vows once more.

"She's watching over us, Tony. I know it. And with her blessing, nothing can destroy our love."

With that, we began our life together as husband and wife.

———

In the muted moonlight, I stared into the same tombstone veil Jen had a year before. After the way I treated her in our apartment, I didn't know if I should beg God for guidance, consult my mom for wisdom, or plead with the devil to release me from his grasp. There I was, married to a woman who loved me more purely than I could ever deserve. I had a beautiful son whose giftedness to the world outshined any shadow concerning his conception's timing. I had memories of an adoring mother whose love held me as unshakingly as the ground holding Jen's buried ring. And yet, I withdrew from all the goodness around me and sulked in stewing fury like a demon-possessed man for whom love's touch comes as a burning stab. I hated the monster I was becoming, but I was powerless before the passions that raged within me. Just what in the hell was wrong with me?

Knowing nowhere else to turn, I prayed.

"Heavenly Father, I don't know what is happening to me. I'm angry all the time. I recoil from my wife. I'm hurtful to a person who deserves only kindness." As if God was underscoring my hardheartedness, Jennie flashed into my mind, sitting on our bed with her prayer journal. "I'm not even moved by your daughter's beauty right in front of my eyes. I'm sorry, God. But I don't know how to stop being this way. When did it all go wrong?"

I already knew. Our premature plunge into carnal oblivion. I traded my soul for a romp on a bluff. And some part of me had been damn glad to do it. "I'm sorry, God. For putting my pleasure above your will. And for hating you for holding us back. Please forgive me. I am so sorry."

I was taught that God always forgave a sincere heart, and I was as sincere as King David bewailing his lust for Bathsheba. But if forgiven, I did not feel it. God, the exacting disciplinarian, withheld the gift of assurance. After all I put Him through, I couldn't blame Him. I proceeded as I was schooled.

"Father, though I don't feel it, I claim your forgiveness by faith. And I know that repentance requires restitution. What can I do to make things right?"

I awaited a reply. As soon as I heard it, I realized its fittingness. Jennie's words voiced it earlier. 'Why don't you tell somebody the truth?' A bitter pill to swallow. But one that promised a cure.

"Okay, Father," I resigned. "I'll do it. I'll die to my pride and stop living this lie. I don't know how I'll be able to go through with it, but I will walk in the ways of righteousness and rely on your power to sustain me."

My resolution stoked a faint spark of confidence, but not enough flame to set me on my way. I stared at the crossed stone at the base of my mom's grave-marker. I rolled it away and reached into the shadow. I felt the buried gumball ring. Brushing it off, I lifted it into the night sky. Even made of cheap plastic it glittered dully in the moonlight. With its sparkle came the memory of my Halloween proposal, and all the promising visions of domestic happiness awaiting us—prayerful lullabies beside Daniel's crib, playful laughter on our dining room floor, lazy walks in the park, Daniel perched in a stroller, tender cuddles in our bed, Daniel feeding between us. That was flame enough for me. "I'll do it," I resolved. "I'll make myself do it. On the souls of my wife and my child, I swear to you, Lord, I'll go straight home, I'll kiss my boy in his crib, and I'll snuggle up to Jen in bed and show her how much I desire her. Then tomorrow, I'll come clean with Danny, with Ruth, with anyone who wants to know. I may have lost my way, but Your forgiving love has brought me back."

I placed the ring back in the soil and sealed it with the stone. I ignored my father's rose and gazed at my mother's name. The pain she bore for all the secrets she kept stoked my determination. For her I would do it too. For all of us. From this day forth, I will follow my Father in Heaven and nothing will divert my step.

I rose from my mom's grave and returned home.

———

I had no idea where my Father in Heaven was leading me. But I soon found out.

My resolute sojourn upon His paths lasted but a few more hours.

It ended with my son's death.

16

I PULLED INTO THE turnout and turned off the truck. The field and far-off grove looked untouched in the eight years since I had been there with Jen. Like then, I retrieved picnic supplies from my truck's bed. Unlike then, I trekked alone.

I crossed the road and stood at the fence. NO TRESPASSING, it warned.

I stretched the barbed wire. And trespassed anyway.

A storm ravaged San Rafael during the final week of Gospel Light's spring semester. A storm ravaged our apartment as well. The card table, coffee table, kitchen table, sofa, rocker, and buffet, were heaped in the corner in a patchwork of desk space with scribbled sheets of paper, splayed-open books, photocopied articles, and earmarked reference materials strewn across them in such thorough disarray they may have been flung there by gale-force winds. The walls had taken the hit too. Pages of notes outlining text and hoards of index cards referencing quotations were plastered about and pinned in place peppered by tacked newspaper clippings touting such atrocities as cancer-stricken children and raping psychopaths, famine-ravaged refugee compounds and warlords feuding over city-states—a veritable rogues' gallery montage of all the suffering and evil inflicted upon the globe.

I was submerged in the middle of it, maneuvering around mugs of cold coffee and plates of stale toast as possessed by my task as a Faustian philosopher brooding over the secret formulas of alchemy. Only I was not turning matter into gold. Quite the contrary. I combed the annals of knowledge, picked through current events, and scrutinized the sacred sources of theology with slanderous intent. I gathered all the shit I could find with which to fling at God.

Jen let slide my workspace mess. She also ignored the mess I had become. I wore the same jeans so long the knees ripped open like gaping wounds. I lost so much sleep my eyes were blood-streaked and hollow. My hair grew so long I sickened of the tangles and shaved myself bald. I looked more like a hardened convict after a rough turn in solitary than a seminarian working on a term paper. I even took up smoking. Ashes dusted my clothes and pages like soot from a belching volcano. I exuded the part I had taken on. I was a theological anarchist—a first mate on a ship piloted by a mad man. The time for revolt had come. Mutiny was at hand. The cozy ark of Christian theology was going down. Along with the God who captained it.

———

I made the mistake of telling Danny I had enough research for a dissertation on the topic Dr. MacIntyre assigned. He took it as an invitation to compare notes. Thursday night before finals week, Jen had gone out. If she told me where she was going, I forgot. I huddled in the corner, the apartment dark but for the desk lamp illuminating my scrawl. Cigarette smoke hung like a gambling den. A knock interrupted me. When I opened the door, my three friends saw my shaved head and stared as if unsure they had the right apartment. I asked their business.

"What's up?"

"Hi, Tony," Blake said. "Danny thought we might talk through MacIntyre's paper together. You up for it?"

"Where's Danny?"

"Parking the car. He'll be right up." I hesitated. I was fine by myself. "Come on, man. We're soaking wet out here." What the hell, I figured. Their foils could sharpen my arguments. I let them in. They hung their soaked slickers on the rack and were fishing books out of backpacks when Danny arrived with a perky tap.

"Hey, Tony. I hope you don't mind us popping in like this. We thought you could help us think through this paper."

"It's fine, Danny." Actually, the debate was growing on me. I turned on some lights and shoved papers off the furniture. Danny sat in the stuffed chair closest to the door. Irby, a six-foot-six good 'ol boy whose Hoss Cartwright gregariousness almost made palatable his theological oafishness, plopped his hulking body on the end of couch by my desk. Blake, the intellectual destined for a Ph.D. from Fuller and certain to be my toughest challenge, positioned himself in the corner of couch opposite Irby. Sandy, Blake's sidekick, who did not share Blake's native intelligence but covered it with a near photographic recall of the Bible, perched himself on the rocking chair across from his crony. I straddled my desk chair backwards and faced all four theological rivals. With the exception of Danny, I hadn't talked to any of them since the day after the funeral.

"How ya been?" Sandy spouted with trademark amicability.

"Good," I said in stoic contradiction to the obvious.

"We've missed you at fellowship."

"Yeah, well. I've been hitting the books pretty hard. In fact, I've still got a lot to do. You guys want to talk about the paper?"

They glanced around as if unsure where to start. Irby finally opened with his befuddled Floridian drawl. "I don't know guys. Seems to me we shouldn't even be messing with this stuff."

"'Woe to him who argues with his maker.'" The Bible verse popped out of Sandy's mouth like a ventriloquist's dummy who can't control the interjection.

"Besides," Irby continued, the gummed up gears of his mental machinery straining to work up steam. "Nobody's smart enough to understand the mind of God."

"'Who can comprehend the ways of Yahweh?'" Sandy blurted, nodding at the floor. "'As the heavens are higher than the earth, so are my thoughts higher than yours.'"

I snapped him a glare hoping he wasn't prepared to parrot every point with a biblical proof-text.

"Maybe," Irby went on, "we're just supposed to worship God and not worry about the rest."

"So," I jumped in before Sandy could volunteer his two verses worth. "You take the Nazi approach. 'Don't think, don't ask questions, just shut up and do what you're told.'"

"No, I'm not saying that. I'm just saying that some things are too hard to understand."

"What's so hard to understand? God can't be all good and all-powerful at the same time. Either God *can* do something about suffering and *won't* or God *can't* and won't *ever*. In the one case, He's a bastard. In the other, He's just plain impotent."

"Now there you go, Tony," Irby responded. "You're twisting it all around. The question is, 'How can a *good* God *allow* suffering in the world?'"

"You're off base already," I said.

"What? That's the question MacIntyre gave us."

"He's off base too. The *real* question is, 'How can God live with Himself when He sees a four-year old girl with her dad's prick up her ass and He doesn't do a damn thing about it.'"

"Jesus God Almighty, Tony." Irby recoiled. "That's disgusting."

"Exactly. Let's be clear about what we're talking about. It's not some tidy intellectual riddle. Disgusting things happen in the world. How does God stand Himself in the middle of it all?"

"But God didn't rape that girl. Her father did. Of his own free will."

"Why didn't God protect her?"

"Because He refuses to violate man's free will. Everybody knows the difference between right and wrong. That's how He made us. It's up to us to choose right. Just like Adam and Eve. They had free choice. They chose sin."

"What do you mean they had free choice? It was a set-up from the beginning. God plants an apple tree, creates people with natural desires, dares them not to touch it, and sends in a serpent to taunt them into it. What's free about that?"

"They didn't have to eat it. They chose to."

"Why tempt them in the first place? Why not create a garden where there's no choice and no problems?"

"Because God wants us to love Him. And it's not love if we don't choose it."

"So God's primary desire is to be loved?"

"Yes."

"So He created people with a choice."

"Yes."

"Between good and evil."

"Yes."

"So God created evil."

"Yes. No. I don't know. Look, all I know is, human beings have free will. We can either love God or hate Him. And God doesn't violate our freedom."

"Now let me get this straight." I was seething. "A young girl's getting butt-fucked by her father and God doesn't do anything because He wants to protect the father's freedom. A ten-year old boy gets shot in the face because his step-dad's too drunk to shoot the beer can off the boy's head, and God doesn't do anything because He's protecting the step-dad's freedom. Six million girls and boys, and moms and dads, and grandmas and grandpas get beaten, tortured and gassed, and God doesn't do anything because He wants to protect the Nazi's freedom. Is that what you're saying?"

"Now Tony, you're not being rational."

"You're not being emotional! This is something you have to deal with from you're gut, not your head. It's outrageous."

"It's human freedom," Irby returned.

"It's divine selfishness. Innocent suffering is too high a price for human freedom. A world without choice is better than a world where children get raped. And a God who would rather be loved freely than create a world where children are safe is not just cruel, He's flat-out egotistical."

Irby didn't know what to say. So I pressed on.

"Okay, so Irby doesn't believe in the Bible. What's next?" That got him talking again.

"What do you mean? Of course I believe in the Bible."

"The Bible's plenty clear. God overrides human freedom whenever He wants to. He even makes people sin. He hardened Pharaoh's heart against the Hebrews."

"He inflicted Saul with an evil spirit." Sandy rifled through the Rolodex of his encyclopedic knowledge. I helped him along.

"He hardened the hearts of the Canaanites so the Israelites could slaughter them."

"He compelled Nebuchadnezzar to crush Jerusalem."

"He closed the Jews' eyes to Isaiah's warnings."

"He closed the crowd's eyes to Jesus' preaching."

Irby looked at Sandy like he wondered whose side Sandy was playing for. Sandy shrugged. "He's right . . . About God hardening hearts, that is . . . sometimes."

"Not only that." I pushed the advantage. "Think of all the times God *does* stop evil. He parted the Red Sea for the Jews. He swallowed Jonah in a whale and turned him around. He raised Jesus from the dead for God's sake. So which is it? Does God refrain from intervening out of respect for human freedom, or does He occasionally step into the fracas and make things happen?"

Irby looked like someone just stole his lunch money.

"God *does* work miracles, doesn't He?" I pushed.

"Of course He does."

"Okay. So what kind of a God saves *some* people from their affliction but other times sits back and does nothing?"

The front door opened as the question reverberated. Jen looked like she just hiked in from Siberia. She was wrapped in my oversized raincoat—an immense parka with an abundance of zippers and snaps, padding and caps, and pockets the size of carpetbags. It covered me like a poncho. It could have sheltered two of her with a fully loaded backpack.

As inconspicuously as she could, she shed the coat, hung it on the rack, and ducked into the kitchen. We ignored her in deference to the question still hanging in the air.

"I got it," Sandy flashed with insight. "A just God. Deuteronomy 30. 'If you walk in the ways of Yahweh, God will bless you. But if you turn away, you'll be destroyed.'"

I turned towards the new opponent. "So God hardened Pharaoh's heart, then punished him for doing what God made him do in the first place."

"I see your point, Tony. But it's not like Pharaoh wasn't hard-hearted to begin with."

"What about babies born with deformities? What did they do to deserve their suffering?"

"I gotcha there too." He sounded like this was a theological chess match. "John 9. They asked Jesus the same thing about a man born blind. Was it caused by *his* or his *parent's* sin? He said neither. He was born blind so God's power could be demonstrated through him. Then Jesus healed the blindness."

"Jesus Christ, Sandy. What kind of primadonna God blinds people on purpose to pump up His own PR? Besides, what about the thousands of other blind people, and maimed people too, people born without fully functioning brains for God's sake, who *don't* get healed? If one blind man 2000 years ago testifies to God's healing power, a thousand thousand testify throughout history to God's gross callousness. If He heals one innocent sufferer, He should heal them all. Or account for Himself."

"But Tony, nobody's innocent. 'All have sinned and fallen short of the glory of God.'"

"That's the best you can come up with? You're going to walk up to a child with spinal bifida and tell him his back's crooked because God *might* use him to demonstrate His healing power but if He doesn't it's okay because the kid's a sinner anyway?"

"No, I'm not going to *say* that."

"You're going to *think* it!? Shame on you, Sandy. That child's done nothing. Look at this world. Good or bad it doesn't matter—some people prosper, others suffer, some get healed, others don't. It's all random. What kind of a God rolls dice to see who gets restored and who's left to rot?"

"How about a loving God?" Blake answered, the guy earmarked for a theological professorship. As I pondered my strategy for the evening's most challenging duel, Jen walked in, laid out several mugs of coffee, and eavesdropped from the arm of Danny's E-Z chair.

"A loving God," I mused.

"Yes. You're right, Tony. Sometimes good people suffer. They follow God dutifully, but they suffer anyway. Their suffering isn't punishment for sin. It's an opportunity to know God's love more deeply."

Sandy changed tacks with Blake. "'If God brings grief, He also brings compassion. For it is not out of His own pleasure that He torments and grieves the human race.'"

"Don't go there, guys," I said. "I've heard it before. Suffering is God's 'megaphone' to get our attention so we can see how great God is. I don't buy it. It's too much like a dad who beats his kid with a belt because he loves the child so much. If God's a child abuser, I'd just as soon report Him."

"No," Blake came back. "I'm not saying God brings suffering to break us down for a relationship with Him. I'm saying that God can *use* suffering to strengthen the relationship we already have."

Sandy lit up like it suddenly made sense. "'Rejoice even though you suffer great trials. They come so that your faith—of greater worth than gold refined by fire—may be proved genuine.'"

"Oh," I retorted. "That fiery furnace bullshit about God refining the choicest jewel out of the fiercest burning. I've got news for you. Look at Auschwitz. Burnt bodies don't refine into gold. They blacken into ash."

"But dead bodies can rise again," Blake rebutted. "Look at Jesus. God can take suffering and redeem it, turn the darkest night into the brightest morning."

Light bulbs flashed as Sandy kept pace with his comrade. "'I know that our present sufferings are nothing compared to the glory that will be revealed in us.'"

Blake ignored him. "In fact, and this is the heart of the matter, those who suffer participate in a special way with the suffering and redemption of Christ."

"Now we're getting to it," I said. "Jesus, the obedient Son who has to suffer to satisfy the Almighty Father. Talk about child abuse. A Dad demands the blood of His own son before He'll accept all the other naughty children. I think someone needs to redeem God."

Blake ignored my blasphemy with the nonplussed persistence of a dialectician cutting away to the original premise. "I'm not arguing that God needs suffering to be appeased or that God instigated Christ's suffering at all. Christ suffered innocently, too. And He showed us the redemptive way through it. Not by explaining it. By trusting God in the midst of it. When a person endures suffering with faith, when he testifies to God's goodness even within the sorrow, God will bring comfort, hope, even joy beyond all expectation. Suffering is our Calvary. Sure, the night of Good Friday is dark. But the dawn of Easter Sunday is infinitely more glorious. Participating in Christ's suffering, we participate in His resurrected life as well."

Sandy vibrated with illumination. "Yes. 'Just as Christ's sufferings flow into our lives, so also through Christ comfort flows. Just as we die with Christ so too shall we rise in Christ.' I get it."

Blake masked his annoyance. His point didn't need the scriptural crescendo. And Sandy wasn't the one who was supposed to get it.

I considered the argument. "So suffering is an opportunity to testify to God's goodness as demonstrated in Jesus Christ."

Sandy was so euphoric verses rattled out of his mouth of their own volition. "'Though I have been afflicted, still I speak of Jesus.'"

"In fact," I continued, Sandy and I now a theological tandem. "It's more than an opportunity to *testify* to God's goodness, it's the way to *know* God's goodness in all of its fullness, to know the hope and joy of resurrected life."

"'Our present sufferings are nothing compared to the glory we know in Christ Jesus,'" he bubbled with living waters.

"Indeed," I bubbled along with him, "the new life we will know is so glorious, we should actually be grateful for the suffering that enables us to know it."

Sandy was ecstatic. I hit the mark precisely. "'Count it all joy when you meet times of trial.'" He glanced around at the checkmate. I let him celebrate.

Then I played my trump card. It was the elephant in the room anyway.

"So tell me. Do you think that Daniel's death and the suffering it has caused are redeemed if someone endures it with faith? Do you think that the God who decided my son's life was not worth living is absolved if somebody guts up resurrected life in the midst of Daniel's extermination? Do you honestly think that the fact that my boy will never grow up to taste the joys of playing baseball with his dad, of dancing in his socks with his mom, of making love for the first time, the fact that his two parents, for the rest of their days, will mark time by the life he can't live, the first steps he'll never take, the first words he'll never speak, the fact that this world will be deprived of the songs he would have written, the cures he would have discovered, the smiles he would have brightened our lives with, do you really think that any of this is going to bring one single person the slightest measure of joy or gratitude or faith in the God who watched His own son hang in the desert and die? Do you?"

Blake met my stare straight on. "That's up to you, Tony."

"Me." I scoffed at the transparent ridiculousness. "Right." But Blake was not making light. He stared with unsettling directness. In fact, so did every other eye in that room. Sandy, Irby, Danny, Jen, they all stared at me, waiting for my response, poised with nervous expectancy as if I was a dying patient in a hospital bed who had only to say the word and I would be healed.

Then I got it. The scales dropped from my eyes. I saw the light. And I felt so Goddamned stupid. This was no theological crib session. It was an intervention. They weren't there to pick my brain. They were there to rescue me. The whole well-concealed plot was designed so my self-destructive reasonings would be exposed for all to see, especially me. They played it perfectly. Good cop, bad cop, right to the point of decision. And I bought into their deception, not knowing I was tying my own noose until the rope was tight to my neck.

So it was all up to me. How was *I* going to respond to the suffering in my life? Well it was all I could do to keep from responding right in front of their fucking faces. I turned from their relentless gazes and stared at the floor. My head pounded as I stifled the urge to pummel them with their theological textbooks. I closed my eyes to think—I had to find a way out of that trap, out of that house, out of that Goddamned life. I opened them again and stared at the living room table. The coffee Jen prepared stared back. Once more, its caramel color betrayed the milk stirred within it. I had my response. With as much calm as I could manufacture, I gripped the cup, walked to the kitchen, and stopped before the sink.

Then I backhanded that milk-infested liquid into the basin with such force it splashed and streaked the walls like blood from a shotgun blast through a skull. The sight of the dripping dung-colored mess incensed me further. I jammed the faucet back, shoved my cup beneath it, and with furious swipes and splashes, shoveled water against the wall, down the counter, around the sink, splattering liquid in all directions until every last drop of that contaminated coffee was cleansed out of that kitchen, out of that cup, and down the drain. Then I yanked the faucet off, seethed at the drenched kitchen, and slammed my mug so hard it should have shattered in my hands.

I willed the return of my self-control. Then I returned to the living room and stood before the dejected faces poised between telling each one of them to get the hell out of my house and flipping them all off before walking out myself. We stared in speechless stalemate.

Danny broke the tension. He walked over and held both my shoulders. I refused to look him in the eye. As he spoke, I glared at the clippings tacked above my corner desk.

"Tony, we're sorry. We love you and we don't know what to do. I don't understand it all. God is good. And there is suffering in the world. I don't know if God makes it happen or lets it happen, if we bring it on ourselves or it's just part of the world we live in. But I do know this. If you let bitterness and rage eat away at you, the devil is going to win. He'll win, Tony. And look around you. He's already well on his way. This isn't you. Something nasty's got a hold of you. And we're afraid you're losing your soul to it. We want the real Tony back. Please, let us help you."

How could he have known? He was looking at the real Tony. The real Tony had switched sides. And no spiritual pep talk, no matter how well intentioned, could pry loose the devil's talons once they've clutched a convert.

I risked a gaze into Danny's eyes. Even in my state I could see his care. But it didn't touch me. I held his stare until he knew I had nothing left to say—not to him, not to any of them. Then I turned to leave.

Gently, Danny held me back.

"We're going to let you go, Tony. But we want to give you something first."

He handed me a book. With its gilded edges and red silk tassel dangling from the bottom, it looked like a Bible. I was close. It was a handmade anthology of Scripture passages printed in a cloth-bound journal. The cover was elegantly engraved, 'Footsteps through the Valley of Shadows.' I cracked the book open and thumbed through random pages. A rainbow of footprints flowed by, each one numbered and ordered in a symbolic path of the Way of Life.

> 2—Wait on the Lord's timing,
>   for His ways are not our own.
> 7—Rest in God's presence,
>   for He dwells even in Sheol.
> 14—Count your blessings,
>   for God's hand provides even as He tests.

Each step was referenced by a psalm or Bible verse and signed with a personal prayer by the disciple who designed the page. On the inside cover, a picture was glued. It was taken on the day of Daniel's baby dedication. He was two weeks old, dressed in white, and held in Jennie's arms while I held them both in my own. The inscription was opposite the picture.

For Tony,

Though the valley of the shadow of death is dark, light shines on the hills. May the Good Shepherd guide you back to green pastures, where love abides, and life endures, and all who have known pain are comforted. (Psalm 23:4)

From those who walk with you,

Your friends in Christ.

"It's from all of us," Danny shared. "The Friday night fellowship, the kids from Young Life, everybody. We're not saying we have all the answers. We're figuring it out as we go along too. But it's everything we know so far. We hope it helps. If nothing else, we hope it shows you how much you're loved and missed."

I closed the book and fingered the tassel. A volume that embodied more good will would be hard to find. I looked up at Danny. He looked like he would lay down his own life for me if it would bring me back to the fold. I looked at the others. Blake, Sandy, Irby, each one longed for Danny's appeal to strike the right chord within me. I looked at Jen. She looked as lost as me, uncertain if the paths really bore life, uncertain of our friends' strategies to reach me, uncertain if a wound that went so deep could ever be healed at all.

I looked at each anguished face. And still, I had nothing to say. I gripped the book, grabbed my parka, and slammed the door when I left.

I don't know. Maybe like Pharaoh, God had hardened my heart. Or maybe the devil had. Maybe my recent tanglings with him so calcified my soul I was impervious to compassion in any form.

What I do know is this, my transaction with the latter would soon be irrevocable.

I sealed it later that night.

As certainly as if I signed an oath in blood.

17

IN THE SPRINGTIME DAYLIGHT, the piles of cow shit splattering the pasture were easy to sidestep. With my picnic blankets and backpack of supplies, I could have been a romantic lad hiking to a remote lover's rendezvous. Eight years earlier, I was.

I reached the grotto of trees and trudged through the brush and branches. The woods were not menacing at all.

What a contrast from the last time I was there.

Then, it was as dark as midnight.

And it had rained like hell.

———

I walked out on the crisis intervention team in my apartment with no idea where to vent my rage. I pocketed their book, hooded my head, and hauled ass for my truck. The icy downpour did not chill me. I was so inflamed the windshield fogged up before I left the parking lot. Despite my rubbing, and the wiper blades thrashing, I had but a narrow portal through which to peer into the dismal night. It was enough to get the hell out of there.

Spraying water behind me, I bolted toward town. Imagining seminarians at the coffee shops made me think better. I hung a U-turn and splashed toward Fairfax. The blues bars would be too raucous, so I doubled back again and hit the freeway north. Sonoma State lay up ahead, as did my mom's cemetery, my Young Life high schools, my childhood home in Petaluma for Christ's sake. What was I going that way for? I got off and circled back toward the city. The Tenderloin had hellholes better to hole up in.

I was half way to the Golden Gate when it hit me. I knew *exactly* where to go. Hellhole was right. It was time for a meeting with the Man. And no piss-ant rainstorm was going to keep me from telling the Bastard off. I pulled off the freeway and circled back again. I cruised the 101 past all my old haunts.

I got off at River Road.

———

The Lord of Sea and Sky was not pleased with my designs. As I navigated the coastal woods, the steady downpour became a vengeful ravaging. Sleet pelted my windshield like stilettos slung from the dark. Tree limbs tossed like frantic watchmen signaling peril. Gusts whipped my truck toward gulches on one side then redwoods on the other. I wrestled for control of the wheel, damned if the storm would deter me. Curse the waters from the sky, and curse the heavens from which they flow. I'd assail to the storm's malevolent center and I defied the Almighty to stop me.

I battled through to Highway 1, forged past the battered bungalows, struggled up the switchbacks, and warred head on into the hurricane blasts assaulting me from the meadows. The more I penetrated the forbidden territory, the more violently the protective tempest attacked. The rain pummeled like machine gun fire. Torrents rushed the roadsides. A typhoonal blast slammed me toward the cliffs as I neared the lane angling up the bluff. Squeezing the wheel, I turned into the monsoon, scaled the tidal wave of hill, and crested the ridge like a monomaniacal captain scoffing certain shipwreck. I drove almost blind. The windshield misted despite my scrubbing; coursing streams overran my wipers; the sheets of downpour repelled my high beams. Even so, I glimpsed the patch of gravel fighting off a flash-flooding wash. I pulled into the turnout, killed the motor, and extinguished the headlights.

Darkness consumed me so absolutely I could not see the fence forbidding trespass across the road. I grabbed my Mag-Lite, bundled up, and plunged headlong into the Cimmerian shade. Once past the barbed wire, a blanket of storm disoriented me. All I could see in any direction was a few feet of pelting sleet and a spotlight's worth of muddy pasture. I groped through the curtain of night trusting that the woods were somewhere within the shadows before me. But though I slogged on, the trees remained hidden— robbed of all form, as if bewitched by eternal darkness. Gradually, the pasture sloped down, then leveled. My feet sloshed in black puddles. I was getting close.

A creepy shade of trunk lit up. Darkness yawned behind it like the mouth of a haunted cave. Another trunk appeared beside the first, the trees forewarning sentinels. I stopped at the forest's edge and shined my beacon within. Shadows shrunk back like disturbed nocturnal creatures. Webs of branch and brush materialized. No clear path led through. I penetrated anyway.

The belly of the wooded cavern was eerily protected from the storm. Water misted and dripped in isolated trickles. Without the dimming rain, my flashlight reached further. I wished it hadn't. A cadaverous tangle of seemingly dead trees surrounded me as I waded through. The twisted trunks and barren branches looked like disfigured skeletons crowding an overgrown crypt. The decrepit forest felt like the breeding grounds for evil. No golden fruit grew from those mangled limbs. No green leaves graced the branches. The cold crops of pestilence were spawned in those woods—poverty, decay, and despair, all awaiting carrion fowl to pluck their fruit then drip its poison upon the sleeping world.

I circled the light to be sure I was alone. The skeletons seemed to move. Gnarled trees and prickly brush closed in from all sides. I stumbled through but they poked and plucked as if intent upon feeding from my carcass. I fended them off, wielding my light like a burning torch. They abated, but continued their terror. With ghoulish taunts, the barren trunks channeled voices, spooky impersonations of my disembodied friends. '*We shouldn't be messing with this stuff*,' Irby howled through a defaced alder behind me. '*Woe to him who argues with his maker*,' a pine-encrusted Sandy cackled before me. '*God uses suffering to strengthen our faith,*' Blake hissed from a butchered cypress at my side. '*The devil's going to win,*' Danny moaned from a hanging branch of poplar. In a whirlwind of sound, their admonitions snaked all around me. '*Trust in God.*' '*You're losing your soul.*' '*Let us help you.*' The words swirled together into a jumbled cacophony as threatening to my sanity as the Siren's shrieks until the babbling backdrop gave way to a single singsong chorus. '*It's all up to you, Tony, it's all up to you.*'

I shook off the noise and pushed deeper. But the woods would not relent. As if the voices were not maddening enough, the grotto hurled snapshots like reeling shards from an exploding kaleidoscope. The memories sliced through me in rapid-fire succession, too fast to evade, too fast to relive, too fast to even register any emotion—my mom kneeling by my bed, my friends staring in my living room, my son laying lifeless in his crib, my dad screaming from the midnight woods. They came more quickly—the caseworker's questions, the paramedic's CPR, the casket's descent, the review hearing's verdict. In a flurrying, condemning barrage, they spiraled around the night of Daniel's death—his smile at dinner, the three of us giggling, a final lullaby, a kiss goodnight, Jen nuzzling my neck, me flinching in response, Jen crying in our bed, me watching from the door, Jen looking at me longingly, me turning and fleeing, my vigil at my mom's grave, pleading before God, digging up Jen's ring, beholding its moonlit sparkle, my graveside prayer, my graveside vow, my graveside boldness to return to my family with love . . . .

Suddenly, the swirl of memories ceased. As did the voices. I stopped still. Within the thicket's silence, one image remained. It held my attention like a bedeviled mirror reflecting my soul in its most disfigured form.

My friends wanted the old Tony back. They wanted me to shake off the coldness, suck up some faith, and step out on the promises of God.

They had no idea.

I tried that once. Hours before my son's death.

But God's promises proved impotent before Satan's passions.

———

I had left my mom's cemetery plot, that night that Daniel died, determined to make everything right at home. I even stopped for flowers. Though the floral department at the 24-hour Safeway was sparse, I made do. I bought three carnations—white in the middle, yellow and red on either side. It wasn't perfect. But Jen would get it.

I snuck back into the apartment and dug out our plastic picnic vase. I arranged the flowers and freshened them with water. After trickling some mood light from the living room, I tiptoed down the hall. A sudden rush of tenderness swelled up within me—for Jen, for Daniel, for the dawn of a new day. I peeked into Daniel's bedroom and saw his empty crib. Jen must have retrieved him for a late-night feeding. All the better. It was time for the three of us to bless our future together.

I crept to our bedroom door and peered inside. I spied them in the shadows. They were both asleep, Daniel snug against his mother's side. Jen's silk pajama top was unbuttoned. Her right breast lay exposed, resting on the mattress. Daniel's open mouth was but centimeters from the nipple. His tiny hand rested gently at the breast's base. Satisfied from his sucking, he had simply slipped his mouth to the side and fallen asleep.

What can I say? Seeing the two of them lying there in such exposed repose, filled me with passion. On the cold, cruel heart of the devil, I swear I wanted to kill. Disgust and rage erupted so volcanically it was all I could do to keep from taking the Goddamned vase in my hand and pounding that bitch into bloody oblivion. I blazed with hatred, twitched with wrath, and squeezed the neck with such trembling violence I nearly beheaded the flowers in my hand. I wanted to charge like a boar. I wanted to flail like a butcher. I wanted to smash every trace of maternal bliss off that face then pulverize every possession in our apartment.

With Herculean resolve, I held myself back. Grinding my rage into granite self-control, I slunk back to the kitchen, shoved the flowers into the trash—vase, water, and all—and ground them into the rotting remains of our spaghetti dinner from but a few hours before. Afraid Jen might see them in the morning, I grabbed a gallon of milk from the fridge, drained the contents down the sink, and buried the flowers beneath the container. Then, with a father's determination upon waking up within a burning house, I went to save my son. With one knee on the bed, I slipped my hands under Daniel. Jen stirred.

"Tony," she smiled drowsily, "you're back." Hunched over the baby, I hesitated while staring at the source of my son's endangerment. She saw me looking at her breast. Her misinterpretation of my gaze could not have been more pathetic. She smiled invitingly, her eyes hopeful with timid seductiveness. I corrected her impression in a snap.

"Why don't you cover yourself up?" My disgust pierced like a bullet to the chest. I picked up Daniel and returned him to his crib.

When I later went to bed, Jen's back was turned. I turned mine as well. I knew she was awake. I couldn't sleep either. We stewed without words in private vigils staring at opposing walls. We didn't nod off until the deathly still quiet of the pre-dawn darkness.

A scream woke me up. As cold and sharp as a blade of ice. It reached up from the frozen fissures of hell and ripped apart the fading fabric of any faith I had left.

I've been falling ever since.

———

Approximating the sea's direction in the stormy midnight, I thrashed through the forest until I flashed on several trunks abutting a vast impenetrable darkness beyond. Hacking to the final perimeter of trees, I stood before a cliff's abrupt edge and shined my light into the black rainy void. The rays dissipated within the depthless darkness like a soul swallowed into Hydra's throat at the abysmal mouth of Hades. When God has turned His back and disappeared, to where else would He run and hide?

Clearly off course, I aimed my light north and sensed more than saw the bluff's silhouette maybe fifty yards away. Keeping a row of trees between the cliff and me, I trudged through until I found it. A tall pine trunk had fallen, bordering the edge of the grassy promontory like a barricade. I stepped onto it and leapt over. I was finally there—the very spot where Daniel was conceived in joyous frolic. It could not have seemed more different. I might have been standing in his tomb.

I sat on the slain trunk and turned off my light. Without the canopy of trees, the storm resumed its unveiled savagery. Rain pounded my parka; wind cut through my clothes; my hands were nailed with sleet; my feet were fixed in mud. I took the tempest's assault and tried to remember why I had come. Maybe I thirsted for a sip from the champagne joy that once bubbled there so abundantly. Or maybe I returned to the scene of the crime to nurse from the source of my life's ill fortune. One thing was certain. If I hoped for an audience with the Architect of the World, it wasn't promising. He was well concealed within the rain-drenched darkness.

More weary than enraged, I bent over and held my head in my hands like a broken man. Affliction is an opportunity to suffer with Jesus, Blake surmised. If that was true, I knew how to start. From within the storm, I prayed.

"Why, God? Why have you abandoned me? Why do you refuse to help? I try to be good but filth just spews right out of me. It kills me what I've done to Jen, to my friends. Why can't I stop? Am I that bad? I'm sorry for how wicked I've been. I'm sorry I took Daniel from his mother. I'm sorry I kept Jen from sleeping that night . . . Please don't turn your back on me . . . Please don't be repulsed . . . I need you, Father . . . I'm begging you . . . Show me you still love me . . . Please, Father, please . . . Show me you still care . . ."

I sat in the rain and ached for a sign. I would have taken anything—a still small voice in the center of my soul or an angry rebuke from heaven, a gentle caress through the downpour's calming or a backhanding blast of sleet—anything to let me know He was there, that He was listening, and that He gave either a hand or a damn now that I was coming before Him.

But I got nothing. The rain maintained its relentless assault. And the night held its silence tight. The storm did not speak a divine word. It just got me wet.

What in God's name do I do now? Without a clue, I sat up and faced the darkness. Something solid pressed against my hip. Reaching into my parka, I felt the book. The gilded edges were slick. The silk tassel promised to secure my place. So that was God's answer. 'Footsteps through the Valley of Shadows.' How do you escape the pit? Just follow the well-marked path, the yellow brick road to the Kingdom of God.

Heedless to the weather, I pulled the book out and randomly opened it. Though swallowed in darkness, I could picture the page—a rainbow of footprints across the top, a numbered admonition with Scripture below, daisies in the margin, a signature at the bottom, closing encouragement to stay true to the path even though the path led nowhere. I felt the rain splattering the page. I imagined the colored-marker words bleeding into one another. I had no idea which platitude was being disfigured. It did not matter. Like a fan extracting a celebrity photo from a magazine, I carefully ripped it from the book's spine and held it out. One footstep to the Heavenly Father, it advanced. Sure it did. Lengthwise, I ripped the page in two. I pressed the halves together and, widthwise, ripped it again. Then I dropped the fractured footstep into the mud at my feet. With assembly-line detachment, I crucified another page, and then each page in turn. I ripped them lengthwise, tore them widthwise, and dropped them in the mud. In quartered fragments, the Scriptural platitudes piled up at my feet. They littered the muck in a heap when only the carcass cover was left. I pictured the family portrait pasted on the side. I tried to tear it into two as well.

It proved too durable. So I simply flung it into the night. Then as best I could in the dark, I booted the pages beneath me and ground the remains into the mud.

Once the Book of Life was sufficiently thrashed, I assessed the mess with my flashlight. Several clumps of soggy pages were scattered about the grass, the largest pile directly at my feet. Many of the pages were defaced from my shoes. Most of the words blotched in the rain. I wasn't satisfied. I kicked a clump across the bluff, then kicked another in its wake. I cocked back to kick a third, but stopped mid-swing. Something did not look right. I was about to punt a picture of a harmonica. The harmonica was in pen, not colored-marker. As were the words now that I looked. Jesus Christ, I even recognized the penmanship. I bent down, peeled the page free, and matched it with the pieces underneath.

Through the crossed rips, I could read it all too well. Beside the harmonica sketch, I saw my name. Some of my favorite foods were listed, colors and music too. Further down, entries scrawled at different times were recorded like a diary.

"Blues harmonica, JT, back-up musician, navy blue and purple, faded jeans, shy kisser, Catcher in the Rye—

"The secret to his soul is his music. He yearns to sing, but he hasn't found the words. So he backs up other singers' words. I wonder what he yearns to sing on his own. Does he know? It is buried deep and hidden well. Bruised words, I'm sure. Maybe that's why his shine is always muted, tentative, hidden in the background. But it simmers with primal power. What a song he will sing when he finds his words."

Further down,

"His words are coming. They are filled with rage. Hard words. And hard to hear. I'm sure he needs to voice them. They're part of his song. As is the pain that lies beneath the rage. Does he know that I'll love him no matter how hard the words? Will he let me?"

Still further down, the last entry on the page.

"Maybe love is not enough. But if not, what is?"

I stared at the soaked paper absolutely stunned. I had not shredded the homemade handbook to heaven made by my God-fearing friends. I shredded a text infinitely more sacred—Jen's prayer journal. A book that included the unique longings and beauties of every person whose flourishing she yearned to nurture. A book that included me. Hoping to God I hadn't fallen that far, that by some sleight-of-hand trickery the pages in the mud weren't really the lifeline of my wife's faith, weren't really my friends' souls being pelted by the sleet, I frantically patted my parka. To my horror, my inside pocket hid something. It cowered in the depths like a puppy afraid of a beating. I fished it out and flashed it with light. The book's unblemished cover boldly mocked the blood on my hands. 'Footsteps through the Valley of Shadows.'

Well, you deceitful motherfucker, I thought. You'll let me debase myself by desecrating something truly pure, but you're sure to protect the pristine Book that bears your infallible Word. So what is it? What's so important in these precious pages? What are you so hell-bent on saying to me in the midst of my darkness? Daring the pages to say something asinine, and craving that the chance throw might roll up something credible, I cracked the book at random.

Something credible rolled up all right. God finally spoke. Not through what the words said. Through what they didn't.

17. Take heart in those who share your pain

Joy has vanished from our hearts,
Our dancing has turned to mourning.
Our hearts are sick,
Our eyes grow dim.
For Mt. Zion is desolate,
Jackals prowl upon it.

Why do you forget us, Yahweh?
Why do you forsake us for so long?
Restore us to you, so we can return;
Restore us as we were before.'
(Lamentations 5:15–21)
You are not alone, Tony.
Luv, Kelli

The words were from the prophet Jeremiah. They were the final verses in a book of sorrowful elegies he composed while his temple was in ruins and his people in exiled slavery. His words, however, were edited. The high school scribe, worried perhaps it would hit too close to the mark, omitted the next line, the actual final verse, the last gloomy note on which the whole book ends. God didn't need a storm to get His last word in. He had Jeremiah's haunting conjecture for why Yahweh refused to help His people.

"Unless God has already rejected us, in an anger which knows no limit."

Yes, indeed. The Master of the Universe plays a cold game.

I stared at the page. The missing words seared into me as much as those inscribed. So He wants to play that way does He, I mused. Well, so be it.

I flung the book across the grass to but a few feet from the cliff. Its unbruised face taunted like an unrepentant convict. I leapt across the bluff and pounded it with my flashlight, wielding as little damage as a sledgehammer against a bronze bust. So I flayed the book open and gutted the pages, disemboweling the parchment platitudes and strewing them throughout the rain-soaked night until I stripped the last page clean and found myself face to face with Daniel on his day of commitment. He gaped in cozy oblivion. His parents beamed as they held him. Their teeth glittered as they stared into the sunny future, their happily-ever-after smiles mocking the crazed man staring back from death's stormy abyss.

And this time, I did kill somebody. I took my flashlight club and, with thrashing arcs of light, I bludgeoned the eyes in that grinning suited bastard, I blinded the all-seeing bitch in black, I decimated that cooing infant in white, the doomed reminder of my rage. I pummeled and pounded until I busted the flashlight's bulb and sealed my captivity in the darkness for good. So I propelled that damaged source of light into the mouth of night and followed it with the battered remains of that book. Then, amputated in the blackout by my fear of falling over the cliff, I screamed from my knees. With the rage of a fallen angel banished to hell's black core and the anguish of a father whose son has been abducted, I let loose on the All-Pure God who turns His disgusted backside on the pleading scum-suckers of earth.

"*You fucking bastard*," I wailed into the cold-blooded storm. "*Keep your Goddamned hands off my boy. I'd rather he burn in the fires of hell than be touched by your bloody fingers. Do you hear me? You can't have him. I swear on Satan's soul, if you so much as look at him, I'll storm the gates of heaven, I'll stalk the ends of the earth, I'll hunt you down through the pits of hell. And when I get my filthy hands on you, I'll hand you over to the devil myself. You better hide from me. Do you hear me now?. . .* I'LL HAND YOU OVER TO SATAN MYSELF!!!*"*

It's true. I was ready to take God down. Screaming from my knees in the darkness, pinned to my spot by terror, battered by sleet, ripped by wind, I made quite an impression, I'm sure. But I took Him down anyway. With nails of blasphemy and a hammer of rage, I handed God over to the devil.

I was hoarse by the time I realized it was pointless. Or maybe the point had been taken too well. God wasn't there. He couldn't hear my words. He wouldn't be bailing me out of the darkness. He and I were done. And I was alone in the rain, entombed within the sepulcher of my rage without even a fellow infidel with which to share my confinement. So I inched my way on all fours, cowered under the fallen tree, and held myself in a ball until daylight.

I would have killed God if given the chance.

No wonder He stayed away so long.

But then again, God is easy to kill—when you don't know what you're doing.

———

I did not get pieces of silver. But I ended up with a gold ring.

About a year later, Jen called, asking to stop by. I expected the worst—another teary plea for reconciliation I'd have to stiffly endure. It was time to end the whole sorry affair for good.

We did.

She came by with no intention to eat. No friends were with her. And only half of our previous belongings adorned my studio apartment.

We had not seen each other since the doomed mediation session required at the courthouse. She sat on the sofa's edge as the awkwardness swelled. I offered coffee. She politely declined. I told her she looked good. She said she was eating again. I told her I hoped she was doing okay. She said she was in therapy—that it helped a lot. Small talk aside, we sat in silence.

Until she broke it.

"I'm sorry, Tony." I tensed. "I know I needed you in ways that weren't always fair. And I didn't understand what you needed from me. I see that now." Her eyes filled with tears. I braced for the inevitable as she pulled a tissue from her handbag. "I'm sorry, I swore I wasn't going to cry." She dabbed her nose and took a breath. Then she looked me in the eye. I held her stare. "I still love you, Tony. After everything. I still see the beautiful person you are." I bit my cheek to maintain my composure. Her composure gave way. "Why, Tony? What happened?" I told her what I knew.

"I'm not the person you think I am, Jen."

She winced with pain. "That's just it," she said. "You are."

I didn't correct her. It didn't matter. She searched me, then looked down. As she regathered her strength, I gathered my own. The two of us would never be together again. This would be her final plea.

It never came.

"I'm done, Tony. I'm done." She slipped off her ring and placed it on the table, then let out a breath as if freed from a spell. With a resolve I had not seen since Daniel was born, she looked me back in the eye. Her words, a twist on my engagement blessing, hit home.

"I don't want it, Tony. It's not an instrument of love anymore . . . only heartache."

Then she got up and walked out.

The trinity of jewels glared at me. Like the all-seeing eye of the Prince of Darkness, its eternal lidless stare burned like a curse.

For some time, I thought that my deepest shame laid in the secrets I hid from one whose rosy naiveté blinded her to the blood-red reality of who I really was. I was wrong. My deepest shame laid in the blood-red secrets I hid from myself, blinding me to the rose that was bleeding right in front of me.

And yet, the searing eye of the ring saw all. From the table, it stared with unceasing condemnation.

That's why I buried it.

But even under stone and soil, its stare continued to haunt me.

It does so still.

18

Trudging through the woods, I came upon the fallen pine barricading the bluff. I had not seen its shadows since I cowered within them during my storm-soaked vigil seven years earlier. I remembered shivering through a night-full of arctic darkness before dawn's fingers brushed the sky with enough gray light to lead me back to my truck. All traces of that night's gusty blackness were gone, however. The sky was as blue as hope, the breeze soft as romance. And the decomposed remains of two shredded journals had long since scattered with the winds.

I set down my bags and walked across the grass where I both made frisky love with my fiancée and consummated the dissolution of my marriage, faith, and friendships. As I had a lifetime ago with Jen, I surveyed the spectacular panorama. After two antithetical odysseys, I was not sure what to conclude. Was this the heath at heaven's horizon, the meadow where gods party with mortals around the bottle of bliss? Or was it the mouth of hell, the cursed necropolis where ghouls prey on despairing souls before abandoning their bloodlet bodies? Sacrament or asylum, it was a cosmic borderland. And the portal through which my son must pass on his way to eternal rest.

I returned to my bags and laid out the provisions that I gathered from both grocery store and storage bin. I arranged the objects with care, each detail sculpted in my imagination beforehand. Then I sat down and waited. Though it was a meal, I did not eat. The food was not for me.

The ancients believed that a soul could not enter its everlasting resting place until its body had been properly buried. I went to Daniel's funeral. I mouthed prayers and heard tell of biblical promises. I tucked his teddy into the casket and closed the lid. I placed him in the ground and dropped dirt into the hole. But I never buried him. He was still out there, somewhere in the expanse between bluff and ocean where I abandoned him so decisively.

On the night that I raged at a rainstorm, I hurled Daniel's picture off the cliff. As I conceived it, his spirit lifted free from the beaten photo and hovered in a haunted limbo ever since. His playground was a prison no taller than a seven-tiered castle, no wider than a castle's grounds. Bound by the sea's border below and the bluff's ridge above, he drifted in conflicting currents—sometimes dropping, sometimes sailing—but never able to sink into the watery bosom of the Underworld nor soar into the vaulted lap of heaven. For seven years he floated alone, his eyes gaunt and gloomy in never-ending wakefulness, waiting in the midst of aborted climbs and dead-ending descents for one to come and remember him, bid him a tearful goodbye, and release him from the forgotten tomb that tethered him to our world.

It was time to set him free.

I pulled my harp from my pack. I moistened my lips with water. Then into Daniel's breezy limbo, I played. As I did, the musical currents wafted into the airy expanse. They caught his distracted attention. They wrapped him with soothing familiarity. And they carried him with a lullaby's tenderness. I played him through his short-lived life—through the night of his nativity where his surgically-garbed dad, scared to death but coached steady, received him into the world; through his first shimmering smile where mirrors of light sparkled with joy as three of us giggled on the floor; through his nighttime feedings where he reclined in our bed with contented rapture, guzzling himself to sleep with milk from his mother's breast. I played him back to the bluff. I played him back to his dad. I played him into my lap.

He was so happy to see me. But he was so tired. Like every night of his brief life, the music coaxed him to sleep.

"Close Your Eyes," I played. It's all right.

Close your eyes. I'm here.

I finished the lullaby. The music's echo dissolved into a cathedral stillness. I held my boy. Until the stillness dissolved into prayer. Then with care not rage this time, I laid him on the blanket, and left him to his sleep. I hoped he would nap for as long as his dreams were sweet. But I also hoped, from *this* sleep, he would wake up. And when he did, I hoped he would feast on the love that brought him into this world.

I hope he is feasting still.

———

For the final time, I trudged through the grotto of trees, crossed the pasture, slipped under the barbed-wire fence, and drove like melting snow drifting toward the sea, down the backside of the bluff, down the rumpled meadows, down the cliff-hewn switchbacks, and back to the mouth of River Road. This time I did not turn. I followed Highway 1 south, past the deserted beach dunes and empty coastal campgrounds, and flowed into the town of Bodega Bay.

I passed the charter boat checkpoint where a crowd of teenagers once crammed a ferry to scout the high seas for Leviathan. I passed the marina where dozens of moored craft watched us return high on victory but eager for solid ground. I passed the Tides Restaurant where the high-schoolers crashed the glitzy souvenir shop and gawked for signs of the man-eating birds Hitchcock once filmed there. I passed it all to the far end of the bay and pulled into Dornan Park.

A paved path atop a chest-high dike stretched alongside a hundred yard channel then descended onto a beach. The path was well peopled—couples strolled and skaters glided, toddlers chased seagulls, parents baited their children's hooks. It was a sunny Sunday afternoon, the week's most bitter stretch for the single and divorced, the childless loners and widowed lovers who have no family with which to recreate before the numbing demands of work return. Fathers play catch on Sunday afternoons, mothers pack picnics, and sweethearts take walks, all of them holding hands or horsing around in the picture-perfect poses that grace Hallmark cards.

After locking the truck, I mounted the dike, paced the path, and found a bench over-looking the beach. Blankets dotted the sand and kites colored the sky; children dodged the surf; teens tossed Frisbees. Down a ways, a family of three looked like a well-oiled walking rig as every few steps parents on either side swung the girl in the middle up, out, and in front of them.

"Daddy, Daddy, catch me . . ." A child squealed behind me. As I turned, a young boy of four or so leapt from the dike toward his father below. The father, his eyes level with the boy's flailing feet, wasn't looking. He flinched with the boy's yell and grabbed as the boy slammed into his chest and slid toward the ground. More afraid than hurt, the boy teared up. "You didn't catch me daddy . . . you didn't catch me."

"Honey, I wasn't looking," the dad explained, crouched on his knees and holding the boy close. "Wait until I'm ready next time, okay?" The boy nodded as the dad stood him up. "Here, do it again."

The boy wiped his nose along his sleeve then scaled the mountain of a dike. When he reached the top, he looked down at his dad to make sure.

"You're gonna catch me, right?"

"I'm gonna catch you," the dad smiled. "Jump as far as you can."

The boy backed a few paces, scrunched his face with pintsized determination, then bolted. At the dike's edge, he leapt into the air and screamed, "Catch me, catch me, catch me." In those few feet he soared, as bright-eyed as if flying to the top of the sky, then he peaked and sloped and settled into his daddy's arms greeting him with a swirling embrace.

That's when the tears came. I hustled down the path before anyone could see. Squeals of "Do it again, daddy," and "Catch me, catch me, catch me," receded behind me as I hoofed it to shelter before the raindrops became a downpour. The downpour came any-way. By the time I reached my truck, I was sobbing. I fumbled through my tears, unlocked the door, and jumped into my cab.

And wept. For all of it. For deploring Daniel's conception and disdaining his mom's desires, for pulling him from his mother's side and failing him when he needed air, for throwing his memory off a cliff and turning my back as if he'd never been born, had never breathed, had never brought the world a smile during his three-and-a-half months of sailing through life's sky launched by heaven's hand and arced toward the steadfast arms in which he longed to land.

I wept for not catching him. And for the haunting fact that I'd never have a chance to redeem myself, never have a chance to 'do it again, daddy,' never have a chance to turn back toward him, keeping my eyes open this time, and stretching my arms wide.

Through my tears, I imagined Daniel waking up from his afternoon nap on the bluff. A school-aged boy by then, he shook off the coverings of sleep and discovered the meal beside him. It was offered to soothe his spirit seven years starved. I fashioned it with precision.

Two blankets were laid out, one wheat-colored, the other off-white terry cloth. A bottle of champagne and a carton of milk peeked out of our old picnic basket. A heap of dainties nestled the beverages—tangerines and golden delicious apples, cheddar cheese and Monterey Jack, lemon drops and butterscotch balls. Across the basket, I draped three flowers—a white rose at the center, an amber chrysanthemum on one side, a rust-colored carnation on the other. At the head of the blankets, a waist-high cross was mounted. Its branches came from the fallen trunk that once sheltered me. A cloth hung from the sticks. Daniel's baby blanket. I draped it over the cross' arms. Like bandages over wounded hands.

Daniel took in the atoning meal. Like the puckish Peter Pan he would be, he swigged the milk from the carton then made straight for the lemon drops, popping two in his mouth while pocketing a handful for the journey. He lingered over the flowers. He studied the crossed branches. He fingered his former blanket.

Then he faced the sea, ran, and leapt right off the cliff. I was not there to catch him. He did not need me. The outstretched eagle's wings of life's breath lifted him aloft. They carried him above the hills. They circled him around the bluff. And they bore him toward the western sun where he was swallowed in a golden embrace.

This time, I cried as he left.

Then I cried for all the other children I did not catch. For Danny, whose simple care slammed hard against the locked arms of my rage. For Jen, whose steady love met my stony scorn. For my mom, whose secret torment went unavenged as I sleepwalked through adolescence.

Each one, then others after them, Irby, Sandy, and Blake, and still others after them, Ruth, Kathy, and Kelli, bubbled up from the dark chambers where they had been hidden in my soul, paused, partook of the meal meant for them as well, then dissipated into my tears, washed away as if carried on a stream out to the cradling sea.

I cried until only the meal remained, an enduring memorial for all who hunger to be remembered by those whose fondness lets them grieve. Then my tears washed the meal away too, and I found myself sitting in my cab.

Like one awakening from sleep, I recollected the park I was moored in. Children still chased after gulls; lovers still strolled the path. The four-year-old boy, perched on his dad's shoulders, bobbed toward me on the dike like a prince atop a camel. I watched him take in the panorama with mounted dignity. He approached my truck. As he passed, he looked over. He smiled. I smiled back. At him and the whole lot of earth's beloved squeezing happiness from the ripened fruit of a Sunday afternoon.

Crying clears vision, I found. Tears cleanse bitterness. I could see again. Maybe for the first time.

Unfortunately, I did not cry again for another seven years.

———

Later that evening, I pulled my truck into my carport like a ship gliding back to port. After a long voyage at sea, I was glad to be back. The darkened house did not distress me. Nor did the ghosts that once haunted my bedroom. Like a sailor coming home to his bedded lover, I slipped between my covers, and welcomed sleep.

The next morning I would go back to work. I was ready. I had followed my doctor's orders. I had visited the Underworld. I had dined with some demons. I had buried the dead.

Little did I know.

I was only at the edge.

Looking down.

PART THREE

Good Friday

19

"GALS . . . you don't want to miss this afternoon's session." Jody and Irene both looked up as I breezed into the nurse's station. Rose didn't. She peered into the locked unit through the observation window. "I've got a story *guaranteed* to blow the guys away." I bubbled so much I grinned. "Literally," I added cryptically.

"Look who's smiling again," Irene greeted. "You look like the old Tony." With the mists of depression for so long cloaking me, I wouldn't have been surprised if they didn't even recognize me.

"What can I say? I had a great weekend."

"Care to tell us about it?" Irene continued.

I turned as coy as a call-girl with a secret. "You're gonna have to wait for the story." To heighten the suspense, I patted the item concealed in my pocket. "And it comes with props."

Irene nodded like she couldn't wait. "It's good to have you back," she said.

I nodded too. Then toned it down as I took in Rose. Registering her somber gaze, a tiny tremor rumbled along the fault-line of my liveliness. "So, how's our boy?" I asked. Rose and Irene exchanged looks like neither wanted to break bad news. "What happened?" I insisted.

Rose looked back through the window as Irene explained. "He's a troubled boy, Tony. And the boys are in a tizzy about who's in the Box. While they were outside yesterday, the ball ended up out back so much their rec time was suspended. They were taking turns daring each other to peek through the tiled windows. It scared Carey to death. He sat through it huddled on the floor across the room."

"I'll have to talk with the boys," I said. "They should know better." Though their curiosity was hardly surprising. "Any word on a bed?"

"Nothing," Irene replied. "Could be a few more days."

At that Rose shook her head. Then she looked at me like I was responsible. "He shouldn't be here," she said like a warning. "That boy needs help." As if charged to go out and find it, she left her perch and strode from the station. I looked at Irene.

"She's right," she said. "He needs to connect with somebody." Her eyes beseeched me. "Do you think you could spend some time with him?"

"I'm not sure it's a good idea," I shared. "If he's leaving soon."

She shrugged. "How good is feeling alone for a week?"

"I don't know," I said. And I didn't.

I went to my office, pulled my work from my backpack, then peeked through my door's meshed window. Carey was back on the floor. His sorrow seemed a gravitational force as he sat slumped over and stared at the emptiness between his stretched-out legs. His wrists bandaged, his body seemed bled of hope. Compassion begged me to enter. Compassion held me back. For the moment, I went to my desk and studied my notes. The story came to me the moment I woke up—the surprise sure to astonish the boys. The flow and climax were nailed, but closing it eluded me. What did the face in the mirror look like? I stared at the pages and waited for inspiration. But the only face I could see was Carey's. How much despair could one boy endure? I decided not much more.

I thought I went in to ease his aloneness. Not find an ending to my story.

Careful not to stir the funereal quiet, I crossed the ward and sat against the wall that cornered Carey's. I did not have a plan—some subtle ploy to pull him out with a Rorschach blot improvised from the linoleum's charcoal flecks. It was just as well. His despair rendered small-talk mute. And words of comfort would clang like tin within the cavernous deep of his isolation. In the midst of his sadness, only the silence rang true. So I followed his lead, and surrendered to the quiet.

The quiet took hold as I stared at the spots speckling the white sea of tile. They looked like drips from ashen haze splattering an ocean surface—fledgling raindrops longing to soar but bled from the sky in a defeated drizzle. They floated in spattered abasement, depleted from their desperate plunge and giving in to the tidal pull from oblivion's darkened depths. As I stared, their hopelessness became overwhelming. They cried to rise in cumulous flight, but they cried into the quiet in vain. For who can raise the drowning drizzle already disappearing into darkness?

Staring into that splattered sea, it came to me. I could not invigorate flight. But I could voice the cry that aches for it.

I reached into my pocket and retrieved my prop. The boy on the floor ignored me. I cupped both hands to my mouth. He stared into the spattered morass. I felt the tidal pull of despair. He gazed without blinking. Then from the sorrow that burdened the room, I made music. A spiritual emerged from the despondent deep, a song that bore the blackened multitude that drifted through the seas of slavery. The words were implied in my harp's troubled tone.

> Sometimes I feel like a motherless child,
> Sometimes I feel so low,
> Sometimes I feel like a motherless child,
> A long, long ways from home.

Line after haunting line, the mournful music seeped into the room. With it, a ghostly echo of field slaves seemed to whimper along. They moaned in melancholic harmony. Homesick runaways hummed as well. Plantation chattel, childless mammies, mindless old-timers sipping moonshine on the porch, all wailed together in wordless sorrow. They cried across the ages of oppression's ebb and flow. And they gathered into their chorus the hollow-hearted howls of all the trampled voices whose misery throughout history joins forces in the single song of suffering. With a blues harp, I played along with them. I played because I knew of nothing else to do. I played because somehow their song was my song. I played because if I didn't, despair's cold silence would drown us all within its silencing abyss. But also I played to cinch the tie that would bind me to a sinking boy. The lifeline of my song offered hope to stay afloat—or an anchor's knot that would take us both down together.

As the final note faded, the song's somber wake settled into a rippleless quiet. The tug of despair still pulled. But for the moment, we were buoyed by our companions' soul. I soaked in the solace, my harp still cupped to my mouth. Then I turned my eyes toward Carey. He remained as still as death.

Until he moved. His body locked in leaden immobility, he pivoted only his head. With eyes pierced by unspeakable pain, he searched every shadow within me. His stare was posed like a question. 'Do you have any idea?' his unflinching eyes asked, 'how evil life can be?' I met his stare straight on. 'Yes,' my eyes answered. 'I sure as hell do.' Without a word, he returned his gaze to the floor and slipped back into the lonely drift of his sorrow. He was done.

Or so I thought. Whether resuscitated by our silent encounter, or flicking the whole damn thing away, the middle finger of his right hand curled back onto his thumb, cocked itself taut, then flicked. Mechanically, it did it again. Curl, cock, and flick. Then again. Curl, cock, and flick.

I did not know what to make of it.

But I knew one thing: for better or worse, we had a connection.

———

Back at my desk, I opened Carey's file. The sheet for detailing his treatment plan was stapled to the inside cover. The form remained blank.

For a suicide level-one temporarily placed in a transitional facility, protocol was clear. The patient should be quarantined in a locked ward and continuously observed. His meds should be monitored, his vital signs recorded. Basic human needs—food, sleep, fresh air two times a day—should be offered even if not received. Beyond that, all therapeutic involvement should be kept to a minimum. It is not in the patient's interests to bond with people he will soon abandon, get invested in a program he'll be quickly yanked out of, and become vulnerable to dynamics that could provoke more acting out. It was simple. Keep him safe, sequestered, and stable until a suitable placement was secured. Indeed, protocol was clear.

But I could not prescribe it. Not yet anyway. Instead, I read through his medical report. There wasn't much in it. And what was there was plenty disturbing. Carey Foster, all of eleven years old, had ripped his wrists with the precise savagery of a surgeon slicing tumorous tissue. From the fleshy underside of his elbow to a tailing streak at his palm, a single laceration tore the length of each arm. The incision where the cutting tool first punctured the skin was as deep as an X-acto knife stabbed to the base of its blade. It pierced both artery and muscle tissue in each forearm and required forty-seven stitches to close.

With the exception of abrasions around the base of each ankle, the rest of his body was sound. His psyche however, was not. Through his round-the-clock suicide watch, he neither ate nor spoke. He went to the bathroom twice. His only movement otherwise was the nervous twitch of his right middle finger recorded with intermittent regularity throughout his hospital stay. Yes, indeed. Carey Foster was one troubled young man.

The report, at the time anyway, seemed straightforward enough. With one exception. The consulting psychologist considered Carey uncommunicative. I disagreed. In fact, I staked my professional career on the premise that such was far from the case. Woody taught me well. Every clinical expression of deviant behavior, no matter how destructive it might appear, was rooted in an authentic impulse toward life. His maxims were planted deep and watered well within the landscape of my therapeutic philosophy. 'Mental illness is the soul expressing itself, the psyche reaching out for healing.' 'Don't fight the disease, befriend it.' 'All symptoms tell a story—listen for its logic and allow it to unfold.' Carey Foster was telling us a great deal. In fact, his healing depended upon people listening with precision.

So what story was Carey's symptoms telling—and what was the impulse for life within it? To be sure, he was living one horrific tale. His self-mutilation hardly a casual cry for help, he clearly knew extreme abuse or abandonment. With a sense of defilement woven into the very tissues of his skin, he sought a savage form of death and came damn close to finding it. The world is a brutal place, his actions were saying, one in which the defiled hero is better off dead. Getting to the bottom of Carey's secrets would be central to his recovery, along with removing the dangers in his environment and equipping him to cope.

But Carey's psyche was telling more than a story of despair. Within the mysteries of his symptoms clues could be found to a life-affirming pulse—albeit faint and misdirected —that begged to be discerned then resuscitated into the throbbing currents of vitality. What was the heartbeat within Carey's brutal self-destruction? Was it a righteous wrath hell-bent on slicing away any thin membrane that veils the blood-red horrors of our world? Or was it an artist's sensitivity aching to feel in his own flesh the pain of a world that slashes its most tender members? Or maybe it was a warrior's strength that wields its sword before monstrous odds to rip open the veins of the world's underbelly, tear away the fibers that enslave, and set free the crimson streams that restore all life. Some hopeful residue of the human spirit beat within the death-drive of Carey's violent actions. He was dying to tell a story deeper than the nightmare narrative screaming at him to take his own life. The hero didn't have to die in the end. He had hidden powers hungering to be accessed. What are your powers? I wondered. Who are your villains? What is the healing story beating within you in a desperate bid for life? Tell me Carey, I really want to know. Staring into the runes of his medical report, I strained for an insight.

Then it hit me.

Of course.

He was already telling me—as certainly as the look in his eye aching for me to listen. Here he was, scared to the brink of death, imprisoned within a traumatized muteness, suspicious of even the most tenuous contact, and yet his body refused to be silenced.

Curl, cock, and flick it shouted. That was the key. Even back then, I saw it. The story was in Carey's finger. And he wanted me to know it.

The form prescribing Carey's treatment remained blank. Protocol was clear. Keep him safe and leave him alone. But even through the security wall that separated us, I sensed it. The curl, cock, and flick of his finger pulsated like a heartbeat. I picked up my pen and inked my instructions.

"Patient is to participate in all therapeutic activities including group therapy, the narrative arts program, and daily sessions with the site psychologist."

The finger had a story to tell.

And I was going to be there to hear it.

20

"So where the hell have you been, Dr. T.?" Hands behind his head on his recliner throne, Virgil's query came off casual. It wasn't. I hadn't seen the boys in five days. Enough to fear abandonment.

"You shouldn't answer that," Fast Eddie interjected like a defense attorney staving off reporters. "Some of these minds are a bit delicate for what you told me."

"Shut up, Fast Eddie," Shadrach exclaimed. "He didn't tell you nothing."

"Sure he did," Eddie countered. "And all I'm saying is, what Dr. T. does with his private life is between him and me."

"That's jack," Shadrach came back.

"Yeah," Blade concurred, glancing at Shadrach like an insecure sidekick.

"Don't worry, guys," I said before Eddie incited a brawl. "I didn't tell Fast Eddie anything. Though I have to admit—I wasn't sick."

"I knew it." Fast Eddie slapped his hands then fluttered them for me to fess up. "Let's hear some dish."

"I don't know," I stalled. "I haven't told a soul what I've been up to."

"So tell us," Blade pressed.

I winced like I wasn't sure. "Let's just say I had some oceanfront property I needed to attend to."

"You gotta do better than that," Fast Eddie scoffed.

"How about some underworld business I had to dispose of?" Fast Eddie smirked like I had to be kidding. Only Virgil sensed that I was and I wasn't.

"Where were you really?" Blade begged.

"You really want to know?"

"Yeah."

I sized them up before deciding. "Okay. I'll tell you."

"The whole story?" Blade implored.

"The whole story."

"With all the juicy details?" Fast Eddie clarified.

"With all the juicy details."

I leaned in. They strained forward. I eyed them all like confidants. "Just as soon as everybody gets here."

"Awww, come on Dr. T.," several groaned.

Virgil only smiled.

We were in the Commons, the regular meeting-place for afternoon groups. Three couches and several stuffed chairs formed a horseshoe. I was in a folding chair at the opened end. Seven boys sat in well-considered locations. Seating position was a matter of pride and social standing. The choice spot was the sole recliner in the room, followed by the stuffed chairs that could be occupied alone, then either end of a sofa. Theoretically, the middle of a couch constituted the lowest rung on the seating hierarchy, but such a debasement was purely hypothetical. A boy would rather sit on the floor than be wedged between a guy on either side. At the moment, three spaces were vacant—both ends of a couch across the circle from me and the end of couch directly at my right.

Virgil, the closest thing to a leader within the ever-vying and perpetually reactive group, claimed the recliner. His stature was neither self-sought nor despotic. Part man of letters, part stand-up comic, part political commentator worthy of NPR, Virgil had the self-secured inner authority of a poet-philosopher. He was the kind of pacesetter who didn't care if anybody followed—which only made the others want to follow him all the more.

Revealing his poetic instincts, Virgil named himself. He identified with the Roman bard after hearing a legend about the latter's nativity. Apparently the Italian poet's mother planted a laurel branch on the occasion of her son's birth. When the stick pierced the earth it spontaneously took root, ripened, and blossomed into a fully flowered tree. Our Virgil's mother also planted a tree when her son was born—a poplar in the woods behind her husband's church. Within two weeks however, before either tree or boy had flowered through a single season, she died.

Few details are known about the eight years he lived with his three older sisters and their country minister father before Virgil ran away. At his intake interview some seven years later, Virgil was as elusive as a beatnik pinned down about politics. When asked about his family he replied, "I am kin only with those whose words can make a dead tree flower."

When asked about his belief system he said,

"I belong to the first congregation of pagans, poets, and the passionately impious."

And when asked about his sexual history he pondered deeply then cited his poetic mentor, "'Immense and soundless regions of the night, allow me to disclose things buried in the dark and deep of earth.'"

Like his namesake, Virgil primarily expressed himself through verse. While the others played ball or watched TV during downtime, Virgil wrote. Curled up in a corner with a spiral notebook and pen, he composed sacrilegious lyrics to popular melodies, fashioned free-verse social critique, or penned a stanza or two for his magnum opus—an epic poem to his long-dead mother. He was compulsively secretive about his work but nobody pressed him. We all knew we'd hear it. During his weekly monologue.

As resident herald, Virgil had the responsibility of warming up the audience every Friday night before the stage presentation of the stories and plays written by the boys in our narrative arts therapy program. Whether in the Crossroads Commons with only a handful of regulars or at the vocational school auditorium with an actual audience, Virgil would stand in front of the crowd, welcome them to the latest performance by the Bitter Truth Players, then preface his opening-act soliloquy with an irresistible grin that said in equal parts, 'I really don't mean to offend anybody' and 'Isn't it great being an artist?' and 'Hold onto your chairs folks, we're gonna have us some fun.'

Virgil always got a rise from the crowd.

The Christmas before he brought down the house with his song to the tune of the carol it mimicked, 'The twelve things of Christmas that truly are pho-ny,' in which he lampooned everything from department store Santas copping a feel to God being born in a pig sty.

A perennial crowd unsettler was his medley of Christian hymns in which, like a degenerate Woody Guthrie, he changed the words though not always the theology to religious classics—the haunting 'Elusive grace, how well you hide,' the bloodedly detailed 'Onward Christian soldiers, kill and maim for God,' and the show-stopping, riot-inducing 'Jesus fucks me this I know, for my butthole tells me so.'

My personal favorite was his Allen Ginsberg-inspired piece titled 'Wail.' Written to commemorate the Rodney King beating, the three stanzas wove together the wailing police clubs that beat up the motorist, the wailing of the one beaten, and the wails that were sure to rise from the multitude of beaten ones doubled over in our urban centers. It was both lament and indictment. And ominously prophetic. Virgil composed the piece in the winter of 1992 during the officers' trial in the affluent Simi Valley. Three months were still to pass before we watched his poem play out on live TV. The city wailed just as he predicted.

Virgil's gifts as a bard and balladeer kept his reputation as seer of the community secure. But his cult-hero authority was sealed during the christening he gave each Crossroads newcomer. Within a few days after their arrival, every residential novice received a new name, divined by Virgil, confirmed by the community, and adopted for use throughout the boy's tenure at our facility. The names were so insightfully crafted and empowering to the boys even the staff addressed the residents through their freshly born identities.

Each person around the circle passed through the waters of Virgil's patronymic baptism.

Malcolm came to us after doing time at the detention center for stabbing his foster father with a mechanical pencil. Virgil saw through the rage and recognized a black militant intellectual in the making. Malcolm so took to his new name he now donned steel-rimmed glasses, toted copies of Malcolm X's speeches, and blamed his wells of aggression on the white structures of power that kept the black man down.

Clint was a diminutive Filipino boy whose deferential manner belied the destructiveness of his acting out. At 14, he drove his dad's BMW to an empty lot, parked it away from some playing children, then pummeled it with a thousand rounds of BB pellets. His assault was so intense the police had to wait behind trashcans until he ran out of ammo, at which point he slipped back into the quietly compliant people-pleaser the courts assigned to us. Whether Virgil glimpsed a loner strength or he found the Dirty Harry stunt brassy enough to immortalize, he made Clint's day when he labeled the kid with the screen legend's monosyllabic trademark. Upon hearing his new name, Clint straightened with self-assurance. Then he glanced around at the others to make sure it was okay by them.

Luke's pseudonymous identity required no otherworldly powers to discern. The tiny Mexican boy came to us from the psych hospital in Marin after passing every test they could throw at him to assess his mental fitness. He was not schizophrenic, delusional, or otherwise psychotic. He was fully cognizant of and functional within the space-time parameters of the real world. But for some indecipherable reason, the pleasant young man inhabited the earth certain he was Luke Skywalker. When Virgil merely sanctified the obvious, Luke received the title as if being knighted. "I promise to complete my training, return to my people, and like my father before me, follow the ways of the Jedi."

The other Mexican boy in our company was decidedly more tortured. His mother, a migrant farm worker, disciplined him at the age of three by submerging his hand in boiling water. Every appendage was lost except the knuckled-length nub of an index finger that glistened in creepy discoloration with a dozen layers of grafted skin. While having the emotional age of a six-year-old, he had the manual dexterity of an accomplished carver. Which was unfortunate. His copper-colored limbs and torso were laced with the bone-white scars of his self-mutilation. Like most cutters, he was not trying to kill himself. He was trying to feel alive. Virgil named him Blade.

Shadrach had a zealot's obsession with fire. He burned playhouses, melted Barbie dolls, and torched stuffed animals. He even seared his own skin. He had the chilling ability to withstand a flame as it burned down a match until it extinguished itself in the dead tissue of his blackened fingertips. If Virgil's name was meant to empower a sense of invincibility within the infernos of Shadrach's life, it fell short. About a year after I left, Shadrach stole a car and drove it to a park near Napa. He doused the interior with two-gallons of gas then lit his final match. In the fiery furnace of his self-destructive rage, no angels appeared to keep him safe. I suspect his wrath is still burning.

The last person with a seat staked out in our circle was Fast Eddie, the slick-talking hustler who could take on Minnesota Fats with words alone. In the world of conning, Fast Eddie Felson's game had nothing on the Fast Eddie Firelli shtick we listened to everyday. Virgil saw it within minutes of Fast Eddie's arrival—right about the time Eddie talked Luke out of the top bunk on account of the force's proximity to the gravitational pull of the ground.

So far we had seven boys on time for the afternoon session. Three of our twelve wouldn't be coming at all. Hannibal, whose psychotic leer rivaled that of Lector, was still at the psych hospital. Corleone, the tight-lipped Chilean with a gangster's temper, was back in juvey for beating up a classmate. And Holden, the white suburbanite suffering a depressive episode, was having a go of it with his filmmaker brother in San Rafael. So we were waiting for two—Boomer and Flash, a pair of twins as inseparable as they were rambunctious. They were our most recent arrivals. And the beneficiaries of Virgil's sole spontaneous naming.

They appeared one afternoon as a winter storm battered the countryside. We were in the Commons, midway through a session, when a sonic boom shook the building. In syncopation with a lightning bolt and thunderclap, the front door burst open and two hulking black teenagers, racing for shelter, popped through with such blundering momentum they seemed cannon-balled straight from the stormy heavens. We stared, jolted both by the weather's blast and the spooky arrival of two identical linebackers battling in our vestibule. Virgil took but seconds to size them up.

"Boomer and Flash," he announced.

And so it was. Our tribe was complete.

———

"So who's the kid in The Box?" Shadrach asked while we waited for the rumbling twins.

"That's something I want to talk to you about. I hear you guys have been spying on him."

"Fast Eddie said he'd make my bed for a week if I touched the back door," Blade complained.

Fast Eddie rebutted. "I said if you *opened* the back door."

"You can't open it. It's locked," Blade responded.

"How was I supposed to know that?"

"Forget it guys," I said. "He's just a kid. I don't want you bugging him."

"What's he doing here?" Shadrach asked.

"We're keeping an eye on him until he's transferred. But the thing is, he's scared and isn't talking much. He's going to join our group but you need to give him his space, leave him alone until he feels like participating."

"Look," Fast Eddie declared, "if he doesn't have to talk at groups then I'm not talking either."

"Anytime you want to keep quiet during groups," I answered, "you've got my permission."

"Come on, Dr. T." He turned on a dime. "I'm just setting a good example by expressing my feelings."

"I know. And the last thing I want to do is stifle your self-expression. I'm just saying let him be. He's only eleven. Take it easy on him, okay?"

"It's cool," Fast Eddie said. The others shrugged their assent.

"Okay. I'll have Rose bring him in." I got up. "And where in the world are Boomer and Flash?"

"I'll get 'em?" Fast Eddie was up off the couch. Sending him after latecomers was like sending Tom Sawyer after Huck and Jim. All three would be out of the state by sundown.

"That's okay, Eddie. Deacon and Willie know we're ready." Former athletes and army cooks, they were the caretakers who slept in the cabins, served the meals, and tossed the ball during down-time. "I'll send Jody just in case."

———

I hadn't been gone for sixty seconds before a cockfight erupted. Blade found a Yahtzee die wedged in the couch and challenged Clint to a roll for the latter's stuffed chair. Clint lost and stood up when Shadrach leapt over and beat Blade to the seat. Blade was no match for Shadrach but he pulled at him with his one good hand trying to force the cheat off his chair. Fast Eddie and Luke egged Blade on while Clint whined that the chair was his in the first place.

"Knock it off, guys," I interrupted. "It's time to get started."

"He's . . . in my . . . chair," Blade grunted between heaves.

Shadrach toyed with Blade like a tiger would a mouse then planted his foot on Blade's chest and shoved him onto the couch next to Virgil.

That's when Rose opened the locked-unit door.

The boys all stopped and turned as if the unseen inhabitant had announced his appearance. But Carey made no announcement. He shrunk in the shadows as if ashamed of being seen at all.

The boys stared amazed. A deliverance from the Box was always an event. Someone was only sequestered there for extreme acts of violence, hysterical acting-out, or persistent signs of suicidality. How they emerged—whether self-consciously nonchalant, proudly unbroken, or stoically restored to saneness—was cause for curiosity even in the most reclusive.

But this was different. The captive freed from solitary was a child—a towheaded tot who should have been out climbing trees. And the macabre explanation for his involuntary confinement was displayed in morbid boldness. His wrists, poised across his chest in cautious self-protection, were gauzed with such self-inflictive allusion and ominous mummification it looked like the kid launched his own slaughter, prepared his limbs for burial, and was now being led, in petrified disgrace, to the site where he would be laid to rest.

"Jesus," Virgil whispered as the others stared speechless. For the first time I wondered if I had made a mistake and exposed him to social scrutiny too soon. Rose was certain I had. With a scowl that communicated he belonged where he was, she escorted him to the side of circle away from me.

"Make way for the kid," Virgil commanded. Blade got off the couch and returned to his original seat. Carey sat down on the now vacant sofa and cowered into the cushions like cornered prey. His finger flicked full throttle.

"Don't worry about it," Fast Eddie chimed in, consigning to oblivion my earlier request. "Blade's cut himself so many times you'd think he was a carving stick."

Carey squeezed his arms to his chest then flinched. Blade stared at the bandages like he was ready to get a knife for himself.

"Welcome to our group, Carey," I said hoping to draw attention from the obvious. "These are the guys."

Two voices clamored from out front. "I'm telling you, you gotta win by two."

"Not when it's time for groups. Then it's next basket wins."

Boomer and Flash jostled in through the door, paused from their argument, and took in the scene. They figured it out in a heartbeat. As if propelled by a starter's pistol, they dashed for the coolest of the two remaining seats—the end of couch next to Carey eternally more desirable than the teacher's pet seat on the couch next to me. While Boomer raced around the sofa, Flash took the direct route, barreled over the back, and thumped into the seat just ahead of Boomer's haunches slamming in from the side. Carey recoiled at the invasion.

"Flash's got it," Fast Eddie called.

"He cheated," Boomer protested.

Flash spread out as Boomer sulked, then crossed the circle and slouched into the space beside me. Now that our merry band was complete, it was time to get started. As Deacon and Willie, Rose, Jody and Irene took seats in the back, I gathered us in for the journey.

"So you guys have been wondering where I've been. Well, let me tell you."

21

“It begins with a story,” I told them. “You’ll never understand the ordeal I’ve been through if you don’t first know who Robert Johnson was—and why some sixty years ago, in the swamplands of Mississippi, he waited in the center of a pitch-black intersection for the precise stroke of midnight to come. The place he stood was called ‘The Crossroads.’ He was waiting for the devil.

—

Robert Johnson picked cotton during the Depression. But he was not your average field hand. Robert had music inside of him, rumbling like a volcano ready to explode. All day long as he and the pickers tore up their hands for but a penny or two a day, the beat pounded through his body all but propelling him to drop the cotton, grab a guitar, and run straight off the plantation. He shouldn’t be slaving in the sun; he should be singing in the limelight—performing at nightclubs, jamming with celebrities, cutting vinyl records, and riding that inferno of rhythm all the way to the top. For he just knew—one day that poor country cotton-picker would perform at the most famous music house in all the world. Robert Johnson would play at Carnegie Hall.

There were only three problems.

First, Robert didn’t own a guitar.

Second, he didn’t know how to play one even if he had one.

But third, and most serious of all, Robert had the wrong kind of music busting up out of his soul. He didn’t want to play no Negro spirituals, not ragtime jazz, no bee-bopping swing neither. He wanted to play the blues. And everybody knew, the blues was the devil’s music.

Blues was what they played at the juke joint on Saturday nights where loose women and willing men drank whiskey and smoked cigarettes and partied so late they missed prayer meeting the next morning. Robert’s family fought to save him. His mother scolded him when he hummed during chores. His stepfather beat him when he snuck to the speakeasies. His brothers smashed his homemade instruments made of wooden crates and bailing wire. But nobody could put out the fire. Not until he fell in love. When the most beautiful serving-girl in Mississippi agreed to marry him, Robert swore off juke joints forever. When she became pregnant with their son, he swore off the music as well. Instead of blues, he sang lullabies to the growing baby in his honey’s belly. For the first time in his life, the devil’s music stopped pounding in the lonely cauldron of his soul.

But not for long. Robert's boy was never born. When his wife went into labor, complications set in. Robert and his wife were too poor to fetch a doctor, too far to make a colored hospital. Before the night had passed, both baby and mother were dead. Robert cursed his life, and he cursed his God. And the music surged back with a rage. Evil or not, he was going to play the blues. No matter what the cost.

He returned to the local juke joint and scrutinized the bluesmen's moves, memorized their words, and studied their licks. When they took a break, he hopped onstage and fingered their warm guitars. But try as he might, he could not get out the sound. The strings pinged like pebbles against a washtub, his riffs screeched like fingernails on a blackboard, his voice screaked like a cat being stretched on a rack. The listeners begged him to stop.

"You got no talent, boy. You can't play the stick end of a shovel."

But Robert refused to give up. He sold his few possessions, bought a beat-up guitar, and traveled the country in search of a teacher. Music shops in Memphis, blues saloons in Arkansas, backwoods old-timers in the bayous of Mississippi, he tried them all, and they all told him the same thing, "You got the desire son, but you ain't got the talent."

For months he wandered, hitching rides on hay trucks, hopping onto railcars, and hoofing it down country highways. But for all the teachers he chased down and all the chords he taught himself, he couldn't play a single song in tune. When his last lead told him he had best go back to cotton, Robert knew he had reached the end. He hopped aboard a random train and buried himself in a darkened railcar. He sat on his guitar case. His head hung low. The broken song of his busted life had nothing left to play.

Until a voice spoke from the darkness.

"What's the matter, son?" An old man sat in the corner with skin the color of night and one bad eye that twitched in time with the train.

"Nothing you can help with."

"No?" said the old man. "Word's out you want to learn that there guitar you be sittin' on."

"I reckon," Robert said staring at his dream lying dead on the floor.

"Word's out you want to play it so good, some day you be playing at Carnegie Hall."

"I suppose," Robert sulked.

"Word's out," the old-timer continued, "you don't want to play just any ol' music, you want to play the devil's music, as good as it's ever been played."

Robert shrugged. "Yeah, that's what I want alright."

"Well," the old-timer hacked up some phlegm and spat. "My question to you is, how bad you want it?"

Robert looked over. "I want it bad enough."

The old man looked back, his bad eye twitching. "You want it so bad you'd leave all your kin, and travel the world alone?"

"I'd say I do."

"You want it so bad you'd sell all you have, and walk the world in poverty?"

"I'd say I do."

The old man gazed at the floor as the bad eye kept twitching at Robert. Then the man looked back. The bad eye stopped twitching. Two eyes, one dead, one living, held Robert in an icy stare. "You want it so bad you'd travel into the cold heart of midnight, face down the devil himself, and trade in your very soul to play his music?"

Without blinking, Robert answered. "Yes sir, I would."

The old man nodded.

"So here's what you gotta do. You wait until the night of the new moon, the darkest night of the month. You walk into the heart of the swamplands, to where two roads form a perfect cross. You stand at the center of that crossroads with your back to the east, and you cradle your guitar in your arms. At the precise stroke of midnight, the devil will come up behind you. Mind you, don't turn around and look at him or he'll kill you on the spot. Just hand the guitar behind you. He'll tune it to the key of evil, then hand it back. You think long and hard see, before you play it. Because the second you do, the deal is done. You'll play blues like nobody ever played them before. But your soul will belong to the devil."

That month, when the moon turned its back on the Earth for a single night of all-consuming blackness, Robert Johnson walked to the center of the Mississippi swampland. It was so dark he could not see his own hand before him, so dark even the crickets defected for the evening. Fifty miles away from the nearest living thing, Robert Johnson stood in the crossroads, and waited for the devil.

At the precise stroke of midnight, an icy breeze escaped from the swamp and slithered down Robert's back. Chilled to the bone, he could neither move nor breathe.

Something crept up behind him. A cold presence pressed against his back. Its voice creaked like a yawning trap.

"So you want . . . to play . . . my music."

Robert was too scared to speak.

"Hand me your instrument."

Robert passed his guitar behind him. The devil took it and plucked each string once. The notes pierced the night like screams. Then he returned the guitar to Robert.

The guitar was as cold as ice. Robert hesitated. He could seal the deal in a second. But his soul would be lost forever.

The music within him ached to come out. Fear gave way to passion. As Satan's breath chilled his neck, Robert lifted his finger.

With it, he plucked the guitar.

Several weeks later, Bobby Hooker and the Black Cats were playing at the juke joint near Robert Johnson's birthplace. In the middle of the second set, when the band was as hot as the bodies on the dance floor, a stranger walked through the door. He wore the hippest clothes to ever shadow a speakeasy. His silk burgundy suit was creased like a knife's edge. His patent leather shoes sparkled like starlight. A white gangster hat with a ribbon of cashmere shaded half his face. Sunglasses concealed his eyes.

He cut through the crowd with the swagger of a celebrity. The dancers stopped their dancing, the musicians killed their music. All eyes stared as the stranger reached the stage and casually unsnapped his case. He pulled out a custom-made guitar with a platinum shell, pearl frets, and diamond studded sockets securing strings that glittered.

The lead singer was impressed. "Can you play that?"

The stranger stroked the length like it was a satin nylon then gently brushed its bottom. "I reckon I could coax her for a lick or two," he said. He removed his glasses and withdrew his hat, then looked back at the singer. "Yeah, I think I can."

The singer looked then looked again. "Robert Johnson? Dang, you had us going... What're you doing interrupting us like you was from Chicago or somethin'?"

Robert was as cool as a Cadillac. "You don't want to hear me play?"

"Just 'cuz a guitar looks fancy don't mean it can play itself."

"Suit yourself." Robert started putting it away.

The singer, suddenly uncertain, turned to the drummer for direction. The drummer nodded.

"Okay," the singer said. "Show us what you got."

Robert Johnson strapped his guitar and slowly plucked each string. The dancers were impatient. "Come on," they cried. "Is that all you can play? We want to dance."

Robert simply smiled. His fingers formed a chord. He strummed. His fingers formed another chord. He strummed again. Then as if a geyser burst forth within him, he let loose. His hands danced down the struts so nimbly they were a blur. His fingers fluttered the strings so fast they could have caught on fire. The notes rippled with such swinging speed it sounded like an entire blues band was playing. Dancers and musicians alike were amazed. Robert Johnson was doing the impossible. He beat his own bass line, plucked his own melody, and rolled his own slides all at the same time. It's like trying to pitch a baseball to yourself, racing to home-plate to hit it, then hauling out to catch it as it's clearing the outfield wall. It can't be done. It's humanly impossible. But here he was doing it, and doing it with a soulfulness never heard before.

"That guy plays blues better than Bobby Hooker and the Cats," the onlookers said.

"That guy plays better than Chicago's Charley Patton."

"That guy plays the devil's music better than the devil himself."

And play it he did. That night, the next night, and every night thereafter. In Saturday night juke houses and riverfront saloons, in backcountry get-backs and big-city speakeasies, cutting records in Texas and capturing crowds on street corners, Robert Johnson washed the South with the poetry and sounds of the greatest blues player to ever work a guitar. And the amazing thing is, no matter how tired he got or how much whiskey he drank, no matter how complicated the chords or how feverish his performance, no matter how long he played, how late the night, or how hard he jammed, in ten years of playing the blues, he never once broke a string, he never once went out of tune, and he never once made a single mistake.

Robert Johnson became a legend. So much so that in the summer of 1938, a certain John Hammond traveled to hear him play. Mr. Hammond was producing a show in New York City showcasing the greatest black musicians from the past fifty years. After hearing him, he invited Robert to headline the concert.

The concert was to be staged at Carnegie Hall.

———

Now some people say that the devil was jealous of Robert Johnson, that he didn't want Johnson appearing at Carnegie Hall because the entire world would know that Johnson could outplay him at his own music. So the devil did something about it. A few weeks before the Carnegie Hall debut, a stranger showed up at one of Robert's gigs. The stranger, whose identity was never determined, slipped strychnine into Robert's drink. The poison burned his vocal cords, then killed him three days later puking like a dog. The devil killed Robert's music before New York City ever heard a note.

But others say different. Robert Johnson died but he refused to be silenced. In hell they say, he faced down the devil. And his music lives on because of it.

I don't know. But this much is true. When John Hammond heard the news of Robert Johnson's death, he wept. That night he had a dream. Robert came to him with a smile and an idea.

On the night of the concert, John Hammond hushed the black-tie crowd. He welcomed them to an evening with the greatest black musicians in two generations. Sadly, the greatest among them, the greatest musician he had ever heard of any age or race, had died but a few months earlier. Nevertheless, the crowd would hear his music.

Hammond drew the curtain. In the middle of the empty stage, an antique phonograph sat on a three-legged stool. Hammond set the needle. For the only time in the history of the most famous music house in the world, a musician played at Carnegie Hall from a record.

The musician was Robert Johnson.

He sang, "Crossroad Blues."

But here's the thing. Carlton Shines was at Carnegie Hall that night. And he was at the Texas hotel where Robert Johnson cut that record. To his dying day, Carlton Shines swore that when Robert Johnson recorded "Crossroad Blues," he didn't have that sly little laugh in his voice, and there weren't no moaning sounds in the background like spooks howling in the night, and he surely didn't sing that extra verse about staring the devil down, and giving the hound a shoe, sendin' him back beneath the ground, so the music could sing on through. No, he never sang that verse on the record.

Carlton Shines was convinced. The phonograph on the Carnegie Hall stage was a hoax. The voice coming through the speaker did not come from the record. It was the real voice of Robert Johnson, reaching all the way from the grave.

His body may have been dead—but his soul was still singing.

———

The hands shot up like quiz kids on a game show. They didn't wait to be called upon.

"Hold on," I said. "One at a time. Clint."

"Is that a true story?"

"You know me. All my stories are true. Even the ones I make up."

"No, I mean, did those things really happen?"

The barrage returned. "Yeah, was there really a Robert Johnson?" "Did he sell his soul to the devil?" "Did they play his record at Carnegie Hall?"

"Okay," I said. "I'll tell you what I know. There really was a Robert Johnson who disappeared for a while then came back playing the blues. Most people said he was the best guitar player they ever heard. When asked how he got so good so fast, he said he went to the Crossroads and sold his soul to the devil. All that's true."

"Did he really die like that?" Shadrach asked.

"Yes, he did."

"Did they play his record at Carnegie Hall?" Fast Eddie followed.

"Yes, they did."

"Was it Robert Johnson singing from the grave?" Clint continued.

"Now that's open to interpretation. As far as I know, there's only one way to find out for sure. So I did it." I waited.

"You did what?" Clint asked.

"Well, Carlton Shines said that the original recording of "Crossroad Blues" doesn't have all that extra stuff on it—ghosts howling, Robert laughing, an additional verse sung live from the graveyard. So I listened to the original record Robert made in Texas. And you know what? None of it's there. Not one sound of it. Now if that doesn't prove that Shines was right I don't know what would."

"That doesn't prove nothing," Malcolm countered. "Maybe Shines just made it up."

"That's why it's open to interpretation."

As they sorted it out, Virgil went for the bait. "So, what's all this got to do with where you've been the last few days?"

They sensed something coming when I held the moment. Even Carey looked up from his corner of couch. "Well guys, it's like this . . ." I suddenly turned serious. "The truth is, I'm a lot like Robert Johnson."

"You're like Robert Johnson." Fast Eddie wasn't buying it.

"I am." I played it straight.

"Okay." He sat back. "Let's hear it."

"Ever since I was young something's burned deep within me." I eyed them all with my soul's desire. "I've ached to make music."

"That's what I was afraid of," Fast Eddie said. "You've got the rhythm of a drunk chicken."

"I know. You guys have seen me. I can't sing, I can't play guitar, I don't have any good dance moves."

"I'll say," Shadrach joined in. "That time you tried to break dance you nearly broke a bone."

"That's what I'm saying. But the desire won't die. I still want to play the blues. As good as Robert Johnson did. So I went out and bought me one of these."

I pulled out my harp and fiddled with it like I wasn't sure which side was up. Fast Eddie settled in for some good comedy. "Oh, this is gonna be rich."

"This is gonna be ugly," Shadrach corrected.

The others looked equally ready to scoff. Carey just looked confused.

I proceeded to make a fool of myself by blowing and sucking a cacophony of notes much like a chimp might who stumbled upon a harp in the wild. The boys groaned.

"Do we have to watch this?" Shadrach begged.

"It's harder than you think," I said.

"I'm sure it is."

"But if you work at it . . ." I wrestled the harp into position then played a single clear 'C'-note.

"Not bad." Fast Eddie was sarcastic.

Shadrach was offended. "You've been away five days and that's the best you can do?"

"Now hold on," I pleaded. "I've worked up a little song." I strained out a rendition of "Mary Had a Little Lamb" that would have shamed parents at a kindergarten recital—a missed note here, a double note there, several seconds between notes as I took the harp out of my mouth and searched for the one I'd already missed three times.

Fast Eddie, Shadrach, and Malcolm each got in a shot. "So much for Robert Johnson." "His *dog* could play better than that." "He'll be returning from the dead just to shut you up." Virgil added the coda. "Now *that's* the devil's music."

"Wait a minute," I said. "I can do better." The boys showed no mercy when I did. As I forced the notes out, woodenly but at least in the right order, they clapped and catcalled in mock tribute, the whole lot of them whooping and hollering like a jeering section at a high-school basketball game.

All except Carey. Still slumped in the couch, he scanned the heckling room and realized what was going down. Nobody knew I could really play that thing. Nobody but him. I was still banging it out when our eyes met. He looked at me like we were the only two scholars in a room full of school-kids who got the song's literary allusions. For just a second, it was him and me. Then he pulled away. He stared at the floor as I finished the song.

The howling subsided. "I know," I admitted. "It's pretty lame."

"Lame!" Fast Eddie was insulted. "Somebody ought to shoot that thing and put us all out of our misery."

"That's exactly how I felt. Then I realized, if I'm going to impress you guys with my blues virtuosity, I gotta find me a teacher."

"Forget about it," Fast Eddie admonished. "You're only chance at virtuosity is . . ." It hit him—where this was going. "You're not selling your soul to the devil are you?"

"Not just yet," I said. "I'm just saying I've been looking for a teacher." The boys grew attentive—this could get interesting. "And it hasn't been easy. For the past few months I've crashed every blues band, jazz jam, and folk festival within a hundred miles of here and it's always been the exact same thing. I go up to this hotshot harmonica player and ask him if he'd teach me how to play. He tells me to show him what I got and I bang out 'Mary Had a Little Lamb.' Then he looks at me like I'm a circus act and he heckles me back to my truck. I've been everywhere—San Francisco, Sacramento, Pescadero, I even got kicked out of a square dance in Calaveras County. I couldn't get a single tip out of nobody and was just about to give up when a hippie in Bolinas told me about a tavern on the Russian River. If I couldn't find a teacher there, he said, then I didn't want one bad enough. So last week, I checked it out. I drove through the woods along the Russian River to a place called The Last Chance Saloon.

"The tavern was tucked in the trees like it was trying to hide from the road. The lot was packed, but a single space was open by the door. The inside was so smoky I couldn't see across the room. I made for the back, hunkered down in a booth, and pulled out my harp to be ready. The only music came from a busted-up radio behind the bar. Willie Nelson sputtered through the static in a country western twang. A waitress saddled up to the table, a cigarette hanging from her lips.

"'Where's the blues band?' I asked.

"'What's the matter,' she said, 'radio's not good enough for you?'

"'No. It's just that I came here to learn the harmonica.'

"She looked at me like I was a hick in a ballroom dancing class. 'The only music we got around here is what comes out of that box.' She looked at my harp and smirked. 'Let me tell you something, city-boy. If you can't appreciate the music right in front of you, you ain't never gonna make music of your own.' Then she snapped her pad shut and stomped away.

"So that was it, I thought. My last chance was a lost cause. I hoped to find a soulful bluesman but all I got was a sassy barmaid. How appropriate. My harp stared up from the table like it was laughing at me. I guess it was time to go home.

"Then her words hit me. Sometimes we get so caught up in making our own music we lose sight of the music sitting right in front of us. Like in the people we spend time with everyday. And maybe the only way to learn to play our own song is to love the song that's already playing in others. I needed a teacher alright, not to show me how to play blues, to show me how to live. And she taught me. 'If you can't appreciate the music right in front of you, you ain't never gonna make music of your own.'"

I pocketed my harp as if I was done then took in the circle of boys. They looked at me like I had to be joking—instead of a story taking on the devil I drop this Cosby Show morality tale? Surely I had something more. Please.

I did. But I let them hang a moment longer. Then I kept playing.

"That's when I heard him." The boys tensed with relief.

"'*I hear you want to learn blues harmonica.*'

"I looked behind me. An old man slouched in the shadows. He stared at a bottle steadied with two hands. With his tousled bleached hair and tattered Hawaiian shirt, he looked like a has-been surfer taken down by a monster wave to places so dark he'd spend the rest of his days drinking to forget about it. As he lifted his head, one eye straggled behind. When it caught up with the other I could see it was dead, the vacant bulb as dark as a haunted house.

"'*What I want to know is . . .*' the old man wheezed, '*how bad do you want to learn?*'

"'I want to learn pretty bad,' I said. 'I got these kids at work who'd think it pretty cool if . . .' His dead eye kept staring at me as the rest of his face looked down.

"'*Do you want to learn so bad you'd turn your back on your loved ones and wander the world alone?*'

"'I'm pretty much alone as it is, " I said to the eye as much as to the man. 'I mean, the kids keep teasing me about my honeys but . . .'

"'*Do you want to learn so bad you'd give up your lifesavings and walk the world in poverty?*'

"'I don't have much money as it is,' I told the eye. 'My line of work doesn't really pay . . .' The eye shut me up as the rest of the man's face rose. Two eyes, one living, one dead, looked straight at me.

"'*Do you want to learn so bad you'd travel to hell and sell your soul to the devil?*'

"To be honest I wasn't sure if this guy was deadly serious or seriously wasted. But something about him forced an answer.

"'Yeah, I guess I do.'

"His mutinous eye circled in its socket as if gathering strength from a diabolical power. Then it bore down upon me. '*Then this is what you gotta do. On the darkest night of the month, drive north up Highway 1 until you come to a deserted road that climbs up into the hills. The road will cross four rivers then lead you to a field with a 'No Trespassing' sign. From there you walk—across the field towards the sea, through a pathless forest, until you come to a bluff at the edge of a cliff. That bluff is the crossroads between Heaven and Hell. Stand at the cliff's edge with your back to the sea and take out your harp. At the precise stroke of midnight the devil will come up behind you. Whatever you do, don't turn to look. The face you see will kill you in an instant. Just give him your harp. He'll tune it to the key of evil. When he gives it back, think long and hard before you play. The second you touch it to your lips, you'll play blues as good as the devil himself. But you'll also have sealed the deal. From that moment on, your soul will belong to Satan.*'"

I had the boys now. Not only was this more like it, knowing damn well I couldn't play the harp, they had no idea how I was going to get out of it. I continued as if the memory still traumatized me.

"Well, last Wednesday happened to be the night of the new moon. Before I could chicken out I got into my truck and followed the old man's directions. Just like he said, a road angled off the highway and disappeared into the hills. I crossed the four rivers, found the field, and turned off my truck. Without a moon, the place was as dark as a tomb. I cautiously crossed the field and entered the woods careful not to rouse any wildlife. I need not have feared. Every living creature had long since abandoned that God-forsaken forest. I trudged through the dead trees, found the shadowy bluff, and inched my way to the very edge. The cliff fell straight down for a thousand feet. Waves crashed against the jagged rocks below. Nothing could survive those waters. Nothing could scale that precipice. I was one step from plunging into hell. I turned my back to the cliff. I pulled out my harp. And I waited.

"At the precise stroke of midnight, a breeze whistled up the cliff and slid down my back like ice. I tightened my coat and fought the temptation to look. I listened for a creature slithering out of the water, for a demon snaking up the precipice, for a cold breath hissing in my ear. But I couldn't hear a thing. I was alone. In the dark. At the edge of a thousand foot cliff. Finally, I had to laugh. That old man got me good. Like the devil was really . . .

"That's when I felt it. A skeletal hand touched my shoulder. A razor of breath slid down my back. A voice screeched in my ear.

"'*So you want to play my music . . .*'

"I was so scared I couldn't speak.

"'*Hand me your instrument.*'

"Shaking, I raised my harmonica. He reached for it and blew into each hole with his dead mouth. No sound came out. Ten blasts of icy breath, ten chills sliding down my spine, but not a single sound. When he finished blowing, he handed me back the harp. It was so cold I could barely hold it. The devil cackled in my ear.

"'*Play my music.*'

"I hesitated."

The boys strained forward as I lifted the trembling harp toward my mouth.

"'*Play my music, I say.*'

"I didn't know what to do. If I blew on the harp I'd become a great blues player but my soul would belong to the devil. If I refused, he'd grab me from behind and plunge me to certain death."

I eyed the boys as if my soul was still at stake. Satan was at my back. I had to choose. Seal the deal with the devil. Or die.

"'*Play . . . ,*' the devil shrieked in my ear. 'PLAY!!'

"So I did."

For a moment, I teased the boys with a slightly more polished "Mary Had a Little Lamb." They were disappointed, even as they figured that such would be the case.

Then I let it rip.

I reached back and played that nursery rhyme with every harp trick I knew. Mary's lamb took the ride of her life. I danced her around the meadows in flowing, effortless melodies; I swooped her down to hell and back with bending, bluesy riffs; I lifted her to the heavens with rising, rolling trills; I wailed and slid, shook and growled, tongue-slapped and throat-popped that children's ditty and transformed it into a blues bit worthy of Robert Johnson. The boys couldn't believe it. They had no idea I could play like that, no idea the harp *could* be played like that. For all they knew, I really *had* sold my soul away and was standing now before them both possessed and eternally damned.

When I finished, only Fast Eddie put words to his gawking. He asked as much as proclaimed, "Man, you were just messing with us."

"No, I'm telling you. I was as amazed as you guys. I was actually playing blues—faster than my mind could think, faster than my lips could blow. I couldn't have been more surprised if I had started speaking Latin. The only one *not* surprised was the devil, and he was still standing behind me as pleased as the papa of a newborn.

"'*Play your blues,*' he hissed. '*But always remember. Your soul belongs to me.*'

"Then I felt him leave. And as he floated down toward the sea, it hit me what I had done. I had sold my soul to the devil. Whenever he felt like it, he could crawl out from under the earth and snatch me away to hell. I had to know. What would he look like when he came after me? After all, what did I have to lose now?

"As he reached the bottom of the cliff, I heard a portal opening in the sea. I dared not look directly. But I found a way to glimpse him. I angled my harp so the plate reflected the portal. I watched through the mirror as the devil slid into the sea. Just as he passed, he looked up. For one cold second, I stared into the devil's eyes. The face I saw was nothing like what I expected. It was not a red demon with horns, not a gory monster with fangs, not some mutilated mask with all the evil features of Judas and Hitler and Charles Manson rolled up into one."

I scanned the circle of boys and caught myself before staring at Carey.

"No. It was the face of a young boy, sad and lonely, who missed the sound of soulful music.

"Then I watched as that face slipped silently into the watery bowels of hell."

The boys looked at me like I had sprouted horns. Then they shook off their ghost story creeps.

"Man, you had us good," Shadrach conceded. But he checked to be sure. "You did already know how to play that thing, right?"

"Of course he did," Malcolm said. "You believe in stories about the devil?"

"I don't know," Fast Eddie weighed in. "I've seen some stuff. How else did he learn to play like that?"

"He knew all along," Malcolm answered. "Didn't you?"

I held out a moment longer.

"Come on, Dr. T.," Blade pleaded. "You already knew, right?"

I finally gave in. "Yeah, I've played the harp for years. I just gave it up for a while."

Fast Eddie wasn't convinced. "I still think we should call a priest and exorcize your ass."

"You had us scared," Blade said. "That stuff's creepy."

"So none of that devil stuff happened?" Clint tried to catch up.

"No," I said. "It's just a story."

"But is it a *true* story?" Virgil asked coyly.

"Yes," I smiled. "It's a true story, even if it didn't happen."

"So are you saying that playing the harmonica is of the devil?" Clint was confused.

"No, of course not. But haven't you ever wanted to learn something so badly you'd do *anything* to be the best there is at it—like Robert Johnson's passion to play the blues?"

"Like what?" Clint asked.

"I don't know—maybe play basketball better than Michael Jordan or be the world's greatest break dancer." They puzzled over the question. "Think about it. If you had the chance to become the world's best at one thing, what would it be?"

"It wouldn't be playing blues," Fast Eddie declared. "There's some bad smack around that stuff."

"So what *would* it be?" I pressed.

"Nothing," he said. "Except score with the ladies."

"Great." I rolled with it. In this work anything can be a symbol for one's unconscious energies. "Fast Eddie would be the ultimate lady's man. Who else?"

"I'd create bombs to blow up bluffs." Shadrach was testing me. I took it.

"Shadrach would be the world's greatest demolition expert."

"How about a sword fighter?" Blade followed now that Shadrach cleared the way.

"That works."

"I'll become a Jedi master," Luke prophesied.

"Okay, you got the idea." I kept going. "Now, what if there was a person who had the chance to become what they passionately wanted, but on one condition—they had to go through the devil to get it? Would they do it, or walk away? And if they *did* do it, what would happen—would they outsmart the devil like Robert Johnson did, or would the devil come back and take the guy's soul forever? That's this week's theme. We're going to write stories about people who go toe to toe with the devil, just like the story I made up."

"What if the devil was Darth Vader," Luke offered, "and you meet him in a cave with your light saber?"

"That's fine," I said traipsing right over where that storyline led. "Run with it. Like always, we'll start with the characters. Today, everyone come up with two and a profile for each. The first is someone who wants to be the world's best at something. The other is the devil. What does *he* want, if it is a he, more than anything else in the world, and why? Tomorrow we'll write scenes where the two of them meet. Okay?"

Once dispatched, the boys retreated to writing refuges around the room. Shadrach and Fast Eddie fought over a note pad until Jody sent them to separate tables. Virgil remained in his recliner, his fertile imagination mulling over the possibilities. Carey sat next to him, as sunk in the couch as ever.

I placed a pad and pencil on the cushion at Carey's side. He didn't have to participate, I told him, but he was welcome to if he wanted. He stared at the blank page as if it was taunting him. Then he looked up. His eyes said it all.

'I've seen the devil too,' he was telling me. 'And I don't think we should be writing stories about it.'

22

I AM LYING IN my boyhood bed, my face to the wall, my back to the door.

Someone enters the room. She approaches my bed, peels my covers to my waist, and places her hand on my shoulder. Her touch tingles with both pleasure and dread. Tenderly, she draws me. I roll over. But as I turn she falls away. Like a body sinking into the ocean, she drifts back through the door, fades into the darkness beyond, then disappears through a distant pinhole of light.

I stare at the pinhole. The light slowly swells. The growing sphere crackles with flame. Gaining both speed and size, it races toward me like a fireball through a tunnel until it engulfs me in an explosion then blazes on past.

My room is charred. Blackness surrounds me. I stare at nothing.

I am lying in my boyhood bed, my face to the abyss, my back to a distant ball of rage.

"Any word from Salve Regina?" I came to work anticipating a response to my call from the day before. Carey needed clothes. I wanted his file.

"Nothing yet," Jody answered from her desk. "But I expect something soon. They were quite concerned about him."

"How's he doing?" I inquired.

"Another hard night," Irene offered. "He was so coiled up in his covers he looked like a linen corkscrew."

"Something's coming uncorked in that boy," Rose shot still miffed at Monday's story. Arms folded, she peered through the security-door window. "It won't stay bottled up much longer."

"Has he talked yet?" I asked.

"Not unless staring at the floor constitutes talking." Her curtness belied her concern. "Or twitching that finger like it's keeping him going."

"Maybe it is," I offered. She huffed at my naiveté and gently rubbed her eyes. "Is he in there now?" I continued.

"What d'ya think?" She sounded like my question was grounds for malpractice. I let it pass.

"I'll see if I can't help him feel settled."

"You might avoid stories about the devil," she warned, sizing me up with her weary eyes.

"I don't think it's the stories," I replied. "He's got a devil all his own."

"I'll give you that much," she said returning to the window. "That much, I'll give you."

———

Carey sat on the sofa, his arms at his side. For the moment, his finger was still.

"Good morning, Carey," I said as I sat in the chair beside him. "I hear you had a hard night. I hope the story yesterday wasn't too intense." He gave no indication it was any more intense than anything else in his life. "Well, I want you to know, we're on your side. We'll see you through anything, Carey. Anything."

Woody liked to tell a story about a prince who crawled under a table convinced he was a chicken. All the king's advisors tried to talk the boy out of it but the boy merely flapped his wings and chirped. So the king sent for the wisest man in the land. The man crawled under the table with the boy, poked around, and clucked. Cautiously, the prince clucked back. The man jerked his head, flapped his wings, and clucked some more. The prince clucked tentatively as if making sure they chirped in the same language. The man clucked on as if he knew exactly what the prince was chirping about. The prince studied the man, flapped a time or two, then clucked away as if recognizing an old friend from the henhouse. For hours the two chirped together—through the day, past dinner, and on into the night. Finally, exhausted and hungry, the prince stopped chirping. The man stopped too. Careful not to be heard, the prince leaned over and whispered in English, "I know where to get us some food."

The man replied in English as well. "Yeah?"

The prince nodded. "But here's the thing. To get it, we have to pretend we're human."

The man nodded back. "I'm in."

"Me too," said the prince.

And from that day forward, the two chickens pretended to be human.

I figured such would be the case with Carey. He'd talk on his own again if held in his silence long enough. I followed his lead and climbed under the table of his quiet. I brought my harp with me. So far, music was the one language through which we connected.

"If it's all right with you," I said after a while, "I'd like to try out a song. The guys were so jazzed about Robert Johnson I thought they'd enjoy hearing 'Crossroad Blues.' If you're up for it, that is."

I sensed his stillness as a sign to proceed.

I set the mood with a bluesy draw then settled into the melody. Spanning a continent and six decades, and the canyons of despair in between, I played us back to a poor country cotton-picker shadowing a Mississippi intersection. Standing with him through the music and aching for a song of our own, we companioned him—as he fell down on his knees and begged God to save him please, as the good Lord passed him by and didn't offer him a ride, as the sun sank down with his soul hung to dry until he drowned it in the swamps of the Evil One. The music seemed so right and Carey so receptive, I played it through a time or two again.

And as I played I wondered, like a steady bass beat in the back of my mind keeping time with the river of song. So who was the devil in Carey's story, feeding him the lie that evil can't be fought but through self-inflicted submission? Was it an interior predator—a sucking shade within the swampland of loss and depression? Or was he threatened by a more tangible phantom—a living hellhound whose violation he still knew and whose reach he still feared? I longed to help him battle his demons but I needed to know what they were. I needed an answer to the most life-or-death question in any of our spiritual journeys—who is the devil with whom we must deal in the shadowy stories of our lives?

Unfortunately, for the moment, Carey wasn't telling. He was only sitting with me, listening to a melody that posed us a riddle. Is it possible to take on the devil and live to sing about it—or would we be taken down by a darkness so deep it swallows every song?

The answer remained to be seen.

The morning quiet had yet to absorb the music's bluesy riddle when Ichabod Eichler dropped by again. I was grateful for the prompt reply.

"Thank you for coming so quickly," I greeted.

"Oh, of course," he sputtered as he jumped up from the sofa. "Monsignor asked me to bring this immediately." A bag crested with the school's insignia sat on the cushion beside him. He frowned with concern. "How's Carey doing?"

"Pretty much the same," I said. "Hasn't said a word." Eichler sat down as if too stunned to stand. I sat down as if in support. "He's an awfully good kid," I continued.

He winced in agreement. "He's as pliant a boy as you'll ever meet," he shared. "I've never conducted anyone like him. He follows my lead like a kite on a string. I take him up then watch him soar. It's beautiful." He blinked his way out of the reverie and fingered the cap in his hands. "I would never have believed him capable of violence—to himself or anyone. I wish there was something I could do."

"There is something," I said, seizing the moment. "You can tell me what you know about him."

"I don't know much," he replied. "Monsignor disapproves of getting close to the boys."

"You must know something," I prodded, "like when did he come to Salve Regina?"

He nodded with awareness of the information he had. "About a year ago. Monsignor went to a hearing with another of the boys and came back with Carey. I've never seen Monsignor so upset. When he sees a boy mistreated he can burn with the wrath of God. But this was different. He showed Carey to his room, which he does for *nobody*—he forbids preferential treatment. Then, when Carey declined coming down for dinner, Monsignor scolded the R.A. who tried to force him, then brought him up a tray himself. He never did it again. Carey had to conform like the rest. But that first night, he tended to Carey as if he was his own."

"Do you know why?"

"With Monsignor, it's hard to say. He's not exactly self-revealing. He cares for all the boys, don't get me wrong. But something about Carey touched him. And he tried a little harder to help him adjust."

"Did Carey—adjust?"

"Sure. He was quiet at first. But once he discovered he could sing, he opened up. Flourished really. Salve Regina's been a great home for him."

"What about his real family?"

He shuddered as if tasting curdled milk. "There's not much to tell there, believe me."

"How's that?"

"His dad's not around at all—in prison for something. And his mom." He looked around as if afraid of being heard. "Let's just say you don't want to be caught anywhere near her." He caught my eye to see that we understood each other. Then flustered that we did, he glanced back down at the cap he fingered.

"Does Carey see her?"

"I couldn't say," he answered, suddenly bothered.

"So why doesn't she have custody?"

"I couldn't say that either." He hid in his cap.

"Do you know how he was mistreated?" He looked at me confused. "You said earlier that the Monsignor was upset at how Carey was mistreated."

He was done. "You know, you really should talk to Monsignor about this."

"Okay," I said backing off. "Of course, it'll all be in his file."

"I'm sure it will."

I waited. "So do you have it?"

"Have what?"

"His file. I asked the secretary to send it."

He looked at me like this was news to him, then recovered. "Oh, his file. Monsignor gave it to me but I must have left it at school. I can mail it this afternoon."

"How about Federal Expressing it so I can get it tomorrow?"

"I can do that." He was still unnerved. "You know," he finally said, "Monsignor wouldn't want me disparaging Carey's mother like that. He doesn't tolerate gossip."

"It's okay," I reassured. "We're all on the same side here. We're trying to help a troubled boy."

"Yeah," he said still distressed, "but if it's all the same with you, let's keep that between us."

"Don't worry, Father."

He stood up like he wanted to flee. "I guess Carey's still not up for seeing anybody." I confirmed his hunch. "Then be sure to tell him we're looking out for him." He handed me the bag. Its weight surprised me. "Monsignor included some books with the clothes. He's of the mind that hard work is good medicine."

"Carey's in a pretty despairing place," I said. "He's not gonna be doing much studying for a while."

"All the same, I best leave them here." He fingered his cap before taking his leave. "You know, Monsignor has definite views on despair. He's preaching about it all week to the boys. You might drop by to hear him. He's quite the commanding orator."

"Thanks," I said. "But I keep pretty busy over here."

"All the same, Monsignor would want me to invite you."

"What you can do is Fed-Ex those files to me. That'll help a lot."

"Of course," he promised. "They'll be here tomorrow."

He lingered a moment unsure what to do. Then he stretched his cap to his head, laid his limp hand into mine, and bolted the hell out the door.

Judging by the speed of his step, it looked like he was the one eluding the devil.

———

Father Eichler was not the only one unnerved by nefarious forces. That night, the entire facility was rattled to the edge of hysteria.

Nothing throughout the day foreshadowed the clamor that was to come. I played 'Crossroad Blues' at the afternoon session then the boys compared takes on the devil. I sat with Carey after dinner and played my harp until his bedtime. Then I participated in Blade's bedtime ritual. Terrified of recurrent nightmares, he approached lights-out pacing his cabin and scratching himself like a man possessed. When Deacon flicked the switch, Blade rushed for the door. Deacon caught him as Blade pelted wildly with his fists and deformed finger. With professional deftness, Deacon followed assault response procedures. He turned Blade to the ground face down and pinned his flailing arms while I secured his thrashing legs. Deacon cooed soothing words until the demon surrendered Blade's body. Blade relaxed, sighed, and gradually controlled his panting. Then matter-of-factly he walked to his bunk and promptly went to sleep. Like I said, nothing unusual happened to foretell the approaching incident. With the boys asleep and the night nurse stationed, I headed home myself.

Rose blamed the rest on overactive imaginations after two days of devil stories. Willie chalked it up to a coyote wandering through the Mayacamus Mountains. The boys were convinced it was a diabolical madman breaking through the Box's back window. Whatever it was, both Rose and I were called out of bed at two. The boys were too worked up to calm down.

———

"You should have seen him, Dr. T." As soon as I entered the Commons, Blade dashed over and grabbed me at the knees. "I swear to God, I've never seen such a mean-looking man."

The others stormed me like a herd of spooked swine.

"He's telling the truth, Dr. T. I heard something too." Shadrach was backing up Blade for a change.

"So did I," Luke attested. "The dark side is near."

"Me too," Malcolm added. "And Clint actually saw him."

"I did," Clint confirmed, buoyed by his role as co-spectator. "Just barely. As soon as Blade yelled, I looked out the window. It was the devil I'm telling you. He just went invisible as he ran away."

"It wasn't the devil," said Shadrach. "It was that mountain-man murderer."

"Then how do you explain how cold it got?" Fast Eddie pushed.

"And the hissing I heard," Luke added.

"And the daggered fingernails . . ."

"Hold on guys." I had to rein them in or I'd lose them altogether. "Let's all take a deep breath and start this from the beginning. I'm sure there's a simple explanation here."

Once back in a chair, Blade, the key eyewitness, began.

"Okay. I woke up and went to the bathroom."

"That's true." Clint had the top bunk to Blade's bottom. "I heard him get up and come back to bed."

Several boys nodded. Clearly they had debated the finer points for the twenty minutes it took me to get there. Separating the real truth from the imagined would take some time.

"When I got back into bed," Blade continued, "I heard something behind the Box. I looked out the window and there he was. He was huge. As big as a giant. With pure evil in his eyes. I screamed when I saw him and he ran away. I've never been so scared in my life."

"I'm telling you, it was the devil," Clint insisted.

"No it wasn't," Shadrach rebutted. "The devil wouldn't run away from Blade."

"How do you know?" Fast Eddie countered. "Dr. T. says the devil doesn't like to be seen."

"He also said you'd die if you saw the devil," Shadrach rebutted. "Blade didn't die."

"I don't know," Blade considered, calmed but still spooked. "It could've been the devil, or the mountain-man murderer. I couldn't tell which."

"What do you think, Dr. T.?" Fast Eddie asked. "Was it the devil or the mountain-man?"

"To be honest," I said, "I'm not ruling out a very vivid nightmare."

"No way," Malcolm argued like a prosecutor. "Too many people heard it. Clint even saw it."

"Even so," I continued. "The devil doesn't just show up in your backyard. And the mountain-man murderer you guys made up. Those mountains are deserted."

"That's where you're wrong," Shadrach claimed. "There are some creepy things out there."

"I'll say," Luke confirmed.

The boys' terror of the wooded hills behind us continued to amaze me. All wolverine bravado within our own walls, they wouldn't chase down a lost ball in those badlands. They so populated them with wild animals, nightmarish monsters, and one-eyed beasts that feed on their young you would have thought that the hills hid the fountainhead for all the rivers of hell. Blade could have seen a squirrel out his window and insisted it was a cannibal hell-bent on blood.

"My guess is you're right," I conceded. "It *was* a creature from the hills. Like a deer. Or maybe a fox. Who knows, it could have been a stray dog."

"I never heard of a dog breaking into a building," Shadrach refuted.

"Maybe not," I said. "But in all the years that people have inhabited these parts, not once has anyone seen this mountain-man murderer. And believe me, the devil doesn't make house calls."

"No," Clint responded. "But he does come after his own. You said so yourself."

"Clint," I implored, "it wasn't the devil. The devil doesn't exist."

"Maybe not," Virgil broke his thoughtful silence. "But it's like your stories. The devil's real, even if he is made up."

We all jumped when the side door slammed open. Deacon stomped in with his flashlight still beaming. A former football player that anchored the line at USC, he was an imposing figure himself.

"Did you catch him?" Shadrach spoke for the group.

"Nope," he said. "There's nobody out there *to* catch."

"Did you see him?"

"Nope. There's nobody out there *to* see."

"Did you find his footprints?"

"Nope. There's no footprints *to* find."

"Well, the devil wouldn't leave footprints," Clint explained. "He's magic."

"Nope. It wasn't the devil neither. I know *exactly* what it was?"

"What?" Shadrach asked.

"Catch a look at this. Found it right outside the Box." Deacon pulled out a plastic honey jar with a gash ripped through it. "And not just this. A whole lot of garbage was trashed around the cans. Somebody didn't bolt down the lids. We had us a bear. A pretty hungry bear by the looks of it."

The boys pondered the evidence like a jury would a smoking gun. Deacon sealed the case with a gauntlet. "I'm happy to take you out and show you if you want." He turned toward the door.

"It's not necessary," Fast Eddie jumped in not about to go out in the dark. "It seems clear enough to me."

"That explains the size," Malcolm affirmed. "And the noise."

"Well I did only see it from the back," Clint conceded.

With that, the verdict was decided. Our intruder was a bear.

Deacon later told me that he made it all up. Finding nothing suspicious outside, he knew that only hard evidence would get the boys back into bed. The subterfuge worked. As the explanation soaked in so did the fatigue. Led by their caretakers, the boys returned to their bunks.

Only Blade hung back. With his hands planted on the upholstered chair's arms, he stared dead ahead like a marbled god of truth. I feared another night terror. We'd had enough visitations from demons already.

But Blade was self-possessed. He gazed sphinx-like into space until all was quiet in the cabins. He wasn't considering Deacon's evidence. He knew better than the bit about the bear. Something more important was bothering him. Sustaining his stare, he revealed what he knew with the clarity of a demoniac whose mind's been restored.

"I don't know Dr. T. It might have been the devil, or a mountain-man murderer, or maybe just some huge guy. But one thing I do know. He was coming after one of us.

"And the one that he wanted, was Carey."

———

In all the commotion, I had forgotten about Carey. I looked for the night nurse to get a report.

The nurse's station, though lit, was vacant. The locked unit on the far side was dark. I walked by the desks and passed through the security door. At first, I saw nothing. Then Mrs. Hawthorne appeared, sitting alone in the shadowed corner. Her terror kept her tears in check.

I peered into the darkness of Carey's bedroom to my left. His cot, though slept in, was empty. I looked back at Mrs. Hawthorne.

"Where's Carey?" I mouthed.

She nodded at his room. I crept toward the door. I could not see him. Until I stepped through.

He was on the floor to my right, curled in the corner, as far from the window as he could get. His face pale, his twitch out of control, he looked like he had just seen a ghost and the only thing driving it back was the furious flicker of his finger.

Fortunately, he was not alone. Sitting on the floor as well, Rose held him to her chest like a mother would a toddler through a nightmare. Her eyes looked up. In them I could see. She was long past criticizing my treatment plan, petitioning for Carey's transfer, or advocating for her own hands-off healing methods. She simply ached for the boy in her arms. And she wanted reassurance from his doctor that his demons could be expelled.

I wanted to give it. But I didn't even know what they were.

One thing was certain, though. Carey heard the same noise as the others. And his conclusions matched those of Blade.

Whatever it was out there, it was coming after him.

23

"WHO DO I HAVE to call on to get through to these people?" I ranted into the nurse's station.

"What people?" Irene asked.

"All of Peckham's minions." It was Wednesday afternoon and Carey's file hadn't come. "They're all scrambling around slamming doors in my face. Eichler won't say more than his secretary Fed-Exed the file yesterday. The secretary says the school counselor has it. The counselor won't confirm or deny because all inquiries have to be cleared through the Monsignor. I tell him I'm the psychologist who's trying to help the boy; he says it doesn't matter, nothing goes on without the Monsignor's permission. Who in the hell is this guy, J. Edgar Hoover? It'd be easier to get the files for the Kennedy assassination."

"Have you tried the Monsignor directly?" Jody suggested.

"Are you kidding? He's been in meetings all morning, now he's lunching with donors. His secretary swore he'd call me the second he gets back, by 1:15 at the latest. But of course that was thirty minutes ago."

"Sounds like his reputation," Irene said knowingly.

"I'll say," I said.

"Who is he?" Jody inquired.

"Someone who thinks he's the Father Flanagan of Sonoma County," I answered.

"Schuyler Peckham," Irene explained. "He came to Salve Regina back when it was Mater Dolorosa. The place was a shambles back then. He changed the name and everything else. Raised lots of money, renovated the facilities, turned it into a prestigious Catholic prep school for at-risk kids. I dare say—he does get results. Most of them go onto college."

"And he's done it all with style," I added. "Which has been quite controversial. Depending on who you talk to he's either a high-brow liberator or a cultural elitist."

"Do you know him?" Jody asked me.

"Never met him. But if . . ."

The phone rang.

"It's about time," I said.

I picked it up. All Irene and Jody could hear from my end was, 'You're kidding . . . *You're kidding* . . .' then a curt 'Fine, I'd appreciate that.' I hung up.

"You're not going to believe this. That was Eichler. Turns out he not only had the file all along, it was out in his car the whole time he was here. This is unbelievable."

"Is he sending it?" Irene asked.

"On his mother's honor, he swears it'll be here by morning. It better be. If it's not, I'm driving out there to get it myself."

I said it with such certainty, I almost believed I'd go through with it.

———

Waiting another day for more clues about Carey seemed interminable. Here was a trauma-tized boy in my care and I didn't know if I was treating chronic dysthymia from parental abandonment or episodic suicidality provoked by bad grades. I returned to my office and called the psychologist who sent him to us. Dr. Carter was surprised to hear from me.

"What a coincidence," she said. "I was just speaking with the sheriff handling the case."

"Sheriff?" I was surprised. "Is there a criminal investigation?"

"Oh no. It's clear what happened. But a child with a knife wound—they've got to file a report." That made sense. "Actually, I was going to call you. We still can't find a bed for him. Could he stay with you through the weekend, maybe the middle of next week?"

"Of course," I said. "But if he's going to be here that long, it would help to know more about his history."

"I wish I could help you. You might try the Boy's Home."

"I did. They're sending his records. I just thought you might have something more."

"Not really." She put her hand on the receiver and called out to somebody. "I'm sorry," she said when she got back, "I have to go. You might talk to the sheriff's department. They seem on top of it."

"I will. Thanks."

"Thank you, Dr. Backman. For taking him. You're helping us a lot."

"No problem."

———

Sheriff Thomas was out of the office. I left a message with the dispatcher. With my sources exhausted and the boys still at school, I had time to check in on Carey. We gave him sleep-ing pills after the night's turmoil. He slept through most the morning. Now he sat in the locked unit with hollow eyes and a flicking finger still unable to wind down. He neither blinked nor broke the beat as I sat down beside him.

"That was quite a night we had, wasn't it?" I said. "Whatever that was outside, it sure spooked everybody." I still had no idea if it was an animal or a strong wind blowing brush against the building. It didn't matter. Either way, it externalized Carey's fears. His feelings were overwhelming, and he was terrified at their power. What he really needed was to express the furies within.

"I realize, Carey, that you're not ready to talk yet, or write a story during afternoon groups. It can take a while for our feelings to find words. But sometimes our body says things before our words are ready. I can't help but think that your finger is trying to tell us something—maybe that something terrifying's trying to attack it, or that it's so mad it wants to attack back. You might just draw a picture, of what you're finger is feeling. Not right now. When you're ready. I'd sure like to know."

His finger kept flicking like it sustained his dissociation. It wasn't going to be talking soon. Not until he felt completely safe.

Then I got an idea.

"Hey Carey. Why don't we check out the backyard? Nobody's sure what it was last night. Maybe we can find some clues."

That broke through. He looked at me like I suggested we enter hostile territory.

"It'll be fine," I reassured. "I'll be with you the entire time."

He lowered his eyes to consider it.

"It's up to you Carey. But it might help you feel safer."

He weighed the dangers.

Then he stood up.

———

There wasn't much to Crossroads' backside. About fifty yards of chaparral separated the buildings from the mountains' wooded slopes. A small garden ringed a live oak where Willie and Deacon often relaxed in the shade—Willie gabbing away and carving wood while Deacon puffed a pipe in silence. At the moment, the garden was empty.

He first, me following, Carey and I wandered through the entire back lot. He was as systematic as a detective inspecting a crime scene. Searching for both tracks and hiding places, he scoped out the hills as far as he dared, then followed the fire-road down toward the parking lot. From the front corner of the main building, he scanned the acres of vineyards that adjoined us, the distant highway they stretched out to, and the breadth of horizon beyond. His finger keeping time with his reconnaissance, he doubled back through the back chaparral, circled the garden at the center, then made for the far side of the building. He stopped before the Box's bedroom wall.

The siding was California stucco with a window the size of a sliding-glass door made of smoky Plexiglas bricks. The window could not be seen through—at best it permitted a wash of diluted sunlight by day, or an opaque shape of shade if someone passed by at night.

Carey examined the entire wall. He tested the strength of the Plexiglas tile, studied the cracks for signs of forced entry, and scowered the base for footprints. Finding a limb lying dead in the dirt, he poked through the surrounding bushes, then returned to the window, held the limb like a staff, and stared with absorbed stillness.

For several moments he did not stir. Then slowly, he circled to take in the panorama around him. With a searching gaze that peered high into treetops and low into bushes, he scrutinized the surroundings as if certain someone was out there. From the fire road to the east, through the woods to the north, on past the reformatory fenced to the west, he perused every cranny, probed every shadow, and pored over every crevice until his circle of scrutiny was complete and he faced the window once more.

He glared as if the tiles were taunting him. Gradually, his breathing grew labored. His grip on the stick tightened. He lips pursed; his head shook; he looked as if ready to spit.

Then he snapped. Before I could stop him, he swung the limb like an axe and smacked the window straight in the face.

"Carey," I screamed, foreseeing shattered glass.

But he was in a zone of his own. Though the stick cracked, he swung it again, pelting the tile like a thug bent on murder, splintering the wood with each pummeling blow until it split at his fist and he slashed as if wielding a knife. I had no idea the villain that Carey was assaulting—maybe the window itself for its vulnerability to attack, or the specter of the predator still watching from the woods, or maybe it was Carey himself, crashing the wall to get to the boy cowering in the corner of the room. Whatever it was, it bore his full fury as he stabbed and pounded the concrete glass until I timed an intervention and ducked in to grab him.

"It's okay," I consoled as I disarmed him from behind careful to avoid his wrists. "Let it go. It's gone now. You're okay."

As quickly as it swelled, it subsided. Carey yielded to my embrace, dropped the stick in his hand, and settled into a panting stupor. The fit having passed, I released him.

"Are you alright?" I asked. "I was worried you would break a bone. That stuff's hard." If he was hurt he didn't show it. He stared at the tile as if the beating became it. "It's good to let out your feelings," I affirmed. "We've got a better place for it though—a room with pads and clubs. You can pound for as long as you want there, without getting hurt."

He wasn't interested. He was done. I turned to the wall he stared at and tapped it with my hand. It was as solid as a fortress. I understood how he felt. I had been there myself. "Well I know what you mean," I said. "Sometimes the world needs a good beating. It's good to know it can take it."

Carey didn't respond. He simply kept staring. For the moment, his finger was still.

I guess it had had its say.

———

After the afternoon session with the boys, I had a message from the sheriff. A woman answered the phone.

"Can I speak with Sheriff Thomas?" I asked.

"This is she."

"Oh." I was a bit surprised.

"What, didn't expect a woman?"

"No, I just . . ."

"Didn't think a woman could wear a badge?"

"*No*. I just . . ."

"What?"

"I . . . expected . . ."

"Well expect differently next time."

It took me a moment to get it. "You're right," I said. "Old assumptions die hard."

"What's hard is not being taken seriously as a cop."

"It must be rough."

"You don't know the half of it."

"I'm sure I don't."

She sighed but was still on edge. "Look, I'm sorry for snapping. You just caught me at a bad time. What can I do for you?"

"I'm calling about Carey Foster."

"You know Carey?" She lightened immediately.

"Yes. I'm the psychologist working with him at the residential facility."

"How's he doing?"

"He's pretty shaken up. He's not talking at all. Dr. Carter thought you could help me figure out what's going on with him."

"About all I know is, he's one troubled boy."

"What's your investigation turned up?"

"The case is pretty routine. He was found with severe lacerations on both wrists. Every indication is they were self-inflicted."

"Where was he found?"

"In his bedroom at school."

"Who found him?"

"Another student. Lucky for Carey, the boy hadn't done his homework. He snuck into Carey's room to copy his."

"Do you know why he cut himself?"

"Not really. He was well liked at school and doing fine in his classes. Monsignor Peckham said he had a history of mental illness. That could explain a lot. Apparently his home life was hell. He was taken from his mother and hadn't seen her in months. I guess it got to be too much for him. It happens a lot I'm afraid."

"Don't I know," I said. "But it still doesn't add up. One of his teachers said he was on top of the world just a few hours before. Something must have happened in between."

"If you find out," she offered, "I'd love to hear. I've seen a few suicides in my time, but never one like this."

"How's that?"

"Well, the ropes for starters."

"What ropes?"

"You didn't know? He tied himself down in his bed—his feet crossed at the bottom, his arms off to either side."

That didn't make sense. "If he tied himself down, how could he cut himself?"

"He tied the ropes first, cut himself, then slipped his hands into the knots he'd already tied. The ropes weren't tightened. They were just for show."

"I don't get it."

"No? He was crucifying himself."

"Oh my God." My stomach sickened.

"He didn't just *want* to die," she surmised. "His sins were so bad he *deserved* to die."

I needed a moment to take it in. "Or maybe he was carrying somebody else's—you know, the Lamb of God that takes away the sins of the world."

"I don't think so," she shared. "Not with what he said to me."

"When did he talk?"

"That night. I arrived just after the paramedics. The place was chaos—kids gawking in their bedclothes, medics treating his wrists, priests untying his feet and applying pressure to the wounds. I rushed in to secure the scene and he looked straight at me. I would have expected him to be faint with all the blood everywhere. But in fact, he was quite lucid. He must have noticed my uniform because he just stared at me with those lonely eyes. Then he spoke as if I was the only one in the room. I'll never forget it. In the middle of all that bedlam, him stretched out like Jesus on the cross, he singled me out, and cut me to the bone with words that said it all."

"What did he say?" I asked.

She hesitated before she whispered. "'Close your eyes,' he said. Then he said it again. "'Close your eyes.'"

Before I left for home, I looked in on him. I wanted to tell him I had business in the city the next day and wouldn't be in until afternoon. He sat at the table in the locked-unit's lounge. The paper in front of him was blank.

I didn't speak as I sat beside him. I just turned it over in my mind. Where did such an innocent boy get the idea he had to die for his own sins?

As usual, he wasn't saying. His only words were the appeal he made to one whose job was to protect him. Well it's my job too, I thought. And this time I'm not listening. Whatever it is we need to take on together, I'm not going to close my eyes.

"I'll see you right here tomorrow," I said as I left. I knew that he'd be there upon my return.

Something else had better be there too. If the file wasn't delivered by the time I got back, I swore.

I'd drive out to the school and get it myself.

24

❝PRAISE BE TO ATHENA," my mentor exclaimed. "I hardly recognize you from last week."

A lifetime had passed since I'd last seen Woody. "But tell me," he twinkled from his office doorway, "is this the real you, or the beggar in disguise?"

"Not to worry," I came back in kind. "Last week was the shipwreck. This week, I'm taking on the suitors."

He laughed as he played the allusion out. "Don't tell me you've been to hell and back."

"Down to the bottom and took on the devil."

"Why do I sense a story coming?" he reveled.

"'Cause what's the point of going down if you don't get to tell about it?"

"Get in here," he bid. "I want to hear it all. From Calypso to Ithaca."

I sat in the office where, seven days earlier, I had dragged myself ashore like a storm-tossed sailor. If I didn't have the swagger of a hero home from exile, I at least had the shine of the Cracker Jack apprentice who just aced the pop quiz.

"I can't thank you enough for these stories," I said, returning Woody's collection of Underworld myths.

"So they pointed the way?" he asked.

"They did better. They inspired my own story—'Tony Backman Plays the Blues after Selling his Soul to the Devil.'"

Beguiled by the possibilities, Woody settled in for a good tale. I gave it to him, leaving nothing out. Robert Johnson's crossroad's rendezvous, my melodramatic butchering of Mary's little lamb, the Underworld episode at the Last Chance Saloon, the cliffside encounter with Satan on the bluff, the boys' shock at my sudden blues wizardry, he relished it all with rapt attention. By the time I sailed into the ending, he absorbed my every word like a seer who discerns the hidden mysteries.

"So here I am, I tell them, as amazed as they are at what just came out of my harp, when the devil decides to go back to hell. But now I'm curious. He's going to come back and claim me someday, and I want to know what he looks like. So I angle my harp toward the portal in the sea, and just as he passes, I catch his reflection. The face I see astounds me. It's not a red demon with horns, nor a monster with fangs. It's the face of a boy, with sad lonely eyes, who misses the sound of soulful music."

Woody cocked his eyes at the surprise revelation then clapped his hands in salute. "That's an amazing story," he marveled.

I radiated like a king restored to full glory. I had a storyteller's afterglow, my mentor's adoration, and the redemption of hitting the cover off the ball after a recent bad outing at the plate.

"And that's just the story," I said, still on a roll. "Then I got the boys imagining their own life's desires and the devils to be encountered in fulfilling them. Now they're writing their own Underworld myths."

"What a great idea." He got it immediately. "The devil's the perfect image for externalizing the shadow, then they claim their vitality in the face of it. It's brilliant."

"Well, it's the method that's brilliant," I said, suddenly self-conscious of my pride. "I'm just riffing off what I was taught."

"But the riffs are inspired," Woody came back, returning the volley of our mutual admiration. "These boys are accessing internal resources to manage their personal demons. It's quite ingenious." I had to admit, I relished his praise. He let me bask in it a while longer. "What are they coming up with?"

"Their stories run the gamut really. In one, the devil turns this nerd into a Don Juan who can score with any lady he chooses. The twist is that the devil's a woman, the only woman who can resist the Don Juan's charms. After cruising the world for a few years, the guy gets bored and realizes that the only woman he wants is the devil. So he goes down to hell, which is this female Playboy mansion, and works all his moves to no avail. Finally, one of the handmaidens betrays the devil's weakness—the world's most romantic flower that only grows on the earth's tallest mountain. So he hikes over, picks a bouquet, and returns to the mansion like a prom-date with a corsage. They dance, he pins the corsage, and they fall in love. It ends with the devil winking to her handmaiden. Turns out it was all a setup. She loved this guy from the beginning.

"Another is from our resident poet who's writing an epic to his dead mother. The devil is this fundamentalist minister who gives the guy the power to write the most beautiful poem in the world, but with a catch. It cannot contain a single word of vulgarity. The problem is, the poem the poet writes is *beautiful*, but it isn't *true*, because the truth can't be censored. So he writes this obscenity-laced exposé that mocks the fundamentalist minister. The incensed devil leaves the pristine chapel of hell and hunts for the poet in this inner-city slum of a writer's colony. Along the way, the minister has to tiptoe over all the homeless and alcoholics because if he merely touches filth his devilish powers wither away. Finally the devil reaches the poet's lair only to find out it's a trap. A band of child prostitutes and drug addicts pounce on him and imprison him in the city's cesspool where every swear word ever spoken is turned to shit and flushed. And since there's a whole lot of truth that needs to be told, the minister's going to be wallowing in it for some time to come."

Woody was impressed. "These are creative kids."

"They are," I agreed. "They've come a long way in two years."

"It's amazing, isn't it?" he mused. "How the imagination makes meaning out of painful experience. Their deepest issues are in those stories."

"It's even more obvious when you know these guys," I confirmed. "They're opening their lives through these stories."

"And not just opening them," he added. "They're discovering their personal power through them. You're doing a great job, Tony."

"Thanks." I stared down as the warmth of his affirmation washed over me. Then came the chill. "I do have one problem, though. We have this new boy, he's only eleven. He cut up his wrists something fierce, I mean he was serious. Both arms, from his elbows to his hands. You should see him, Woody. He's the gentlest boy I've ever seen. And apparently he's this amazing singer, a soloist in a Boy's Choir. But right now, he's absolutely mute, hasn't said a word in nearly a week with us. He just sits in a chair and stares at the floor like he's sorry for taking up space in the world. I have no idea what's bothering him or even how long he'll be with us, but we made this connection. You should have seen his eyes after I told this story. He knew *exactly* what I was talking about—yearning to find your song, but having a devil to go through to claim it. I've got to find a way to help him. Do you have any ideas?"

Woody nodded as he listened. I thought he was taking the threads I spun and weaving a lifeline for Carey. Little did I know. He was coiling the ropes with which I would hang myself.

"I guess what I'm curious about is," he offhandedly misdirected, "what's been going on with you? Last week you were having a hard time caring anymore, now you're determined to help this boy. What's happened?"

Whatever this had to do with Carey, I knew we'd get to me eventually.

"Actually, something big happened," I admitted. "I told you once that I lost a child when I was married. As I was thinking about what you were saying, the demons I needed to dine with, I realized I never grieved his death. I just locked it all away. So on Sunday, I drove out to the place where he was conceived, and I said goodbye to him. It was pretty powerful, really. I brought a bunch of baby things, made a memorial, played him a lullaby. And for the first time, I cried for him."

Woody held my words as one who's cried through a few goodbyes of his own. "It must be excruciating to lose a child like that." I nodded. "I can see why you've been carrying it around for so long." I nodded some more. Then he wondered, "That place you went, it wasn't by chance the bluff in your story, was it?"

I squirmed as if caught with my pants down. He was good. "As a matter of fact, it was."

"Well, that only makes me all the more curious," he continued, "about something I wanted to ask you before."

"What's that?"

"The boy in the story, on the face of the devil, who is he?"

"It's nobody. It's just a story."

"Sure, but you know as well as I do, these stories come from *some*place."

I should have seen this coming, hoisted by my own narrative petard. I knew the drill. He had me. "Okay," I played along. "Let me think. Yeah, I guess you're right. Maybe it *is* Daniel. My devil's been my own boy, longing to be remembered after all these years."

"That seems like an obvious connection," he concurred.

"Yeah," I agreed. "It rings true."

"But I have to say," he continued, "I'm not sure it was only Daniel you saw in that devil."

"What do you mean?"

"Who else could the boy be?"

"Come on, Woody," I cautioned. "You're reaching now. I can buy that I made an association with Daniel, but that's it."

"That's the thing about stories, isn't it? They work on multiple levels."

"What are you getting at?" I suddenly felt like a psych patient being considered for an involuntary hold.

"I'm wondering," he prodded, "if the boy is you."

"Now Woody, don't go making more out of what's really there."

"Maybe I am, but what's the harm in playing around?" Woody was gentle but persistent, like a deep tissue massage therapist caressing a muscle before bearing down with the pressure that blinds you with pain. "Imagine for just a moment that the boy longing to hear his song *was* you. Who would the devil be in his life?"

I spit my response. "You've got the wrong boy, Woody."

"Stay with me," he pressed. "What was the first thing that popped into your head? Something hit you."

"Look. I haven't seen my dad in over ten years. I have long since left that hell."

"What was so demonic about your dad?"

"Are you kidding? He was a monster. Violent, vindictive, he terrorized us."

"He abused you?"

"Not physically. He never touched us. But emotionally? He was downright sadistic. Maybe not so much to me, but my mother, he despised her."

"So if this boy went to the crossroads, and his father came up behind him, what would he want from him?"

The very image of that bastard behind me made me recoil. "You've got it wrong, Woody. I want nothing from that man."

"Stay with it a second."

"*I told you!* I don't want *anything* from him."

He held me with his eyes. Then he gently pressed again. "What do you want from him?"

"*Fine!* I want an accounting. That's what I want. I want a fucking accounting."

"For what?"

"For hating us so much. Me, for wanting to be with my mother. My sister, for wanting to be out of that house. My mother, for being alive at all. I want him to finally account for himself."

"Have you ever asked him for one?"

I stared at Woody like *he* was the Prince of Darkness. "Are you insane? My father is pus. I'll be damned if I ever look at that boil of a man again." I turned away as if he were there. How in the hell did we get into all this? I just wanted to tell Woody I was back in the game, and secure some professional advice. Why did he have to dredge all this up?

"Look, Woody. It's dead and buried. My dad no longer exists." I stood to go. Then I scolded him. "If you'll excuse me, there's a boy who needs my help."

Even as I said it I knew.

He was trying to help the boy.

Both of them.

25

"He's coming uncorked, I tell you. We're going to lose him."

"That doesn't mean you just dope him up, Rose."

"I'm not trying to dope him up—Dr. Carter should be consulted." She was indignant.

"You should've talked to me first. You don't just call in the psychiatrist behind my back."

"You didn't see him unravel, Tony. A child's ego is fragile."

"Don't lecture me about a child's ego. He's a long way from a psychotic break."

"How do you know? You weren't there."

"Well I am now. And I'll take it from here." I turned to leave. Then I remembered. "What about his file from Salve Regina?"

"It hasn't come yet. They're sending it tomorrow."

"*Goddamn it!* Doesn't *anybody* care about this kid?"

Rose glared. "We care, Tony. And caring means putting *him* first."

I glared back. But I didn't say it. My obvious rejoinder wasn't worth the effort. I turned my back and made for the Box.

——

As far as I could gather, Carey went ballistic while outside with Deacon. The two were out for air when Carey wandered down the fire-road and gazed toward the highway. Something either flashed into his field of vision or bubbled up from his subconscious for all of a sudden his face contorted with terror and he fled as if being chased. He tripped in the dirt, recoiled at Deacon's aid, then eluded all captors by bolting for the building. Without slowing down, he sped for the padded room and hurled himself against the wall, turned, raced, and hurled into another, then still another, exploding into walls throughout the room until, flinching in circles with fright, he circumrotated around the center as if assailants advanced from all sides. Whatever they were, they must have oozed from the walls, for he attacked again, flicking both middle fingers along one wall, then another, as if picking off spiders seeping through the pads, snapping with increasingly frantic abandon until, all but running around the room, he finally spent himself and stumbled into the corner. Deacon locked him in; Irene watched from the window; Rose called in the psychiatric cavalry—only Carter could determine a need for meds.

When I spied him through the window, I saw why Rose was alarmed. He looked crazed beyond all connection with reality. His finger flicked absently in futile exhaustion. His mind sought refuge in a world far away.

———

He did not return from his distant retreat as I quietly entered the room. I slipped the door closed, then eased to the floor careful not to rile him. I did not have a plan, only my presence. And a need to find respite of my own. Everything swirling with gale-force ferocity, the padded-room seemed opportune.

The room had an electric stillness about it, like the charged calm that follows a lightning storm. The quiet gave me space to think. Carey's checked-out terror gave me a reason to. Why was my every move undermined, as I tried so hard to reach him? The school, Rose, even Woody poking at my personal life, all seemed determined to resist me. Carey too rebuffed my efforts, even as his body screamed to be understood. Why couldn't they see I was on his side? Could it be that I really wasn't—that I was mixing him up not only with Daniel but me in the face of my father? And if so, just what in the hell should I do?

We sat in the squalls of our respective tempests, he eddied in one corner, I in the other. We swirled without bearings and took on water as we waited for the beacon that would point us the way.

He was the first to see it.

Slowly emerging from his hypnotized refuge, Carey turned his head and stared at my side. I turned to see what engaged him. He studied my hand. Without my realizing it, my middle finger mimicked Carey's tic. Apparently, my body needed to voice its turmoil, too. So it picked up the twitch, the flick at the world that seemed to say it all.

I considered the tic. Then I spoke.

"My finger's saying, 'I'm scared. Things are coming at me from all sides and I don't know what to do. Please, will somebody help me?'"

Like a wind-up toy that had spun itself out, Carey's flick slowed, then stilled. Mine stilled as well. Then he looked up. His eyes looked scared as they studied me.

'Who's it going to be?' they seemed to ask.

My eyes held the only answer I had.

'I don't know.'

———

It was time to make right by Rose. For the first time in two years, she sat out in the garden.

"I'm sorry I jumped on you," I said after sitting in the shade beside her. "I know you only did what you thought best for Carey."

"Is he feeling better?" She was unusually pensive.

"He's quiet anyway."

She absorbed the garden's cathedral calm. Then she whispered as soft as a prayer.

"You have a gift, Tony. You really are great with these kids. But sometimes the best way to help is not to help so much."

I absorbed the calm as well. "I don't know Rose. Maybe he would be better off elsewhere."

"That's just it," she confessed. "Maybe he wouldn't."

———

Dr. Carter had trouble getting away. She didn't arrive until well after groups. Carey opted out of them anyway, though he joined us for the consultation. He sat at the head of the locked-unit table like a boy so forlorn he didn't care what was to become of him. Carter and I sat on his either side. Rose sat next to me.

"I just came by to see how you're doing," Carter said to Carey. "And talk about where you should stay. I hear you've had a rough couple of days."

Carey stared down, his hands in his lap. His only response was his finger's flick.

"I guess the main thing I need to know is," she continued, "do you feel safe here?"

Carey didn't stir. The mute sanctuary of his inner world seemed all the safety he knew.

Carter gave up. "He really should be at Ross," she said to Rose and me. "Or St. Mary's. But they simply don't have any beds. The only other possibility is to take him back to the hospital. I'd hate to do that, but there aren't many options. And if he's not feeling safe here . . ." She trailed off with indecision.

Carter held the cards so I was careful how I responded. I didn't want to sound defensive. "There may be another way to look at his behavior," I suggested. "Perhaps he's been so expressive because he *is* feeling safe here."

"That's the question, isn't it?" she puzzled. "Whether his acting out is cathartic release or damaged impulse control."

"Or a veiled attempt to communicate with us." I was shocked to hear this coming from Rose.

"He's so dissociated," Carter dismissed, "I don't see how any of his behavior can be an attempt to communicate."

"On the contrary," Rose came back, "Dr. Backman's work recognizes every bodily impulse as a form of communication, no matter how arbitrary it might appear."

"He couldn't be any more *in*communicative," Carter rebutted.

"I'd have to disagree." Rose sounded like a disciple defending her teacher's work. "The twitch in his finger is certainly expressive."

"His twitch is an involuntary anxiety reaction," Carter contradicted. "Hardly Morse code." She looked to me to see if I condoned such nonsense.

"I wouldn't be so sure," I said. "It's not an accident that his body picked this particular way to release anxiety. It isn't Morse code, but it's communicating something. There's a story in that finger, I'm convinced of it."

"And a bid for healing," Rose added.

"Yes," I allied. "We actually take great hope in its persistence to be heard."

Carter raised her eyebrows like this was precisely the kind of flakiness California was famous for, a theory to bandy at a hot tub party but hardly one to stake someone's healing upon. "Well it's not his finger I'm worried about," she moved along. "It's his acting-out. Did you ever get his records from school? That would at least tell us his history."

"Not yet," I answered. "We're still waiting."

She thumbed through his sparse medical chart and sighed. "I hate to do it but, I think I should take him back to the hospital."

"Are you sure?" I said. "We could see how he does for another day or two."

"No," she decided. "If he acts-out again, I'd like him in a hospital." She closed his chart to settle it.

So that was it. We were through. After less than a week, Carey was leaving.

The other's got up. I stayed back. Carey stayed beside me. I stared at the table and struggled for words as I realized how much I would miss him. I wanted to tell him he'd be in good hands, that someone would restore his song. But my sadness kept me quiet. The flick of his finger was all I would hear, and the silence in those longing eyes.

"I would have loved to have heard it," was all I could say for fear of choking up. His voice, his song, the story of his finger, I left for him to interpret. I glanced once more at his downcast eyes and ached that he couldn't look back. Then I nodded my farewell, flicked my finger for luck, and followed the others out.

I made it as far as the door. Rose held it as I passed but stopped me with her hand. She pointed behind me and I turned. Carey had picked up a pencil and was staring at a blank piece of paper. His brow knotted, his eyes intense, he looked like he was cracking a code.

Then he drew.

In the upper left-hand corner, he traced a house—a single square, a triangle roof, a boxed door, and two cubed windows with crossed panes in each. Nothing else—no people, no trees, no picket fence, no curl of smoke coming out of a chimney. Just a house. Or maybe a mechanical face—a coned head, a boxed mouth, and two crossed cubed eyes. A cold face that doubled as a house, a house that bore no life.

Next to it, Carey drew another, an exact copy of the first, then another, and still another, filling the top of the page, a row underneath, and several more rows below those, until the entire page was filled. A battalion of head-like houses stood in formation peering absently into the distance. The paper filled, Carey stopped drawing, and studied the frozen faces.

But he was not done.

He gazed at the paper as if peering into a pool whose waters were as still as glass. Slowly, the waters trembled. A mesmerizing power rumbled from the depths. A hidden presence beckoned the boy and demanded to be known. As if caught in a spell, Carey returned to the paper and scribbled right over his picture. A large swirling circle defaced several houses as a single eye materialized in the corner of the page. Carey's pencil slid across with another distracted swirl as a second hungry eye insisted on being seen and appeared boldly beside the first. Back and forth between them, Carey spun the two coils, the eyes devouring houses in their whirling unblinking stare. Then another circle surfaced defacing another cluster of houses, a hollow mouth opened-wide but poised in a swirling silence. And then a crown, and a chin, and snake-like cheeks, slicing more houses and scribbling into place as a skull took possession of the page. Though now fully present, the skull was not satisfied. Carey furiously retraced the profile. With feverish strokes and dizzying spirals, he circled the eyes, sliced the cheeks, and arced the crown and chin as if the face on the page only lived so long as the pencil kept spinning on the paper. But Carey could not keep the skull alive. His scribbling became manic, the features grotesque, as he wildly swiped the page, then he lost control altogether, turned his pencil into a knife and erupted with an explosion of scratches that obliterated the picture in a slashing disfiguring frenzy.

Only then did the spell break and the pencil stop. The whirling energy of the face receded. But not entirely. For peering through that battlefield of scribble, like a hacked casualty that refuses to die, the swirling eyes of that relentless skull glared on. Angry, hollow, tearless and silent, they screamed in their stabbed, all-seeing stare.

Carey gazed at the eyes while we gazed at him. Then he set the pencil down, picked up the picture, and walked it across the room. As he placed it into my hands, his head bent low like a toddler who had soiled his pants. I studied the picture as my mind flooded with questions. Like why did the windows have crosses but the doors were devoid of knobs? Why were the houses so lifeless while the deathly skull was so vital? And who was that skull seething through the scribble—a boy who saw too much, a God who saw too little, a devil hell-bent on blinding both boy and God alike? But mostly I wanted to know, what had those eyes seen? For I was absolutely certain of one thing. Whatever it was, Carey wanted me to see it too.

"This is your finger's story, isn't it?" I asked still taking in the picture.

As faint as a whisper, Carey nodded.

"I can see why it's hard to find words for it. It's a hard story." The truth self-evident, he didn't nod again. "If it's okay with you, I'd like to keep it a while. There's a lot to understand in this story."

He paused as if considering, then turned and walked toward his room.

"Carey." He stopped. "Thanks for showing me." He didn't respond. The picture said it all.

If only I had the eyes to see.

Rose kept her 'I-told-you-so' smirk to herself. Carter didn't need it. As far as the doctor was concerned, Carey had communicated for the first time in a week. He was staying at Crossroads.

For my part, Carey did more than communicate. He commissioned me. He wanted me to know his story. And I knew exactly where to begin.

First thing Friday morning, I dropped by the office to confirm. The file hadn't come. After a week of empty threats, I made good.

I left for Salve Regina.

It was some time before I found out, I did not go alone. An olive green camper lurked just off the highway.

From the moment I left Crossroads, it followed me.

26

Not Darkness, Light.
Not Sorrow, Joy.
Not Despair, Hope.
Come, Choose Life.

THE INSCRIPTION WAS ETCHED across a stately stone archway. Two chiseled cherubs mounted pillars on both sides. A planked bridge met an ornate iron gate like the moated entrance to a fortress. As if expecting me, the gates were wide.

Salve Regina was open.

I crossed the stream, passed through the gate, and drove onto grounds as spacious as a Victorian country estate. Grassy slopes stretched for acres all but begging for children to roll down. A lane lined with flowers meandered along then disappeared behind a hillock speckled with live oak. On a distant plateau, majestic stone buildings towered into the morning sky. The only anomaly to the tranquil splendor was well disguised along the perimeter. A wrought-iron fence, spaced by brick columns, appeared to protect the grounds from intruders. Closer inspection revealed otherwise. Inches below the wrought-iron spikes, camouflaged razor wire crowned the fence's inside face. The threat of breach came from within.

I followed the lane around the hill then climbed to the parking lot atop the plateau. The panorama was breathtaking. A valleyful of farms and vineyards stretched out to hills in three directions. Only one thing spoiled the scenic view—the spastic dread in my stomach. I still did not know what I would say if I braved a long-belated reunion.

I got out of the truck and surveyed the grounds to get my bearings. Schuyler Peckham was true to his reputation. The compound had the sparkle of fresh money. And plenty of it. A state-of-the-art athletic complex, the price-tag all but dangling from the computerized scoreboard, soared alongside a manmade lagoon. A recently renovated concert hall glistened at the end of a rose-lined walkway, its silver marquee heralding the recital a few weeks away. A meticulously maintained flower garden blossomed in multicolored splendor, the centerpiece to the rectangular academic building that circumscribed it from three sides. And with a bird's eye view of both the campus below and the vista to the west, a brand new three-story tower of an administration wing adjoined one end of the academic building like a turret to a castle. The mirrored windows on the top floor had Peckham's name written all over them. I made my way for the tower.

I was halfway through the parking lot when I felt a vague creepiness. The campus was quiet. Too quiet. In fact, the unnerving realization soaked in that I could not detect a single other person anywhere on the premises. Cars were parked in the lot. A flag drooped from the pole. A groundskeeper's cart was stranded by the garden's fountain. But not a single sound whispered through the dead-sea calm of that school—not out the classroom windows, the concert hall door, nor even from the sports fields off in the distance. Like an abduction episode from the Twilight Zone, the entire campus was devoid of human life.

I approached the administration building with the foreboding that inside would be just as desolate. I cracked the door and heard my first sound. From a series of speakers spaced throughout the impressive lobby, a boy's choir sang in staticy falsetto. *Tears and sorrows, they caroled, only make us strong.*

The music, meant to soothe, only intensified my dread. It played to a completely empty building. The desks in the offices held half-eaten doughnuts on napkins, untouched coffee in mugs, computer consoles ponging in screen-saver mode, but the entire place was militantly deserted. The mass exodus was so eerie I sensed some sinister cause, like terrorists rounding up hostages now held at gunpoint in the basement. The evacuation was so hurried they neglected to disarm the stereo. Reverberating from an intercom system that encompassed every corner of the building, the choir sang on, oblivious to the emptiness for which it was playing. Surrounded by the polyphonic echo, I ascended the stairway at the center of the foyer. With each step, the choir thanked God for solving every problem the storms of life bring on.

The musical miasma was seamless. Its currents absorbed me from hidden speakers above as I drifted past the second floor and emerged at the third—the walnut-paneled reception area to Peckham's office suite. It too was uninhabited, the absence so oppressive I imagined a knife to my neck at any given second. I was torn between calling in a missing person's report and bolting down the stairs while I still had the chance. But I also had an opportunity. Making sure that nobody was watching, I approached the secretary's desk and peeked through her papers. As I nosed around, the choir climaxed with the chorus, their harmonizing admonitions mocking the death pall vacantness that pervaded.

> Through it all, through it all,
> I have learned to depend upon God's Word.

As the music ended, a shuffling noise filtered through the speakers. Finding nothing on the desk, I noticed Peckham's office door ajar. Inside, wall-length windows framed an elegant handcrafted desk. The veneered desktop was strikingly ascetic—the furnishings limited to a golden penholder centered at the front, a sleek black phone to the side, and an upholstered chair tucked neatly into place.

And a single manila folder centered precisely in front of the chair.

I checked the stairs to see if I was followed. Then I tiptoed into the office. I was just past the door when I heard it. Thundering through the speaker at my back, a booming baritone so impressively impersonated the Lord on high I jumped as if the rebuke was directed at me.

> "*See now that **I Myself** am Yahweh.*
> "*There is **no God** beside **me**.*

"'*I put to death, and I bring to life.*
"'*I have wounded and I will heal.*
"'*And no one can deliver another out of my hand*.'
"*Thus sayeth the Lord*."

Shaken as if being watched, I vacated the office while the voice continued through the speakers. It roared throughout the empty suite and the deserted floors below with the commanding authority of Napoleon preparing his troops for battle.

"*For over a hundred and forty years a man-eating beast has stalked the seas of American literature. Indeed this creature's malevolence has proven so invincible it has leapt off the page and into the dark regions of our collective unconscious. If you are alive, it lurks in your soul—a savage that so personifies evil its appetite for flesh rivals that of the devil, a leviathan so large its belly harbors the legions of ships it has swallowed, a killer whale so albino white it blinds you with its glare as it springs up out of nowhere, grinds you with its ivory daggers, and plunges with your carcass into the darkened depths of the sea.*

"*I speak, of course, of the notorious Moby Dick*."

Something in the headmaster tone told me it was Schuyler Peckham. Something in the political rally intensity told me he was speaking live. I put the pieces together. Peckham had gathered the community and was preaching that very moment. With his rumbling cry reverberating throughout the cavernous vacancy of the building, I descended the stairs from his suite and set out in search of him.

"*Some of you boys have read of this menace. And you know he is stalked by one of the most misunderstood characters in all of the classics through which questing minds are schooled. Captain Ahab was one of the few whalesmen who took Moby Dick on and survived. He was chasing the brute when Moby Dick dove and disappeared, then turned back on Ahab, and leapt from the sea with homicidal rage. His skyscraper hulk blinded the sun as he crashed toward Ahab's dory. About to be pulverized, Ahab launched his harpoon, forcing the whale to swerve and explode by his boat like a bomb. With primal fury, Ahab grabbed a blade and lunged at the mountain of beast. With a mere dagger attacking a tidal wave of terror, Ahab hacked the albino hide until Moby Dick snapped like a giant snarling dog. Ahab dove to escape but the beast bit down and severed the captain's leg. The body-part but a morsel in its mouth, the fierce whale simply sneered. Then limb and all, it disappeared into the sea.*

"*Ahab shrieked with such rage the entire voyage home he had to be tied up like a mummy in his hammock. But the second he was landbound, he snagged a whalebone for a leg, gathered a fresh crew, and set out to sea once more. Searching throughout the infinite depths, he burned with all-consuming purpose—he would track that beast around the globe if need be, but he would not return alive until he rid the world of the demonic Moby Dick.*

"*Some say Ahab was insane, a monomaniacal madman whose madness was maddened in his demented obsession for revenge. Others say he was allied with the devil, his psychopathic single-mindedness inflamed by satanic lust. Still others say that he thought he was God, a megalomaniac usurping the power to condemn one of the Maker's Titans.*

"*But I say, they're all wrong.*

"*In Moby Dick, Ahab encountered pure depravity. And when he did, he did not turn away and flee; he did not capitulate in desperate surrender; he did not despair at the odds and take a blade to himself. No. Ahab fought back like a first-century Christian with a gladi-ator's courage. When his stick of a blade proved feeble, he marshaled his resolve, replenished his forces, and righteously returned to battle. His crew, his ship, his own life if he had to, he would sacrifice it all in his holy war campaign to purge the world of evil.*

"Mark my words, young lads. Captain Ahab was a hero."

The words pounded from all directions as the administrative wing gave way to the ground floor of classrooms. The academic building was barren too, like a deserted ghost-ship listless at sea. As I boarded, the voice blared on.

"Today's world needs another Ahab. For a creature as insidious as it is destructive still stalks our seas. Its feeding grounds include our own placid waterways. It lays in wait in our bedrooms' pools poised to consume us whole—a leviathan more dangerous to us than Moby Dick was to the whalesmen of old. Moby Dick could destroy your flesh, but he could not devour your soul. The savage that preys upon our school threatens body and soul alike. It poisons us with the one affliction for which there is no cure. It seduces us into the one sin for which there is no pardon. It swallows us into the one belly from which there is no escape.

"The beast that stalks Salve Regina, is Despair."

The classrooms seemed abandoned in haste. Each door I passed betrayed lessons unfinished on whiteboards, notes splayed out on desks, pencils askance, chairs shoved back, windows left open for air. The entire community was either summoned or scared away by the all-commanding voice on high. I was the only one left. And the voice was still summoning. From every room I passed, every hall I wandered, around every corner I turned, it hounded me alone as if determined to subdue me. An all-seeing eye was spying. I was its stalked prey. Like the dreaded white whale being hunted, I crept through the lifeless hallways.

"Despair has a natural habitat, a scummy section of sea where it scrounges for lost souls to feed upon. Its coal-black hide swims most abundantly, most invisibly within the filthy dark waters of depravity. Those of you that house yourselves in the safe harbors of Christian goodness, who persevere with prayer and hard work, moral vigilance and sensual prudence, you will not suffer but an occasional sighting of this menacing creature off shore. But those of you who sludge in the foul seas of lust, who squall in the crosscurrents of unnatural appetites, who gust about in the tempests of deceit and vindictiveness, greed and gluttony, you drift in the indigenous waters where despair preys with abandon.

"Beware as it steals up behind you. There is something sinisterly seductive about its coat's obsidian darkness. It sneaks from the shadows with the face of self-pity, enticing you to bemoan how much suffering you've known. Then it sucks you into its orbit with the sapping lure of sloth, overwhelming you with how hard it is to row your way to righteousness. Your will gets drowsy, and your heart stops caring if you ever see another day. You let go, and drift to sleep, wrapping yourself in the dark warm blanket closing in around you.

"But now it's too late. You're already caught. For make no mistake about it. The seduc-tive undertow of sloth is the riptide of a monstrous appetite. And the beguiling face of self-pity is a gaping mouth in disguise. The leviathan of despair is bearing down and few swim free from its pull. The jaws promise torture as the teeth taunt with a way out. They turn into razor blades and hanging ropes, sleeping pills and pistols, and they beckon you toward the self-destruction that leads to the belly of the beast.

"Hear my words and hear them well. Despair means to kill. And from this death, there is no resurrection."

The relentlessly echoing Jonestown charisma created a bewildering effect. Around this corner, that corner, behind me, before me, from empty rooms on either side, Peckham's booming oratory swirled around me through the disorienting twist of hallways. The leviathan itself could have borne down upon me and I would not have noticed its approach. The only lifeline out of the reverberating vertigo was the voice reaching through the spiral of speakers. I fought on, determined to find the body to which it belonged.

"What then do we do when we find ourselves sucked into this all-consuming black-hole? In the end, there are but two choices—the way of death, or the way of life.

"Suicide takes many forms. Some people kill themselves over time, dragging out a slow death for years from drugs or alcohol. Others kill themselves more precisely. They poison themselves. They leap off bridges. They even slice their own wrists.

"Don't misunderstand me. People caught within the jaws of such murderous despair deserve nothing but compassion. A more agonizing death does not exist. But the heart's compassion must be tempered by faith's perception. Suicide is sin. God's Word is unequivocal—'I bring death and I bring life. And noone can deliver another from my hand.' The taking of one's own life, like murder, is a usurpation of God's prerogative to take or give life as He wills. But unlike murder, from suicide there can be no repentance. Its punishment will be as self-induced as its chosen form of death. And just as eternal."

The final corridor of classrooms emptied into a formal dining hall. The tables were set for lunch. The room, however, was as void of food as the rest of the school of people. Such did not deter the voice. It roared in quadraphonic stereo from each corner of the room. Peckham was luring. I had to find him. I made for the doors on the far side of the tables.

"Hell's lowest region is occupied by one whose contempt for God constitutes the debased standard by which all sin is measured. Judas Iscariot committed the most despicable act in the history of psychopathology that has polluted our planet. He handed the very Son of God over for crucifixion. And yet, it is not his betrayal of our Lord that confines him to the bitterest depths of hell. It is his self-infliction. Three times Jesus offered his traitorous friend mercy—at the table of the Last Supper, in the Garden of Gethsemane, even from the cross on Golgotha. But Judas refused Jesus' forgiveness. He hung himself in despair and consigned himself to hell. Christ could forgive betrayal. But He could not forgive suicide. For the way of suicide is the way of death—a death that lasts forever."

The dining hall doors opened into an enclosed walkway. I passed through then slipped into a spacious narthex. I was close. The walls seemed to pulsate from the energy within. Though the double doors to the sanctuary were closed, the voice on the other side bellowed. Schuyler Peckham was building to his conclusion.

"But there is another way.

"The way of a man who did not surrender to despair's insidious undertow. The way of a man who sighted the leviathan then spent two days confined to a raft before rising on the third to stand for life. The way of a man who like Judas died from a rope wrapped round his neck, not the cord of a cowardly hangman however, but the rope of a harponeer boldly spearing the beast that would slay him.

"I speak of the way of Ahab, the captain who in the face of despair kept his weapon sharpened and greased with wine, who spied the demon's shadow in the murky black water and defied it, cursed it, attacked it, and gave himself to a martyr's death as he refused its rapacious assault."

I stood at the doors too intimidated to enter. I imagined Peckham a replica of his hero. With crazed eyes and rabid flourish, Ahab blasted from the prow of a pulpit. And there, sitting in the captive audience . . .

"Take heed young whalesmen and listen to my word. There are only two ways in this world. The way of death. And the way of life. The way of Judas. And the way of Ahab. And make no mistake about it—you will have to choose. Look into your soul right now if you dare and you will know of what I speak. The black beast is lurking there, and your death is what it seeks. It's lulling you into the melancholy of a world where fair ones fall. And it's draining you of the fortitude to fight back with faith's true call. The shadow's drawing near I fear, its jaws are opening wide. Its teeth are stained with blood from here, and its thirst's not satisfied.

"But before you surrender to the pull of its bite, before you reach for blades or rope, look more closely and you will see. There's a ship bearing down inside you like a cruiser clad for war. And on its prow a captain stands, who to despair says 'Nevermore.' Can you see him in the putrid waters of your soul? Can you hear his call to arms? There's an Ahab in each of you! And he's showing you the way! His eye is on the spyglass and the beast is pinned in his gaze. His maimed leg is planted and his sharpened blade is raised. His aim is keen, his throw is true, as he thrusts with God's cold rage. And he pierces that scum in its eye now stunned then spits in its blinded face.

"Watch the whale cringe and twist with pain, watch it buck then dive. And watch my fellow whalesmen, as your captain is swallowed alive. His dead-center aim is the cause of his demise, his neck is caught in the line. That whale is plunging back to hell and it's towing him behind.

"Do you see him as he races? He's looking back at you.

"Do you listen as he cries? His final words are true.

"Even as he drowns, he bids you from the hole.

"With the only words that have a chance to save your endangered soul.

"Do you hear him as he roars through the suffocating surf?!

"Do you hear him as he sinks into the bowels of the abyss?!

"Do you hear him as he echoes from the other side of death?!

"I ask you all right now. Do you hear the hymn of Ahab?!

"'Choose Life!' his dying words resound!

"Face despair down, and choose!

"'For the sake of Christ and your own mortal soul!

"'Choose . . . the Way . . . of Life!'"

Like the Pequod crew rallied to a frenzy to face their certain death, the boys in the sanctuary erupted. Though their applause pounded through the doors with the force of a standing ovation, I still had not peeked in on the crowd, or the man at the helm inflaming it. For all my hesitation the jaws of Moby Dick could have been yawning wide within. Only the cheering's contagion bolstered my resolve. And the urge to see Peckham in action. I gathered my courage and pulled on the door. A hand out of nowhere blocked it.

"Just what do you think you're doing?" a voice snarled behind me. I spun around in terror and recoiled before a gargantuan custodian. A six-and-a-half foot Native American had me pinned to the door with an arm the size of a tree-limb. "I've been watching you," he grunted. "What're you doing here?"

"I'm Dr. Tony Backman," I sputtered. "I'm here to see Monsignor Peckham."

He eyed me as if I was armed with an assassin's rifle. "He expecting you?"

"No. I just drove over. I'm Carey Foster's psychologist."

He betrayed no recognition of Carey's name. "Monsignor don't like people poking around. A lot of troubled kids here—scared of strangers. I suspect you'd know that, if you was really a doctor."

"You're right," I said. "I wasn't thinking. I just drove up and tried to find everybody."

The applause within the room abated. Peckham's voice drifted through the doors. "Now as we choose to follow life, we celebrate the feast that sustains it."

"Look," I said. "I don't mean any harm. I really am Carey's psychologist and I need to talk with the Monsignor. How about I just sit in the back and speak with him when he's done?"

"Chapel's not open to the public." His arm kept barricading the door. "You best wait for him back at his office."

I wasn't about to argue. I eased around his hold and started walking. He didn't relax his arm until I was well away. Then he followed me. "I know where it is," I told him, rattled at his hulking shadow.

"Monsignor would want me to stay with you." He obeyed, several steps back.

As we retraced my path through the dining room and on down the halls, the speakers broadcasted the words of institution. Back in the sanctuary, Monsignor Peckham transformed bread and wine into the body and blood of Christ. As I settled down, I looked back at the custodian. 'Shuk Ocampo' was stitched above his pocket.

"Do you know Carey?" I inquired.

"Everybody does."

"What can you tell me about him?"

He glanced at a speaker as if it were a two-way intercom. "Monsignor wouldn't want me talking about the boys. He's very particular about that."

I knew better than to ask again. The Monsignor had been emphatic. All inquiries were cleared through him. And for the moment, he was preoccupied. Echoing throughout the halls, Ahab invited all within earshot to partake of the Eucharist.

All but two.

Shuk and I would have to wait.

27

MRS. MERIWETHER, MONSIGNOR PECKHAM's scattered secretary, had the annoying habit of repeating your every word in the form of a question. She skipped up the stairs after Mass then stopped and squeezed the handrail when she saw Shuk and me sitting in her workspace. The Monsignor was not with her.

"I'm Dr. Backman," I said rising to greet her.

"You're Dr. Backman?" she echoed, rattled by the intrusion.

"Yes. I'm treating Carey Foster."

"You're treating Carey Foster?"

"Yes. I'd like to talk to the Monsignor about him."

"You'd like to talk to the Monsignor about him?"

"Yes. I would."

"I see." The request confounded her. "Well, he's not here right now." She scooted to her meticulously ordered desk and shuffled through a stack of papers as if instructions for such a contingency were hidden within them. "He's saying his prayers," she thought out loud. "And he doesn't tolerate interruptions." She stopped mid-shuffle and concentrated, determined to get this right. "But he'll want to see you right away. Shuk, would you take Dr. Backman to Monsignor's chapel?"

Shuk hesitated as if this wasn't such a good idea. Their combined uncertainty made me uneasy. The last thing I wanted was to rile Captain Ahab. "Are you sure we should bother him?" I asked.

"Am I sure you should bother him?" her echo returned.

"Yes. I don't want to disturb his praying."

"You don't want to disturb his praying?"

"Not unless he wouldn't mind."

"Not unless he wouldn't mind?" She considered the consequences. "No. He'd mind more if you wait. You better see him right away."

I turned to Shuk. He made for the stairs as if dreading a flogging. I felt like the one strapped to the post. Looking for a way out, I turned back to the secretary. She was restacking her papers into a precisely shaped pile. "All I need is Carey's file." I said.

"All you need is Carey's file?" she repeated.

"Yes. Monsignor said he'd make it available."

"Monsignor said he'd make it available?"

"Yes, he did."

She wasn't biting. "Then you better talk to him." That seemed inevitable. But still, I wanted the file.

"Can you at least have it ready for when I return?"

"Can I at least have it ready for when you return?"

"Yes. I need it to treat Carey."

"You need it to treat Carey?"

"Yes. I do."

She fussed with the pile until it formed a perfect right angle to her nameplate. "Then it'll be here when you get back."

I picked up her quirk to make certain. "It'll be here when I get back?"

She snapped me a look as if stung by a smart ass. "Yes," she curtly assured. "It'll be here when you get back."

———

Shuk led us through the lobby, out the front doors, and up a path between the gardens and the concert hall. I felt like a trespasser being convoyed to the compound's commander. I was surprised when we passed the sanctuary.

"Aren't we going to the church?" I asked.

"Monsignor's got his own church back in the woods." His words intensified my disquiet—the meeting would take place out of earshot of the campus.

"Why does he need his own church?" I inquired.

"Monsignor's a man of prayer," he answered. "Likes to pray in private." Then he added as if it explained things, "Made it special for his mother."

"Will the interruption bother him?" I hoped he would ease my anxiety. He didn't.

"We'll see soon enough," he intoned. "Monsignor lets you know when he's bothered."

Shuk left the sidewalk and strode a path sloping up into the woods. Within moments we seemed miles from the school. Thick trees swallowed us into a shadowed haven. All sound dissipated. The limbs were still, the air hushed. A solemnity swelled as if sacred ground was near. Or the sorting site for Judgment Day.

About a hundred yards in, a redwood walking bridge spanned a trickling creek. As we crossed over, I glimpsed a sunlit clearing in the distance. I sensed it without seeing it. The clearing enclosed Monsignor's chapel. We continued to the trees' edge. Before stepping out of the shadows, Shuk stopped.

"One thing you should know," he prepped without turning. "Monsignor doesn't shake hands. He's got a bad paw."

"You mean it's deformed?" I asked over his shoulder.

"Not exactly. Scarred's more like it. Runs clear through his hand."

"What's it from?"

"Depends on who's doing the telling." Shuk was suddenly talkative now that we were close. "I've heard it all ways from the boys. Some say he stopped a bullet to save a kid's life. Some say he did it to himself, ran a spike clear through before he got religion. Some say he got stabbed by the devil when he chased him with a Bible. Some say it's the wound of Jesus that bleeds whenever he prays. They all say it's got special powers. It burns when it's around evil. That's why he massages it so much. For all the misbehavin' that goes on around here."

The stories sounded typical of school kids. "What's it really?" I asked. "An unusual birthmark?"

Shuk turned and glared like I was mocking a truth beyond me. "Just don't shake his hand," he warned. Then he turned back and stepped into the clearing.

A building the size of a single-room schoolhouse shimmered in the sunlight. It resembled a tidy English cottage. A white picket fence enclosed a freshly mown lawn. Blooming flowerbeds brightened the border. Country shutters and boxed planters adorned windows etched in cast-iron. The only religious symbol was a plaster Virgin Mary perched atop a gurgling fountain. A plaque was mounted at the base.

Dedicated to Miriam S. Peckham
A Woman of Prayer
and Purity

En Aeternum Pace

Shuk delicately passed through the arbored gate, tiptoed across the stepping-stone path, and scaled the front steps as quiet as a supplicant tardy for church. He paused at the door as if second-guessing our intrusion. Maybe the Monsignor was better left alone. Or maybe not. Shuk turned the knob and entered. I followed right behind.

The chapel was as aesthetic a worship space as I had ever seen. All the woodwork—the pews, the font, the altar, lectern, and railing—was handcrafted out of Alaskan cedar. The windows on either side were floral designs rivaling those of Tiffany. Quilted tapestries of royal blue were trimmed with golden thread. And above the chancel, where a crucifix would usually hang, a larger than life stained-glass Madonna loomed in maternal majesty. She was framed on either side by a column of panels depicting her life with Jesus. On one side, Mary celebrated with Elizabeth the news of her pregnancy, glowed over a manger in Bethlehem, and held her arms wide as a toddler learned to walk. On the other, Mary beamed at her boy teaching in the temple, marveled at the miracle of water become wine, and raised her arms in ecstatic bliss beside the stone rolled away at the tomb. But these panels paled before the mammoth Madonna poised like the Queen of Creation. Robed in white, crowned with rubies, wreathed by a canopy of roses, she spanned two stories with arms outstretched, holding each scene on the stained-glass panels and any that played out in the chapel with the Mother-of-God compassion that embraces the entire world.

Her embrace even held death. Freestanding and off to the side, a crucifix was forged out of slender notched nails, the kind to hammer shoes to a horse. The iron spikes were coiled like a barbed rope to form a cross with spurred tapered tips. More spikes were entangled to create a jaggedly contorted body, the corpse of nails nailed to the cross of nails. The symbol was fitting. Weapon and victim were entwined as one when God became wedded with death. The spiked crucifix was mounted on a polished hickory pole and planted in a leaden base. Beside it, eyes closed, head raised, hands serenely interlaced but for the thumb massaging the hollow of his palm, Schuyler Peckham knelt in prayer.

Peckham's calm demeanor so completely contradicted my preconceptions I questioned if it was him I had heard through the speakers. He was immaculately groomed—black clerics pressed and white collar starched, dress shoes polished and silk socks taut, silver beard and matching hair so precisely manicured they seemed trimmed with the aid of microscopic instruments. He bore an infinity of refinement, an unsurrenderable self-control, a princely poise so perfect in posture his inspiration seemed drawn from an Episcopalian aristocrat not the raving madman that ransacked the seas for revenge. Whatever fire had blazed during his rabid oratory, it dimmed to the quiet incandescence that burns in the deep center of a pearl.

He so sustained his prayerful repose he might not have heard us come in. But after a moment, he raised his blemished hand, silently signed himself with the cross, then stood, bowed before Mary, and turned our way with a smile of disarming paternal affection. Stepping with the dignity of a studied cardinal, he descended the altered dais and approached with wide welcoming arms.

"You must be Dr. Backman," he greeted with unexplained prescience. Instinctively, I held out my hand. With practiced grace he ignored my sleight, squeezed my fingers with his left hand, and patted Shuk on the back with the marked one. "Thank you, Shuk. We'll be fine now." Dismissed, Shuk glanced at me then left. "He's a good man," Peckham continued, looking me squarely in the eye. "We're standing on his land, you know. The Pomo Indians lived here for centuries—peacefully until the Franciscans came and offered them conversion before slicing off their heads. The Russians arrived soon after and raped their women and children while forcing the men to hunt for fur. Then the ranchers settled and used the Pomo as slaves. Two Indians led an uprising—killed some ranchers, freed some slaves, then fled into these hills. The U.S. Army came in and massacred an entire village—188 Pomo who had nothing to do with the uprising. They hunted down the two liberators, hung them on a tree not far from here, and left the bodies to rot in the sun. Shuk was named after one of them. I figure the least we could do is let him work on the land that belongs to his people."

I couldn't tell by Peckham's stare if he considered me an ally or was castigating a racist. "You don't read that in the history books, do you?" I cautiously responded.

"No, you don't," he replied. "Which is why it's on us to remember." His smile was warm but his eyes seemed to dare a rebuttal. Then they snapped on. "But come. You're not here for a history lesson." He walked toward the chancel, motioned me to sit in the front pew, then leaned against the altar rail. As I slid into the seat, the polished wood seemed to conform to my body.

"Impressive," I admired, sliding my hand along the sensuous surface.

"It was crafted by a student of James Krenov," he shared. "All the wood was. It's flawless. Like pressed satin." He caressed the rail like a connoisseur would savor a sip of wine. "Sometimes," he confided, fingering a seam imperceptible to the touch, "when I celebrate the Mass, the artistry overwhelms me. It's part of the prayer really—to delight in one's ability to take raw timber and mold it with such exquisite beauty."

"It could go in a museum," I observed.

He smiled. "For what they're worth, many museums couldn't afford them."

"You have a taste for fine things," I acknowledged. "The whole school is first-class."

"My philosophy is, damaged kids deserve the best. A child becomes what he's surrounded by. Surround him with great things, he becomes great himself. Wasn't it Coleridge who said, 'Plant a strawberry seed in a bed of weeds, you'll grow a weed. Plant a strawberry seed in a garden, you'll have fruit for dessert.'"

"I'd hate to see the price-tag for such surroundings," I said.

"Raising money's easy," he shrugged. Then he took me under his wing. "I'll give you a tip. Most non-profits think it's all about the heart—tell a sad story about underfed children and people'll start reaching for their change. That's not where the sell is, not for the real money. You sell it the second you walk into the CEO's suite. These guys step over the homeless on their way to lunch at Scoma's. They respond to professionals. Portfolios with cost tables and customized schematics, long-term sustainability charts and statistically calibrated success indicators—it's all in the presentation. You walk in with class, you walk out with a check in your pocket. And a seat on their board."

"Crossroads could use the tip," I played along. "We're lucky to pay our heat."

"Let me know if I can help," he offered. "Like I said. Our boys deserve the best." He eyed me certain of just who the best was. "But you didn't come to talk fund-raising either. What's on your mind?"

I answered as if he didn't know. "Carey Foster's been assigned to my care."

Concern covered his face in an instant. "How's Carey doing?" he asked.

"He's traumatized—withdrawn and scared to death."

He winced as if feeling the pain. "Father Eichler says he hasn't spoken a word."

"That's right. Though he did draw a picture yesterday, which was quite a breakthrough."

Peckham shook his head. "He was doing so well, too. I tell you, despair is one insidious beast. Coddle it, and it will destroy you."

"Did Carey coddle his despair?" I asked.

"Don't we all?" he answered. "That's why I've been preaching on it all week."

"I heard. You make quite an impression through an intercom, even to one who sees things differently."

"We see things differently?" I couldn't tell if he took offense or wanted to talk professionally.

"Well, I don't believe in a literal hell for one, or that suicide is unpardonable. But mostly, I don't think despair can simply be willed away, not even by impassioned oratory however persuasive it might be. The causes are too complex. They need to be explored, not repressed."

If Peckham felt challenged he didn't show it. He studied me like a schoolmaster. "Let me tell you a story," he said. "Where I first started teaching, a boy became depressed. Turned out he was sodomized by a priest. As far as I am concerned, hell was created for just such a person. Anyway, the boy asked his confessor if suicide was a sin, and if so could it be forgiven. The confessor told him that God has compassion for those who kill themselves whether it's a sin or not. The boy did kill himself, jumped off the chapel roof. His note was to the point. 'I was told that you would forgive me. Please God, let it be so.' Tell me, Dr. Backman. Wouldn't that boy be better off if the confessor had been unequivocal, told him that suicide was a sin to be resisted under threat of eternal death?"

Like Woody, when told a story I always wonder. "Before I answer, can I ask—were you the confessor?"

His stare was impenetrable. "No. I was not."

"What I would say, then, is that the boy would have been better off if the confessor heard the cry for help hidden within the question. He could have validated the boy's feelings and helped him discover the resources for healing found even in the darkest despair."

"I must confess," Peckham responded. "I find such views aesthetically compelling, but under the circumstances, therapeutically inadequate."

"How so?" I asked.

"Consider Carey. Coddling his feelings did not diminish his despair. On the contrary . . ."

"So Carey's been despairing for some time?"

"That's how he came to us. Carey tried to kill himself before. He cut his wrists about a year ago, when he lived with his mother. An investigation was done, the mother deemed unfit, and he came here. Some of the staff were of the opinion we should affirm his fixations, validate his feelings as you would say. I wanted to surround him with a more positive environment—plant the seed in a garden if you will. I gave in. Carey responded so well, I let it go. Unfortunately, it turned out I was right. Plant a seed in weeds, it will die."

"How was he planted in weeds?" I asked.

Peckham pondered how best to make his point. Then he stood up.

"Let me show you."

Without a word about where we were going, Peckham hiked an alternative trail toward campus. Tree limbs as smooth and straight as javelins hung low across the path, their budding tips fragrant with the blossoms' promise of fruit. Careful not to snap them, Peckham brushed them back and trekked down the hill to the last of three dormitories lodged behind the academic building. Entering through the far side, we climbed to the second floor and stopped before the door next to the stairwell. Peckham retrieved a single key from his pocket. He did not need to reveal where we were. His gravity betrayed it. As he opened the door to Carey's bedroom, I braced for signs of suicidal horror—puddles of blood, discarded blades, caution tape draping the bed. I found worse. I stepped into a macabre recollection of a Holocaust concentration camp.

A string of contorted paper clips, reminiscent of barbed wire, was strung below the perimeter of ceiling. A travel-poster of Auschwitz, defaced by black swastikas, was pinned to the bedside wall. Above the desk a chart of Nazi patches was tacked—pink triangles for homosexuals, purple for Jehovah's Witnesses, red for Communists, and so forth. The books on the shelf included Holocaust classics—the comic books *Maus* and the novel *Night*. "Arbeit Macht Frei" was stenciled to the back of the door.

But the most disturbing display in the horrifying room was the mirror on his closet. A collage of Holocaust victims was pasted out of newspaper snapshots. Striped prisoners with shovels and piles of naked bodies lined the outer edges. Within their circle, a cattle-car crowd of cadaverous faces stared in silent futility. Their skulls were shaved, their shoulders unclothed, as they awaited their rendezvous with the showers. The hollow eyes knew their fate and they searched in vain for someone who cared—a guard, an inmate, the callous bystander taking in the picture, anyone at all who would have the humanity to hallow them before their death. Their eyes were not alone. In the middle of the crowd, a patch of mirror was left uncovered. In its reflection, I saw myself, my own face nestled among the faces of the others, my own eyes knowing they were marked for death, my own despair searching for care before my hope turned to ash in the ovens. The effect was chilling.

I turned to Peckham and caught him fingering the one emblem that had nothing to do with the Holocaust—the crucifix above the foot of Carey's bed. It was a replica of the one that bid St. Francis to heal a dying church. Its distinguishing feature was the eyes of Jesus. They were open. From their hooked perch, they took it all in—the entire breadth of horror endured within that room. Peckham stared into the eyes as if aching for what they saw. Then he turned and sighed at their work-camp backdrop.

"It goes against everything I stand for," he said. "I should never have allowed it."

"Why did you?" I asked, shaken by a primal recognition.

"He seemed to be doing fine, even thriving in the choir. It was rather prosaic really—such a transcendent voice rising out of this darkness."

"I'm surprised he could sing at all," I said. "I'd be melancholic." That much I knew.

"No," Peckham considered. "Carey was not melancholic. Quiet perhaps, and serious. But always compliant without complaint. And when he sang, he lit up. Last week, he was a hero. This competition's a big deal to the boys. Carey was as proud as can be."

"So what happened?" I asked. "Why did the bottom fall out?"

"Look at what he came home to."

I did. It was a home all too familiar. "How long has he been interested in the Holocaust?"

"I couldn't say," Peckham answered. "It started at his mother's."

"What can you tell me about her?"

He sighed as if watching his words. "The court decreed her unfit. They cited gross negligence, frequent abandonment, and sustained exposure to promiscuity. I think that says enough."

"Does Carey see her?"

He retained his composure but the question upset him. "She's entitled to supervised visitation once a week. She came twice the first month, once last Christmas, and she hasn't come since." He retrieved from Carey's drawer a glossy red change purse with a blue and yellow ice cream cone stitched to the side. "It's enough to break your heart," he continued. "From two to four every Sunday, Carey waits in the lobby fingering this—a coin pouch she made so he'll always have money for any ice cream truck that came along his way. He cherishes it like an heirloom. It's the only capital he has on the illusion that she really cares." He fingered the pouch himself. "I tell my boys never to speak bad of others.

Sometimes it's hard. You'd be bitter too if you had to watch that boy all alone every week, sitting in his Sunday best, composing excuses for why she didn't come while comforting himself that it's really okay because look at what she made for him. Phyllis Foster loves her son enough to supply him with ice cream. She just can't find the time to visit him once a week. If it were up to me, the court would deny her visitation altogether."

I stared at the pouch as well. Unfortunately, I had seen it all too often—kids clutching a keepsake, a ball cap, a stuffed animal, the intangible vapor of a single memory, anything that will hold at bay the unlivable reality that your mother or father simply doesn't give a damn. I understood Peckham's bitterness. Carey deserved better.

"How about his father?" I asked. "Where's he?"

"He's been out of the picture for some time—in prison for child molestation. Unrepentant from what the mother says. He claimed she lied to spite him and swore he'd be back for his boy. She moved here to get away from him."

"Was Carey the victim?"

"Apparently. Though he must have been quite young."

It made sense. A father's abuse and a mother's abandonment could certainly explain Carey's cutting. But the abruptness of it all still hung me up. "Could Carey have been abused by somebody here?"

Peckham tensed. "Why would you suspect that?"

"I don't suspect it. I'm just trying to make sense of his mood swing last week, and the severity of his dissociation ever since. A repetition of early trauma could explain it."

Peckham studied me carefully. His reply was as clipped as it was emphatic. "It would never happen. Not at my school."

"How can you be so sure?" I asked. "Abuse is more common than you think."

"Dr. Backman," he answered. "There's not a thing that concerns my boys I do not know about. I guarantee you—they are well cared for."

"I'm sorry if I suggested otherwise . . ."

"No apology necessary," he said. "After all, we're all on the same side here. We're trying to help a troubled boy."

The words were precise, the exact ones I used with Eichler. Peckham wasn't kidding. He knew *everything* that concerned his boys.

"That we are," I agreed. "And I've appreciated your help." He nodded that it was nothing. "Before I go," I added. "Can I get Carey's file?"

"Of course," he said. "I know right where it is."

I had no doubt that he did.

—————

We passed Father Eichler on our way to Peckham's suite. Perusing a video with a boy on either side, he stood outside a classroom door as kids scuttled the halls. I was so concerned about seeing someone else I almost didn't recognize him. He recognized us though. He looked up, saw the Monsignor, and blanched. As Peckham glared, Eichler shoved the video to his side and scooted the boys along. Peckham's stride never slowed.

When we reached his office, he handed me the file from his desk. I thanked him for the cooperation. He asked if there was anything else. I told him there was—I wanted to talk with Carey's teachers. He studied me as if sensing my deception. Then he told me I could talk to whomever I needed.

I left his office before opening the file. My trembling would have betrayed me. Like I knew I would, I spotted the name in Carey's class schedule. Seeing it in print was like sighting a ghost.

Room 22 was the far classroom on the academic building's second-floor. With everyone off to lunch, the hallway was empty. I walked the length fearing Carey's teacher would pop out at any moment. My belly erupted, its rumbles throughout the week mere foreshocks to the earthquake now that I was so close. How long had it been? How would I be received? How many ways could this blow up in my face?

I saddled up just shy of the room. The door was open, the light within lit. My heart pounded as if warning me to flee. I did not listen. I took a breath, then stepped into view.

Carey's Religion teacher was staring out the window. As I appeared in her doorway, she turned. Her face looked confused, then opened in astonishment.

For several seconds we stared.

Then I broke the silence.

With words I hadn't used in nearly seven years.

"Hi, Jen."

28

"WHAT IN GOD'S NAME are you doing here?" Jen's alabaster face always betrayed the faintest hue of emotion. Her shock surged forth in a crimson blush. Why not? Seven years without a word, then her ex-husband materializes in the middle of her lunch period.

In spite of my bass-drum heartbeat, I tried to sound casual.

"I was here to see Monsignor Peckham and . . ."

"You know Schuyler Peckham?!" She spat out the name as if it sickened her. I recognized the Gallagher ire, but the feistiness in her eyes could not mask the pools of pathos. She could have been crying just moments before, with tears seasoned for years. And she could have started all over again after tossing me out for being in league with a man she clearly detested.

"No," I fended. "I just met him today. He had something I needed, and I thought I'd drop in to see you. I'm sorry if I upset you."

"No, it's not . . ." She shook her head to take it in. "How do you know Schuyler Peckham?"

"I'm a psychologist in Santa Rosa. I'm working with Carey Foster."

"*You know Carey Foster?!*" This was too much. She pressed her hands against her head as if trying to contain all the impossible convergences. Then a more troubling thought occurred. "Has something happened to him?"

"No. He's safe. I just came by for his records."

She covered her eyes as she shook her head. "I can't believe this."

I couldn't either. With one step in the door I stumbled into a tempest the prevailing winds of which I couldn't figure out. "I should have called first, Jen. I didn't realize how unsettling this would be."

"It's not that," she said her eyes still closed. "This is *not* the time to tell me you're involved with Schuyler Peckham."

"But I'm not. Honestly. This was the first time I ever laid eyes on the man. In fact, I'm reeling from it myself. That guy's unbelievable." She opened her eyes to gauge my sincerity, then folded her arms in self-protection while shaking her head at the floor. Her hand bore no trace of a wedding ring. "He sure has gotten to you," I tried to soothe. "What's going on?"

She rolled her eyes and sighed. Her uncertainty about my trustworthiness vied with her need for a sympathetic ear. "Let's just say the Monsignor and I have different ways of seeing things."

"I can understand why," I affirmed. "The guy thinks he's Captain Ahab."

Her head shot up with surprise. "You were there?"

"I heard from the halls. I wandered around looking for everybody while he thundered through the intercom. It sounded like the voice of God."

"I'm sure *he* thought so," she bemoaned, looking back down at the floor. Something about it hit her close to home.

"It was actually quite chilling," I related. "This invisible madman vilifying everything I believe in."

She looked at me as if aching for support. "Wasn't it awful?" I couldn't help but be moved. To see her was to love her.

"It was. I felt like he was staining me with the sign of Judas."

"Well," she allowed, "the staining was meant for me."

"Why you?"

After pondering whether to or not, she opened up a degree. "I don't know if you've seen Carey's room."

"Peckham just took me."

She brooded as if in it right then. "I'm the one who lobbied for Carey to keep it like that. I thought we should hold his experience with compassion, not condemn it. For me the only hope that's secure is one that's honest about how dark the world can be. Peckham only gave in because others agreed. And Carey seemed to respond. He was doing great, until last week. Ever since, Peckham's been in rare form. Today was the climax. When he leaned over the pulpit and scolded that there are only two ways in the world, the way of Judas and the way of Ahab, he was pointing his finger at me. Holding darkness is coddling despair. And despair is the way of Judas."

"If it's any consolation, Jen. I couldn't agree with you more. I never thought of it as the way of Judas before, but why not? He represents the darkest realities of all. If healing comes through holding the darkness, maybe it means holding the Judas in each of us, finding a way of forgiving him and restoring him back to life. It works for me. We can start a new religion." My tepid attempt to find humor in our heresy coaxed a weak smile from her face. But Peckham's wrath still left a shadow. I wanted to wash it away. "Anyway," I continued, "it's Peckham's way that's the way of death as far as I'm concerned. Repressing despair is psychological suicide."

"I'd love to hear you tell him," she sighed.

"I did. I told him despair can't be willed away, even by impassioned oratory."

She took vicarious pleasure in my boldness. "You said that?"

"Yeah. And that healing has to validate despair until hope is discovered from within."

"What did he say?"

"He found such views 'aesthetically compelling but therapeutically inadequate.'"

"Sounds like Peckham," she said from experience.

"Well, rest assured," I heartened, "as long as Carey's at Crossroads, we'll be validating his despair, even if it is the way of Judas."

Trusting I was not in concert with her boss's condemnation, Jen relaxed a tad more. She unfolded her arms and leaned against the window, holding the sill to steady her. As the tide of professional distress receded, I wondered what would flow into its place—a wave of lapsed bitterness from the pain I once brought her, or could I hope for a wash of fondness at seeing me again? The face that unfailingly betrayed her emotions was suddenly indecipherable. I hoped I wouldn't misstep.

"You look great," I dared. "You're as beautiful as ever."

She smirked as if unsure such a sentiment was possible. Her self-deprecation stung. I wished I could retrieve every word I said that ever made her doubt her beauty.

"So how *is* Carey?" she asked, returning to safer shores.

"He's pretty troubled. His cutting was vicious, and he hasn't said a word since."

"Do you think you can help him?"

"Up until yesterday I wasn't so sure. I've just helped him feel safe, tried to connect in some way. He's been completely shut down. Then yesterday, he finally communicated. He drew me a picture. It doesn't sound like much, but it's huge. He's starting to trust me. But more, he wants me to know something, I can feel it."

She smiled. "You were always great with kids, Tony."

I was too anxious to take the tenderness in. "You'll appreciate how we connected. For two days, I did nothing but sit with him and play blues. I think he felt if I could play such sad songs maybe I'd understand something of what he's going through. I hope so anyway."

She stared at the floor as if listening to sad songs still singing. "So, you're still playing," she said.

"To be honest, I just picked it back up. I hadn't played for years. It was just too hard." Brushing that close to the grief that both bound us and tore us apart caused us both to pause. Though his ghost hovered all around, neither of us was ready to acknowledge our dead son's presence.

"Well, I hope you can help him," Jen said, returning to the other boy we had in common. "He's special."

"It would help if I could ask you some questions."

"Sure."

"The thing I can't get over is his mood swing. From what I understand, he was ecstatic about the choir competition just a few hours before."

"I know," she cringed with bewilderment. "That afternoon he was as happy as I've ever seen him."

"Did something happen later in the day?"

"Not that anybody noticed. He hung out after school, had dinner, then did homework until bedtime."

"Could some of the boys have teased him, or picked a fight?"

"Not that night. Carey's voice is the jewel of the choir. With the news of the competition, he was a celebrity all day."

"How about his teachers—did anybody chew him out over forgetting his homework, or flunk him on a test?"

"No. Carey's conscientious to a fault. He's quiet in class and painfully well-behaved. He's afraid to upset anybody. Like he ever would. You can't help but feel for the boy."

"Could one of his teachers feel too much?"

"You mean like abuse?"

"*Something* caused him to crash. I'm just exploring everything. When I suggested it to Peckham, he was personally offended I even considered it."

"I bet he was." She could imagine.

"What do you think?"

"I don't know, Tony. Peckham is vigilant about boundaries. It's one of the few things we agree on. A couple months ago, several priests who live on campus had some boys to their apartment to watch videos. They said it was harmless, a way of bonding with the boys. As soon as he found out, Peckham blew up. Refused to tolerate it. He's fierce about even the appearance of impropriety. And I agree with him. If I saw any signs of abuse, I'd be all over it."

"Was Carey close to any of them?"

"Father Ike, the choir director, was one. But that was weeks ago. Peckham would have his balls if he thought Ike was still entertaining kids. And believe me, few people take Peckham on to his face. Especially Ike."

"What do you think made Carey do it?"

She sighed and stared away. "I don't know. I've been over it a thousand times to see if I missed a signal. He was elated that afternoon. He came running over right after school with the news about the choir. I was so happy for him I would have hugged him if he didn't mind being touched. Then I had to go—I was late for an appointment. I told him I had another book for him I'd bring the next day. I've been giving him Holocaust literature then we discuss it. He's so bright, and sensitive. I knew he'd love this book." She paused at the echo of a much deeper wound. "Maybe that was it. I wasn't really there for him. Instead of celebrating his great news I was still holding onto the darkness."

"Just because you recommended a book," I reassured, "doesn't mean you triggered his acting-out."

"No, I know it's not that simple. But this whole thing has me second-guessing it all. Maybe Peckham was right. Maybe we reinforced his fascination with suffering instead of helping him let it go."

"I don't think so, Jen. I take the same approach as you. These boys live in some dark places. Until we connect with them there, we'll never help them discover any lasting hope. We'll just teach them to repress it, which is the recipe for depression." Jen's darkness was that of self-doubt. It pinched to stay for long. "What was the story you were going to give him?"

"It's called *The Trial of God*," she shrugged, "by Elie Wiesel. It's about a group of Ukranian Jews who put God on trial for all the pogroms they've endured. It has a rather dark ending. But it makes you think."

"Could I borrow it? I use stories to help kids connect with their experience. Maybe I could use it while Carey is with us."

"Sure," she said absently. She picked up a book from her desk then walked it over. I met her half way. We were so close when she passed it I could have stroked her apricot hair. I avoided her eyes by glancing at some pages. I didn't register the words. Only the nearness of her presence. And the sweet familiar scent of her skin. I closed the book.

"I think you've been great with Carey, Jen. He obviously likes you. And trusts you, too."

"I know," she said. "You just caught me at a bad moment. That sermon really got to me." She shyly smiled. "I can't get over you're a therapist."

"I've grown a lot," I shared. "Finally went to therapy myself, studied with a man who works wonders with stories and wanted to be just like him when I grew up." I longed to brush her freckled cheek. At one point in our lives it would have been the most natural thing in the world. "How about you? What have you been doing?"

She raised her brows like it too had been quite a journey. "I met some women who taught me a lot about myself, about *life*, went back to school, got a PhD in Religious Studies at Berkeley, started teaching here while writing my dissertation and just stayed on."

"Wow. *Dr.* Gallagher. Congratulations." A whisper of the power she discovered along the way washed across her face. "What did you write on?"

She smiled. "What else? A feminist response to the problem of suffering. The male God who rides in and makes everything all right didn't make much sense after . . ." She caught herself and grimaced. "Well . . . that God doesn't seem to show up when you need Him. I found more hope in a feminine God from the Jewish Scriptures. She's not spectacular. But She's there in ways that keep you going."

I wanted to hold her through all the times *I* failed to show up, all the times *I* made it hard for her to keep going. "I'd love to read it sometime."

"Yeah, well. One of these days I'm going to publish it. My advisor's quite the advocate. I just haven't had time to work on it."

"I'm sure your hands are full keeping Peckham in check."

"That does take energy." Something in her forced smile told me that her inability to write was more complicated than finding the time from work. The life I once knew still beat deep within her. But something precluded its bloom. I feared I played no small part in it. "Well, it's good to see you again, Tony. My next class starts soon, and I better get ready."

"Of course, Jen. I need to get back, too." Neither of us moved. I was as scared as a man at the side of a cliff. The next step could be fatal. I took it anyway. "With all that's happened these last few years, would you like to catch up over coffee?" I felt it the second I said it. My stomach was in my mouth at the speed I was falling. Jen winced and looked away. Like a camera's flash revealing demons in the shadows, a blink of an image foretold my doom—me in all my disfiguring fury pelting this poor woman with pain. She looked back. Her eyes were moist.

"I didn't realize until now how much I still care about you. It looks like you've grown in some important ways. I have too. It's been a long journey, and I'm in a good place. I will always love you, Tony. But I can't be hurt like that again, not by you. I wish it didn't cut so deep. But it does. And I just can't do it again."

She spoke the truth. I could see it in her eyes. I wished it wasn't so, but it was. I looked as far into her pain as my shame would allow. Within it, I searched for words—words I would have shared with her had we gone out, words I wished I would have shared long before that day when the wounds became too deep for anything more than an impromptu remark in passing. Amidst the pools of tears, I found them.

"I understand, Jen. Because you're right. I hurt you, I know. I wasn't there for you, not before either, but especially when Daniel died. I wasn't there to hold you, to cry with you, to question God and scream with you. But mostly, I wasn't there to tell you what I knew to be true even though I couldn't say it.

"You were a great mom, Jen. You were a great mom. And just in case there is any doubt, I want you to know that I know—Daniel did not die because of anything you did or did not do. The truth is, he died because his dad could not see the beauty right in front of his eyes. I'm sorry I wasn't there to tell you that. And I'm sorry it's taken me seven years to show up and tell you what I should have told you the very morning we found him in his crib and every single morning since. It was not your fault, Jen. You were a great mom."

Midway through my words, tears coursed down Jen's cheeks. By the end, her head was in her hands. I wanted to hold her crying to my chest. But I knew she wouldn't want me to. So, for once, I simply stood beside her.

When her sobbing eased, she walked to her desk, pulled a tissue, then blew her nose and gazed outside. I knew her class was starting soon. And I knew that the pain cut deep. A handful of words, however heartfelt, could not heal a wound seven years bleeding. Her back was telling me it was time to go.

"Goodbye, Jen," I said. "I really am sorry."

I lingered a moment longer, wishing there was a way to finally be present but knowing that my time had long since passed. I turned to leave.

I was at the door when she found words of her own. They weren't much more than a whisper.

"Tony . . ."

I turned to look. Her eyes were swollen and streaked. They said more than the words that followed.

"If there's anything I can do to help Carey, please call."

My eyes said more as well.

"Thanks, Jen. I will."

29

MAYBE I SHOULD HAVE eaten first. With food in my stomach, I might have slept. Then I wouldn't have read the story. Nor fed my nightmares.

Yes. I should have eaten first.

—

The day was such a whirlwind I didn't have time for a meal. I rushed back to Crossroads for a silent session with Carey—he drawing rows of box-faced houses while I doodled picnics and birthstone wedding rings. Then it was time for afternoon rehearsals—the Bitter Truth Players had a performance to refine. Stories were polished, stage lighting cued, the Commons rearranged as a makeshift theater. The boys beseeched me for musical interludes so I spent the dinner hour preparing Robert Johnson material. The show came together but moments before curtain time. The audience was small but they reveled in a devil of a production. Literally. Seven stories of taking on Satan introduced by Virgil's monologue on the Lucifer in the Governor's mansion and my rendition of the swampland soul-selling that inspired the theme in the first place. The boys were so possessed after their diabolical performance it took two hours to unspell them enough to get them down to sleep. I didn't get home until well after midnight. Too tired to satisfy my belly's craving for food, I went straight to bed and sought sleep myself.

Unfortunately, my own devils were not so easily expelled. The coat of my busyness no longer protecting me, images pierced me like a pin-pricking imp—Peckham's self-righteous sneer castigating the coddling of despair, Carey with a coin purse awaiting a mother who wouldn't come, Jen's wounded eyes declining a date over coffee, and poking throughout with an ominous persistence—black-markered swastikas and paper-clipped razor wire, Holocaust comic books and death-camp signposts, triangular red badges and yellow stars of David, all the front-line strike for the advancing eyes in a mirrored collage of hell.

Sleep was impossible. Giving up the battle, I grabbed a blanket and bunked down on my living room couch. I needed to find refuge from the demons. Little did I know I'd only invite them into my nightmares. Shunning late-night TV, blues on my harp, or the pleasures of a midnight snack, I turned on the light and holed up in a good read—Elie Wiesel's *The Trial of God*.

Several hours later, I was still on the sofa. The book lay finished in my lap. Its spell so entranced me, its world blurred with my own. I was not lost in the bombshell ending, nor mulling how to adapt it for the boys. I was mesmerized by the characters' faces. Even as they followed me into sleep.

———

I am walking through a forest. The woods are as black as death. I come to a country inn. A voice is shouting through a speaker. I open the door. It is the dining room from my childhood home. The table is set for Passover. Seated with heads bowed, my mother, sister, and Jen absorb my father's rabid screams. As I step in, all four turn. They are shocked to see me. They stare—mute and unmoving—as I walk toward my mother. She follows my approach with bewildered suspicion. I bend down and kiss her frozen lips.

Instantly, torches burst in through windows on all sides. The room blazes with fire. The four at the table are engulfed in flames until the inferno explodes, obliterating the room and my family in a final volcanic blast.

I stand alone in the smoldering ruins. Ashen remnants of the table and its meal are scattered about my feet. The centerpiece is covered in soot. Bending down, I brush it clean. Singed photographs line the edges of a mirror. One bears my mother's face. Her mouth is open as if struggling to speak. She stares at me without comprehending.

I look into the mirror and see why.

I am wearing a Nazi uniform.

———

I snapped awake and trembled, my single layer of blanket anemic against the living room's chill. As the dawn's gray hands snuck into the napping cover of night, I laid on the sofa and stared. The nightmare image persisted past sleep. My mother's face haunted the horizon. She stared in the pose of the hollow-eyed hordes aching to be seen in Carey's mural. She aimed her stare at me. I had either to respond to her longtime plea, or wear the costume of those who persecuted her.

In the cold dawn of my restless night, I decided to acknowledge her suffering. I decided to acknowledge Carey's as well. Peckham would detest it. But the boy's experience would be validated.

What would it hurt to validate them together?

———

The boys barely registered my appearance—I often dropped by on Saturdays. They were caught up in basketball out on the court, a game marked by trash-talking more than ability. Blade hit the tetherball off by himself, his deformed fist as fierce as his whole one in coiling and uncoiling the ball around the pole. Virgil's writing absorbed him in the Commons. Carey was alone in the Box. He was the one I sought out.

I had something to show him.

———

The muffled noise of the boys playing ball seeped into the Box's silence. Carey looked so forsaken he mocked the vapidity of sport. He sat on the couch and stared at the floor. A tuna fish sandwich and fruit cup laid untouched on a tray beside him. I sat in the chair cornering the couch and held a folder to my lap. I spoke as if coming from a death-camp.

"Hello, Carey. I see you opted out of rec time." Shadrach screamed for a pass outside. "I don't blame you. I don't feel much like playing myself." Fast Eddie taunted Shadrach's missed shot. Carey would have killed for nothing more than an errant toss of a ball to mourn.

"I stopped by Salve Regina," I revealed. "I got a chance to go by your room. I see the Holocaust intrigues you. Me too. Not many know this, but my mother was in it. She spent two years at Dachau. She didn't talk about it much, but the anguish stayed her entire life. It's horrifying how brutal human beings can be."

Fast Eddie called for a foul on the court. Carey was not distracted. He followed me so completely he nearly turned to look.

"She gave me something I thought you'd like to see." I slipped from the folder an aged military envelope. An elastic band looped it closed as if securing classified documents. '42 Rainbow Division' was printed on the side. The World War II vintage bore its own authenticity. Carey did look, with guarded fascination.

"It's all she kept from Dachau. My dad made her burn everything else. He saw it first-hand helping the allies liberate it. He detested everything to do with the place. But my mother kept this. I guess she needed something to remind her it wasn't just a horrible nightmare."

I slipped off the elastic, opened the envelope, and pulled out a plastic bag. It contained a blood-red triangle patch stitched to a remnant of a black-and-white prison uniform. The sight of it always chilled me. It had been there. It had seen it all. Hugging my mother's sleeve, it weathered the banalities and witnessed the brutalities of a real-life Nazi concentration camp. Carey stared as if viewing a holy relic.

"It's the badge she wore while she was there. It's red because she was a Communist. She wasn't Jewish. My dad was, but she wasn't. They were actors in Munich involved in Marxist political theater protesting Hitler's government. She got caught. He didn't."

I freed it from the plastic and allowed Carey to hold it. He fingered the fraying thread as if touching the hem of Jesus' garment.

"Sweeeeeet Mama! Nothing but net!" Fast Eddie sang after scoring. "Now *that's* what I'm talking about!"

As if afraid he would spoil it, Carey delicately passed it back. We stared at it staining the palm of my hand. I spoke as much to it as I did to Carey.

"This world is filled with suffering. I don't know how people take it. I guess that's why I do what I do. I'd really like to know. How do people go on living after stomaching so much brutality?"

I hoped Carey wanted to know as well. Maybe as much as I did.

———

I was back in my living room digging up the drive to cook up some dinner when Harry shuffled up to the door. He wore the same jacket from the Saturday before with a fresh tie clipped to a pressed shirt. He carried a Tupperware bowl.

"You look ready for singles night at the senior center," I quipped.

"Oh no," he bemused preferring not to josh about it. "My heart's already taken."

I took back the joke. "Well, she's the lucky one." He nodded but his gaze said otherwise—truth be told, *he* was the lucky one. "You want to come in?" I asked.

"I suppose I got a minute. Mass don't start 'til seven." It was quarter after five. That was Harry—all decked out for church two hours before it started. "Here." He held out the bowl. "I tried my hand at cioppino. It don't hold a candle to Martha's but I thought you might like to try some."

"Thanks, Harry. I'd love to. Can I get you a soda?"

"A Shasta would be fine."

When I returned from the kitchen, Harry was sitting on the sofa's edge like he wasn't too used to calling on folks. His conversation was a bit rusty too.

"So, how you doing?" I asked.

"Oh, getting by."

"Your yard's looking good."

"Yeah, it's coming along."

"Ready for spring?"

"I suppose so."

I sipped my soda and regrouped. Harry would never be accused of being gabby. "You think the Giants will have a good year?" I tried.

"Maybe so. Roger Craig seems okay."

"Even if he was a Dodger, huh?"

He snickered. "Even so." I was striking out. Just what I needed—another guy I couldn't get to talk.

"Well, I had quite the week," I swung away. "I've got a new boy at work whose tried to kill himself twice, eight others who heard the devil in the middle of the night, and my ex-wife turned me down to have coffee together." It was a lot to blurt out, but anything to shock life into the flat-line of our conversation. Something started beating.

"So you was married once?" Harry asked.

"A while ago. I hadn't seen her in seven years."

"That's too bad."

That's *exactly* what it was. Too much bad. "I don't know Harry, how do people do it?"

"What's that?"

"Stay happily married with the person you love."

"Don't reckon I know."

"You seemed to do it. You and Martha were married what, thirty years?"

"Forty-three."

"Forty-three! So what was your secret?"

He sighed. "Findin' someone like Martha, I suppose."

"But it takes two to keep it alive."

"I don't know about that. Everything good about me, I owe to Martha. Like becoming a churchgoer. That was all her."

"What, she up and converted you?"

"I wouldn't say anybody got converted. I just went 'cause I wanted to be close to her."

It hit him how far her closeness had become. I wondered why he bothered. "So if she was the religious one, why do you still go?"

He gazed into his glass like a seer would a ball. "I don't know exactly. It just feels right somehow." I gazed as well. Maybe that was the poignant truth. After forty-three years with the woman you love, it just feels right to take Eucharist alone. We all have our ways of hanging on.

Then Harry bobbed up with a gleam. He sounded like he was changing the subject. "I ever tell you about our fortieth wedding anniversary?" He grinned just thinking about it.

"Boy oh boy, what a night."

———

I wanted to do something special for all that time she put up with me. So I looked around for the classiest restaurant I could possibly find. I asked everybody—people who'd know too, my boss at Ma Bell, people at the bank—and I found out about this place out on the ocean where all the rich folk go. A fancy chef from the city started it somewhere's south of Bodega Bay. It must have been fancy 'cuz they told me on the phone they don't even have menus there—you just eat whatever they cook that night. Which sounded kind of strange to me, but I figured that must be what the rich folk do. I asked how much it cost, and they said fifty dollars a plate. Now for a guy like me, that could buy groceries for a week. But I knew Martha would be tickled so I reserved a table for two and sent in a check for a hundred dollars just so there wouldn't be any problems.

Martha was tickled. She got all dolled up in her best gown and a necklace that looks like real pearls. I put on my suit and we headed off for the coast. Now we had never been there before, so we started looking for it as soon as we passed Bodega Bay. We drove so long I thought we must have passed it. Then sure enough, there it was. You couldn't miss it. It was built right on the beach, so close the waves went underneath during high tide. 'The Watch' it was called 'cuz you could see into the ocean for miles.

Now we was a little early, it was only a quarter to six, but I didn't see no harm in it. We walked in and there's this guy in a tuxedo at the door. I tell him we're there for dinner and he says that's fine but they aren't even open yet. Can you imagine? This place was only open for dinner. Denny's is open twenty-four hours a day—you can get a Grand Slam for breakfast at two o'clock in the morning. This place, only dinner. Now that's classy. So I say,

'Could we just wait someplace and have a glass of wine, you see today's our fortieth wedding anniversary?'

And as I'm saying this, the owner walks by and says, 'You two been married forty years?'

'Sure have,' I say.

'Get outta here, forty years today?'

'Yes sir. And ready to do forty more.'

'Well come on in.' He takes off our coats like he's our butler or something, then in we go.

Man, you should have seen this place. It was like walking into Paradise. All the tables had white tablecloths and crystal wine glasses and four or five forks and knives all lined up next to their best china. They had plants coming out the ceiling, a fishpond with a waterfall, a grand piano so shiny you could see yourself in the reflection. They even had a sculpture made of ice. I'm telling you, this place was classy. The owner takes us to this big round table by the window, the best seats in the house, helps us into our chairs like we was movie stars and says he'll be right back. Well me and Martha are still figuring out what all the forks are for when he comes back with the guy in the tuxedo, a bottle of champagne, and four glasses.

'We're gonna have a toast,' he says. 'Tonight, we celebrate forty years of wedded bliss.' Well, he's working the cork off the bottle when one of the waiters walks by.

'What's going on?' he says. 'We aren't even open yet.'

The owner says, 'These two been married forty years.'

'Get outta here,' the waiter says, 'forty years today?'

'Yeah,' the owner says, 'get yourself a glass.'

He runs off and another waiter walks by.

'What's going on? We aren't even open yet.'

'These two been married forty years,'

'Get outta here, forty years today?'

'Yeah, get yourself a glass.'

He runs off and a waitress walks by.

'What's going on? We're not even open yet.'

'These two been married forty years.'

'Get outta here, forty years today?'

'Yeah, get yourself a glass.' Then a bus boy comes, and a few more waitresses, and more waiters too, with more glasses and more champagne 'til there's so much commotion going on they hear us way back in the kitchen. This guy with a chef's hat leans out the door and hollers,

'What's going on out there? We're not even open yet.'

'These two been married forty years,' everybody says.

'Get outta hear, forty years today?'

'Yeah, get yourself a glass. Get the other cooks. Get Joe and Julio doing dishes in the back. Get anybody who's around. We're celebrating forty years of wedded bliss and every-body's part of the toast.'

The next thing you know, there's thirty people standing around our table, some of them wearing tuxedos, some of them in jeans and aprons, all of them with a glass in the air as happy for us as if we was family. And they didn't even know our names. I looked over at Martha. She looked over at me. We clinked our glasses like we was the King and Queen of England, and I thought to myself, I don't care how much this costs. This is a party we'll never forget.

And that it was. Pretty soon, people started coming in, so everybody got back to work. But they didn't forget about us. We didn't have one person waiting on us, we had a whole restaurant full. Every waiter that walked by stopped to fill our glasses and take our dishes. We asked for coffee and they gave us cappuccinos. We asked what they were serving, the chef came out with dish after dish for us to try. The owner sat down so many times to reminisce about our courtship, people started looking to see if we was somebody famous. And the way they treated us after dinner, they probably thought we were.

The owner got the piano player to play the song from our wedding. Then Martha and me danced the same dance we danced forty years earlier to the day. Everybody stood around and watched—the people from the kitchen, the customers, the waiters and waitresses. I still had a move or two and gave Martha a dip, then I kissed her right there in front of everybody.

They all cheered, and sang, 'Happy Anniversary,' and the chef brought out a cake to cut. Then the owner pulls out this shiny bottle and pours us something older than our marriage. He lifts a glass, we lift our own, and he finishes the night with one last toast—'To forty years of marriage . . . and forty more just like it.' I tell you what, if you don't count the one on my wedding day, it was the best party I'd ever been to in my life. We didn't leave 'til eleven o'clock, and me and Martha had work the next day.

But here's the kicker. Before we left, I asked about the bill. I knew it cost a whole lot more than a hundred dollars. And darn if that owner didn't put his arms around us and tell us it was already taken care of. I told him at least let me add a little tip. He wouldn't hear of that neither. Wouldn't even look at my billfold. He says, 'What you've given us is more valuable than money. We'll be savoring this evening for seasons to come.' That's just how he talked.

So what could we do? We thanked them for the dinner, got a picture with the owner out front, then waved goodbye and left. Martha took my hand, and hummed our song, and all the way home I thought to myself, we just got the deal of a lifetime. A hundred dollars for a night like that—it was worth a hundred times that.

Well, I had no idea.

About a week later, I get a letter in the mail from some restaurant I don't remember.

'We're sorry you didn't make it for your fortieth anniversary. We hope you'll try us for your next special occasion.' And out drops my check for a hundred dollars.

Me and Martha went to the wrong restaurant! They weren't even expecting us at 'The Watch.' That whole meal was entirely on the house.

I tell you what, that was one classy restaurant.

———

Harry chuckled at the story as if it had happened last week, the check just found in the afternoon's mail. The brightness of his beaming could have given off warmth.

"What a great story," I said. "You must have laughed about that for weeks."

His smile sobered as he gazed faraway. "We never did stop laughing about that."

The poignancy caught me. "I can see why," I empathized. "Those are the things that warm your heart."

Harry nodded in palsied reflection. Then he looked over and corrected me.

"Warm your heart?" he said. "No. Those are the things that keep me alive."

———

After he left, I warmed up the stew. I lit a candle in my dining room, opened a can of diet Seven-Up, and supped on Harry's homemade cioppino.

If it wasn't spectacular, it was enough to keep me going.

30

CCSo, you guys got game against the devil, I'll give you that. But do you got it to go against the Big Guy Himself?"

We were debriefing the performance during Monday's group session. The boys were all abuzz about their title fight with Beelzebub. Swatted the devil silly, they said. Took him down for the count like Muhammad Ali in Zaire. To hear them tell it, the Rumble in the Jungle was a tea-time social compared to the Rumble with the Devil that Crossroads hosted. They were flexing to rope-a-dope a rematch.

Until I switched the opponent.

"What're you talking about?" Fast Eddie bit.

"I'm talking about the Main Man," I teased. "The Master of the Universe. I'm talking about *God*."

They looked at me like satire was one thing, sacrilege another. Virgil was intrigued. "Go on," he coaxed from his recliner.

"Since we gave the devil his due," I reasoned, "it seems only right to give equal time to the Almighty. I found a story that's the perfect counterpoint to the one last week. But I have to warn you, it's rather dark."

Virgil smiled like that's how he liked his stories—dark and hard to chew. Carey was attentive from the outset—I told him earlier the afternoon's story came from Ms. Gallagher. The others were open to sparring, but they kept their protective gear close by.

"A Holocaust survivor wrote it," I introduced, "a man named Elie Wiesel. He was fifteen when he witnessed a scene in Auschwitz that so haunted him he wrote a play about it thirty years later. A group of rabbis accused God of conspiring with the Nazis. Why else wouldn't God deliver them—He saved the Jews from Pharaoh, after all. Either God supported the Nazis, or He didn't care enough to get involved. Either way, He was an accomplice to genocide. So they did the unthinkable. They put God on trial."

"That's messed up," Fast Eddie shuddered.

"That ain't right," Shadrach concurred.

"That ain't nothing," I added. "Wait'll you hear the ending."

The play takes place in seventeenth-century Eastern Europe. It's Purim, the holiday where Jews tell stories to celebrate how Esther saved their ancestors from a Babylonian massacre.

Three strangers come to an inn at a Jewish village. The inn is deserted, except for the testy innkeeper who feeds the three strangers dinner. After they have eaten, the strangers call the innkeeper over.

"We must be honest," they tell him. "We have no money. But fear not, we will bring you bucketfuls before the night is through."

"No money?" the innkeeper shouts. "I'll have you swindlers thrown into jail."

"But we're not swindlers," they say. "We're minstrels. And tonight is Purim. Gather the entire Jewish community to listen to our stories. They'll laugh, they'll cry, and they'll eat and drink until your pockets, good sir, are bulging."

"Ha!" the innkeeper snarls. "Look around you. I **am** the Jewish community—the only Jew left in this village but for my daughter who's half-dead and mad."

"But how can that be?" the minstrels exclaim. "We've seen menorahs in all the windows."

"Let me tell you *a story*," the innkeeper scorns. "Two weeks ago a Jewish 'community' is celebrating a wedding. My daughter, seventeen years old, is marrying the rabbi's son. Two hundred Jews—men, women, and children—gather in this room for the wedding feast. Unfortunately, it is the night the Christians call 'Good' Friday, the night they claim we Jews killed their God. In the middle of the feast, a mob of Christians storm in. With clubs and axes, they hack their way through the crowd until they have butchered every Jew but two. Me, they tie to a table—it takes ten to subdue me. They stand it against a wall and pry my eyes with sticks. I am forced to watch as twenty, forty, sixty men rape my daughter then spit in her face. Then they left us to bury the dead and live with the nightmare. Tell me, God's minstrels, what kind of Purim stories will you tell that do not insult the dead who begged your God to deliver them?"

The minstrels are shaken. "But what are we to do? It's our sacred duty to extol God's goodness through story tonight."

"No such stories will be told here. God doesn't deserve to hear them."

"You accuse God, then?" they ask.

"That is exactly who I accuse. God abandoned His people when they cried to Him in their suffering. What does He have to say for Himself?"

The minstrels are stunned. "We do not know."

"Then that is what we'll find out. You want a story for Purim? This is it. You be the judges. I'll be the prosecutor. Tonight, we put God on trial. Let Him listen to that."

Just then, a priest bursts in through the door. "Hurry," he warns. "Trouble is brewing. A mob is forming to kill any Jew that still lives. You must flee to the woods until it is safe."

"We're not going anywhere," the innkeeper threatens. "We're celebrating Purim, aren't we, minstrels?"

The minstrels are terrified and talk it over. Then they agree. "Fine, innkeeper. We will celebrate Purim as you wish."

The priest runs out to talk sense into the mob. The Jews convert the inn to a courtroom. A judge and two advisors are seated at the center. The prosecutor has a podium to the side.

"Are we ready to proceed?" the judge commences.

"We are," the prosecutor replies.

"Where is the defendant?" the judge inquires.

"Absent," the prosecutor sneers. "As usual."

"Then where is His defense attorney?"

"There isn't one."

"But there must be somebody with faith enough to justify the ways of God."

No one moves. "It's God's own fault," the innkeeper denounces. "He killed them all two weeks ago."

"Well, we can't have a trial without a defense attorney," the judge insists. "Somebody must answer the accusations made against God."

Once more, the door blows open. This time a stranger walks in, wearing a Purim mask. "I must warn you," the stranger says, "a mob of Christians is coming this way. Their priest is unable to stop them. I suggest you flee at once."

"We will not flee," the innkeeper insists. "We have a story to tell for Purim."

"Yes," the judge concurs. "We are putting God on trial. But unfortunately, we cannot find a defense attorney."

The stranger considers the matter. Then he removes his coat. "I would be honored to defend God's ways. What precisely are the charges?"

The prosecutor begins. "I accuse God of conspiracy with every murder, rape, and genocidal slaughter the world has ever seen."

The defense attorney responds. "But surely you cannot consolidate every atrocity into a single lawsuit. Each act of violence is unique unto itself."

"Fine," the prosecutor comes back. "I accuse God of massacring this village, of violating my daughter, and of defiling a faithful Jewish home."

"Very well. Bring on your witnesses."

"I am the witness."

"But that will not do," the attorney responds. "You are the prosecutor. In your mind, God is already condemned."

"Then I bring the shrieks of all that were killed as testimony against God's silence."

"But you cannot testify for the dead. Maybe they rejoice to be rid of this world."

"I heard their screams as their children were hacked—nobody rejoices at such a horror."

"Precisely my point," the attorney rebuts. "Death brought relief from violent suffering. Maybe they rejoice now to be with their God."

"A God who condoned their death?"

"A God who spared your life. Should you not be rejoicing now, since you were not killed as well?"

"Rejoicing!" the prosecutor spits. "That my loved ones were slaughtered, my people exterminated, my daughter defiled right in front of my eyes? How dare you suggest I rejoice in that." The innkeeper looks ready to attack. The stranger calmly looks back. Cries are heard in the distance; the Christians, lusting for blood and armed to spill it, are getting closer.

"Okay prosecutor," the stranger continues, "for the sake of argument, I will concede that your village witnessed a sinister night. But theologians and rabbis for centuries have concluded that God's goodness prevails even in the midst of evil. If you wait with faith, God will make things clear in the end."

"I waited for God," the innkeeper refutes, "killers came instead."

"God's reasons are mysterious, man cannot understand them."

"Evil is not, even a child flinches when stabbed."

"God uses suffering to punish the wicked, sin brings violence upon itself."

"What is the sin of a newborn baby impaled to a door with a spear?"

"Then, it's the sin of the killers that is to blame. God does not impale children."

"God does not stop it."

"God is not able."

"Then, God is not God."

"God is not willing."

"Then, God abets murder."

"God preserves freedom."

"God deserves death."

The two men glare as they pause from their sparring. Outside, the cries of the mob grow louder.

"You are a hard case, Prosecutor."

"As is your defendant, Stranger."

The stranger patiently contemplates the innkeeper. "You are right," he says. "God's ways are difficult to comprehend."

"They are more difficult to defend," the innkeeper responds.

"Perhaps. But the holy one believes in God's goodness despite God's absence."

"I despise God."

"He glorifies God in the midst of persecution."

"I find God contemptible."

"He turns to God in times of darkness."

"I turn my back on God."

"The way of life is to trust God despite it all."

"I choose death, to protest God in the midst of it all."

"I see that," the stranger says. "Pity. For the death of a godless man never ends."

The door flies open. The priest rushes into the room. "Quick!" he pleads. "I can't hold them off. They'll be here in seconds. They'll kill you all."

The innkeeper looks at the judge. "I offer our deaths as my final testimony. Surely, God's silence now proves my case."

The judge turns to the stranger in terror. "But God has not abandoned us yet. Surely He will listen to you, holy one—you who alone have defended His ways."

"But what can I do?" the stranger beseeches.

"God hears the prayers of the righteous," he says. "Beg Him to spare us."

An axe-blade thunders against the door. Rabid cries surround the inn.

"Prayers are useless," screams the innkeeper. "I demand a verdict before I die."

Another axe-blow pounds the door. "Please holy one," the judge pleads, "pray for God to deliver us."

The door splinters as the axe breaks through. An arm reaches for the lock. The prosecutor screams at the judge. "I demand a verdict, I tell you."

The minstrel stares at the stranger. "If you won't pray for us, at least tell us who you are."

The stranger reaches for his mask. The innkeeper shouts again. "A verdict, I tell you! Now!"

"Please holy one, reveal yourself."

"A verdict!"

The door crashes open. Christians rush in. The stranger rips off his mask. The minstrels and the innkeeper are aghast. As the mob consumes them, they cannot stop staring.

The man before them, the only one who dared defend God, is Satan.

———

The boys gaped as if confronted with an enigma as distasteful as it was impenetrable. Even Virgil furrowed his brow as he pondered the surprise revelation.

"I don't get it," Shadrach blurted. "The good guy is Satan?"

"What makes you think he's the good guy?" I asked.

"He's the only one watching God's back."

"Maybe God's back shouldn't be turned in the first place."

"That's not what I mean. He's the only one on God's side. If that doesn't make you good, what does?"

The others were as stumped as Shadrach. Except Virgil. His wheels spun as if anticipating a delicious insight.

"So, why would the devil take God's side?" I nudged.

"Well, somebody had to," Blade said. "Everybody else is just blaming Him."

"But what does he stand to get out of it?" I continued.

"Nothing," Fast Eddie said. "It doesn't make sense. The devil should be glad everybody's dissing the Guy."

Virgil closed his eyes to focus his thoughts.

"Maybe the devil's just making them madder so they'll hate God more," Shadrach offered.

"Maybe the devil feels sorry for God," Clint considered.

"Or maybe," Virgil gushed as it suddenly became clear. "The devil's making them *less* mad by explaining it all. Ohhh, this is good. The devil is the one who's got all the answers."

"But what's wrong with that?" Shadrach asked.

"The answers make you stop asking the question." Virgil's excitement grew as he rolled along. "People give explanations when they should be protesting the facts. It's an outrage God lets evil exist. Anything that takes the outrage away is from the devil."

"So God is guilty?" Clint was confused by the dialectical subtlety.

"That's what's so brilliant about it." Virgil bubbled over like a lit-up tutor. "The story leaves it open. *Any* answer is demonic."

"I get it," Fast Eddie sparked. "The audience decides for itself if God is guilty or not."

"Is that it, Dr. T?" Blade asked.

I turned it back. "What verdict does the story give?"

"It doesn't," Fast Eddie said. "The judges are killed before they decide."

"As far as I'm concerned, that makes God guilty," Malcolm concluded.

"But God didn't kill them," Fast Eddie defended.

"Maybe not," Malcolm countered. "But He didn't stop it either. That's what Virgil's talking about."

"No, it's not," Virgil corrected. "Don't you see? Even declaring God guilty is answering the question. *Any* answer is of the devil."

"But you yourself said it's an outrage that God doesn't do anything," Malcolm grappled.

"It is. But I'm not going to let God off the hook by declaring Him guilty."

Fast Eddie was lost. "How does declaring Him guilty let God off the hook?"

Virgil started over. "Look, I don't need to tell you guys that shit happens. Look at Blade's hand—his own mother did that. It's just as bad as Christians gangbanging an innkeeper's daughter. And God just goes about His business without doing a damn thing about it. What would you like to say to God about that?" The boys just looked at him. "What would *you* say, Blade?"

"I don't know."

"Well I know what I'd say—'Open your Goddamned eyes and take a good look at all this pain.' Then I would demand a response. And if He doesn't give me one, I'd cry out for a verdict, and I'd keep crying out until my cry drives Him mad."

"So you want Him declared guilty," Malcolm confirmed.

"No."

"You want Him innocent?" Clint asked.

"*No!* Don't you see? Innocent or guilty either way, the case is closed and everybody goes back to business as usual. I want the case perpetually opened. God's not condemned, God's not absolved. He has to just sit there and face the suffering until the horror of it all finally gets to Him and He does something about it."

"But Virgil," Blade said. "You don't even believe in God."

"It's not about God. It's about whatever's out there—the life force, the collective will of humanity, just one person in the audience if nobody else. But that one person has to look suffering in the eye and has to keep looking at it until it finally gets to them. And anybody who lets them off the hook is on the side of Satan."

"So how do you make them look suffering in the eye?" I led.

Virgil smiled. He knew he was onto it. "You tell the story. Isn't that what this is all about, Dr. T.? You tell the Purim story. You take God or humanity or whatever the hell you believe in and you sit them down in the defendant's chair and you tell them the story of suffering in the world. Then you demand a verdict, but you don't accept one. Innocent or guilty, they don't get out of the chair until the truth of the story compels them to actually do something."

The boy's pondered Virgil's words. They did not grasp all the subtleties but his voice spoke with authority.

"So what do you say?" I asked. "Are you up for it?"

"For what exactly?" Shadrach clarified.

"For putting God on trial."

"How would we do it?" Blade asked.

"Like Virgil said. We start with the stories. This is the theme for the week—create a character that has a reason to put God on trial. They've experienced evil first hand and they want some kind of an accounting. Then we'll see what happens when the characters come forth with their complaints. Are you game?"

Virgil was more than game, he was half way down the court. His pencil scratched his pad as if trying to keep up with his thoughts. The others were still warming up to the idea. They'd need more time before it took hold.

But one boy wouldn't.

I had no idea what massacre he witnessed, no clue about his grievance against God. But the innkeeper within him had a story to tell. And apparently, it was time to come out.

Carey picked up a pencil and reached for a pad. He stared at the blank page.

Then he wrote.

31

L UKE SUMMED IT UP for us all. "The Force is strong in that one." The rest of the boys were speechless. I had just read Carey's story from the day before, the seed for a play he sketched into the evening. The outline was rough, but the images were chilling. Luke was right. *Something* was strong in that boy.

Virgil smiled at the ceiling, bemusing the possibilities. Taken by the impiety, he broke the spell with his imprimatur. "Brilliant," he declared. "Absolutely brilliant."

Then with the aplomb of a bankrolled producer, he took charge. Roles were delegated, sets were imagined, costumes and props conceived. By the time the afternoon session was over, the boys bustled with the purpose of a small-town acting troupe bucking for a Broadway debut. With an inspired concept to work with, they dispersed to develop their parts. Virgil however, remained in the circle. He relinquished his recliner and huddled next to Carey on the couch. Though Carey remained mute, the two became a team. Virgil, the veteran writer, crackled with ideas; Carey, the concept's originator, scribbled more of his own. The two sparkled with artistic chemistry.

For the first time in two weeks, Carey smiled.

———

"I can't thank you enough, Jen." She returned my call after school. "Your story was the perfect catalyst. Carey's been writing up a storm since yesterday."

Delighted, she asked what he was writing.

"A play with the boys," I answered. "Inspired by Wiesel's. In fact, they're working it up to perform at their school this Friday."

She wondered if Carey would be in it.

"Oh, he'll be in it," I assured. "He has the most haunting role—though it's not exactly a speaking part."

She asked for the elaboration I didn't want to give.

"To be honest," I hinted, "I'd rather not spoil it for you. I was thinking you might like to come see it."

That took her aback.

"It would mean a lot to Carey," I deflected. "He lit up when I told him the story came from you."

She hesitated as if surmising whom else it would please. Then she said she'd have to think about it.

"I understand," I let out. "But it'd be great if you could."

By Wednesday, the commons looked like a backstage prop room. From the vocational school maintenance department, the Crossroads supply shed, and assorted Bitter Truth supporters, the boys scrounged up paints and butcher paper, full-length mirrors and plywood panels, set dollies and toga costumes, and boxes filled with everything from religious memorabilia to shackling irons. The real find was the play's central prop. Virgil remembered an activist guild that reenacted Chinese slave conditions during turn-of-the-century railroad construction. The guild donated a padded-rubber sledgehammer they used for pounding wooden spikes into Styrofoam ties. Of course, the kids had to engage in impact tests on our plywood portrait and each other. I took a swing or two myself. I had to admit—pounding that plywood was satisfying.

The script proceeded as well as the prop acquisition. We fine-tuned adjustments as we improvised each segment. My only hesitation came with the ending—the darkness was disturbing. I urged the boys to present more hope but they insisted it would cheapen the play. They did come up with one idea. To extend the mood as they took their bows, they wanted some blues from me. I told them they didn't need it; the final scene would stun a circus crowd. Then I had my own idea. It took my breath away to think about. I told them I'd do it, if I could choose the piece. I shared the words and played the tune. The chorus suggested that our play was our song; and once we were gone, the song would play on. The boys turned to Virgil. Virgil turned to Carey. Carey reread the words, then nodded. We had our ending.

Now I had to go through with it.

I had two messages Thursday afternoon. One was from Jen; she was coming. The other was from Dr. Carter; a bed had opened in Marin—Carey would be transferred on Saturday. I called them both back. Jen, I gave directions, Carter, an update. Carey was doing so well I contested, he shouldn't be shipped someplace else. I invited her to the performance to see for herself. She said she would consider it.

Thursday night, we set up the school auditorium and had our dress rehearsal. We all sensed the coming intensity. Friday evening would feature the most powerful production we ever performed. But even we were unaware of how intense it would be. We only knew what the programs portended. The Bitter Truth Players were introducing their newest member. And with his inspiration, they were presenting an original piece. The world premiere of . . .

'The Night That God Got Nailed.'

"Jesus Fucking Christ! What's the big deal about cussing?"

I couldn't believe Virgil's first words; I had no idea they were coming. All that he said was his opening monologue would be particularly relevant to the play. Then his wicked smile promised a dose of his signature irreverence. But of all nights to come up with this. I leaned back to gauge Jen's reaction. I couldn't read her across the room. But Dr. Carter was transparent. Her eyebrows stretched in shock. Which was just what Virgil wanted. He may have had a Seinfeld smile; but he was all Lenny Bruce inside.

"Why would parishioners go apoplectic if their priest looks up from his homily and says, 'Hell if I know why the world's so fucked—talk to the Son-of-a-Bitch in charge'? Why do we wash Suzie's mouth out with soap when she spills Kool-Aid on her dollhouse and says, 'Shit.' You'd think she just spoke from her butthole.

"'*Straight* to the *bathroom* with *you*, young lady. Gonna *scrub* that *filthy* little *mouth* of yours.'

"I'll tell you why—it's true. The eyes may be the mirror of the soul, but the mouth is its rectum. And nobody wants to be reminded—the cesspools of profanity are in each of us.

"Admit it. You hit your thumb with a hammer and what spews out? Not 'Dog gone it.' Someone takes a hammer to your head, who's going to retaliate with, 'Oopsie daisey?' Somebody fondles your boy, rapes little Suzie, hammers your God to a tree for Christ's sake, and all you're going to pull from your underbelly arsenal is 'Gosh darn you?' I don't think so. We've got heavy artillery ready to go and now's the time to use it—'Go-to-hell-you-*God-damn*-MOTHER-FUCKIN'-*COCK-SUCKIN'*-SON-OF-A-BITCH!! . . . AND FUCK YOURSELF WHILE YOU'RE AT IT*!!*

"No, show me someone who's satisfied with 'Rats' and I'll show you a school sniper in the making. Ask their children, they'll tell you.

"You don't think Jesus ever took the Good Name in vain? The guy was human for God's sake. He's strapped to a post with a spike at his hand and a sledgehammer ready to fall, you don't think he's got a few 'feelings' about this?

"'Forgive them Father for . . .' BAM! 'Goddamn it, that hurts. I'm trying to pray for . . .' BAM! 'Piss off already. God, are you catching this . . .' BAM! 'GO TO HELL YOU BALLBUSTIN' PRICKS . . . JESUS CHRIST!!'

"It might not stop the nailing, but a verbal enema cleanses the soul. Besides, it's the most reliable form of prayer I know.

"And what an inspired lexicon of expletives we have. Whoever said swearing's for people who can't express themselves properly just isn't listening. These words are crafted with a poet's perceptiveness.

"When life's spike's being pounded into you, 'Shit' communicates perfectly—'I find this pain so offensive I turn my backside to it and consign it to a sewer's fate.'

"You call the person pounding the nails a 'son-of-a-bitch', you're diagnosing him with textbook accuracy—'You are the product of a quick lay; your mother never loved you so you have no love to give.'

"You're hanging in the desert when vinegar's shoved into your face, calling the guy a 'Goddamned cocksucker's' just shorthand for saying, 'You're draining the juices of my dignity; may the King of Glory condemn you to the darkest regions of hell.'

"I defy you to find more exact forms of expression. 'Asshole'—'You're the portal through which filth enters the world. 'Bastard'—'Your father abandoned you and left you to degenerate.' 'Jesus Christ'—At once a confession of complicity in a crucifixion and a prayer for God to make things right.

"I'm telling you—when people cuss, listen carefully. They're speaking with precision.

"Which leads me to our cultural obsession with the word, 'Fuck.' It's the most versatile word in our four-letter armory—a noun, a verb, or an adjective, each with a bunkerful of applications—Fuck you, fuck me, fuck off, fuck your mother, fuck your dog, fuck yourself, I don't give a fuck if you fuck your sister's brains out but don't you fuck with me you fuck or I'll fuck up your fucking face.' Try it; it's as much fun to say 'Fuck' as it is to do it.

"But conjugate it any way you want, there's soul in that word—sex and violence. It lays bare our most primal human longing for connection, and the rage that erupts when that connection is violated. When our soul-mate moves into the bed of our best-friend, 'Fuck you' pays riddance with decisive eloquence—'I once ached to feel you skin to skin and savor the communion of making-love. Now I want to penetrate by force, thrusting my prick until you scream from the pain.'

"'Fuck' is the word of the wounded lover.

"Which makes the most wounded word of all, all the more poignant.

"'Mother-Fucker.' A more derogatory obscenity cannot be composed. A person fucked by his mother is more pitiable than the infant dumped in a dumpster. The mother-fucker's been molested by life's very womb. The lap they yearned would hold and suckle, spread its legs and sucked. From that fondle forward, every person that touches is suspected of seduction; every hug becomes a hand-job. Broken and betrayed, their longing for love becomes a rage that would rape the woman that bore them.

"Maybe that's why these words are so hard to hear. There's something of the mother-fucker in each of us. And Goddamn the son-of-a-bitch who ever tries to remind us.

"Jesus Christ.

"It's enough to make you cuss."

———

The play begins when Fast Eddie stumbles into view in front of the curtains as if shoved from offstage. He glares back at the culprit that expelled him, then brushes off his clothes. With a black suit and red dress shirt, a matching silk pocket-handkerchief, and a deviously painted pencil mustache, he looks like a cross between Snidely Whiplash and a used-car salesman from hell.

"Huh," he huffs, extending his cuffs. "I never liked the Old Man anyway—always playing favorites." He looks around. "So where in the hell have I landed?" Picking up a chance newspaper, he scans the front page. "Let's see—war, lynching, parents abusing their kids . . . Must be Earth. Well, what's a guy to do?" He tosses the paper and looks around to make a quick buck. Spotting me at the far end of the front row, he opens his jacket like a huckster hording stolen watches. Religious memorabilia dangles inside.

"What can I interest you in?" he asks. "Rosary beads, praise music, prayer cards? I got it all. Guaranteed to take your mind off things. What d'ya say? I'll throw in eternal life for an extra ten-spot."

I hand him twenty dollars and he slips me an icon, pockets the bill like a con on the make, then turns and confides in the audience. "Greatest scam in town—a guy could get rich in a place like this. But enough of the petty cash; we've got bigger fish to fry. From what I hear, the peasants are revolting. Come, look for yourself." He reaches for the curtains then looks back. "But I'm warning you. Keep your eyes open at your own peril. For tonight is the night . . . that God gets nailed."

He pulls the curtains open.

The stage is set like an ecclesiastical courtroom. A two-tiered judge's bench dominates the center; its front panels are stenciled, 'The Truth shall set you free.' Shadrach sits magisterially behind it in a judge's robe with a priest's collar. He has a glass of water on one side, a Bible on the other. Three chairs angle from the bench; Blade, Clint, and Malcolm sit expectantly as witnesses. A prosecutor's table, littered with law books and folders, juts out from them with Virgil rifling through the documents. Across the stage, a bare table faces off with Virgil's, a gap separating it from the judge. Fast Eddie eavesdrops off to the side.

Shadrach drowsily bangs his gavel. "Hear ye, hear ye, hear ye. Court is now in session. The Honorable Pius Pontiff presiding. Come and ye shall be heard." He sips his water and sighs. "Today we hear the matter of . . ." He searches for the docket. "The People of the State of Affliction versus the Lord God Almighty." Surprised, he looks down at Virgil. "Is that right?"

Virgil spots and retrieves Fast Eddie's newspaper. "Yes, your Honor. We the people from the State of Affliction have a grievance against the Supreme Architect and Divine Governor of the Cosmos. We're putting God on trial."

"On what grounds?"

"Capricious neglect, criminal abandonment, and conspiracy to commit child abuse, racism, and murder."

"These are severe charges, son." Shadrach swigs his water. "With serious implications. You sure you want to go through with this?"

"Yes sir. We've been preparing for some time."

"Okay," Shadrach shrugs. "It's your neck. So where's the defendant?"

"He didn't show up," Virgil sneers. "As usual."

"A word from the wise," Shadrach admonishes. "In my courtroom we show the Creator respect. I'll have you do the same."

"I'm sorry, your Honor. But He hasn't responded to any of our summons."

"You should've come to me first. That's what guys like me are for." He pulls out a cardboard papal miter, places it on his head, grabs a staff, stands, and faces the curtained backdrop. Glancing at the audience, he ad-libs, "Children, don't try this at home." Then with the dramatic solemnity of the high priest of Ra parting the Red Sea, he turns back to the curtains and intones, "Ominy Dominy, Hocus Pocus, Abracadabra, and Mother

May I." He dips his hand into his glass, sprinkles water on the curtain, and makes the sign of the cross.

The stage lights go off, a spotlight flickers, pounding feet create an expectant drum roll. The curtains flutter, then open. Boomer and Flash, dressed in white togas, wheel out a prop the size of two sheets of plywood and position it between the judge's bench and the vacant table. It is God—a giant eight-foot face painted on butcher paper, a cross between the Almighty Oz and the longhaired head of the shepherd Jesus. The eyes are open, the mouth straight. Neither smiling nor frowning, it faces off with the three witnesses across stage, a guard poised on either side. The lights return.

"How did you do that?" Virgil asks.

"That's what separates us sheep from the goats." Shadrach lifts his glass in mock salute, drains the contents, and sits down. Removing his miter, he proceeds. "Now all we need is a defense attorney." He looks at the witnesses. "Which of you would like the privilege of defending God and all His ways? . . . Come on . . . Think of how your faith will please Him . . . Lots of perks—blessed assurance, a get-out-of-hell-free card, eternal life in Shangri-La."

The three shake their heads. The judge's tone changes.

"Then think what'll happen if you don't—God's back to you 'til the end of time, an eternity of scorn and torment."

The three shrug as if such would be a step up.

"So be it," Shadrach gives in. He scans the courtroom. "Is there no one with faith enough to defend the Almighty Creator?" He spies Fast Eddie leaning against the far stage wall. "How about you?"

Fast Eddie is amused. "Believe me, you've got the wrong guy."

"I can make it worth your while."

"I'm listening."

"If you get Him off the hook, I'll see that you're restored to your former glory."

"You can do something about that?"

"I have connections."

"And the other guy goes?"

"The other guy goes."

"You're on." Fast Eddie saddles up to the defense table, sits on the edge, and folds his arms like this'll be a snap.

"What shall we call you?" the judge asks.

Fast Eddie smiles. "Devon'll do."

"Then it's Devon for the defense. Let's get started. Prosecutor, do you have an opening statement?"

"I do," Virgil says.

"Fine," Shadrach answers. "But I'm warning you, anything you say can and will be used against you in the court of Kingdom Come."

Virgil picks up the newspaper and, with Clarence Darrow dignity, strides center stage for the speech he's waited a lifetime to deliver. Reading from the headlines, he begins, "Racism, child abuse, genocide. We live in a violent world."

"Objection," Fast Eddie interrupts.

"What do you mean, 'Objection'?" Virgil says. "I'm just getting started."

"The prosecution's making assumptions, your Honor. No evidence of a violent world has been submitted."

"Good point," Shadrach nods.

"But I'm reading a newspaper," Virgil protests. "It's filled with facts about . . ."

"Don't confuse the court with facts," the judge interjects. "Objection sustained."

"Fine." Virgil sets the paper aside and regroups. "I'll begin with a story—a *true* story . . ."

"Objection," Fast Eddie cuts in. "Stories are worse than facts, your Honor. Highly prejudicial."

Shadrach scolds Virgil. "What're you trying to do, bias the court? Objection sustained."

Virgil checks his irritation then plays along. "Okay. During this trial, the prosecution will provide evidence that violence exists. Now the question is, why did God create such an imperfect world?"

"Objection," Fast Eddie interrupts again.

"Now what?" Virgil's getting exasperated.

"Prosecution's assuming that God created the world."

"He's God for Christ's sake."

"That may be so," Fast Eddie countered. "But the prosecution's introduced no evidence that God created this or any other world within the legal parameters and statutory venues of this court's jurisdiction. Simple case of locus temporalis, your Honor."

"Very good," Shadrach enthuses. "Objection sustained."

"But you yourself called God Creator," Virgil appeals. "Aren't you an authority within your own courtroom?"

Shadrach bangs his gavel. "Watch yourself, young man. I don't like your attitude."

"Of course, your Honor." Virgil sighs then tries again. "I'll rephrase. The question is, why doesn't God stop violence in the world He may or may not have created?"

"Objection." Fast Eddie is relentless. "Assumes God has the power to stop violence."

"But it's *God* we're talking about!"

"No evidence, your Honor."

"He's right," Shadrach rules. "Objection sustained."

"*Fine!*" Virgil fumes. "The question is, how do we reconcile the contradictory facts that both God and evil exist?"

"Objection," Fast Eddie breaks in. "Circular reasoning. We're right back where we started—assuming the existence of evil. And quite frankly, I represent that."

"Objection sustained," Shadrach pounds. "Listen to me prosecutor. If you're going to run this court in circles, you're statement is finished."

"But your Honor," Virgil implores. "Every word I say is objected to."

"And that is why your statement is finished. It's too objectionable." Shadrach turns to Devon. "Does the defense have an opening statement?"

"I do, your Honor." Virgil sulks to his seat as Fast Eddie slides off the table and points to the butcher paper. "God is God."

"Objection," Virgil interrupts. "Assumes that the identity of the defendant is the identity of the person in question."

Shadrach seethes. "Are you making a mockery of my courtroom?"

"No," Virgil responds.

"Then let the man speak."

"But you didn't let me speak."

"*I* determine who's worthy of being heard, not you. Understand?"

"God, you're just like my father."

"Excuse me?"

"I said, you know best, your Honor."

"That's better." Shadrach turns to Devon. "I apologize for the interruption."

"Think nothing of it."

"I try not to."

"As I was saying," Devon resumes. "God is God. His ways are as mysterious as they are irreproachable. He commands respect not contempt, faith not cross-examination, praise not scrutiny by the insufficiencies of finite human reason. The heart must trust what the head can't know, and receive all, good and ill-fortune alike, with humility and acclamation."

"Bravo," Shadrach raves. "We have a theologian in our midst."

"Thank you, your Honor. I've hung out with the best."

"I'll have to invite you to my pulpit. My flock would do well to hear your wisdom."

"Why, of course. I would be honored too."

"Well, that should settle matters," Shadrach concludes. "Is there anything else?"

"Yes," Virgil insists. "I haven't presented my case yet."

"Oh that," Shadrach begrudges. "But I'm warning you. I'll have no impudence in my courtroom."

"Certainly not. My first witness is the millions of children born with deformities." Blade hobbles forward, his shoulders hunched, his hands hidden in his sleeves. "Please state your name for the court."

"I am Legion."

"How old are you?"

"As old as mankind."

"And what is the nature of your complaint?"

"I was born with acute skeletal deteriation. My bones are disintegrating. My hand's already decayed."

"Would you show the court."

Blade starts to, but Shadrach interrupts before the hand can be disclosed. "Stop right there. There'll be no obscene displays in my courtroom."

Blade complies; Virgil proceeds. "What is your prognosis?"

"My bones will crumble until I die in a splintered mass. They already chip whenever I'm touched."

"Why are you here today?"

Blade motions toward the butcher paper face. "Is that really God?"

"It is."

Blade cautiously looks over. "I'd like to know why You made me this way."

"Objection." Fast Eddie leaps off the table. "Witness can't address the defendant."

"Sustained. Address the court, son."

Confused, Blade glances at Fast Eddie. "Don't look at me, I didn't do it."

He peeks at the judge. "You accusing *me*, boy?"

He darts back to Virgil. "It's okay," Virgil consoles. "Talk to me."

"But I want to talk to God," Blade says.

"Absolutely not," Shadrach warns. "He can't be defiled by you. He's holy."

"But look at what He did to me." He pulls out his hand. His splotchy stump makes the courtroom gag. Shadrach pounds his gavel. "Put that away this instant!" he yells.

Blade slumps toward God, waving his deformed fist. "Why God," he asks, "why did you make me a mutant?"

Shadrach explodes. "*Guards!*" he screams. Boomer and Flash intercept Blade. Blade cringes at their grip. Shadrach grabs a giant sledgehammer and dashes around the bench. "How dare you bring such foulness before God."

Writhing, Blade squeals, "I just want to know why." His fist flails toward the face.

Shadrach reaches him and whales on him with the hammer. "Hide your rot, right now!" he screams. Blade buckles at each blow and is beaten to the ground. Shadrach keeps pummeling until Blade lies on the floor in a splintered mass. "God shouldn't have to see such filth," Shadrach fumes at the courtroom. Then he storms to the bench as the guards return to their post.

"I *object!*" Virgil exclaims. "You killed my witness."

"I didn't like the look of him," Shadrach sneers. He hides the hammer, pulls out a tequila bottle, pours a shot into his glass then chugs it. "Do you wish to continue?" he dares.

Virgil beseeches the paper God to see if He's going to intervene. The face stares blankly. "Yes," Virgil avows. "I call my next witness—the countless victims of child abuse." Clint, painfully aware of Blade's body on the floor, cautiously steps forward. "Would you state your name for the court," Virgil directs.

"Jesús de la Cruz."

"What is the nature of your complaint?" Clint lifts his shirt. Bruises and burn marks scar his chest.

Shadrach's gavel pounds. "Hide it, or you'll pay," he warns.

Clint does. Virgil resumes his questioning. "What happened?"

"My father said I had the devil in me. He beat me with beer bottles and burned me with cigarettes. Then he locked me in the closet 'til I had my right mind."

"What did you do to bring this on?"

"He said I sassed him, and looked at him bad. I didn't mean to, honest."

"What did you do in the closet?"

"I asked God to stop it."

"Objection." Fast Eddie breaks in.

"For what, praying?" Virgil asks.

"His request implies disrespect."

Clint is frightened. "I wasn't sassing, I promise."

"Didn't you see that smirk?" Fast Eddie impugns. "Nothing but disrespect."

"Objection sustained," Shadrach barks.

"But I wasn't sassing," Clint pleads. "I just want God to stop it."

"Don't start back-talking me," Shadrach warns. "Or I'll teach you some respect."

"But my dad keeps hurting me," Clint appeals.

"Are you defying me?" Shadrach boils.

Clint turns to God and begs. "Why won't you stop this?"

"*How dare you challenge my authority!*" Shadrach rails.

"Please, God. Stop it."

"*Guards, subdue that proud spirit!*"

Boomer and Flash go after Clint. Shadrach gets the hammer. Clint's face twists with pain as the guards stretch his arms for the beating. "Why have you forsaken me?" he cries to the blank God.

"Wipe that smirk off your face," Shadrach screams as he batters Clint with authority. Clint falls, but Shadrach keeps pounding until he's pounded the smirk clean off. "That's more like it," he scowls. "I don't tolerate disrespect." He storms back to the bench.

Virgil is aghast. "You can't keep killing my witnesses," he challenges.

"I will not tolerate back-talk."

"But it's against the law."

"Not my law. As the Good Book says, 'Spare the rod, spoil the cross.'" He lifts the Bible from its perch. A Playboy magazine slips out. The judge slams the Bible, picks up the magazine, peeks at the centerfold, then slams it down too. "Never mind that. Get on with your witnesses."

"But . . ."

"Get on with it, or you're next!"

Virgil looks to Fast Eddie. Fast Eddie shrugs uncertain which side to play. The massacre's helping his case, but the passive God next to him is proving the prosecution's.

"Your next witness!" Shadrach commands.

Virgil reluctantly complies. "I call the victims of violence committed in the name of God." Malcolm steps forward with a martyr's boldness. "What is your name?"

"Mohammed Elijah."

"What is the nature of your complaint?" Malcolm lifts his hands. Chains hang from each wrist. "Are you a slave?"

"I once was."

"But you still wear chains."

"We may be slaves no longer, but the chains of racism still bind us."

"Are you a Christian?"

"As a Black Muslim, I reject the white man's God."

"Why?"

"For three hundred years the white man used his God to oppress us. 'Slaves be submissive to your masters.' 'The Black Man bears the mark of Cain.' 'Take up your cross and submit to your suffering.' The words of Christianity are harsh for my people."

"Why are you here today?"

"I want to ask the white God why He condemns us."

"Objection," Fast Eddie interrupts. "Argumentative."

"Sustained."

Malcolm argues anyway, directing his words to God. "In your name, Christians have persecuted my people—Arabs slaughtered in the crusades, Africans hunted by colonizers, Negroes enslaved by white church deacons. Now your priests promise riches in the afterlife while we remain poor in this one. We're offered Heaven but we suffer on Earth. When will you stop the oppression? *When will you let my people go?*"

"That's it!" Shadrach screams. "I will not tolerate blasphemy. *Guards!*"

Malcolm turns to Boomer and Flash. "Don't you see what's happening? The white man's using his God to keep us down. Stand up and resist."

"GUARDS!!" Shadrach grabs for the hammer as Boomer and Flash take a hesitant step toward Malcolm. Malcolm approaches them with pride.

"Look at their God. He does nothing for us. Our only liberation comes from ourselves."

"*Don't listen to that infidel,*" Shadrach screams as he races around the bench, "*or your Black hide is mine.*"

"Our power is in our brotherhood," Malcolm proclaims. "Don't be God's nigger anymore! Join me in the fight for freedom!" Shadrach reaches Malcolm and pounds from behind. Malcolm falls, exhorting his brothers, "The white God is dead . . . Black Power."

"Power this, you cursed son of Cain," Shadrach spits as he beats Malcolm senseless. Boomer and Flash are confused. They look back at God; God's doing nothing. They look back at Shadrach; the judge is still pounding.

Boomer innocently wonders, "Sir . . ."

"*You too, you ignorant mule?*" Shadrach turns on Boomer.

Flash is horrified as Boomer falls. "Brother . . ." Flash laments. Shadrach turns on him too, flailing his hammer between them until they both stop quivering. Panting wildly, Shadrach surveys the mound of death. Within it, a spark of life still pulsates. In trembling defiance, Boomer raises his fist. Shadrach attacks like a mad dog, beating it down then bludgeoning the whole pile until all hope of life has been obliterated.

Virgil is outraged at the bulk of barbarity. Even Devon finds it mildly distasteful. "I demand a mistrial," Virgil declares.

"This is the only trial you get."

"Then I demand a judgment," Virgil insists.

"Please. You've got to be joking."

"Am I?" Virgil steps toward Shadrach. "Look at your God. He's as callous now as He's been throughout history. He neither weeps nor smiles. He doesn't cry for the slaughtered; He doesn't delight in your handiwork. He simply does not care. Not for them. Not for you."

The judge considers Virgil's words and turns to face his God. Virgil is right—God's eyes are dry; and He does not smile. Shadrach scans the bodies. He studies his hammer. He stares back at the face. "All the work I do for You, and You don't even care? We'll see about that!" He wheels around and slams Virgil, bludgeons him to death, then towers over him and spits, "Prosecution rests!"

Still burning, the judge starts toward his bench. He stops cold. A boy's head, terrified and bewildered, peeks over the top. Slowly, he stands. It's Luke, wearing a black suit and red shirt with a matching silk pocket-handkerchief, a younger version of Devon. Distractedly, he wipes his mouth clean.

"Oh no." Devon is repulsed. "Don't tell me . . ."

"You suckin' tease!" the judge seethes. "I told you never to come out from under there." Shadrach breaks for the bench. Luke races the other way. He makes for Fast Eddie and leaps into his arms yelling, "Save me." Fast Eddie is too stunned to move. Shadrach catches up and swings at Luke's back.

"How dare you expose me," Shadrach rages as he pounds. Luke slides to Fast Eddie's feet, his eyes pleading for help. Fast Eddie watches as Shadrach keeps thrashing. He watches until Luke's eyes are closed. Then the sight of his abused protégé makes him snap.

"You sick degenerate. How could you?" He snatches the sledgehammer and pummels the judge with his own weapon until Shadrach too is beaten to death. Still fuming, Fast Eddie takes in the carnage then turns and sneers at God. "So," he spews, "it's you and me once more. How can you just sit there? How can you let this happen? Well this time, you're going down." Raising the hammer like an axe-murderer, Fast Eddie lunges after God. He slashes away as the butcher paper rips, each blow slicing another gash across God's face, each swing shredding the face to pieces until it litters the floor in a pile of scraps. Then he stops, steps back, and looks at what is left of God.

Beneath the paper, an eight-foot square mirror stares back marred by spider web cracks as if cast at by stones. Graffiti scars the surface, its red letters dripping like leaking blood from a wound. 'Nein Juden!' 'Colored Only!' 'Spare the rod, Spoil the child!'

Devon gazes into the mirror and shakes his head. Horrified by his reflection in God's butchered face, he slowly backpedals, trips over a body, and falls. Still stricken, he whispers, "No." Then louder, "*Noooo!* . . ." Then a piercing howl, "NOOOOO . . . !" as he bludgeons himself with the hammer and he too, the last living member on stage, lies cold on the battered heap of corpses. For as long as a last breath, he's still. Then his arm swings up, arcs across, and like the final gasp from the gavel of judgment, the hammer slams to the floor.

The hammer's ring fades into silence. The pile of bodies is still. For several moments, nothing moves.

Then the curtains part. A small boy creeps out. From shoes to gloves, he is dressed in black. It is Carey. Moving with the presence that could still a heartbeat, he positions himself behind the mutilated God then slowly, like the sun inching into a canyon of darkness, rotates the mirror toward the audience.

The glass surface fills with faces as the spectators are gathered into its gaze. The slogans swell into cold clarity as they come more fully into view. The spider web cracks sparkle in a collage of disfigured facial fragments. With its relentless turn, new faces are captured as old ones fall off behind. I watch it approach. A woman near me is caught. The man next to me. Then me.

A cold shiver pierces me as my face slides onto the surface. A bloody slogan castigating Jews sweeps across my forehead. My face splinters in a spider web of broken glass. 'Colored Only' drifts across me, then more broken glass before the stain of words that abet the abuse of children. Finally, my face appears in unbroken purity as a clean stretch of surface sweeps by, then mercifully releases me as the face of God moves on.

In stoic persistence, the glass keeps moving until its back is completely turned. The boy behind it pauses. His arms are stretched wide in their sober grip. His head is bent low. His back bears the weight of every incriminated stare that saw its own face reflected in the marred mirror of God. As if nailed to the spot, he waits.

Then he pushes. The curtains give way. Both mirror and boy recede, then disappear into the darkness. The play is over, the final scene suspended—absent God, piled victims, stricken spectators.

A timeless moment.

A portal into hell.

That's when I played, softly, without riffs, a single line of melody leaking from my harp. Like a trail of vapor, it rose from my seat, drifted across the stage, and coiled through the corpses. For the length of a verse, the boys remained still. With the sound of the chorus, they moved. Solemnly, Fast Eddie eased from the pile and walked to the stage's edge. He was supposed to bow, the cue for applause, but instead he simply stared. The audience stared back. Shadrach got up and stood next to Eddie. Luke followed. Then Virgil. The effect was stunning. The music seemed to restore each boy to life, carry him across the stage, then sustain him as his grave eyes became the new mirror into which the audience peered.

I played another verse and returned to the chorus. Boomer was revived, and Flash. Then Malcolm, Clint, and Blade, each one following suit in the unrehearsed final scene. The audience kept staring as the last of the corpses took their place in line. Still, they did not applaud. Still, the boys did not bow. One presence had yet to appear. All of us wondered. None of us knew. Would God show up, or at least the boy that moved Him?

I eased through another verse; the curtains did not stir. I held the last note as a bridge before a final pass through the chorus.

Only then did he come. Not in form. In voice.

From behind the curtains, a clear note sounded and merged with the one from my harp. We held the pitch like a seasoned duo, then descanted into the chorus together. As he stepped into view and took his place with the others, his words sang out in soprano purity. They cut like a lullaby played at a baby's funeral.

"So close your eyes . . ." I could hardly hold it together.

"You can close your eyes, it's all right . . ." I spied Jen across the room.

"I don't know no love songs . . ." Her tears flowed freely.

"And I can't sing the blues anymore . . ." I knew why.

"But I can sing this song . . ." Our boy could make a stone cry.

"And you can sing this song . . ." I wish I could have cried too.

"When I'm gone." I still do.

Carey's song was primal. It could have moved the devil to tears. It could have raised a dead God from Hades. It could have raised a dead boy back to life. I know. I was there. The crowd was too. And we all watched in silent awe.

Then we exploded. In a single ecstatic outburst, the crowd leapt to its feet. People whistled, people hollered, people clapped their hands while wiping their eyes. The boys, released from the moment, broke into grins, and slapped high-fives. Boomer and Flash lifted Carey to their shoulders and led a line dance through the courtroom. When they disappeared through the curtained backdrop, the ovation only swelled; so the boys came back for a curtain call.

This time they did bend. The defiantly undemonstrative boys even held hands. They motioned me up, grabbed each other's fists, and like they do it on Broadway, soaked up the ovation with a final group bow.

I was on the end next to Virgil. Coming up from our dip, he looked over. His Cool Hand Luke smile was in full bloom.

"How's that for hope?" he said.

"Not bad," I grinned back. I looked down at Carey on the other end. A timid smile adorned his face.

"Not bad at all."

———

Jen's tears still sparkled when she found Carey and me savoring the moment in front of the stage.

"You two make quite a team," she said. "I'm still tingling."

Carey smiled self-consciously. He still hadn't spoken since singing. "He's something else, isn't he?" I said.

"He sure is," she relished. Then she looked at me.

"I'm glad you liked the song," I said. I longed that she got what it meant— the song that once buoyed our deepest hopes still sang, even though the singer was no longer with us.

She nodded. "There's something healing about it, isn't there?"

"Yes," I agreed. "There is."

She sighed. "Well, you two have given me a lot to think about." She turned to Carey. "I understand this was your idea."

Carey shrugged it off. "The basic concept was," I said. "But the boys fleshed it out together. He has an incredible imagination." Instinctively, I patted his shoulder. His reaction was instinctive as well. He wasn't impolite, but at my touch his back stiffened. I withdrew my hand.

"You sure do," Jen said. "What a haunting story." She looked at me again. We both knew how haunting stories can be.

"I'd love to hear your thoughts about it sometime," I dared.

She smiled slightly. "I'd like that."

"Dr. Backman." Dr. Carter jostled into our circle. "I have to say, in twenty years of practice, I've never been more challenged by a group of kids. Your work is impressive. Unorthodox, but impressive." She turned to Carey. "And you, young man. I can't tell you how moved I was when you sang." She turned back to me. "You've persuaded me. I'll ask the court to keep Carey at Crossroads."

Carey looked up as if realizing he'd just dodged a bullet he hadn't known was coming. "How long is the hold?" I asked.

"Thirty days. He'll be with you through April 19th."

"That's Easter Sunday," Jen recognized. "The day of the recital."

"Is that all right with you?" I asked Carey.

He nodded.

So that was it. Carey would stay at Crossroads. And his last day would be Easter Sunday. It all seemed so appropriate.

Of course, we hadn't counted on one thing.

God was hidden backstage.

Where would our splintered mirror be when we needed to glimpse ourselves again?

32

COUNSELING KIDS WHO'VE GOT a secret is like coaxing testimony from a gangland informant. Their words are a maze of half-truths, obfuscations, and unconscious self-deceptions. They ache for the relief of opening up, but they're terrified of reprisals. Discerning fact from evasion is painstaking. Making a mistake can be fatal.

Though Carey told the truth during our first conversation, he lied to me as well. I tried to see between them; but my perception was clouded.

I had secrets too.

———

"That was quite a show last night. We could take it on the road."

I dropped by the Box on Saturday morning hoping Carey's song would give way to speech. He sat at the table and stared at his lap as sunk in his shell as a tortoise who had seen too much sun. I sobered the banter and sat down beside him.

"Seriously, Carey, accompanying you was incredible. I'd love to do it again sometime." He started to look, then stopped; eye-to-eye contact was still too big a leap. I suggested a less direct way to connect. "For today though, what would you say to some drawing? I have an idea for a theme. I've been thinking about the play, and that image of God's face as a mirror that reflects the world's evil. Why don't we each draw something the mirror would see if we could point it anywhere we wanted."

I took his silence for consent and retrieved supplies from the cabinet. Grabbing some paper and a black colored-pencil, I trifled with what to draw. My own picture wasn't important; I was priming the pump for Carey. I doodled randomly, scribbled a box, then lined the sides with Xs. Reaching for a red pencil, I sketched two upside down triangles inside the box's upper corners, then a third at the bottom midway between them. As I trailed gray curls from the upper two triangles, it hit me what it was—a barbed-wire face, the features communist Dachau patches, tears leaking from the eyes. Fury ripped through me. Snatching orange, I scribbled out an eye with streaks of flame, scribbled the other eye too, then burned out the whole damned face. I was grabbing for black to obliterate the blaze when I sensed I was being watched. My drawing so consumed me I hadn't noticed that Carey wasn't drawing at all; he stared at mine with grave fascination. I felt like we had agreed to both drop our pants but I was the only one with my boxers exposed. I was composing an explanation when he whispered his first words:

"My mom gave me something, too."

Our contact felt as fragile as timeworn thread. I collected myself and whispered back. "Yeah? What was that?"

"A pouch," he said, as pensive as a mourner remembering a loved one. "Filled with money. She wanted me to get ice cream whenever I wanted it."

"That's quite a gift," I said, speaking to the picture that held us.

"Yeah," he answered. "Not many moms let their kids have ice cream whenever they want it."

"No, they don't."

"It's probably the best present a kid could ever get." He sounded like he longed to believe his own words. I didn't contradict them.

"When did she give it to you?" I probed.

"A long time ago," he toned, still talking through the picture. "Before I had to leave her."

"Why did you have to leave?"

"The judge said I had to." He continued as if sharing the gospel truth. "I still see her though—every week. We usually get ice cream, or do puzzles. Once we went to the fair. That was our funnest time."

I often found such illusions moving, but Carey's was disappointing—he still was hiding his feelings from me. I was toying with a response when he surprised me.

"Did your mom do nice things for you?" he asked.

"Sure," I said, "but she didn't let me have all the ice cream I wanted."

He took that in, gazing at my mother's patched eyes peering through the scribble. "What's the funnest thing you ever did with her?" he wondered.

"Gosh, I'd have to think." I scanned the blank canvas of my childhood. The kind of life my mom had, the word 'fun' didn't generate many memories. I wanted to mirror honest disclosure but I couldn't remember a single moment of gaiety. Then out of nowhere, a memory surfaced. It wasn't fun, but at least she was smiling. And it sustained Carey's and my connection.

"I remember when *Mary Poppins* came out—I must have been seven or eight. Julie Andrews was my mom's favorite actress so she couldn't wait. She had it all planned out, got the tickets early to take me and my sister to opening night—which was a big deal because it was a school night and I'd get to stay up past my bedtime. So on the day of the show, she made me come straight from school to take a nap before the movie. I got home all excited for our big night out, and I'm in my mom's room getting ready for my nap, when I pull off my pants and find out I'm still wearing my pajamas underneath. I wore them all day without even noticing. Boy did she laugh about that—her big boy wearing pajamas to school. That was fun, seeing her laugh like that."

Imagining it, Carey weakly smiled. "Was the movie fun, too?" he asked.

A trap door gave way and my memory's pleasure plunged into dread. "Not really," I shook off. "For some reason my father went too . . . He was not a good man."

Carey creased his brows as he absorbed my candor. My revelation made way for his own. "My father was not a good man, either," he said, clouded by the admission's pain.

I sensed we were close to his trauma. Baring his wound was the linchpin to healing. "How so?" I gently pushed.

Apparently, I pushed too hard. His mouth clenched, his eyes glared, his lips pursed so tightly they whitened. Something in him wanted to burst into daylight but his body's rigidity restrained it. Under the table, his finger twitched, its curl, cock, and flick either prodding him to revelation or castigating him for revealing too much. I waited with the hope that the pressure would build and he'd blurt out the truth that pained him. But the truth didn't come. Slowly his breathing settled, his face relaxed, his finger stopped its twitching as his stranglehold on silence won out.

I masked my disappointment. "It's okay," I soothed. "You can tell me another time."

He didn't register my words. He was gone. He stared through my picture as if it transported him to another world. I gathered the pencils, placed them in their box, then turned to him before I left.

"I'm glad we talked today," I affirmed. "I look forward to more on Monday."

My picture on the table his only anchor to the room, I left it with him as I made for the door. Carey's whisper stopped me.

"Dr. T," he pled, as if afraid of being abandoned.

I looked back. His eyes held a drowning boy's terror. I ached for him to hold fast. He did for a second, then turned back to the table. Once more, his jaw stiffened as words fought for release. This time, they broke through.

"I didn't do this," he blurted.

"Didn't do what?" I asked.

Under the table, he turned his wrists upward. "I didn't hurt myself."

I checked my discouragement. "I'd understand if you did," I assured.

"Maybe," he replied. "But I didn't do it."

I rolled with the setback. "Can you tell me who did?"

His finger resumed its flicking, more frantically this time. Defiance hardened his face. His words spit with insolent shame.

"I just didn't do it."

The leaden weight of his denial sunk the remnants of our connection. The strands dissipated as I ended the session. "Okay," I reassured, "you can tell me when you're ready. But whatever's going on, I'll see you through it all the way."

As it turned out, we both lied that day. And not just to each other.

Our downfall lay in the lies to ourselves.

———

'Hold whatever the psyche gives you,' Woody's healing path admonished, 'for the psyche always reaches for life.' There was one flaw in the theory—what if the psyche gives you bald-faced lies? Woody was undaunted. 'Every lie reveals a truth,' he professed. 'We must hold the lie until the truth is revealed.'

As I wrote up the session at my desk, Woody's words seemed insulting. I didn't want to hold the lies; I wanted to punt them out of my sight. Why didn't Carey trust me with the truth? I knew he didn't see his mother; she was too busy making ends meet to drive out for a single weekly visit. And the purse he fingered while he sat all alone was hardly a symbol of love; it was a pathetic attempt to buy off the heartbreak that she didn't even bother with his birthday. I knew he was only expressing his need to fantasize a loving mother, but fuck it—he could've come clean with me. And why the denial about cutting his wrists? He could externalize his rage to more securely engage it without pushing me away in the process. Didn't he realize what these games were doing? He may be reaching out for healing but he's alienating the only ally he's got.

I was so infuriated I couldn't finish the report. Besides, I had a date. I slammed the file shut and stuffed it into my backpack. Unfortunately, the session wasn't stifled so easily. As I drove to Caty's Cavern, one face bedeviled me. Not Carey's mother. And not Carey's make-believe assailant.

Mary Poppins.

Fuck her too.

33

"I'M GOOD," I LIED. Jen clenched her coat to her chin as if my pat reply carried a chill. I volleyed back her greeting, "How are you?"

She answered sincerely. "To be honest," she said, "I'm a little scared. I almost didn't come."

Her transparency chastised me—especially since I called her up so I could finally tell her the truth. I tried again. "I'm glad you did," I opened up. "I'm scared too." She looked at the decaying railcar across the street from Caty's as if uncertain she was staying. After all the ways I betrayed her, I could understand why. "The last thing I want to do is hurt you again," I said. "I was hoping a talk would be more healing than painful."

"That's just it," she sighed. "Healing doesn't preclude pain. Like that song last night. It brought back a lot."

"It did for me too," I confessed. "Including parts of me I've been too ashamed to face. There are some things I never told you, Jen. Maybe they can be healing, too."

She nodded like her head was assenting before the rest of her was ready. Then she looked at me with eyes I swore I'd never bring to tears again.

"Okay," she said. "Let's talk."

———

None of Caty's goodies called to us, only two cups of decaf. We took them to the cavern's dusky interior and settled into two upholstered chairs. Jen unbuttoned her coat then slipped it off. Her apricot hair was pulled back. A freckle floated like a lily pad on the pond of neck behind her ear. How she once purred when I caressed it.

"How's Carey?" she asked, stirring cream into her coffee.

"He started talking today." I sipped mine black. "Though it's something of a mixed bag; he's in denial about his cutting."

"What do you mean?" She set the spoon down and sat back.

"He says he didn't do it."

She looked up stricken. "You're kidding. You mean somebody else did?"

"He didn't elaborate. He just said he didn't do it."

"My God," she worried, "how do you know he's not telling the truth?"

"I don't see how he can be. The police, the paramedics, the doctors, nobody's seen a thing to suggest it wasn't self-inflicted. He even had the knife. Besides, he's done it before."

She brooded with maternal concern. "I can't imagine Carey lying like that."

"You'd be surprised how common it is," I assured. "They're so ashamed, they can't admit it to themselves."

She stared at the unsipped coffee in her lap. "It makes you wonder what he's been through to do something like that."

"I know. I'm sure it's plenty dark."

"How are you going to find out?"

"Wait for him to tell me—give him ways to express himself and listen to what he says. I don't think it'll be long. Something in him wants to be known."

"Well, he's in good hands," she encouraged. "You're great with those boys. I can't get over what you get them to express."

"I don't do much," I deflected. "They've all been through hell. I just invite them to tell about it, and hold what they have to say."

"It's amazing how healing that alone can be." She said it like she knew. "Or how painful it is when it's absent." She knew that too. I wasn't sure where she directed it, but it stung me all the same.

"I've spent some time in our own hell," I said, inching toward the edge. "That's why I played Daniel's lullaby last night. One thing I've found—somehow the song plays through it all."

We grew quiet as if listening to the lullaby's echoes. "You know," Jen shared, "I hadn't heard that song since the night Daniel died."

"I know," I empathized. "It brings it all back." The echoes carried us to Daniel's bedroom, the last time the song held the three of us alive. "That's the night I want to talk to you about."

Jen set her coffee on the table, drew a breath to settle her, then looked at me with a gentle strength I envied. I hoped the song wouldn't drop me now.

"We were quarrelling, remember? About how withdrawn I'd become. I stormed off to finish my paper but I never went to the library. I drove around in a fury then ended up at my Mom's grave. I knew how awful I was being to you, but for the life of me I couldn't make myself stop. So I made a last-ditch effort; I begged God to soften my heart. I dug up that Cracker Jack ring—it was still there—and I remembered that day on the bluff. I swear it was the happiest day of my life. I thought about your engagement ring, and the color-coded picnic, and those two whales humping in the ocean, and I felt this huge surge of love for you. It was like God was giving me a second chance to care for you like you deserved. And I dashed home determined to; I even stopped for flowers. I couldn't find mums or roses so I got three carnations—yellow, orange, and white. I got back to the apartment, put them in a vase, and tiptoed toward our bedroom. I couldn't wait to nuzzle your neck and make love to you again, I really couldn't. But when I got there, I just froze. I was so consumed by self-disgust I couldn't stand it. So I trashed the flowers, came in and scowled at you, said something cruel, then snatched Daniel and plopped him into his crib. We were both so upset, we didn't sleep for hours. That's why we didn't wake up on time. It wasn't you; it was me. The shameful truth is, Daniel died because I was too cold to love you."

Jen stared down as if considering my words one by one. I couldn't read her feelings. She could as easily have been relieved that it wasn't her fault or been convinced that she knew better otherwise; she could have empathized with my shame enough to assure me of my innocence or detested my coldness enough to walk off in disgust. As it turned out, she felt none of those things. Or maybe she felt them all then settled into that space where feelings dissolve into stillness. Either way, she spoke with neither comfort nor rebuke. She simply shared her story. For the first time since Daniel's death, I listened.

"I still have nightmares of that morning. I'm in bed, alone, and he cries out for me from his room. He's gasping for breath but I can hardly move. It's like a gale-force wind is crushing me to the bed. I fight to get up then strain for every inch down the hall. He keeps crying for me, his cry getting older as the years go by, five, six, seven years old . . . But he's always an infant when I find him in his crib. He's as peaceful as can be, sleeping on his tummy, his tiny hands on the mattress . . . Except he's blue, like he suffocated in a plastic bag.

"It's hard to explain how that affected me. I should have been in there—holding him to my breast, watching him drink his fill. Instead he died alone, without me. It didn't matter who kept who awake or how tired I had a right to be; I was his mom, and I wasn't there to feed him. You didn't know it, but I produced milk for weeks. Each drop was like acid mocking me as a mother. Then, when you wouldn't touch me, or even talk to me, I felt condemned as a wife, condemned as a *woman*. And not just by you, by every man in my life—my father, my stepfather, even God the All-Powerful Knight in shining armor was too revolted to hold me. I stopped eating not just because I couldn't stomach food—I wanted my breasts to dry up, my periods to stop, my womb to shrivel away. I was ashamed to be a woman anymore.

"Fortunately, a group of women took me in. They couldn't bring Daniel back, or you; but they fed me, and cried with me, taught me that I didn't need a man to legitimate me, that there are different ways to claim one's womanhood. But that wound goes deep. They could say all day I'd make a great mom, but they weren't there. They didn't see Daniel cold and blue. They didn't see the look in your eyes the last time you took him from me. They couldn't stop him crying out for me from his bedroom in my nightmares.

"Then after all these years, when Carey's trying to kill himself, another boy finding my care inadequate, and Peckham's going ballistic, of all the people in the world, you walk through my door and cut me to the bone with the words I've ached seven years to hear from you, 'You were a great mom.' The play last night only sealed it. After God is so gruesomely silent while we suffer, you and Carey sing the lullaby we used to put Daniel to sleep by. It made me realize, the choice was mine—to sing or not to sing. So I did. I got Daniel's baby pictures out. I laid them all over my living room floor. And I sang him his lullaby all through the night. Just like a mom would."

I stared at Jen's lap as her words soaked in. Her hands rested gently, one on another. They were delicate, as if softened by years of tears, yet strong with the power that can hold one's own pain. Once, it would have been only natural to slip my hand into hers. Now it seemed like a faded dream.

"I know I've caused you enormous pain," I said. "I hope there's been healing too."

Jen nodded like it was all true—me being a source of pain and healing both. Then she looked up. "What happened, Tony?" she asked as if wondering for years. "Why did you withdraw like that?"

My panic returned with my remaining confession. I hoped to God Jen wouldn't hate me. "When Daniel died," I unburdened, "my whole world fell apart. Everything I believed in didn't make sense anymore. God was supposed to bless His servants; and if He didn't, we were supposed to trust Him anyway. Well, I couldn't. I cursed the Bastard. Remember that night Danny and the guys gave me that book of platitudes? They meant well, but that pushed me over. I drove off to our bluff, I hiked to our spot, and in the middle of a pitch-dark storm from hell, I spit every obscenity I knew at God, told Him I was done with Him forever. Then I ripped up that book right in front of His face. Only it wasn't that book. You must've borrowed my coat and left your prayer journal in the pocket. I didn't mean to, but I tore it up and stomped it in the mud. When I realized what I'd done, I felt like the curse came back on me. I didn't see how anyone could forgive me after that. So I walked away from it all."

Jen sighed at the irony. "You're not going to believe this," she said. "I tried to throw that journal away, too; but I couldn't find it. I thought I must have tossed it by mistake and that it served me right."

"You didn't toss it," I assured. "I had already used it to defile myself."

"I don't think you were defiled," she comforted.

"It was ugly," I insisted. "Talk about the way of Judas. I all but pounded in the nails myself and was glad to be rid of Him."

"You don't think God can hold our rage?" she asked.

"Not in my Bible. Judas ends up in hell. If God can't hold *him*, how can He hold the Judas in the rest of us? The sad truth is, I don't believe in God at all anymore. He died a long time ago."

Jen nodded knowingly. "Well, if it's any consolation," she said, "I don't believe in God, either."

I had to laugh. "Jen, you're a religion teacher—how can you *not* believe in God?"

"Like you said, He died—at least the Father-in-Heaven God who's supposed to make everything alright. That God died the night Daniel died."

"What do you believe in instead?" I asked, really wanting to know.

Jen smiled like she was betraying her membership in a cult. "I believe in the Shekinah."

She had me intrigued. "What's that?"

"She's a female deity described in the Jewish Scriptures. I constructed my own Midrash about Her for my dissertation. It's another story to put alongside last night's. I'll tell it to you sometime."

"Why not now?"

She collected herself like a Hasidic tzaddik then handed down her tale.

"As legend has it, the world was created when the Lord God, the Master of the Universe, wed His Queen, the Shekinah, in whose womb the earth was conceived. Born from such love, the world was pure and good. But the people turned wicked, and the earth was consumed by darkness. The Master of the Universe was incensed at the depravity yet refused to violate human freedom to stop it. Paralyzed by rage, this God of glory shattered into a thousand shards of light that spewed throughout the darkened world and faded in the foulness. The Shekinah was likewise horrified; but instead of exploding with rage, She was overcome with grief. She wept for the suffering that evil inflicted and for the pain of Her broken marriage. Moved by love, She forsook the Heavens for the desecrated earth and searched for the shards of Her splintered husband.

"She wandered the world as a compassionate presence—soothing the wounded, nurturing hope, inspiring the people to acts of kindness in resistance to evil's dehumanizing pull. In a world of excremental assault, where overlords exterminate races, parents abuse their children, homes are rife with death and poverty, any act of kindness and compassion, justice and beauty, is a miracle. It's a miracle that a work-camp inmate would share food with another. It's a miracle that a man would apologize to his ex-wife then play her a lullaby. It's a miracle that a mother would care for unwanted children after losing a child of her own. They're not the spectacular miracles of a Master of the Universe dividing the Red Sea; they're ordinary miracles, birthed by the Shekinah who holds everyone with compassion through whatever hell they happen to live in. And as people participate in these simple miracles of kindness, they shine with the glory of God's image, a tiny light is illuminated, and one of the shards hidden by darkness is discovered in the world's muck. The Shekinah gathers each of these shards and wanders the world for more. When all the shards are gathered, so many they've been found in every sordid crevice evil can create, the Shekinah will remake the Master of the Universe. She will place each piece in position until His patchwork frame is assembled. Then She will bathe those shards, and the cracks that hold them, with the tears of Her compassion. The cracks will fade and disappear, the shards will come back to life, and the Master of the Universe with His Queen, the Shekinah, will wed once more, and delight together in a world of radiant goodness."

As she shared the tale, Jen glowed like one whose own life was restored by the Shekinah hidden within kindness.

"It's a beautiful story," I affirmed, appreciating Jen's hard-found truth. "I've never looked for God in such simple acts of care."

"They're so simple, it's easy to miss Her." She said it as if grieving a neglected friend. "But when you're in pain, simple care is sacred." She knew this friend well. "Anyway," she wrapped up, "She gives me something to believe in. How about you, what have you found to believe in?"

"That's a good question," I mused. "I'm still a man without a God. He's just too holy for me. All the dark things in life—despair, rage, lust, whatever, He relegates them all to hell. Hell is where the healing is. The only way to find life is to face the darkness within ourselves. Until God gets dirty in the shadows with the rest of us, He's only the whitewash on hypocrisy."

"You really do endorse the way of Judas," Jen smiled.

I smiled back. "Yeah, I'm holding out with the reprobate. Give me a God who embraces Judas even after the guy's killed His son and killed himself in despair, and I'll be the first one in line at the altar."

Jen shook her head. "You are an enigma, Tony. Your withdrawal can be so absolute; then there are times when you hold so much."

"I've grown quite a bit," I admitted. "I found a mentor who can walk through the darkest places imaginable. He's taught me a lot."

Jen recognized the truth; but a shadow still troubled her. "So tell me," she said, nagged by a wound not yet closed. "Why did you withdraw from me before Daniel died? You only talked about afterwards." Like plunging into an icy pond, my breath caught short. An image stabbed me with shame—Jen in our bed, her breast exposed to Daniel's touch. "You can tell me," she reassured. "Did you stop finding me attractive?"

"God, no," I recoiled. "Is that what you think? You're the most beautiful woman I've ever known. I still get knotted up around you."

"Then what happened? Once I got pregnant, you acted like I repulsed you."

I stared at the floor as if hardening against the cold. My mind grasped for something to hold. But only that morning's image emerged—me in my mom's room with my pajamas on. Why didn't I see anything wrong with that? Someone else did though. His sinister presence brooded in the hallway. Goddamn it. I was not letting that bastard come between me and another woman.

"Sexuality was another thing God couldn't accept," I recovered quickly. "I was so ashamed when we got pregnant, and angry at God for punishing us, I just turned it all off. It kills me you thought I didn't find you attractive. It was exactly the opposite. I was *so* attracted I felt despised by God for it."

It made sense enough to Jen. But I knew better. My father was still at the bedroom door. I was with Mary Poppins. He couldn't stand that I was closer to her than he was. So he sabotaged every connection we had.

Well, not this time.

I was casting him back into hell.

My worries about Jen's reaction to my confessions were dispelled several days later. I received a card at Crossroads. A Chagall print graced the cover; a bride and groom hovered over a starlit countryside. Inside, she penned a message.

"May your healing song play through the night—until its serenade weds God with God's world once more."

She included a photocopy of a page from a book. A paragraph was highlighted in yellow.

According to one early church legend, Jesus descended into hell after His death and scoured the abyss for Judas. He found him crucified upside down in hell's darkest depths, the wood of his cross fashioned from the tree on which he had hung himself. His eyes were swollen, his body gutted; Satan gnawed on his spilling entrails. Jesus banished the devil, righted the cross, and recognized the tree from which His own cross was made. He removed the nails, healed the wounds, then embraced his friend with tears of compassion. That night, the two shared bread and wine within the gates of Heaven.

My response was simple. I sent Jen three flowers—an orange carnation, a yellow chrysanthemum, and a white rose. My words were few.

"Seven years late, but even Judas can say he's sorry. Keep singing, Tony."

34

"I'LL BE BACK."

Carey's stare was deadly serious. The villain in his story had spoken the truth. He'd be back to finish the job.

This time . . . the boy would die.

———

To lighten things up after two weeks of devils and dead gods, I told the boys a Jack tale Monday afternoon. The oafish lad of beanstalk fame used his native half-wittedness to ward off thieves defrauding a village. Though the story was light, my aim went deep. I asked the boys to write about the most menacing villain they could imagine, and how a hero used his natural talents to fend the foe off. I hoped to gain insight into their personal demons. And Carey's phantom assailant.

Carey didn't take to the assignment; the probe was too direct. So I went back to the story his body was telling already. "If your finger was the hero," I prompted, "what villain could its powers take on?" Carey did an end around. He made his finger the villain.

On Thursday, he told me his story.

———

"A boy and his mom live in the woods. But the woods are haunted. A giant hand sneaks around with a middle finger that shoots electricity and has a nail as sharp as a razor—one slice and you bleed until you die.

"One night, the boy and his mom are praying beside her bed. They feel something evil sneak up behind them.

"'Keep your eyes closed,' the hand hisses. The boy and the mom don't move. The hand starts breathing, heavier and heavier. Then it shoots electricity at the mother. She groans as her body twitches all over. Slowly, the boy turns and peeks.

"'Ahhhh,' the hand screams like a vampire in the sunlight. 'Close your eyes, I said.' But the boy keeps staring, so the hand gives up, and runs back into the woods.

"The boy puts his mom to bed, then goes to sleep in his own room.

"Later that night, the hand returns. The boy wakes up tied to his bed and blindfolded. He hears the hand breathing.

"'Thought you could escape me, eh?' it says. The boy's too afraid to scream. The finger slices both the boy's arms then shoots him with electricity. The boy twitches as he bleeds to death. But his shaking works the blindfold free and he stares straight at the hand. The hand cringes. It wants to attack but the boy's stare beats it back. So it finally gives up and slithers out the door.

"But before it leaves, it turns.

"'Don't think you'll ever escape me,' the hand warns the boy.

"'I'll be back.'"

———

"That's a scary story," I responded. "That hand is terrifying." Carey nodded like he knew. "I wonder why it's so evil?"

Carey had it all worked out. "The hand came from a murderer who was crucified next to Jesus. While he was dying, he flipped Jesus off. God shot him with lightning and sliced off his hand. It's terrorized the world ever since."

"Why's it after the mom and the boy?"

"It doesn't like people praying."

"This hand is mean," I replied. "I worry about the boy." Carey's brow shared my concern. "I wonder what part of him it electrocutes."

Carey barely whispered. "Down there."

"You mean his privates?" His face screwed up with shame. "That makes me feel sad for him," I shared.

"Me too," he said to the floor.

"What's he going to do when the hand returns?"

"Keep his eyes open." He spoke with resolve.

"That's a brave boy," I affirmed. "Maybe he could reform the hand."

Carey shook his head. "The hand is evil," he declared. "It belongs in hell."

———

Every symptom tells a story. Carey's tale was a window into his inner world. Right after the session, I deciphered its symbols like a cryptologist cracking enemy code.

'3-26-92: Carey shared his finger's story today. It encapsulates both the clues to his trauma and the impulse for healing within him.

'The hand is his externalized rage—it flips off Jesus, electrocutes his mother, and terrorizes people who pray, perhaps because their prayers are never answered.

'Unfortunately, he thinks his rage is bad—murderous feelings deserve crucifixion, God strikes obscene gestures with lightning. So he turns the rage on himself—it slices his arms with razorblade fingernails and electrocutes the body parts that betrayed him, his genitals. These are classic signs of sexual abuse—rage at being violated, self-loathing for doing something shameful (remember his father is a convicted pedophile).

'But the rage is his strength—a life-force that revolts against what's happened and defiantly refuses to give up. If he could recruit the finger as an ally instead of repressing it into an unconscious hell, he could turn the rage away from himself and direct it where it belongs. He needs a story to help him—one that's willing to enter hell and subjugate the rage's power.

'His open eyes could help.'

———

Carey's phantom finger made no further appearances that week. I didn't push it. That he named his rage at all was breakthrough enough. But the following week came time to encounter the finger again. As long as Carey repressed his rage, the victim would always be himself. I paved the way on Monday. To set the week's theme, I took the boys to hell. Woody's myths provided the archetype, but the tale I adapted from Dante. The story destined to plot our descent chronicled the pilgrim whose only hope of paradise laid in a journey through the abyss.

I played up all the gory parts—the crowd of corpses mobbing Acheron, the reptilian flight into Dis' depths, the sadistic tortures of the more notorious inhabitants—heretics entombed in burning sepulchers, murderers boiling in rivers of blood, inciters of violence walking through the dark, dangling like lanterns their decapitated heads.

Then I took them to hell's frigid core. Imprisoned in a lake of ice, pierced by bitter winds, the traitors of God and comrade gnawed one another's heads, their eyes stabbed by the daggers of their frozen tears. A glacial pit gaped at the lake's numbing center. A colossal petrified Satan was perched within. His three heads gazed in frozen rage like gigantic sentries paralyzed by the cold while bat-like wings, the source of hell's calcifying gusts, frantically flailed with razor-sharp tips threatening to slice all who trespassed. The only path to paradise was through the chilling cyclone of hate, clawing down Satan's torso like a mountaineer descending a cliff.

Dante clasped a boa-sized hair and inched down a frozen head. He made it as far as a crystallized eye the size of a full-length mirror. Dante stared into the thin sheet of ice glazing the eye's surface. In the reflection, Dante saw himself. With unblinking eyes, he felt pity for the creature staring back.

In that instant, the cold black tomb of Satan's eye flickered with recognition. The film of ice moistened. His wings stilled. The winds of hell stopped howling. And with the calmed wings a webbed rigging, Dante descended the devil's body and slipped through the bottom of hell. On the far side, he found himself on the shore at Heaven's gate.

It was morning.

———

I asked the boys to imagine hell, populate it with notorious creatures, then tell of a hero who journeyed through. The assignment didn't capture Carey. On Wednesday morning, I caught him doodling as defeated as trapped bait resigned to impending capture.

"A story isn't coming, huh?" I sat beside him in the Box.

"Not really."

"Are you having a hard time imagining hell?"

"No." He knew hell plenty well.

"Are you having a hard time populating it with creatures?"

"No." That was hardly the problem.

"What is it?"

"I'm having a hard time knowing why go there in the first place."

"Because it's filled with phantoms like the flicking finger?"

He looked at me like I still didn't get it. "The flicking finger doesn't live in hell; it lives in the real world." He thought again. "Unless that's the big secret. The real world really is hell."

Carey never did write of a journey through hell.

He left that up to me.

I, too, had no problem populating it.

On Thursday morning, Carey left the premises for the first time since 'The Night that God got Nailed' debuted. Even if imaginary, his phantom seemed real enough. As we left the safe refuge of Crossroads and pulled onto Highway 12, he scrutinized the abandoned gas station on the corner then scouted the road behind us with the intensity of a runaway convict.

"Don't worry," I reassured. "I'll keep an eye out for you. Besides, I've got a surprise when we're done." Carey feigned being comforted. He turned forward and buckled up, but studied every building and billboard we passed as if certain his assailant was close. He didn't relax until snugly settled deep within the hospital waiting room.

Carey's appointment with the surgeon went well; his wounds were healing nicely. The doctor removed the stitches near the palms but left those binding the deeper cuts in Carey's fleshy forearms. When we returned to my truck, I revealed my surprise.

"What would you say to us getting some ice cream?"

He was so pleased he didn't bother checking our backs. Such was the power of Carey's love for ice cream; it vaporized fictitious assailants. We traveled west past the freeway and pulled into Coddington Mall. Baskin-Robbins fronted the entrance. We skipped in as if inaugurating a father and son getaway weekend.

The shop was void of customers, the decadence of our treat enhanced by it being an hour before lunch on a school day. The college-aged clerk interrupted his studying long enough to fill our orders—a double cone of chocolate-chocolate-chip with sprinkles for Carey, a scoop of kona in a cup for me. We started to sit outside but the wintry chill discouraged us. So we strolled into the mall. Where the foyer hit the mall's main artery we found a bench and sat down. Apart from a housewife with a stroller and a clerk hanging dresses, the entire place was deserted. Apart from some white noise Muzak, the entire place was quiet.

"Sure beats a math quiz, huh?" I said dabbing at my scoop with a pink plastic stick.

"Oh yeah," Carey mumbled as he mouthed his mountain-peak of a treat. He couldn't have been more tickled if it came with the keys to the Magic Kingdom.

"You ever play hooky?" I asked savoring the conspiratorial feel of our outing.

"Never," he smacked with chocolate lips. "Not just for the fun of it . . . Did you?"

I downplayed my high-school excursions to Lew's cabin. "Not really. Once in the twelfth grade, but only after I knew I was graduating."

"Did you *ever* do anything bad?" He asked as if his ice cream savior was incapable of sin.

"Sure I did."

"Like what?"

"I don't know. The usual things—hiding peas in my pockets, sneaking cookies into my bedroom. Stuff like that."

He dug out a sprinkle with his fingers then wiped his shirt. "What's the baddest thing you ever did?"

I rolled my eyes at the question. Truth be told, everything I did as a child felt bad; my dad seemed disgusted by the way I breathed. "I snuck my dad's heirloom pocket-watch once. I used it for a Halloween costume."

"Did you get in trouble?"

"He got me back."

Carey cocked and recocked the cone to his mouth with the rhythm of a metronome, a swivel and a lick timed to each beat. "Your dad was pretty mean, huh?"

"He was pretty mean."

"What was so mean about him?"

Where did I start with that one? My dad's meanness was so cosmic it defied a single snapshot. It could seep into an empty mall fifteen years from my last sighting of him.

"I'll give you an example. Remember how I told you my mom was so excited when *Mary Poppins* first came out? My dad *hated Mary Poppins*, hated all those sappy Disney movies. But he went anyway just to spite her." It came back so clearly I could spit. "He insists on sitting between us so we can't enjoy it together. There's this stranger on my other side so I have to ball myself up in my seat not to touch anybody. Even though it's a musical, the movie makes me cry. I look to my mom for comfort but she's scared of my dad too, and just stares straight ahead pretending to enjoy the movie. My dad barks at me to stop crying like a baby, which only makes me cry all the more. So he orders my mom to stay put with my sister and marches me out to the lobby." God I forgot all about this.

"So he's fuming and pacing while I'm crouching on a bench trying not to make him any madder when what does he go off and do? He buys me ice cream. Go figure. A box of cherry Bon-Bons. It was the last thing in the world I wanted, I didn't even *like* cherry ice cream. But he scowls at me and makes me eat it anyway, like if I don't I'm insulting his token stab at parenthood. But I can't. I'm scared to death it's going to make him madder but for the life of me the ice cream makes me gag.

"'*What kind of a boy doesn't like ice cream?*' he snarls. '*Eat it!*' I tried. But then I just threw up—dry heaves because I hadn't eaten dinner but this acidy slaver's dripping from my mouth. One of the ushers comes over with napkins but my dad chews him out, tells him there's nothing wrong with me and that it's all my mother's fault. Then he drags me out to the car, drives me home, and makes me go to bed. He sulks all night in the living room refusing to go back for my mom and my sister. They find their own way home past midnight. He was cruel like that."

I stabbed at my scoop with the pathetic piece of plastic. The ice cream made me nauseous all over again. That bastard ruined everything.

"I'm sorry, Carey. I didn't mean to get into all that." The bathroom was in front of our bench. "I need to clean up. I'll be right back."

Once inside, I shoved the ice cream into the trash and pelted my face with coldwater as if the splash could wash my memory clean. But my father was not shaken so easily. As I toweled myself dry, his sinister presence loomed at my mother's bedroom doorway hours before the movie. I stared into the mirror still fuming. What was he even doing there, anyway? Why wasn't he at work? Was he *that* jealous of me and my mother? What a prick. I deep-sixed the wet towel into the trash and walked out.

Carey was gone.

Goddamn it! How could I be so stupid! I scanned up, down, and around the mall. The stores were as still as morgues, the walkway so deserted it could've been cursed. I glanced at the bench for a clue. His cone was crushed to the floor, his napkin splayed on the seat. Where the hell could he be? Did he bolt or did somebody nab him? It's broad daylight. Goddamn it, which way did they go?

I raced up the mall, frantic for a sighting in the stores. A grandmother was fifty yards ahead.

"*Did you see a boy in a jean jacket?*" I screamed.

She shook her head. Quick. Don't waste a second. I doubled back. They'd make for the car. I tore down the walkway and out the doors. I begged for a glimpse of something unusual—movement in a car, his face through a window, a truck speeding off into the distance, *anything*. Like gunfire ripping into my belly, I flashed with visions of grotesque possibilities—Carey raped in a van, Carey dead in a ditch, Carey a child prostitute a thousand miles away. How could I be so *stupid*? I burst into the Baskin-Robbins.

"Did you see the boy I was with?" I pleaded.

The kid blinked up from his book. "I thought he was with you."

Goddamn it. Where the hell could he be?

I raced toward my truck, the panic cinching me like a chokehold to the neck. I wanted to puke, I wanted to scream, I wanted to gut myself for ever leaving him alone. What was I *thinking*? He wasn't in the truck. He wasn't *anywhere*. I ran to the street screaming like a madman,

"Carey, Carey."

Cars were stopped at the light, others sputtered along, people stared with alarm, but I couldn't detect even his fleeting shadow. How could he just disappear like this? I darted to the corner and scanned the cross-streets. *JESUS! Please!* Don't let him get hurt! I sprinted down to the far side of the mall. Nothing. The traffic just bustled like ants over a carcass. The perimeter of escape was widening beyond my capacity to cover. I hauled back to ground zero and dashed into the ice cream store.

"*Call the police*," I panted. "*A boy is missing.*" The attendant looked at me like I was an over-protective parent. "*CALL THEM!!*" I shrieked.

I ran back through the mall, screaming at the top of my lungs,

"*CAREY! CAREY!*" Some clerks poked out of the stores. "A boy's missing. Have you seen him?" They shook their heads with regret. Damn it! He's not in here. I ran back to the parking lot, my chest burning from the chase. I scanned the horizon. Futility bled the landscape of color.

"*CAREY!!!*"

A clerk rushed out to help. "What does he look like?"

"Eleven years old," I sputtered. "Jeans and a jean jacket."

"There!"

I followed his finger. On the far side of the lot, across the street, Carey tore down a sidewalk and raced toward the mall like a jackrabbit chased by hounds. From a hundred yards away I could see the whiteness of his face, the panic in his eyes as he peeled into the street with careless abandon and made for safety as fast as his legs could carry him. I dashed towards him. He saw me and cut in my direction, leaping a bush at the sidewalk and scurrying between parked cars, down the lane, in front of a mini-van then into my outstretched arms. He clawed me in his embrace, his legs still pumping uncertain if he was really safe.

"You're okay," I cried. "You're okay. I've got you."

I sensed movement in the distance and glanced at the road. An off-white truck with a green Chinook camper raced along the boulevard from which Carey ran. The driver was huge, a bullish beast of a man cramped within the camper's cab. For a split second, he caught my glance, his malignant eyes smoldering. Then he looked at the road, accelerated to the corner, swerved right, and squealed into the distance.

Carey panted into my shoulder, his fists in a vice grip on my jacket. Kneeling, I held his shoulders and pulled him away. I stared him straight in the face.

"Carey," I stressed, "I've got to know. Did somebody just try to take you?"

He was too terrified to talk, too terrified to control his trembling body. His quivering head nodded once.

"Carey." I could not have been more serious if asking for the identity of my own killer. "Is it the same person who cut you?"

His wide-open eyes were crazed with fear, pleading for me to believe him.

"Carey, is it the same man?"

He looked like his despair would implode if I didn't trust him. But I did. I could see it in the abducted terror in those eyes.

"Carey, somebody's trying to hurt you, huh?"

Shivering, he nodded again.

"Okay." I pulled him into my arms. "Okay. We're gonna get him. I promise."

He squeezed me so hard his bandages pressed against my back.

I looked into the car idling before us.

The woman at the wheel was crying.

35

"HE'S TELLING THE TRUTH. I'm sure of it." I tried to convince her by conviction alone. Unfortunately, evidence trumps conviction.

"There's not much corroboration." Deputy Sheriff Thomas was a petite black woman, not more than thirty, with the kindness that could calm an hysterical child and the punch that could take down a truck driver. She also had a cop's need for procedure. She questioned me in my office after looking in on Carey. He hadn't talked since the incident—not to her, not to me, nor the officer who showed up at the scene. "Did you actually *see* Carey with this man?"

"No, but believe me. Carey couldn't stage a prank like that. He couldn't fake that kind of terror."

"And nobody else saw him either?"

"No, the officer questioned everyone he could find."

She contemplated her pad and shook her head. "You know, even if someone abducted him today, there's nothing to suggest the same guy cut Carey a month ago."

"True," I admitted. "But you should have seen the look in his eyes when I asked him."

Deputy Thomas sighed like she did when she first saw Carey bandaged and dissociated in the Box. "You're asking me to take a pretty big leap—turning a routine suicide attempt into a homicide investigation on nothing more than a look in the eyes."

"I know, Sheriff. But believe me. He's telling the truth."

She saw the look in *my* eyes. "Okay. We'll do it. We'll check Salve Regina—see if we missed anything. I'll need you to come. Monsignor Peckham'll have a few questions."

"Fine," I agreed. "When do we go?"

"First thing tomorrow morning."

"Should someone call the Monsignor?"

"I will. After all, it's an official Sheriff's investigation."

———

That night, I coiled my covers in such sleepless distress Carey's hand could have been coming after me. It didn't have to. I had phantoms of my own.

My dad's shadow dominated my doorway. My mom's ghost knelt beside my bed. The face in the truck promised terror's return. And to top it all off, Schuyler Peckham would have questions in the morning.

———

As I entered Salve Regina and drove atop the compound's plateau, I sensed Peckham's searing stare from behind his mirrored window. I didn't dare look up into his tower. I knew he was pissed. His boys didn't get assaulted. Not under his vigilant eye. I parked my truck and waited for backup. Only with a police escort did I ascend the steps to his suite.

Deputy Thomas paused at Peckham's door and invited me to enter first. The Monsignor laid in wait. He leaned against the front of his desk, his hands cupped and raised to his mouth as if harboring a trapped insect. His stain glared like a crimson eye that insisted on seeing everything. He watched me without moving as I stepped inside and discovered we were not alone. Father Eichler fidgeted on a divan like a schoolboy called to the principal's office. At his side, Jen stood alert and professional.

"Good morning," Peckham opened, pressing his fingertips to his desktop so forcefully they turned white. "You remember Father Eichler, Dr. Backman. I believe you already know Dr. Gallagher." He said it like we were adulterers he'd caught on tape. I had no idea what he knew nor how he came to know it. Which was precisely how he wanted it. "Deputy Thomas, let me introduce you. I took the liberty of inviting them as they both work rather closely with Master Foster." I glanced at Jen. She widened her eyes not knowing what was going on. Peckham turned to me.

"I understand that Dr. Backman has reason to believe Carey's suicide attempt was really an attempted murder. Perhaps he could enlighten the rest of us to the source of this disturbing revelation."

He was as controlled as a prosecutor poised with a surprise eyewitness. Sensing he'd love to fillet me on the stand, I cut to the chase. "Somebody tried to kidnap Carey yesterday."

"Goodness." His response was calculated. "I was under the impression he was in a locked unit."

"It happened off-site."

"Off-site?"

"At a mall. We were getting ice cream." Peckham raised his eyebrows in implied bewilderment—why would anyone unsequester a suicide risk for something so inconsequential as ice cream? "He had a doctor's appointment," I explained. "His therapy's been going so well I took him for a treat. The main thing is, we were followed. And someone tried to abduct him."

"Thank God you were there to stop the rogue." The bastard—he already knew that I wasn't.

"Actually, I was in the bathroom."

"And where was Carey?"

"Waiting on a bench."

"You left him alone?" My dereliction bordered on the incredulous.

"I did. It was poor judgment on my part." He let me hang until it sank in. *Nobody messes with Schuyler Peckham.*

"Well, I'm sure you feel horrible," he feigned compassion. "Any of us would after being so negligent." I did not retort. I deserved it. "So how did you find Carey?" Apparently, he wasn't done exposing my incompetence.

"He escaped somehow and ran back. Terrified as you can imagine."

"I'm sure he was." Peckham humored my commentary but seemed otherwise confused. "Am I to understand then, that you never actually *saw* Carey with this alleged abductor?"

"No. I didn't."

"So, all we have is Carey's word that he was accosted?"

"More or less."

"More or less?"

"He didn't exactly tell me; he nodded when I asked him."

"He nodded."

"Yes."

Peckham shook his head as if genuinely perplexed. "Please forgive my questions, Doctor. I know you would never deliberately distress my boys with a murder investigation in their home without having sufficient cause. I'm merely trying to understand what that cause is."

"Of course." I caved like I would have with my father.

"What I don't understand is, even if Carey did not simply run away when left unattended, what makes you think this alleged abductor infiltrated Salve Regina and harmed Carey weeks ago?"

"Carey told me he didn't cut himself."

"He did." Peckham said it like only a chimp would be surprised that a disturbed boy would deny his own cutting. "And did he say that this abductor was the same person who cut him?"

"It was implied."

"Implied?"

"I could tell by the look in his eyes."

He smiled as if my transparent ineptitude defied rational discussion. "I think I understand now," he condescended. "The eyes *can* be surprisingly communicative." His own were as satisfied as a surgeon specializing in swift emasculation. Without a compelling response, I silently seethed. "So Sheriff." Peckham was done with me. "I know you're required to investigate every allegation of impropriety. How can we help you?"

"I'd like to reexamine Carey's bedroom."

"Of course. It's very important to us that Carey receive the attention he deserves." He brushed by me as if the procedure was finished—though I was still on the table, my legs fully spread.

Once at Carey's dorm room, Deputy Thomas opened her investigator's satchel and slipped on latex gloves. Peckham unlocked the door careful to avoid smudging the knob. The sheriff rashly grasped it.

"You don't want to check for prints?" Peckham inquired.

"A common misconception," Deputy Thomas answered. "Usable prints are seldom found on doorknobs. Especially one that's already been handled, even by you, I suspect." She let him know; she wouldn't be messed with either.

Peckham's grin was unfazed. "Of course you're right, Sheriff. On both counts." She entered the room while we huddled in the hallway. "I wish I could say," Peckham continued, "that the room has remained undisturbed. We thought it best to launder the sheets. And Dr. Backman probed about when he dropped by." He sounded like an unwilling accomplice to yet more of my blatant malpractice.

"I was grateful you suggested it," I came back. "It helped in Carey's therapy."

Peckham was amused at my dignity's meager revival. "Anything to help our boy," he smiled. Like a shark smelling fresh blood, he turned. Father Ike cowered behind us as if the sight of Carey's room made him squeamish. "I'm sorry, Ichabod. I'm blocking your view. One can always learn from a professional."

"I'm fine, Monsignor," Father Ike answered.

"Oh, I insist."

Eichler hesitated as if being in the hallway was penance enough then dutifully stepped toward the door.

"Jennifer, would you like a better look?" Peckham asked.

"I'm fine where I am, Schuyler. Thank you for your concern."

"It's nothing."

The Sheriff examined the floor, the bed-frame, the closet, dresser, and desk. Nothing looked unusual. Peckham pressed his advantage.

"So tell me, Dr. Backman. How will you proceed now that you've 'validated Carey's experience'?"

"I'm not sure I follow." His contempt gave off fumes.

"Surely the reason you put us through this was to presume Carey's honesty until he violated your trust. How will you address his, what . . . his evasion of the truth?"

"I believe that people can't help but tell the truth—even the games they play betray their story."

"So you won't hold him accountable for his deceptions?"

"Children become what they're surrounded by. Surround them with trust, they will become trustworthy."

Peckham smiled, if nothing else admiring my audacity. "It seems Carey has found a most trusting caregiver."

"Now this is interesting." Deputy Thomas was at the window. "Has anyone touched this since Carey was cut?"

"Not that I'm aware of," Monsignor allowed, alert for a shift in the winds.

She nudged it open with two metal prods. "It's been pried from the outside. Maybe by a laborer. Do you have a ladder available?"

"Ichabod," Peckham ordered, "have Shuk bring a ladder immediately." Eichler scurried like a lackey sent to fetch.

Deputy Thomas dusted the inside panes, lifted several prints with tape, and labeled the samples. Then she led us outside. Eichler, Shuk, and ladder were waiting.

The dormitory backed to a grove of trees. The wall was laid with rough-hewn stone, a narrow ridge separating the two floors. From ground to roof, a stretch from Carey's window, a silver electrical conduit was cinched by brackets. The base was secured by rope where the bottom bracket had come loose.

"Did you do this?" the deputy asked Shuk.

"No, Maam. It didn't come from the grounds crew."

She had Shuk place the ladder to the window then climbed up. She dusted the panes, inspected the sill, worked the window up and down, then leaned over and studied the conduit's underbelly. She gave her verdict when she climbed down. "No doubt about it. Somebody scaled this conduit and broke through Carey's window."

Jen held her hand to her mouth; Eichler winced with worry; Shuk flared with wrenched resolve. Peckham however, showed no reaction at all. His steely gaze gusted through the Sheriff. So cold it could have iced her to the spot.

———

Deputy Thomas was sobered by her findings. After an hour at the window gathering clues, then another along the fences searching for forced entry, she shared her results with Peckham and me in the Monsignor's office suite. Jen and Ike had long since returned to class.

"I found more prints all up the conduit, a few might be usable. Several brackets were caked with dirt. More prints were on the windowpanes, most of them worthless but one or two might hold up. In the southwest corner of the property, the fence's razor wire was snipped then jury-rigged to escape detection. A log was angled on the outside to climb onto a pillar. I found more prints on the brass fixture they used to pull themselves up. I don't know if the prints will substantiate a positive identification, but this much is true for sure. Somebody climbed over the fence, scaled the pipe, then slipped through Carey's bedroom window. There's no doubt about it."

———

"It's all so heartbreaking. Who would want to hurt such a beautiful boy?"

Jen lamented on Crossroad's front steps. She was so unsettled, she came by after school, stayed through the Friday night story event, then spent an hour with Carey before he went to bed. The others down too, we were leaving for our respective homes.

"I don't know, Jen. But the guy I saw in that truck oozed venom, even from a hundred yards away."

"Who do you think he is?"

"It's anybody's guess. Carey's not saying a word." His withdrawal chastised me. "To think I thought he was externalizing his rage. I even encouraged him to engage it. He must've felt like I was throwing him to the lions."

"You couldn't know, Tony. It was all so cryptic."

"Maybe so, but I violated my own principles. I didn't hold what he was saying. I mean he flat out told me he didn't cut himself."

"It *is* hard to believe," Jen consoled. "Somebody sneaking in and knifing an eleven-year old boy."

"Maybe if Peckham wasn't so adamant that Salve Regina was safe."

"Oh, Peckham's an asshole."

"Jen, I've never heard you talk like that."

"Well, he is. The way he treated you today was inexcusable. I told him so later."

"What did he say?"

"That the current threat to Carey's life was far more pressing than any interpersonal incivilities that might have occurred during the investigation. Like he gave a damn about Carey when he was baiting you. All he cared about was the slight to his command if there was a murderer running around."

"He did seem more bothered by not knowing it happened than he was by the actual assault."

"And don't think it isn't eating him up. He's been prowling around campus all day. And hounding Father Ike."

"What's up with that? Eichler's like his personal minion."

"Honestly, I don't get them. Eichler despises Peckham, but he fears him too. They go back a long time." Jen scanned the night's horizon then changed the subject. "Do you think that guy's gonna try again?"

"I don't know," I admitted. "He seemed most determined. We called in an extra night nurse in case."

"What do we do in the meantime?" Jen wondered.

"We wait for Deputy Thomas," I said. "She hopes to know more by Monday. Hopefully the prints will turn out, and the guy will be in their files."

Jen sighed at the weekend of waiting. "You'll let me know when you hear?"

"Of course," I promised. "And thanks, Jen. I'm glad you were there today, even if it was ugly."

She smiled sympathetically, then made her first allusion to our cards. "Well, we followers of Judas need to stick together."

"Yeah," I responded. "That we do."

———

Carey was still silent on Saturday. We spent a session drawing fingers that flicked electricity. I could have flicked myself for reducing his story to its intrapsychic dynamics. On Sunday he opened up enough to recount his escape. He pried the camper door with a tire iron, then leapt while stopped at a light. On Monday, he rejoined the group. After that, he talked with ease.

It was a good thing.

As it turned out, we had a few things to talk about.

I caught my breath when I heard the voice-mail. Deputy Thomas phoned during groups. 'Call back', she demanded. 'It's urgent.'

"Are you sitting down?" she asked.

"No, I'm pacing too much."

"Well, you better."

"What's up?"

"We made a positive identification—twelve minutiae points, a core, and a delta for two prints from the fence and the conduit, eight points and a delta from a print on the window."

"In layman's terms?"

"It's enough to hold up in court. But here's the thing. I also lifted a print from the knife. It's a partial match, but plenty conclusive. All the prints from the fence, the pipe, the window, and the knife—they come from the same hand. And we know exactly who it is."

"Who?"

"They all come from Carey. It looks like he's been lying after all."

36

"I DON'T KNOW WHAT to believe anymore." I had driven for hours and was still in a fog.

Jen's message greeted me when I got home. She already knew. Peckham caught her as she left for home.

"Well, let's figure it out." She mobilized with a detective's sense of purpose. "We'll separate what we know from what we don't." I imagined her making a list. "We know someone tried to kidnap him, right?"

"It sure seemed that way. I can't imagine Carey faked it."

"So he didn't. Somebody tried to get him, but we don't know who."

"We also don't know if the guy knew Carey," I added. "Maybe he was just on the prowl and Carey was the only kid around."

"Okay, that's something else to find out. What else do we know?"

"We know that Carey was cut in his room, but we don't know by whom. It could still be Carey for all we know."

"So who cut Carey? And if Carey didn't do it, how did the assailant get into the room? Maybe he came through the door, or through the window with gloves."

"Perhaps," I continued, "but still, we only have Carey's word that somebody else did it."

"So we need more evidence of an assailant. What else do we know?"

"We know that Carey snuck off the property, but we don't know where he went."

"That seems like a place to start," she suggested. "I bet you anything he left the night he was cut. And wherever he went, it had something to do with the cutting. It would certainly explain his mood change. Do you think Carey would tell you that much?"

"Maybe. It's not as threatening as who's trying to hurt him. Of course, that's another thing we know. He's a frightened boy, traumatized by something."

"How is he?"

"Settling in, I suppose. I didn't see him after I talked with the Sheriff. I was afraid I would yell at him for lying to me."

"You know," Jen reminded. "We're not sure he's lied about anything."

"No," I conceded. "But his silences can sure be deceptive. So how was Peckham? Gloating?"

"I'm not sure how vindicated he felt. One of his boys sneaking out is as offensive as somebody else sneaking in. He rubbed that birthmark like it was on fire and grilled me for all I knew. He did ask if you were a capable therapist."

"What did you say?"

"The truth. It's amazing what you do with those boys."

"Thanks, Jen." Her words were soothing.

"How are *you*?"

"I'll be okay. I just need the whirlwind to settle down a bit. This helped a lot. I'll talk to Carey in the morning and see what I can find out."

"Keep me posted."

"I will."

"Tony."

"Yeah."

"I care."

The whirlwind didn't stop spinning. First thing Tuesday morning I found a message at the office.

Schuyler Peckham wanted to see me.

I called Mrs. Meriwether and told her I was booked all day; yes, I was booked all day. I'd come by Wednesday morning at eleven; yes, Wednesday at eleven. I was only stalling but I didn't care.

I'd rather have been summoned by my father.

Carey was drawing another hand when I joined him in the Box. After sleeping on the sheriff's news, I could honor the finger for what it was—a fitting symbol from a boy surrounded by assailants, both from within and without.

"I'd love to hear more about the hand," I began. "Did it ever come back for the boy?"

"Not yet," he said.

"Does the boy still think it might?"

"It's still out there. He knows that much."

Carey wasn't elaborating so I eased into my agenda. "Carey, do you know the difference between stories and the truth?"

He looked up confused. "I thought stories were true even if they didn't happen."

I had that coming. "They are," I admitted. "Do you know the difference between a story that may be true but it didn't really happen from a story that happened for real?"

He resumed his drawing, anxious about where this was going. "Yeah . . ."

"Carey, it's very important to me to find out if some things really happened or not. Could you help me?"

He shaded his hand's nail marks with purple as if bracing for something painful. "Yes," he whispered.

"A man in a camper tried to kidnap you at the mall the other day. That really happened, right?"

He nodded as his scribble intensified.

"Your wrists were cut. That really happened."

He nodded again.

"It happened by a person who isn't you, right?"

Another nod.

"Not a pretend person from a story, but a real person."

A nod.

"And you know who this person is."

He hesitated, then nodded.

"Is it the same person from the camper?"

Carey kept coloring. He didn't move his head.

"Are you afraid to tell anybody who really did it?"

He nodded.

"I understand. This person that did it, they did it in your school bedroom, right?"

He nodded.

"Did they sneak in through the window?"

He kept drawing.

"Did they come in through the door?"

He kept drawing.

"Did they seep through the walls like a ghost?"

He looked at me hurt, like he took this seriously and I treated it like a game.

"I'm sorry, Carey. You already answered that. This was a real person."

He returned to his drawing.

"Carey, did you ever sneak out of your room through the window?"

The question hit. He stopped drawing and stared.

"You won't get in trouble, I promise. But it's very important that I know. Did you ever sneak out of the school?"

His head barely moved, but he nodded.

"Thank you for telling me. This will help me get this guy. Did you sneak out the night you were cut?"

He nodded.

"Did you see the man in the camper that night?"

He stared.

"Carey. Where did you go?"

He kept staring.

"I promise you. I'll see you through this. But I need to know. Where did you go that night?"

He stared at the picture as if invoking courage. Then he mumbled.

"I'm sorry. What did you say?"

"I went to see my mother."

Jesus. I was stunned. "She lives close enough to walk?"

He shook his head.

"How did you get there?"

"I rode my bike. I hide it by the fence."

"Do you see her often?"

He nodded. "Every Sunday after bedtime."

My God. He wasn't lying about seeing her. "Why doesn't she visit you?"

"She doesn't like that place."

"Carey, the night you were cut was a Wednesday. Was your mom expecting you?"

He shook his head.

"Why did you go?"

He stared at the picture, then barely whispered. "I wanted to tell her about my solo. I knew she'd be happy."

"Was she?"

Carey kept staring. His eyes started to water. But he pushed the tears back—with his middle finger. Curl, cock, and flick, it pierced the air. Then he grabbed a red pencil and resumed his drawing.

He didn't say either way.

On my way to Schuyler Peckham the next day, I made a detour. I parked on the roadside then trekked cross-country to Salve Regina's southwest corner. In the gully where Carey directed me, a sheet of plastic was camouflaged by branches and brush. A blue stingray bike with rusting wheels rested underneath. A flashlight was tied to the handlebars with laundry line.

I resolved never to doubt Carey's word again.

Mrs. Meriwether delivered Peckham's message. He was expecting me in the prayer chapel. I hiked through the woods determined to resist his dressing down. I hesitated at the door for strength. Sucking up my resolve, I walked into the Monsignor's chapel.

He was kneeling at the altar's rail, his head raised prayerfully toward the stained-glass Madonna. I waited at the door, expecting him to turn the gloating face I'd crave to harpoon. He let me wait. Then he crossed himself, stood up, and turned around.

"Dr. Backman, Tony, thank you for coming." He motioned me to a front pew, sat on the edge beside me, and leaned in with his hands folded as if contemplating a heart to heart with his son, a posture he saw once on "Father Knows Best."

"It seems you and I have gotten off on the wrong foot," he opened. "I apologize if I appeared . . . ungrateful the other day, for the interest you've taken in Carey. I'm a bit sensitive where my boys are concerned. I'm sure you understand."

"Of course, Monsignor." I understood that I trusted him as much as I did a guillotine poised for a beheading.

"How is our boy doing?" he inquired. "I neglected to ask last time."

"He's doing much better. He's talking again."

Peckham nodded like a master admiring his apprentice. "You have cultivated a copious amount of trust with him. A tribute to your technique."

"As I recall, Monsignor, you found my technique therapeutically inadequate."

"A regrettable first impression." He frowned then rethought his gambit. "I'll be straight with you, Tony. I had a long talk with Dr. Carter yesterday. As Carey's guardian, I considered requesting a change of venue for his treatment. I must say, she's rather impressed with you. In two weeks, you took Carey from being defiantly incommunicative to singing again in public. I was forced to reassess my appraisal of your work."

"In other words, she denied your request to remove him from my care."

"Would you believe me if I said I rescinded the request on my own?"

"Did you?"

He smiled evasively, then looked away to consider taking me into his confidence. "I know the satisfaction of restoring another to song. I once ministered to a singer as violated as Carey. Unspeakable what his mother did to him. Fondled him while he said his nightly prayers then snapped him when he became aroused. Hissed that God detests impurity. A twisted lesson to be sure. The man became a priest, for complicated reasons, and sang the most haunting Mass you'll ever hear. Unfortunately, he was tortured—started drinking, gave into unnatural appetites, stopped celebrating Mass, even tried to kill himself. He came to me as his confessor and I agreed to oversee his recovery. I developed boundaries for him, held him accountable to a priest's discipline, kept watch over his impulses and passions. Over time, it worked. Now he not only sings a beautiful Mass, he's helping others sing as well. It's a gratifying feeling, isn't it—restoring someone's song that it might inspire others?"

Being teamed with Peckham in a common project was as attractive as sharing a sentence in hell. "I didn't restore Carey's voice," I demurred. "His soul wants to sing. I just sat with him in the darkness until it sang on its own."

"Validated his experience."

"Yes."

"Well, I appreciate your work. And I'm willing to set aside our philosophical differences to further the task at hand."

"What task is that?"

"Why, getting Carey home."

"My task is getting Carey healed."

"One hopes that a child's home *is* healing."

"In my work, that's an assumption I cannot make."

He smiled like a fencer who had yet to break a sweat. "I consider Salve Regina healing for the children whose only home it is. After all, we nurtured Carey's song in the first place."

I wasn't backing off. "Carey's not ready to come home, Monsignor. Besides, the court's hold lasts another two weeks. He's not returning before then."

"Oh I concur," Peckham insisted. "He'll benefit enormously from your care." One trifling detail though, troubled him. "There does seem, however, to be some question about the date of his return. I was under the impression that Carey was coming home on April 19th. Dr. Carter understood it as the 20th."

"I don't see what difference a day . . ." Then it hit me. The two-faced bastard was playing me. "I get it. You want Carey to sing at the Easter recital."

He grinned like a wolf with Red Riding Hood's sleeve in its teeth. "I won't deny that Carey's presence would reap great dividends for Salve Regina. But mostly I'm thinking of the boys. Imagine how inspired they'd be to see Carey rise up and sing after all he's been through."

"My responsibility is to Carey, not your boys."

"But I'm thinking of Carey, too." He frowned. "Can you imagine him coming home the day after the recital having let his classmates down? While the pride of singing for a national competition could be worth weeks of actual therapy. I wish you could've seen him when he heard about his solo."

Who did he think he was fooling? "Monsignor Peckham. What you say may be true —I'll consider it with Carey. But make no mistake. I don't give a damn what good it brings you or your school. I have but only one interest—what serves Carey's healing. And I will not let Carey be used. He's more than a voice, you know."

He smiled like I was a hick who didn't appreciate Picasso. Then he closed his eyes as if Carey's voice was singing deep within him. "Do you have any idea how rare it is to hear a voice like his, a soprano as pure as Eden's innocence?" His countenance changed as the song rose. He softened and radiated like a conductor savoring an incomparable sound, yet he winced and ached at the haunting fear he may never hear it again. "God holds His breath when that boy sings, then remembers to heal the world's wounds. Depravity is washed away; goodness blossoms into full bloom. Dostoevsky once wrote, 'only beauty will save the world.' He was right. Carey's voice kindles salvation."

To watch him, it seemed true. His hand covered his other's stain as if the song shamed imperfection. The hair on his neck stood upright. His lips trembled as if anticipating ambrosia. And from the veiled curtain of his closed eyes, a single tear slipped free, and dripped to the chapel floor.

Me? I felt like I needed a shower.

———

"The guy pushes my buttons, Jen. He's slimier than my father." I paced with my cordless phone. "You should have seen the way he played up to me. The only reason he respects my work now is because Carter's leaving Carey's release date to me. It makes me sick."

"That's self-serving even for him," Jen concurred. "I take that back. It's *transparent* even for him."

"And the way he drooled over Carey's voice. He had a religious experience just thinking about it. It's creepy."

"It's Peckham. Beautiful music enraptures him."

"Does he get that way when Mass is sung?"

"It depends on who's presiding."

"How about Eichler? Does he sing the Mass."

"Actually, he does. It's really quite lovely. Why do you ask?"

"Something Peckham said. I wondered if it was Eichler. If it was, he's had it pretty bad." I paused before my living room window and stared at the streetlight's shadows. The indecision that plagued me all day gnawed for resolution. "I think I'm going to do it, Jen."

"Do what?"

"Visit Carey's mom."

"Isn't that something the Sheriff should do?"

"That's just it. Thomas closed the case. Carey's word he was assaulted is all we have and that's proved unreliable. As far as she's concerned, there's nothing to investigate."

"Could you get in trouble?"

"I don't know." I really didn't. At what point do you cross the line between professional interest and meddling out of personal involvement? "But his mom's got to know something. Carey left school excited about his solo and came back either suicidal or stalked. *Something* happened."

Jen weighed it. "I'll go with you," she offered.

"Thanks. But it'd be cleanest if I go alone as Carey's doctor."

"Will you let me know what you find out?"

"You'll be the first person I talk to."

"Be careful, Tony."

"I will." An awkward silence hung between us. I said as much as I dared. "I'm glad we're working on this together. It feels good."

"Yeah," she replied. "Me too."

———

Jen and I were talking every night now. I castigated myself for being attracted to her and was damned if I would let her know. Why pollute a great working relationship? Besides, she made her disinterest clear that first day in her classroom.

It reminded me of my one and only fling—if you could call it that—my freshman year in college. I was too petrified to ask anyone out, so my roommates arranged a blind date. Billi and I had such a great evening I sputtered up the courage on the drive home to ask her to go steady. Being more seasoned in the rhythms of romance, she politely turned down my premature proposal with the standard line, 'I just want to be friends.'

I took her at her word. We started hanging out, occasionally at first, then more frequently as fall turned into winter. By early spring, we were inseparable, hitting the books over coffee on school nights, movies and concerts on weekends. My crush flared into an all-consuming fever but I was as chaste as a eunuch. My friends begged me to kiss her, or at least declare my feelings, but I told them. True, she accidentally brushed her hand against mine when we walked, and she doodled on my leg with twigs as I proofread her papers in the grass, but she had made it clear that very first night—friendship was all she wanted.

Word must have reached her, or libidinal frustration. After three seasons with me yet to take my hands out of my pockets when we walked around the pond, she took the initiative.

Tony," she whispered as we watched the play of moonlight on the water. "Remember when I told you I just wanted to be friends?"

"Of course, Billi."

"Well, I've changed my mind."

"Yeah?" I said, worried she didn't want to be my friend anymore.

"What I mean is," she hemmed, "if you want to date, each other, I'd really like that."

"That's great, Billi," I gushed.

She waited, deftly concealing any platonic exasperation. "You know what that means?" she hinted.

"What?"

"Well, if you want to, you can kiss me now."

I wanted to. And I did.

But two weeks later I was in over my head. She brushed my crotch and I broke up.

Jen had made it clear too. If she changed her mind, she'd have to let me know. And she wasn't brushing her hand against mine.

All she was doing was calling every night.

37

CAREY'S MOM LIVED ON the seedy edge of northern Calistoga. I parked at a single room church on the highway that looked like an abandoned outpost. Its Puritanical austerity permitted but a bolted door out front and three battened-down shutters on the sides. The alabaster clapboard was so grimed with exhaust, painting it would be pointless. From its peeling planked stairway, I gazed across the street. I faced a potholed cul-de-sac so shadowed by decay the sun seemed permanently repelled.

If hell had a front door, that street could take you to it.

Peculiar bedfellows with the church, two suspicious establishments flanked the cul-de-sac's corners. A liquor store caged in steel advertised the coldest beer in California, while a dilapidated cocktail lounge proclaimed an evening show flashing as much flesh as is legal within the city limits of Calistoga. The single-laned court in between housed a handful of decrepit shacks constructed so hastily they seemed supported by the trailers butted on the ends or the crutches of carports anchored by poles.

As I crept in, the hovels seemed devoid of life. The windows were tacked by sheets within and barred by steel without. The rampant weeds across the lots blurred the un-fenced lines of ownership. Gutted cars and decaying washers, rusted oil drums and skel-etal laundry lines marred the yards more dirt than lawn. The sole creature in the slummy confines was a mangy mutt too bored to care about whoever had dealings on its turf. The place bore such blind disregard for human activity one could slink the length into the deepest bowels of the block, do one's business, and depart.

And no one would know you were there.

The house burrowed at the far end was shadowed by eucalyptus trees stripping their bark like snakes shedding their skin. The storm door was missing its screen. The porch lamp lacked a bulb. Cobwebs draped the overhang like a passage to a castle dungeon. Though it was late afternoon, the place felt as dark as death.

I reached through the screen-door carcass and knocked. Nothing in the house stirred. I knocked again. The cemetery silence heightening my senses, I listened for the slightest rustle. Nothing. I walked onto the yard. Apart from the Impala parked in the carport, the place appeared abandoned. I snuck back onto the porch and knocked once more.

Without a sound slithering within, the door eased open. A dopey-eyed woman slid to the edge, her breasts exposed to the nipples in the full-length satin housecoat tied by but the lazy knot at her waist.

"Does little Dickie want to come out and play?" Her seductive slur could have been laced by pot, Bloody Marys, or a doubled dose of sedatives.

"No, Mrs. Foster. I'm Dr. Tony Backman. I'm the psychologist treating your son."

"Does little Tony want to come out and play?" Her naughtiness was unabashed.

"No, Mrs. Foster. I'm here about Carey."

She squinted as if trying to remember. "Carey's not here."

"I know. He's in my facility. I'm here to talk to you about him."

She eyed me to see if I was serious, then smiled as if it could go either way. Cocking her head, she enticed me in, then disappeared into the house. Stepping in, I almost gagged.

The living room looked more like a stag party den than the parlor of a single mom. Men's magazines were scattered across the coffee table—sports and automobile periodicals on top, *Hustlers* stashed on the shelf below. E-Z chairs and a couch faced the TV console where a cardboard placard of a blond in a bikini displayed her cleavage over a beer between her legs. Ashtrays with racing-car decals and coasters sporting female derrieres peppered the end-tables while a cabinet of videos stood in the corner, one shelf devoted to titles in red, another to classic children's movies. On the walls astride the tunnel of hallway, dozens of bumper stickers were randomly pasted—'Shake off the dust before entering,' 'If you hear screaming, wait in line,' 'Schoolgirls do it for their daddy.' A photo montage of Phyllis Foster arrayed the hallway within—costumed as a girl in need of a spanking in one, a high school co-ed pumping pom-poms in another, still others in a showgirl's dancing tights, a farmer's daughter's shirtless overalls, a nun's habit, a maid's mini skirt, a man's suit, and several other alluring ensembles arranged like entrees on a menu. Shaded in the unlit recesses beyond, a freshly laundered cheerleader's outfit hung from the doorjamb to the bedroom. Carey's mom grazed it with her hand as she sashayed into the room, her bare ass brushing against the caressing satin of her robe. I hoped to God she wasn't expecting me to follow.

"Do you mind if I get some water while I wait?" I stood ground. A bare arm waved me permission. With feline instinct, she sensed my discomfort.

"Don't worry, Sugar. I'm just changing into something a little less comfortable."

Strands of beads hung in the kitchen doorway. I ducked through like game in need of cover. The counters and stove were bare but for an opened box of saltines. An office desk held a sewing machine in the corner, the drawers bulging with patterns. Bins of fabric were stacked on the side, topped by a tackle box for buttons, baubles, scissors, and X-acto knives. A card table hugged the wall. A bag of coin purses hid underneath. On top, an unfinished jigsaw puzzle lay scattered. The box's cover disclosed 101 types of ice cream bars.

I walked to the sink and regrouped with a glass of water. Three pictures on the sill absorbed me. Carey beamed before a brand new bike in one. He and his mother laughed before a county fair merry-go-round in another. The last was vintage black and white— a young girl, blond and in braids, sat on a pony and glowed into the camera without the slightest premonition of the hell her life would become. I stared at the young Phyllis Foster and wondered how that playful child had turned into the chilling plaything she was now. And what would change her back.

The beads rattled behind me. She followed my gaze. The pictures stopped her too.

"Do you know what it's like to be told you're not fit to mother your own child?" I turned around. She wore a staid housedress though her slinky manner could make burlap seem seductive.

"I can't imagine a more agonizing thing," I said.

She stared at the boy on the sill. "Do you know what it's like to have your own child wish he were dead?"

"No, Maam. I don't."

She grimaced and blinked sleepily. "When God is in an especially foul mood—when He tries to think of the cruelest thing He can do—He makes a woman like me. Then He gives her a son. And He lets her love him." She snickered like she could imagine God's self-satisfaction. Then she shook it off, and sauntered to a chair at the table.

"I saw the coin purse you gave Carey. I didn't realize you made it."

She winced as if salt stung her wounds. Lifting a bottle from the floor, she poured into an iced glass perched within the puzzle. Margarita mix. Without the tequila.

"I wanted Carey to get his own ice cream," she said with defeat. "So I found a pouch at the flea market and made the cone for it."

"Well, he loves it," I encouraged.

She responded wistfully, talking to the puzzle as much as to me. "It got me started. I made others. Sold them at the flea market. Thought I might start a business." She snorted. "But it's not what sells in this world. Then once they took my boy, it didn't much matter." She studied a puzzle piece. "How is he?"

"He's coming along. He's a good boy."

"My good boy," she reaffirmed dreamily.

"You can help him a lot if you would answer some questions." She waited, avoiding eye contact like shut-ins do the sun's glare. "Carey told me he came here the night he was cut. Is that true?"

She closed her eyes. "He always comes to see his mother."

"He said he came to tell you about the choir competition."

She smiled. "Is that what he came for?"

"He didn't tell you?" She slowly shook her head. "But he did come, right?" She grimaced. "Can you tell me what happened while he was here?" She sipped from her glass like she was drinking to forget. "It would help him a great deal."

She circled her tongue around her lips as she sat the glass down and stared. "In his whole life, I only scolded him once, for running away and making me find him. It's not that he never did bad things. All boys do. But I didn't want him to leave me. So I never scolded him again." She sighed at the irony.

"Did Carey do something bad that night?" Her eyes clouded like a mist of senility threatened to swallow her. Trying to retrieve her, I changed tacks. "Carey's a good boy, isn't he?"

"He's my sugar," she drifted.

"What do you most love about him?"

"He takes care of his mother. He's always thinking of his mother."

"Like coming to visit you every week."

She pined at the puzzle. "He misses his mother"

"And sharing his news with you."

"He tells his mother everything."

"When I was a boy, it upset my mom when I did bad things."

"All boys do bad things. Then they become men, and do sick things."

"I'm curious, what's the baddest thing Carey ever did?"

She winced like it still grieved her. "I told him, I have to work hard for us. He must never interrupt me with a client."

"Mrs. Foster," I eased. "On the night Carey was cut, were you alone when he came over?"

She rubbed her eyes trying to massage the memory away. Then she opened them, and glared at the puzzle.

"Men are pigs."

"Was there a man here?" I could see. I lost her. "Okay, Mrs. Foster. I have only one more question. Did a man come here driving a green camper?"

She sneered. "The men I see don't drive to my door. They don't want to be seen with me."

"I see."

"Why would you ask?"

"I think the person who cut Carey's wrists is driving a green camper."

Deep within her dementia, some tumbler of coherence clicked into place. "Carey cut his own wrists."

"I don't think so. Somebody's trying to hurt your boy."

She shook her head as a she-bear fury flickered. She pursed her lips as she spat. "Men are pigs."

"Are you sure there isn't more you'd like to tell me?"

She flared at the busted-up puzzle. "Oh, I'll tell you more. And you'll know it when I do."

"You can't tell me now?"

"You'll know." She brought it home. But it wouldn't be then.

By the time we reached the front door, her flicker of fury simmered to a doped-up despondency. A school picture of Carey in a blazer and tie was nailed to the wall. She paused before it, her face twinged with both longing and regret.

"What a yummy boy," she purred. "Couldn't you just eat him up?" Distractedly, she took her middle finger and caressed the length of his chest like a lover.

Then she looked me in the eye for the first time since she invited me into her home. "I could just eat you up too." She pulled herself into me and pressed her lips against mine with as sensuous and probing a kiss she could indulge in before I pulled myself away.

"Don't worry," she teased with eyes that could recognize perversity. "I kiss all the men I love."

If she was telling me more, she picked the wrong way to do it.

38

THAT SLUT'S SALIVA IN my mouth poisoned my system like acid. I should have debriefed the buttons she pushed, but instead I let it fester. By the time I got home, I reeked with rage. I tried to contain it, but it bled through my speech and infested my sleep.

And then, it contaminated my work.

———

"It was disgusting, Jen. 'Sustained exposure to promiscuity' doesn't do it justice. It turned my stomach." I paced my house with the phone. "Not to mention the clientele that comes in and out. Some of those guys must be brutal."

"Did you find out what happened that night?"

"No, but *something* did. And she wouldn't share it. My God, here she has a chance to save her son's life and she'd rather keep her dirty little secrets. What kind of a mother is like that?"

"Did she give any hints?"

"Boy did she! Carey's been a '*bad boy*' for '*interrupting her clients*.' Can you imagine? She's acting out fantasies of schoolgirls screwing their daddies and *he's* bad for interrupting the sexcapade. Goddamn it."

"So you think it was one of her clients?"

"I'd bet money on it."

"And she knows who."

"Damn right she does! And she might say more later. I mean, Jesus Christ! Wake up lady! Somebody's trying to kill your son and you're protecting the bastard. I'm sorry, Jen, but she's trash. Slutty trash."

"Poor Carey."

"Poor Carey's right. I wanted to cut myself after thirty minutes around her. And that was before she said goodbye. This is gonna make you *sick*. She caressed Carey's picture with her middle finger and said she could just eat him up. Isn't that *nauseating*?"

"It's heartbreaking." I was too worked up to register the difference. "What did you do?"

"I did nothing. I turned my back and bolted."

I neglected to mention how she tongued me.

———

Carey's mother gave me nightmares. A reprise of the one I had as an adolescent. With a wicked twist.

I'm lying in my childhood bed. My bedroom door opens. A woman comes in and kneels beside me. Though her face is shadowed, she's dressed like Mary Poppins. She feels my forehead as if checking for fever, then pulls my blankets past my chest. The familiar bestial shadow fills my doorway. The Victorian nanny sits up. I turn to look at the menacing presence. SMACK! My face is slapped. The woman glares, her hand poised, threatening to slap me again.

Casually, I lift my hands from my covers. I cock my middle fingers. Then into her face, I flick electricity. She falls back. I rise. My fingers let fly as her face blisters and blackens and is charred unrecognizable. I fry her until she stops writhing. Smoke curls from her scorched face. With my middle finger I stroke the charcoal mask. It peels away like tissue. Behind the blackness, my mother's cadaver stares.

I stare back. The bestial presence approves. Then disappears.

———

I woke up hounded—how dare I hurt my mother! What in God's name was that nightmare about? The pitch-black world, checked out in slumber, was not disclosing. The night's promise of rest a tease, I splashed myself with water then sat in my living room's darkness. Like the premonition of a tombstone with your name upon it, the source of my nightmare materialized. Jesus, I had forgotten all about it.

Like Carey's, my mom only scolded me once.

I was thirteen.

She slapped me in the face.

———

The slap seemed to rise from the dead. My mother had sobbed into such broken oblivion, she looked like a beaten corpse. My father had already slunk from the table with the shame of an exposed degenerate. Our unblessed Passover provisions lay tossed on the floor in a napkin. The cryptic pile of communion wafers, the half-dozen blades of grass, and the single raw potato glared from the table like taunting false idols. The items had shattered my mother. As my father sadistically unveiled them one by one, she begged him to stop, screamed in terror, then wailed into her empty plate. No Shekinah gathered her tears. She wept alone. My father bent down almost repentant. Then he came back to himself. He gazed at the desecrated shambles of our meal and said to no one in particular, "The trouble with the Jewish God is not that He fails to come for those who perish. It's that He fails to come for the ones He saves." Then he scowled at the food as if it was rotten. "Catherine, Tony, clean this mess up. You can eat later." With that, he left.

Catherine and I complied. We scraped the matzoh and lamb into the trash as if it were sprayed with insecticide. My mother remained in her chair. Her crying ceased, yet it made her immobile. Just minutes before, she had bounced to the meal with the vigor of spring hope. Now she couldn't have chewed if mush were spooned into her mouth. I wanted to comfort her but tenderness eluded me. I was removing her plate when I spouted off.

"I *hate* the Jewish God."

The slap came so quick I had yet to flinch. The woman at the table glared as if possessed.

"Don't ever denigrate your father's God," she spat. "You have no idea how he's protected you."

I didn't know if the 'he' she referred to was God or my father. Nor why she stuck up for either prick.

I never saw her again to ask. The next day, she was dead.

Twenty years later, I was just as clueless. I stared out my window until the dawn stole her tired fingers into the fold of the night sky.

Even with the sunrise, I was still in the dark.

———

One bit of good news greeted me at work. The Bitter Truth Players were invited to perform once more 'The Night that God Got Nailed.' A teacher from a Catholic high school in Sonoma was at the premiere and asked us to stage it in their theater the following week. The boys would be thrilled. And it would get Carey singing in public again.

Besides, the timing was irresistible.

We'd perform it on Good Friday.

———

I found Carey in the locked unit hacking through "Shenandoah" on a harmonica. Several of the boys had taken an interest in the harp, so I bought a few Hohners to have around. Carey was one.

"That's pretty good," I said. He stopped with a self-conscious shrug. "'Jingle Bells,' right?" He looked like I told him he flunked the first-grade. "I'm just kidding. It's coming along. You should have heard me butcher it when I was first learning."

"It's hard to get the notes clear," he acknowledged.

"Try putting it deeper in your mouth—not like you're whistling; pucker like a fish." He tried a couple notes. "Yeah, that's it."

"It's hard. How did you learn?"

"By doing what you're doing right now. I used to sit for hours and just blow. Drove everybody crazy."

"I want to get as good as you."

"You will. You obviously have a gift for music. Speaking of which—we just got invited to reprise our play. What d'ya say? You up for our duet again?"

"You mean you want me to sing again?"

"Of course."

"But it's not really part of the play."

"It is now. It's the perfect ending."

He hesitated. "Well, if you really think it's okay . . ."

"Why wouldn't it be?"

"I don't know." He was clearly uncertain.

"Carey," I wondered, "do you like singing?"

He thought a bit. "It's not that I don't like it. I'm just not sure it's a good thing."

"Why not?"

He sought a way to explain. "Sometimes I go far away in my mind, someplace really peaceful. And when I come back, I don't know how long I've been there. When I sing, I have to go to that place. And I'm not sure that's good."

"A lot of musicians experience that. It's the zone an artist gets into when they hit that sweet spot of music. That's why many start playing in the first place. Sometimes we need a little break from the world."

He took it in. "Well, if you really think it's all right."

"Of course I do. I'd never ask you to do something that wasn't good for you." He nodded like he knew that much. I segued into our session. "This plays into my idea for today. How would you like to tell a story as a duet?"

"What d'ya mean?"

"We'll make it up together. I'll start, and you add parts along the way. What d'ya say?"

"Okay."

"Good. There once was a boy who loved to . . . what?"

"*Fly.*"

"Exactly. He loved to lift right off and fly through the sky, watching all the trees get smaller and smaller until he was so high they looked like little dots."

"*Sometimes he flew into outer-space.*"

"Right. Sometimes he flew right into space, admiring the stars, visiting other planets . . ."

"*That was his favorite.*"

"He *loved* visiting planets. In fact, his favorite planet to visit was . . ."

"*The sun.*"

"Because . . ."

"*It's always light there.*"

"Yeah, it's never dark and scary there, always bright, with lots of fun things to do."

"*The children play all the time.*"

"They never go to school."

"*And they eat as much ice cream as they want, special ice cream that never melts, and never runs out.*"

"How this boy loves to visit the sun and eat ice cream. And one day his fairy godmother comes and tells him that the best thing in the world is going to happen . . ."

"*He gets to fly to the sun and live there forever.*"

"Exactly. And this boy is so excited he can't wait to go home and tell his mother because . . ."

"*She gets to go with him.*"

"Of course. They're going to live on the sun together. So he gets home and he finds his mom . . ."

"*Sewing him a magic cape so he would never lose his flying powers.*"

"She's sitting at her sewing machine making the boy this beautiful cape. But when the boy gets there, he senses something evil . . ."

"*A mean giant.*"

"A horrible giant's there . . ."

"*Watching the mom sew.*"

"He's just sitting in the shadows watching the mom sew. In fact, she knows he's watching her."

"*No, she doesn't know.*"

"She doesn't even know he's there, but he's watching her all the same. And the boy walks in and something terrible happens."

"*The giant takes the mom's thread and ties them both up.*"

"He wraps them around and around until they can't move, they can hardly breathe. But the giant's not done."

"*No. He attacks them with his finger. He snaps them all over until every part of their body hurts.*"

"It's horrible. It hurts so bad the mom and the boy start crying."

"*The mom cries, but the boy doesn't.*"

"Yeah, the mom's crying, but the boy doesn't."

"*No, it hurts too much. He just lies there and wishes he could fly away.*"

"But he can't, because the mom never finished the cape, and the fairy godmother's nowhere around. So he lies there until . . ."

"*The giant snaps him one last time then runs into the woods.*"

"The giant runs away and waits for when he'll come back for the boy. But the boy knows who the giant is. So he uses his special powers to get rid of this giant once and for all."

"*No. The giant's too big. The boy just hides and waits.*"

"Yes, the boy waits until the giant comes back, and then he uses his powers . . ."

"*No. The boy is hiding, and waits for the mom to take care of the giant.*"

"Yes. The boy waits. But the mom doesn't do anything, so it's up to the boy . . ."

"*Yes, she does; she tells the boy she'll take care of everything; and she does.*"

"She *tells* the boy she'll take care of everything, but she doesn't really do it."

"*Yes, she does. She tells the giant to stop.*"

"She tells him to, but he doesn't."

"*Then she goes to the police.*"

"They don't do anything, either."

"*Then she buys a gun and kills the giant.*"

"But she doesn't really do it."

"*Then she runs away with the boy.*"

"No, she doesn't."

"*Yes she does. She takes him to another state.*"

"No. She doesn't."

"*Another country.*"

"No! She doesn't!"

"*Another planet! She takes the boy to the sun!*"

"Carey. The mom doesn't do anything. It's up to the boy to stop the giant."

"*But there's nothing the boy can do. The giant's too big.*"

"The boy can tell somebody."

"*The giant's too big for him, too.*"

"The boy has friends. They'll gang up on the giant."

"*He's too big for that, too.*"

"He'll set a trap and catch the giant."

"*The giant's too smart.*"

"Carey, the boy has to do something. He can't just wait for the mom."

"*But the mom is taking care of it.*"

"Not in this story. The mom's not doing a thing."

"*Then it's a stupid story!*"

"It's not a stupid story. The truth is, the mom doesn't give a damn."

"My *mom gives a damn and* she's *taking care of things.*"

"No, she's not."

"*You don't even know my mom.*"

"I saw her yesterday. She wouldn't even tell me who's hurting you."

"*Then she has her reasons.*"

"She's protecting the guy! She's giving him time to get you!"

"*She'd never do that. She loves me too much.*"

"Well, she doesn't love enough."

"*She loves me plenty.*"

"How do you know?"

"*I just know.*"

"She doesn't even come and see you. She doesn't care."

"*She gives me things.*"

"Like what?"

"*She just does.*"

"Like what!?"

"*Things.*"

"Name one."

"*Ice cream money.*"

"Carey. A silly coin purse is not love. Love is protecting your child from evil people. Your mom's going to bed with them."

He looked at me like I slapped him in the face. His finger flicked with vengeance. He checked his tears as he clung to his illusions..

"*My mom's taking care of things.*"

"Your mother's a whore, Carey. It's time to face reality."

A bubble of a tear swelled then burst, skipping down his cheek like a stone across a pond. He slapped at it with the back of his hand. Then he skipped away too, disappearing into his bedroom's refuge.

He left the harmonica on his chair.

So much for our duet.

39

"Looks like you got hooked."

"I know. I can't believe I was so cruel."

"It happens, Tony."

"Not like this. I can't imagine *you* laying into a child."

"Every therapist gets hooked. I've said inappropriate things."

"And what did you do?"

"What you're doing now. Talked with someone who's been there." I knew I could count on Woody. Thank God he squeezed me in on a Friday afternoon. "Why don't you catch me up with what's going on."

I did. I told him everything—how Carey started talking and said he didn't cut himself, how he concealed his window desertions so the sheriff thinks he's lying, how I abandoned him in the mall and about lost him to an abductor, how Jen sustained me, Phyllis disgusted me, Peckham enraged me, and Eichler creeped me out, my fantasies about my ex-wife, my nightmares about my mom, my recollections about my dad, and my sudden aversion to Mary Poppins. My God, how did it get so complicated?

He received every word without judgment, but raised his eyebrows when I finished as if the complexities impressed even a man who had seen it all.

"You know, Tony. It's alright to refer a patient when they bring up too much in us."

"Jesus, Woody." I couldn't have felt more defrocked if he had torn up my license. "You're saying I can't cut it as a therapist?"

"Of course not."

"Then help me. I've got to find a way to make things right with Carey."

He gauged my seriousness then raised his brow like a physician considering the horsepill in his pocket. "The best way I know is through a story."

I was game, so I thought. "Okay. Let's go."

"A guy has a dream. If he sells everything he owns and travels the continent, he'll find a house that's an exact copy of his own. Buried in the backyard is a chest of gold that'll make him wealthy beyond belief. So he does it. He sells his possessions, travels the continent, and finds this house, exactly like his own. But as he's digging his hole, he strikes a sewage line, and up springs a geyser of filth. A stranger walks by, is disgusted by the stench, and asks what the guy is doing. The man tells the stranger his dream.

"'HA!' the stranger mocks. 'What a foolish man to trust in dreams. Why I had a dream myself—if I sold all I had and traveled the continent, I'd come upon a house that's a copy of this one and find treasure in the backyard too. You don't see me covered in filth.'

"The man thanks the stranger and journeys back home. He's digging in his own backyard when he breaks another sewage line and once more is covered in filth. Disgusted, he gives up and storms into the house.

"That night he has another dream. A voice speaks but two words.

"'Dig deeper.'

"So the man goes back and digs through the sewage. Sure enough, he discovers the treasure that has been in his own backyard all along."

Often Woody's stories required decoding—this one had me stumped. "I'm not sure I follow," I said.

"It's simple," he explained. "You've found a house that copies yours. There's treasure to be found, but not in *its* backyard. In your own."

"You're saying my family's just like Carey's?"

"Something's got you hooked. You know how the shadow works. Our repulsions and attractions are mirrors of ourselves. It's messy stuff. But there's gold to be found."

"How are they even remotely alike?"

"That's where we have to dig deeper. It's hard work—the hardest you'll ever do. Are you up for it?"

He looked like a trail-guide warning his party that the only way forward was straight down a cliff and the time to turn back would be now. Though something warned of an impending fall, I went along. "Sure."

"Okay. Tell me when you became annoyed with Carey."

"That's easy. When he told me his mother was taking care of everything. It's ridiculous. His mother's this whore who caresses his picture like he's her Goddamned lover and thinks of him as some yummy piece of candy. She's playing screw the cheerleader with the guy who's killing her son and he thinks she's going to rescue him. It's preposterous. Where's the gold in that?"

Woody furrowed with concern, like a doctor with a lab report betraying worse news than he thought. "Are you sure you want to go there?" he asked.

"Come on Woody. If you see something, come out with it." If he had the Golden Bough I wanted the pass-key.

"Okay. So why so you think you're so angry with your mother?"

I felt like he'd pulled my pants down. I considered rebutting, but my shame was there for all to see. It had already invaded my sleep. "I don't know," I confessed. "It's awful. In my dreams I electrocute her with rage. I torch her face. I was even dressed up like a Nazi once. What in the hell is wrong with me?"

"It sounds like your mother hurt you."

"But she didn't. She's a Dachau survivor for Christ's sake."

"That doesn't mean she was a good mother."

"She wasn't a *bad* mother. It's not like she was Phyllis Foster."

"Why her—what is it about Phyllis Foster that most repulses you?"

I knew where he was going. "My mother is nothing like Phyllis Foster." I shivered with revulsion, as if the finger caressing Carey's picture was caressing my own bare skin.

"What just came to you—what made you shiver?"

"Nothing to do with my mother."

"Then what?"

There was no question—her touch sickened me. I could still feel it. "The way she stroked her son's photograph, then came onto me. It was disgusting."

Woody weighed whether to prod any further. Whether for my sake or for Carey's, he did. "Did your mother ever touch you like that?"

Though I should have seen it coming, I didn't. The very idea—her finger's touch—was so repugnant, I took the offensive. "That's my mother you're talking about."

"I mean no disrespect."

"No? How would you like it if I suggested your mother fondled you? What would you do with that filthy image contaminating your mind?"

He let it in. "I would find it distasteful. But it wouldn't repulse me. That's the test. If the image sticks in your gut—there's some experience it's hooked onto."

"Or maybe the image is just abhorrent," I came back. "Or your mother's already endured one hell, and you don't want to drag her through another."

"Fair enough," he said, though there was nothing fair about it. "Then you wouldn't mind me asking."

"Asking what?"

"In these images, why is your mom beside your bed? Why is she unbuttoning your pajamas? Why are you taking your pants off in your mother's bedroom?"

He had no idea what it was like to conceive of your mother engaged in a fictitious perversity. The fantasy alone was enough to render the pitiless son untouchable. How sick would I have to be? How disdainful of one who suffered enough? "Look," I said, too near a truth so painful it defied consideration. "I messed up. I yelled at a patient. I came here for some help, not to speculate about things too disgusting for words."

"I have one idea," he offered.

"What?"

"You could let someone else treat him."

It pierced as if with a bronze-tipped arrow. "So that's it, huh? Turn in my badge and my gun?"

"It's just, sometimes our issues make it hard to see things clearly. Someone could get hurt. It could be you."

I stared like an intern deemed too damaged to practice. "Thanks anyway," I dismissed. "I think I'll take my chances."

I never saw Woody again. He died before I could make amends. My only other contact was the note I sent the following week. 'Sometimes our issues help us see in ways no one else can.'

I included the newspaper clipping. I wondered what he would say to that.

I still do.

Friday afternoon traffic on the 101 fed my fury like dead timber would a California brush-fire. Half of San Francisco must have knocked off early. I burned with scorn over Woody's insinuations through the clog of cars that glutted the Golden Gate, then blazed with rage at the pyloned lane closing where Caltrans—with inspired timing—removed graffiti off a Mill Valley divider. I was sputtering through San Rafael before my verbal barrage at Carey finally simmered into contrition. The poor kid was simply clutching the plastic remnant of a world where your mom really loves you and I had to blowtorch his fantasy beyond recognition. One thing was certain. I had to follow Woody's advice, or win Carey's trust back.

As I sped by the Petaluma ghosts, the idea came to me. I knew exactly how to make it up to Carey. I pulled off at Rohnert Park and called in to Crossroads. I'd be a little late, I told Irene. I had an errand to run.

I needed to stop by Salve Regina.

Dusk had cast the school in shadows by the time I reached the gate. It was well after five but I didn't fret. I knew Peckham would be around. I glimpsed his silhouette in his office tower as I pulled into the parking lot. Like the lord of a manor scanning his domain, he watched me leave my car. I avoided his gaze and entered the building. The wing was dark and empty. With the dread of a prodigal returning home to dad, I crept up the stairway. Peckham's floor was as gloomy as a swampland at midnight, his chrome-plated desklamp the only source of light. Peckham was seated at his desk, buried in a document like a scholar poring over a manuscript for hours. I softly rapped the door. He marked a spot with his finger and looked up with feigned surprise.

"Why Dr. Backman. What a pleasure to see you." He spoke like a litigator with all the leverage. I had driven out on a Friday evening. I wanted something. "I trust all is well with Master Carey."

"Carey's fine. We have a strong rapport."

"Marvelous." He waited, his finger poised on the page.

"I was hoping to retrieve an item from his room—the coin purse from his mother. I think it could have therapeutic value."

"How much therapeutic value?" His mind whirled with Machiavellian efficiency.

"Excuse me?"

"How much value would this item have? As you can see, I'm a bit pressed. Would the value justify an interruption?"

His question threw me. "I'm not sure how to determine such a thing."

"Would its regenerative properties, say, restore Carey's ability to sing?"

The snake. I couldn't believe he was bartering Carey's trinket for a solo at a recital. "Monsignor, I cannot make Carey sing if he's not ready to."

"No. But I suspect you have some influence over how ready he could be."

"Are you telling me you won't give me Carey's purse unless I guarantee he sings?"

"I'm simply saying that you caught me at a bad time. But an interruption could be in order if the therapeutic value was significantly promising."

"How promising?"

"Let's say I tell Father Eichler he need not prepare a back-up."

"Let's say Father Eichler prepares his back-up and I'll see what I can do . . . No promises."

He smiled like a card shark who'd just turned up an ace. "Good enough. I'll take you myself."

———

Speak of the devil, we saw Father Eichler moments later. He scooted around the corner of Carey's dorm-room hallway and recoiled as if he had slammed right into us. Peckham's face turned the color of his stain. He forced his words through clenched teeth.

"My office . . . Five minutes."

Eichler did not answer. He grimaced as if receiving a death sentence then scurried out the building. I retrieved Carey's purse then scurried out myself. I couldn't wait to get off that property.

I hadn't done anything wrong. But I still felt party to a back alley drug deal.

———

The stage was set for the Friday night event by the time I returned to Crossroads. The boys were fine-tuning the line-up. Virgil was channeling his monologue. The staff and some regulars were milling around including Jen who had frequented the last several shows. Everyone was there but Carey. After having a bad day, he went to bed early.

I listened to the boys' stories, played my harp, and mingled with the post-show crowd. Before heading out for coffee with Jen, I slipped into the Box.

Carey was asleep on his side. His face tilted upward and his mouth hung open like a baby bird poised to be fed by its mother. Even at eleven years old, and after all he had been through, he still looked as tender as an infant trusting the cradle to hold him through the night. I pulled his disheveled covers to his chin and tucked his arm under the blanket. I brushed a curl off his forehead and said a prayer for restful slumber.

Then I left. After leaving my oblation on his bedside table. A plastic coin purse with an ice cream cone stitched to the side. And a note.

'I'm sorry, Carey. You were right. Your mother loves you more than I'll ever know. We'll talk in the morning. Tony.'

40

THE LOCKED UNIT WAS as quiet as a cathedral. Carey's breakfast lay uneaten on the table. His bed was unmade, his room vacant. The absence hung like a forsaken sacrament—a confessional absent an absolver, communion devoid of communicants. I stepped toward the seclusion room and spied through the doorway. He sat on the floor against the far padded wall staring at the purse in his hands. His dazed eyes showed no comfort; he could have held a telegram bearing news of a slain loved one. I sat down beside him as solemn as one shadowing the sanctuary where such news is shared and shouldered. With penitential remorse, I whispered.

"I feel sick about what I said yesterday. I am so sorry."

He gazed at the purse as if it was a portal through which he witnessed some distant scene. He recounted it with a reporter's detachment.

When I was little, I used to make forts with the couch cushions then watch the kids play outside. They made jumps for their bikes and played war with dirt clods for hand grenades. But my favorite was when they played baseball. They used the gutter lids for bases and our end of the street was the outfield. Whenever somebody hit a homerun, the ball would roll all the way into our front yard. Sometimes the boy chasing it would stop at the sidewalk and look around. I'd wave and he'd wave back. Then he'd sneak up and get the ball and run back as fast as he could. I loved watching them. My mom wouldn't let me go out when she had a guest over but it was okay. I could hide in my fort and stare out the window and watch the kids play baseball.

One day they were playing when this ice cream truck came by. You could hear the music from down the street. All the kids dropped their mitts and ran home for money. I knew it was bad—my mom told me not to bother her when she was playing grown-up games with a guest. But the truck had these pictures of rocket Popsicles, and everybody looked so happy, I couldn't help wanting some ice cream too. So I went to her room and opened the door.

She and this man were doing things on the bed. They didn't see me at first but I kept standing there hoping the music wouldn't go away. Then my mom jumped up.

"What're you doing here?" she said. I told her I wanted some ice cream. "Well you can't have any right now."

But the man was looking at me too, and he smiles kind of creepy, and says, "Oh, Phyllis, I think we should give the boy some ice cream."

My mom looks at him, she's not wearing any clothes, and starts kissing him and says, "I'm all the ice cream you need."

But he pushes her away and says, "No. I want to see you give your boy some ice cream."

So my mom looks at me and says, "Come here, Sugar. It's alright."

So I went over. I thought they were going to give me some ice cream like the man said. But they didn't. The man watched as my mom pulled me up on the bed and took off my clothes. Then she started doing things to me. And she kept doing it until she's making all this noise and the man pushes me away and says, "Now let a man show you how it's done." And they went back to doing things to each other.

I laid there on the bed. I could hear the ice cream music going down the street, but I didn't feel like ice cream anymore. I just stared at my mom's dresser. She had this picture of Jesus there. He was naked too, up on a cross, except something was covering his privates. His head was bowed like he was dead, or he just wanted to close his eyes to it all. But as I looked at him, hearing the ice cream music get further and further away, he opened his eyes and looked at me. He looked like he was real sorry, like he wished he could come over and help me but couldn't because he was nailed up on that cross. Like a dog I once saw who got run over and tried to crawl to its owner across the street but just couldn't. That's how he looked at me.

And then he started to cry. His eyes filled with tears until they spilled out and dripped down his cheeks. And he kept looking at me, and crying, as the tears made puddles on my mom's dresser. And he kept looking and kept crying, the puddles getting bigger and bigger until they dripped off the dresser and onto the floor. And then the water came pouring out, gushing out his eyes like a dam broke, filling the room higher and higher until it swirled around like a hurricane and smashed everything in the room then crashed through the walls and flooded outside carrying me and Jesus down the street in a great big river of tears.

Except it didn't really happen. I was still in the bed and the man was all dressed. And he looks at me real creepy and says, "You liked that didn't you?" And he squeezes my worm. It gets bigger, I don't mean it to but it just does. And he says, "Lookee here, Phyllis. His pecker's ready to hunt some more bush." Then he turns mean and says, "Better get that boy dressed before someone finds him like that." And he leaves the room.

My mom's still lying on the bed kind of sleepy-like and sad. And she gets my underwear and starts pulling them up my legs. But she stops halfway and looks at my worm. It's still big from when the man squeezed it. Then she takes her finger and slides it down my chest and leans down and kisses my worm like it has an owee. Then she kisses it again like it's dirty and has to be cleaned off. Then she sits up and looks at me like she's real mad. And she says, "Men are pigs. Do you hear me? Men are pigs."

Then she goes into the bathroom and leaves me there with my underwear halfway pulled up. I couldn't hear the ice cream music anymore. But I could still see Jesus on my mom's dresser. Only his eyes were closed now. And he didn't cry. And I just wondered.

Where are those crying eyes now?

I wanted them to carry me away more than I wanted ice cream.

He shared his story without emotion, as if pathos from a listener was as unlikely as tears from a crucifix. His only affect was a weary twitch. He let the coin purse drop to the floor like an amulet that had lost its powers. Then he lightly flicked his finger once, bidding farewell to a fantasy outgrown.

Do you still seek those crying eyes, Carey? If they cry, they cry for you.

41

I CLOSED MY EYES that night aching for sleep. All I could see in my hallucinatory fatigue was Carey in his mother's bed. I imagined him straddled by his mom, underpants around his knees, feeling the tingle of her finger down his chest, gazing at Jesus as she tended his wound, listening to the drift of ice cream music slipping into the silence.

My exhaustion so muddled me, I blurred that bed with the one in his dorm room. The barbed-wire encircled us like a crown of thorns as the rope burned our feet and hands, a pair of malicious eyes paralyzed us, and that wild boar of a man punctured our skin, sliced our flesh, then sneered as the blood leaked from our wrists.

In my dream state delirium, I fused a third scene into the kaleidoscope of horror. I'm in my childhood bed, lying on my back. A woman sneaks into the room. She pulls my covers down to my knees. With a courtesan's cunning, she unbuttons my pajama tops then slips down the bottoms exposing my chest and privates. My arms at my sides unresisting, she slides her middle finger's nail along my underbelly of wrist, elbow to palm, in a sensuous scratch that yields no blood. Teasingly, she slides her nail along my other wrist, elbow to palm. Then she places the nail in the hollow of my neck and slides it down my virgin chest. My skin tingles along the finger's trail. Cool whispers stir my member. The finger continues its carnal plunge, down my boyish stomach, below my baby skin abdomen, sinking ever closer to the charged tickle of my . . .

Goddamn it!! I bolted out of bed. How could I not see this?! Of course, Carey didn't cut himself. His arms all but shouted that someone else did it. And I knew exactly how to corroborate it.

I looked at the clock. 2:15 a.m. I called Sutter's Emergency Room. The physician on duty confirmed my suspicions. I called the Sheriff's office. Thomas would be in at seven. I was so keyed up I paced my house. Why hadn't anybody noticed? It was obvious once you saw it.

I tried to resist but couldn't stand it. I called Jen. I apologized for waking her then shared my speculations. She shouted her affirmation. Of course. It made total sense. And there was another way to prove it. She got dressed and drove over. As we waited for dawn, we drank coffee and penciled our suspicions. We left at 6:30.

The resplendently streaked sky announced the sun's triumphant arrival.

It was Palm Sunday.

The Sheriff's office was located one exit north on the 101. Within ten minutes, we were standing in the lobby. The receptionist said Sheriff Thomas was already in and summoned her on the phone. Jen and I were so roused by our discovery we could have had the solution to the Lindbergh kidnapping. As soon as Thomas arrived at the counter we rushed her with our excitement.

"Sheriff Thomas," I gushed, "there's no way Carey could've cut himself. When a person slices their wrists they start at their hand and cut inward. Carey's wounds start by the elbow and cut *out*. I even checked with a surgeon. *Nobody* cuts themselves like that. It's way too awkward."

Thomas was a seasoned investigator. She did not leap with the endorsement Jen and I expected. "Now hold on. Let's think this through. First, can a doctor determine the direction of a knife wound?"

"Yes. At least in this case. It's harder to break skin than you'd think. It takes pressure which leads to a puncture wound. The end that gets more shallow suggests a blade's release point. That's exactly the kind of wound Carey has. The knife punctured him at the elbow then trailed out at the palm."

"Okay, but how do we know Carey didn't cut himself that way?"

"Sheriff, you have to admit. The only natural way to cut yourself is to pull the knife towards you."

"I see that, but what if Carey wanted it to look like somebody else did it? He's already lied about his window."

"Actually, he admits to sneaking out. And he never said that the person who cut him came in through that window."

"Still, Carey could have done it himself."

"There is a way to find out for sure," Jen suggested.

"How?"

"Do you have the evidence from the hospital?"

"Of course."

"Let's take a look."

Sheriff Thomas retrieved a plastic bag with Carey's name and case number labeled in black. His nightclothes were folded inside. She donned white gloves and laid on the counter a powder blue pullover pajama top with three Power Rangers—red, yellow and blue—posing on the front. Surgical scissors had sliced up the sides. Blood, the faded color of my mother's Dachau patch, caked both sleeves so thickly it cracked as it dried.

"My God, it's true," Jen gasped.

"See, Sheriff," I explained, demonstrating as I went along. "Think about it. He's lying in his bed on his back, his feet are tied down, ropes are in place on either side to slip his hands into. He cuts one wrist, *away* from himself, with such severity it requires nearly thirty stitches to close. Then he leans over, switches hands, and slices the *other* wrist with equal severity. Then he reaches *back* over and places his hands into the ropes. Where's the blood on his pajama top? His wrists would've been bleeding all over his chest. But there's nothing. Except on the sleeves. Don't you see? Somebody tied Carey's hands down and cut one arm then the other, both towards himself, trying to make it look like a suicide."

Staring at the sobering shirt, Sheriff Thomas came around. "Have you thought about who it might be?"

"That's all we've been thinking about for hours. We have one idea that, if nothing else, should be easy to rule out. Carey's father. He was convicted of sexually abusing a minor when Carey was young. Apparently, he insisted on his innocence and swore he'd be back. We can find out if he's still in prison, can't we?"

"Do we know his name?"

"It's in Carey's file. Tauren Astor."

She studied the shirt another moment. "Come around to my desk."

———

Jen and I sat in front of the desk while Thomas typed on her computer. It didn't take long. Tauren Astor had been incarcerated at Soledad State Prison. Seven to ten for involuntary manslaughter and child endangerment. He was released January 17, 1992. He failed to meet his parole officer on February 28. He'd been missing ever since. "Hold on a second," Thomas said. "Let me print out his picture."

She typed some more then scooted out of the room to retrieve the photo. I looked at Jen with dread. She clasped my hand like we were awaiting a terminal diagnosis from a doctor. Thomas came back. She handed me the printout.

"You recognize him?" she asked.

Recognize him. He had already appeared in my nightmares. I stared at the face from the Chinook camper.

It was Carey's father.

42

"Dr. T'll back me up, right?" Virgil sounded like a sheriff fending off a lynch mob.

Whatever he was defending, I wouldn't be helpful. If there was a posse being formed, I wanted to be in it.

So far, Deputy Thomas didn't need one. She put an APB out on Astor, increased the patrol around Crossroads, then dug for clues in Astor's past. For my part, I notified Carter, hired a security guard to stand watch outside the boys' view, then drove out to Crossroads to brief the staff. With nothing else to do, I considered staying over. For one night anyway.

The boys were spending their Sunday afternoon free time embroiled in controversy. All except our previous day's arrival. Hannibal had come back from the psychiatric hospital. His meds were recalibrated but the soporific side effects of his competing antipsychotics had yet to completely dissipate. He sat on a chair and stared out the front window with such paranoiac intensity he could have been eyeballing Tauren Astor hidden in the vineyards. With Hannibal however, the stalker would have friends—a battalion of ninjas creeping through the bushes with machetes strapped to their backs.

I had greeted the inert Hannibal then approached the boys in the Commons. With Shadrach and Fast Eddie as spokesmen, they held common cause against Virgil. Carey sat next to Virgil's recliner as attentive to the debate as Hannibal was watchful. I sauntered in and acted natural.

"What's Virgil advocating now, guys?"

"A mass murderer's freedom," Shadrach blared with indignation.

"Not his freedom. Just his life," Virgil set straight. "And he's not a mass murderer. He only killed two people."

"Kids for God's sake," Fast Eddie weighed in. "They were *our* age. The guy should fry."

"We don't fry in California," Virgil corrected. "We gas. With the same cyanide canisters the Nazis used to kill Jews. I'm telling you, the death penalty's barbaric. Come on, Dr. T. *You* at least have a social conscience." Virgil was so riled up he could've been the civil-liberties lawyer working the case. Any other time, I would've been sympathetic. But having just identified Carey's would-be killer still on the loose, my ideology gave way to castigation. Hang the guy for all I cared.

"What are you guys talking about?" I was clueless.

"Robert Harris," Virgil declared as if anyone not catatonic should know. "The first man to be executed in California in 25 years. He's sentenced to die two days after Easter. Don't you read the paper?"

"I can't say I've been following it. What did he do?"

"Get a load of this," Shadrach took over, lead counsel for condemning the man to a swift and certain death. "He kidnaps two boys eating burgers in their car, takes them out to the woods at gunpoint, and forces them to beg God for their lives. Then he shoots them anyway, laughs at their whimpering, and munches down their half-eaten hamburgers while watching them slowly die. The guy's a sociopath."

"Sure," Virgil rebutted, "but there are reasons why he's that way. He was born premature when his father kicked his mother in the crotch so hard she went into labor three months early. When he was two, the dad punched him so hard he knocked him out of his high chair and broke his jaw, then looked at his wife and laughed, 'Your baby's bleeding, Evelyn.' And for kicks, when he wasn't molesting the two daughters, the dad got his loaded shotgun and screamed that everybody had thirty seconds to hide before he hunted down the first person he found. You'd be a sociopath too with a childhood like that."

"I'm not saying he grew up with silverware at the table," Shadrach came back. "I'm saying, if you do something horrible like kill kids, you deserve to die."

"Don't you have compassion, guys," Virgil pleaded. "He could be one of us."

"How can you say that?" Fast Eddie reacted. "None of *us* are going to become mass murderers. Except maybe Hannibal, and he don't count. He's crazy."

"Maybe not," Virgil conceded. "But some of us had dads as mean as Harris'. Mine beat me with a Bible."

"Which is exactly the point," Shadrach jumped in. "*You* didn't become a murderer. He *chose* to kill; he deserves to die. It's right there in the book your dad beat you with. 'An eye for an eye, a tooth for a tooth.'"

"An eye for an eye leaves everybody half-blind and aiming for the other one," Virgil argued. "It leads to vengeance not justice. What about the part that says love your enemies? When are you Bible-thumpers going to preach that one?"

"You want us to *love* this guy?" Shadrach was incredulous.

"Why not? At least have compassion for him."

"And what kind of message does *that* send? It's no problem if you kill children because we'll love you no matter what?"

"No. It says we're going to lock you up for life, but we're not going to kill you. We're not going to perpetuate hatred."

"So you're telling us," Fast Eddie picked up, "if you were in those woods and you came across this guy eating a Big Mac . . ."

"It was Jack-in-the-Box."

"Jack-in-the-Box then, and he's laughing at these boys begging God for their lives, you wouldn't do everything you could, even kill him if you had to, to help those boys because that would be perpetuating hatred?"

"You're switching the subject," Virgil insisted. "We're talking about how to punish a man who's already caught."

"We're talking about whether killing a killer is justified," Shadrach returned. "Even necessary at times to keep him from killing again."

"But he's in jail. He can't kill again."

"What if he gets out? What are you going to say to the kids he kills that time?" Fast Eddie turned to me. "Come on, Dr. T. You'd kill this guy wouldn't you?"

"I don't know," I demurred, "if the guy's in jail . . ."

"But what if he was *here*? What if Robert Harris showed up at Crossroads and tried to kill *us*? You'd kill him then, wouldn't you?"

The boys all looked at me to see what I would say. Their eyes made clear where they saw themselves in the story. Maybe Virgil could identify with the abused-child-turned-killer, but the rest were the boys in the woods being murdered.

"Listen guys," I swore, "and listen carefully. If somebody ever tries to kill one of you, they'd have to go through me first."

Virgil still fought for the guy on Death Row. "But you wouldn't want him killed in cold blood, would you? Then you'd be just like him. And evil wins."

I looked at Carey taking it all in. "I don't like it anymore than you do, Virgil. But if a kid gets killed, somebody's going down. Let's hope we're not there when it happens."

———

"Well that was a gruesome conversation." Carey and I debriefed in the locked unit. "Did it scare you?"

"No," he shrugged.

"So what do you think?" I asked. "Should Harris die or be locked away?"

He pondered the possibilities. "I think he should have to watch our play."

"How come?"

"It'd be pretty bad punishment to have to look in that mirror."

I was taken by his insight. "Would that be punishment enough?"

"No," he considered out loud. "He should have to stare in that mirror every day he's alive. It should be the last thing he sees before they kill him."

"So you think he should die."

"Oh yeah," he said with certainty. "The guy should fry."

I let his sense of justice ring before identifying the other killer in our midst. "I wanted to tell you, Carey. I've been doing some investigating. I know who's trying to hurt you." His eyes searched me with both fear and hope. "Your father's the one who tried to kidnap you, huh?" He looked down as if the identification caused him pain. "He's trying to hurt you, isn't he?" He nodded. "I'm really sorry, Carey. I know what it's like to have a father who's a bad man." That I did. "Well, don't worry. You're completely safe here. The police are patrolling the area around the clock and we have a security guard stationed outside." He showed little comfort, seeming certain his father could elude any dragnet. "I was even thinking of staying over myself. I can take the room next to yours."

He looked up. "Really?"

"Yeah. We'll have a slumber party. Do you like playing games?"

"I like doing puzzles."

"Me too. We'll do a puzzle together, maybe watch a movie."

He half-smiled before the dread shadowed his face.

"Carey," I reassured. "I promise you. Nobody's going to hurt you. I won't let them."
He nodded as if he almost believed me.
Almost.

———

As he would all evening, Hannibal kept watch by the front window, certain the predators would pounce the second he averted his eyes. The others, I gathered in the Commons.

"Something's come up, guys. I'm spending the night here."

"What's the matter," Fast Eddie teased, "you got kicked out on the couch but you got no couch?"

"No, Fast Eddie. It's not a domestic matter."

"I got you covered." He said it like we both knew I was lying.

"It's a pest problem," I offered. I didn't want to scare them with the truth.

"Yeah," Fast Eddie smirked, "you been pesting her a bit too much."

"You're lucky I haven't fumigated here."

"Whoa," he recoiled, "you always hurt the one you love."

"So where are you sleeping?" Blade asked.

"In the Box."

"What d'ya think of that, Blade?" Shadrach ribbed. "Dr. T.'s gone psycho."

"I'm not psycho," I defended. "Not anymore than usual. I'm just bunking in the extra room."

"Watch out, Carey," Virgil intimated, still smarting over Richard Harris. "I hear he talks in his sleep."

———

It turned out to be quite a party. Carey and I completed a puzzle, some cutthroat capitalists bankrupted me in Monopoly, then we popped some corn, dimmed the lights, and screened *Home Alone*. Midway through, Jen dropped by with homemade snickerdoodles. I walked her to her car between Macaulay Culkin pranks, then fended off the boys' cheap shots about Jen and me being lovers. When the movie was over, Mrs. Hawthorne escorted Carey to the Box, Deacon and Willie led the boys to the bungalows, and I ambled up front to get Hannibal to bed. The room still dark, I stole up behind him and peered into the night.

The landscape seemed molded for stealth. No light shined between the feeble reach of our porch lantern and the occasional headlight in the highway a half-mile away. Even the stars abetted concealment, conspiring to cower behind the cover of cloud. Our rural remoteness was so shrouded by darkness, a specter could suddenly materialize in the window, cackle while he shot us, laugh while we prayed, eat our food while we bled, and nobody would hear our screams.

I had little insight into the phantoms Hannibal feared were lurking in the blackness. I knew which ones I did. Like glancing through a looking-glass into the shadows where nightmare apparitions are poised to invade one's sleep, I sensed those out there certain to invade my own. Tauren Astor was but one at the head of the line. Jakov Backman, Schuyler Peckham, Ichabod Eichler, they all threatened imminent appearances. Why not Robert Harris as well, a week from death and hungry for a last burger to devour? I placed my hands on Hannibal's shoulders as we stared down the darkness.

"See any psychos out there?" I asked.

Hannibal didn't flinch; his leer didn't waver. "We're all psychos," he said, "the good guys just got it working for them."

I squeezed his shoulders, affirming his struggle to be one of those good guys. He knew it was time for bed. So he narrowed his gaze for one last span of the horizon.

"But they're out there," he said. "And they're coming after us."

You have no idea, I thought.

You have no idea.

T HE TALK OF THE town during Holy Week was the Harris execution. Though his date
with death was destined for the Tuesday after Easter, his hopes for reprieve rested on
hearings spread throughout the Christian calendar's seven most sacred days. The state
and federal courts had a petition apiece, but the focal point was the clemency hearing
Wednesday with the governor. Pete Wilson was mayor of San Diego when the murders
occurred there and had publicly expressed outrage at the belabored appeals process. A
swift answer was expected. By Good Friday at the latest.

Virgil followed the story with the indignant idealism of a social crusader. To hear
him tell it, Robert Harris was a sympathetic victim being rushed to death by a system so
corrupt it would have crucified Jesus. The rest of the boys were equally passionate—Harris
was the Judas who already condemned the sympathetic victims to death.

Crossroads had another drama playing out that week. Our own sympathetic victim
had a week left of recovery.

And his Judas had yet to be found.

On Monday, the *San Francisco Chronicle* set the stage for the week by recounting the
epic battle the Harris case had already endured—thirteen years that included four separate
execution dates, each stayed in the final days, and dozens of appeals on everything from
the prosecution's withholding the accomplice's initiating gunshots to the constitutionality
of death by gassing. The Astor investigation discovered evidence of a stakeout behind the
abandoned gas station on the highway—footprints, tire tracks, fast-food debris, and a
busted strap from a pair of field glasses. I encouraged Carey to express his feelings about
his trauma. We drew pictures of crying crucified Christs.

On Tuesday, the papers reported protestors going public—celebrities like Martin
Sheen condemned the execution, Mother Teresa wrote an open letter pleading for clemency, and dozens of abolitionists arrived at San Quentin for a weeklong vigil with placards
and cardboard tombstones. Deputy Thomas discovered a Santa Maria stolen car report—
a friend loaned out a Chinook camper that never made it back. Carey and I discussed how
Jesus felt hanging over his mother's dresser. We drew pictures of flooded bedrooms.

On Wednesday, the paper detailed the defense's argument for the clemency hearing
that afternoon—Harris had suffered brain damage from fetal alcohol syndrome and the
beating-induced labor that thrust him into the world. Deputy Thomas questioned the
camper's owner and confirmed that Tauren Alton, obsessed with his son, had discovered the whereabouts of Phyllis Foster just before borrowing the vehicle. I took Carey to

the padded room with batakas hoping to ignite the Stygian rage that had to be bubbling within him. Carey tapped a wall or two, then requested to do something else.

On Thursday, front-page pictures—one of the killer's sister, the other of a victim's mother, both of them weeping at separate press conferences—offered a glimpse of the emotionally-charged clemency hearing to determine Harris' fate. Deputy Thomas reported that the Chinook camper had been found, abandoned at a supermarket parking lot in Petaluma. Carey, either feeling the increasing tension or lamenting his return to Salve Regina, resumed his finger's flick. We didn't share stories; nor did we draw.

On Good Friday, the Chronicle headlined Harris' fate in bold type—'WILSON DENIES HARRIS CLEMENCY.' In foreboding irony, an unrelated article peeked from the front page's lower corner—'Scholars Say the Resurrection Didn't Happen.' Even if Jesus didn't rise with Easter Sunday's song, we were going ahead. Carey rehearsed for the evening performance of 'The Night that God Got Nailed.'

Tauren Astor was still at large.

———

Jen had the idea of turning Friday's dinner at Crossroads into a Seder. By virtue of a rare convergence in the two religions' calendars, Passover fell on Good Friday the spring that Carey was with us. Like she had when we were married, Jen insisted we honor my half-Jewish background.

"Nothing elaborate," she promised, "just some matzah and a lamb spread to go with whatever's being served. And a cake. It'll be like a cast party before the performance."

Salve Regina ended classes at noon in deference to Good Friday services. Jen skipped out, came to Crossroads, and pitched her idea to the only boy not in school at Vo-Tech. Carey lit up like it was his birthday. He had never baked a cake before.

Jen decorating a holiday cake was like Rockefeller Plaza dressing up for Christmas. Our Seder table centerpiece would be a custom-made commemoration worthy of being memorialized in marble. Jen and Carey drafted the design then sent me off for supplies. When I returned they were as giddy as elves with free rein of Santa's toy factory. Flour powdering their faces, their fingers sticky from taste tests, they had transformed the kitchen into a secret-lab confectionary with variously shaped cake pans dusted and ready for batter, trial bowls of icing colors spanning the hues of the rainbow, and a carving space cleared for the fairyland assortment of Easter candy they requisitioned from me. They grabbed my bags, snickered at the wares, then swooshed me out declaring the galley off-limits for all but cleared personnel.

Inspired by their merrymaking, I draped the ping-pong table in the Commons with a cloth and made preparations of my own. As the boys came home that late afternoon, they found me pouring water into glasses on a table already decked out for a banquet. With dishes and silver for the dozen or so staff and kids on-site, platters of fish sticks, bowls of succotash, plates of matzah and lamb dip, uncorked bottles of sparkling grape juice with plastic goblets for toasting, couches and chairs around the sides, and candles on either end, even the jaded Crossroads castaways were amazed at the feast that awaited them. The boys rushed the food and fought over the grape juice while Jen and Carey sprayed finishing touches onto the centerpiece dessert. Then Jen came out and requested our attention like a maitre d' announcing a chef extraordinaire ready to unveil his culinary masterpiece. She held the door and Carey emerged.

He balanced a wax-papered board the length of two cookie sheets placed end to end. Spanning the entire breadth, an edible reconstruction of the parted Red Sea was mounted. Crafted with carved layers of cake, multi-colored frosting, and enough candy to fill a dozen Easter baskets, it looked like a Sunday School miniature of a children's Bible story laced with the sweets from a gingerbread house. The sea was a sheet-cake with choppy blue frosting bound on either end by mounds of milk chocolate desert. The water was parted with cake piled high and frothing whipped cream waves. Poised within the perilous path, Snicker bar chariots chased Gummy bear Hebrews, the carved Hershey horses reined by black licorice whips. Jelly Belly fish leered from the sides, Rocky Road rafts rode the waves, taffy twist cactus adorned the desert, and two leaders vied from either end—Pharaoh, sculpted from a chocolate Easter bunny, raced into the sea around Tootsie Roll boulders while a marshmallow Moses, cut from a candy Easter chick, climbed out through Heath Bar cliffs.

But the most beautiful part of the entire creation was the beaming artist holding it. Carey grinned with such pride he glowed. Never had I seen him radiate such joy—serenity yes, the night he sang our lullaby, pleasure to be sure when he indulged in conspiratorial ice cream, contentment perhaps when he savored a nesting Sunday afternoon over jigsaw puzzles and board games. But never had I seen him like this. Displaying his hand-fashioned Seder centerpiece as if it were at once a gift to his short-lived family, an illustration of the Promised Land bliss he tasted with us, and an homage to the God who frees and leads and parts the way toward such sweet liberation, he sparkled in the childlike purity of happiness. He could not have shined more brightly had God Himself smiled His glory from His Sinai perch above.

Carey's glow continued throughout the meal then only swelled when the cake became a performance piece. To everyone's surprise, the whipped cream waves atop the sea walls began to melt getting the cake underneath so soggy the walls started sagging together. The watery death portended for those still trapped on the path caused Virgil to proclaim,

"Looks like God's sealing things up."

Clint jumped in, "We better eat that thing before we're digging through cake to get to the candy."

"Carey," Jen asked, "do you want to serve everybody?"

"Sure," he said, smiling like a groom before his wedding cake. "And Dr. T. You get the first piece."

He cut me the slice with the marshmallow Moses. The transparent symbolism touched me. So much so, I stood up to say a few words.

"Do you guys know why Carey and Jen baked such a beautiful cake today?"

They looked at me and feigned ignorance even if they knew.

"Tonight is Passover," I said glancing at Carey. "Let me tell you a story."

My father would have been proud.

———

St. Dymphna's Catholic High School had a thousand-seat theater so professionally de-signed that neighboring drama companies used the facility for all their major produc-tions. The boys gaped in wonder when they first walked in.

"Whoa, balconies," Blade exclaimed.

"Looks like we hit the big time," Fast Eddie marveled.

The others were too star-struck to speak. Even Carey stared like a farm boy with his first look at Manhattan.

I distracted the boys into unloading our gear then scoped the place out. I couldn't imagine Astor storming after Carey in a crowd, but I took no chances. I checked all the locks and noted all the exit routes. I had Deacon and Willie stand guard backstage. And I called in reinforcements—Deputy Thomas to roam the aisles, her deputy to screen the front entrance, and the Sonoma P.D. to stake out a squad car on the side street that bor-dered the parking lot out back. Each had a copy of Astor's mug shot.

After we set up, Jen and I tried to keep the boys focused backstage. Carey and Virgil found a quiet spot to center but the others were tempted beyond all hope of will power. Overwhelmed by the amply stocked make-up rooms and high-wire scaffolding, the packed wardrobe closets and bulging prop barrels, an entire row of ropes for the cur-tains and the irresistible orchestra pit that surrounded the stage like a moat, they horsed around like monkeys at a carnival. Blade and Clint played tag in the rafters, Boomer and Flash swashbuckled with swords, Shadrach and Malcolm measured jumps into the pit, but Fast Eddie in drag trumped all the squirrelliness. Luke and Blade scurried down the ladders and rifled through the costumes to do him one better. Then the three of them paraded as the others whistled like cabin-fever judges at a backwoods beauty pageant. We didn't get them into their places, and their appropriate stage apparel, until moments before Virgil's monologue.

I needed to take my seat out front but I indulged in a final check. Virgil flipped through note cards at the center of the curtains while Hannibal, acting as stage manager in the absence of a role, took an all-seeing position to the side. Deacon and Willie kept watch by the back doors at either end. Jen stood next to Carey behind the Wizard of Oz backdrop to help hold the curtains when it appeared. They were the last two with whom I touched base.

"Are you okay?" I asked Carey.

"Yeah." He was bright-eyed and ready to roll.

"Good. I'm looking forward to our song."

"Me too."

"How are we going to play it?" I asked like we'd done this a thousand times. He had the comeback.

"So sad, they weep."

I winked. "You got it."

I looked at Jen. She kissed me on the cheek. Nothing romantic. Just a peck. "Go get 'em," she said.

"We will."

Then I left them, Jen and Carey, poised to make way for God.

———

The one restriction the high school placed on us was that Virgil had to expunge his monologue on cussing. I expected him indignant at the censorship. He was unfazed. He had new material.

I should have seen it coming.

"*Jesus* was a victim of capital punishment. The headlines told all about it. 'Pilate Denies Christ Clemency.' 'Attorneys Argue Brain Damage from Unnatural Birth.' 'Appeal to Supreme Ruler Dismissed.' The people buzzed in the marketplace, 'I heard he laughed when he called himself God,' 'I heard he forced others to pray then tried to destroy their temple,' 'I heard he finished their half-eaten loaf while making them drink his blood.' The mobs even rallied at the jailhouse. 'Kill the Jew,' they screamed, 'Nail the Bastard,' 'Let His Father save Him now.'

"Can you imagine how primitive those people were? That would never happen today—Christ scheduled to die at San Quentin and mobs showing up with posters, 'Gas the Jew,' 'Drop the Pellets,' 'Plop, Plop, Fizz, Fizz, Oh what a relief it is.' It'd never happen. We're way too civilized. Besides, Jesus is on *our* side. He's the one weeping in the garden."

Even Virgil's in-your-face blasphemy could not nullify my uneasiness. I scanned the auditorium to check once more. Deputy Thomas spied from the corner, her deputy watched from the lobby, the chains secured the push-handled doors, the crowd disclosed nothing suspicious. The only way Astor could penetrate the defense was if he had hidden in a cubbyhole since early morning. Carey was as safe as a crown jewel.

I missed the remainder of the monologue but I caught Virgil's final words. "The way I look at it—we already let six million choke on it. What's one more?"

Like wider public opinion, most of the audience sat in silence while a few catcalled and clapped as if trying to make up for the rest. Virgil dispensed with his self-deprecating smile. He signed the cross, then disappeared through the curtains.

The play got off on a wrong foot when Fast Eddie was pushed so hard he flew onstage and fell onto his face. He jumped up, realized he forgot to stash his coat, and looked back for help. As if flung from heaven, rosary beads shot through the air, hit the floor, then slid past Fast Eddie and into the orchestra pit. Fast Eddie looked over the edge like he was damned he was going after them then ad libbed, "Well, the things never worked in the first place."

He walked right by the newspaper making Virgil's later retrieval seem like someone accidentally dropped it onstage. Shadrach called us to order then tried to kick-start the floundering performance by hamming up God's epiphany—he banged his staff like it wasn't working, then intoned the magic words. It proved anticlimactic. Even with help holding the curtains, Boomer and Flash couldn't budge the plywood deity. They grabbed it from the sides thus tearing the construction paper, prompting Blade to spill the beans from across stage, "Be careful or they're gonna see the mirror underneath."

Hannibal, taking his duties seriously, matter-of-factly walked out, kicked the wheels free, and dragged God into place from underneath. Then he realized he was standing onstage. He glared at the audience like an angel of death interrupted during a mission then stormed back out of view.

But the real problems began when the bodies started piling up. Blade and Clint went down okay but Malcolm stepped on Clint's hand then fell over Blade's head. Though they were supposedly dead, the three jockeyed for more comfortable positions. Boomer and Flash went down then elbowed each other until all five were shoving in a grunting mass. Virgil played on, got beaten, fell, then hushed the squirming bodies so loudly Fast Eddie had to repeat his lines. Luke thought it was a game and leapt onto the heap like it was a dog pile inspiring another round of wrestling. Shadrach too, launched himself backwards like a rigid corpse flung from a catapult then fought for position on top of the pack. By the time Fast Eddie exposed God's face then immolated himself, all hell broke loose. The pile of bodies writhed and crawled like a mound of worms fighting for air. The effect was totally lost. Instead of gaping at the marred mirror of evil's victory, the audience watched a king-of-the-hill free-for-all.

I waited for Carey to come out, swivel God, and put an end to the Bitter Truth follies, but he suspended his appearance until the boys settled down. After a few hushes and several final elbow jabs, the mound calmed, convulsed, then calmed again. They didn't recover the mood but at least the crowd knew we weren't done.

Carey took his time. The audience waited. He took more time. The audience grew uneasy. He took too much time. The audience knew something was wrong.

Then we heard him backstage. Not Carey. Hannibal. In the high-pitched wail of a schizophrenic whose demons all lunged at once.

"*HE'S HERE*!!"

Jen screamed.

The audience assumed it was part of the play, a backstage theophany to scare the hell out of any unbeliever. I knew better. I was well-schooled in hellish theophanies. Tauren Astor was backstage.

I hauled up the steps and hurdled the bodies making straight for the curtains where Carey should have appeared. I almost reached them when the lights went out. I fumbled through the veil and into a blackness so dark I could not tell up from down. I crouched to the floor and anchored my hands. Screams wailed from the frenzied audience but backstage was as quiet as a crypt. I realized why. Nobody wanted to give away their position. Astor could be armed.

I tried to make out a shape, a movement, anything, but I couldn't even see my hand as I felt out in front of me. So I listened. It was surreal. Carey and Jen, Hannibal and Astor, Deacon and Willie were all within twenty yards of me. But they were so silent they could have already perished.

I inched forward. Then I heard it. Deeper in the darkness ahead. Breathing. Deep and bestial. Like a caged boar not about to be taken down. In a whispered grunt, it spoke.

"I want my boy."

I stopped moving. Goddamn it, I thought, don't come after me.

In a flash, the lights flicked on. I saw him. Five steps in front of me. A huge-bellied man, more bullish than obese, in black coveralls. And cowering behind him, under a table, his black clothes no longer protecting him, Carey was curled up in a ball. Astor followed my gaze. In an instant, he recognized his boy, charged after him, hoisted him on his shoulder with a single heave, and dashed out the one unmanned door in the dead center of the building's rear. I was paralyzed with fear. They were out before I could react.

Suddenly, bodies materialized from all sides. Jen crawled out from a table beside Carey's. Deacon and Willie raced from either end. Deputy Thomas leapt through the curtains behind me and shouted to get out of the way. She ran to the door, poked her head through, then chased after Astor and his quarry.

I sprinted to the door behind her. She had already radioed the patrol car. It pealed into the parking lot and made for the man lumbering toward a pickup. Astor spied the car and kept heaving. Deputy Thomas stopped running. She lifted her gun and shot into the air. The patrol car skidded in front of the truck.

His one chance at escape blocked, Astor stopped. I expected him to turn with Carey as a shield. He didn't. He set the boy down, kneeled, and looked him in the eye.

"Let Carey go," the Sheriff yelled. Carey stared at his father. Astor whispered into his son's ear. Carey nodded blankly. Astor swatted him on the rear and motioned toward the Sheriff with his head. Carey hesitated. Then he ran.

I did too. We met beside Deputy Thomas, Carey leaping into my arms like he had at the mall.

Thomas kept her gun on Astor as the other officer ordered him face first on the ground and cuffed him. Thomas holstered her gun, walked over, and recited his rights. Then she stood him up.

Astor looked in our direction. He stared at his boy in another man's arms. Then he spoke. Not to Carey. To me. Looking me straight in the eye as he said it.

"I wasn't gonna hurt him. I just wanted to get my boy."

Yeah, I thought. And take him straight to hell.

Astor couldn't hold my stare. He looked down like a defeated warrior then walked to the back of the cop car.

The bastard never looked at his son again.

I had to swallow my words.

I hope they gas your ass.

This very night.

What could have been more appropriate?

PART FOUR

Easter Sunday

44

THE LAST FULL DAY Carey was with us, his mood swung from the dolor of Good Friday to the rapture of Easter Sunday.

Though I had been up until two—first processing the night's pandemonium with the boys, then again with Jen at her house—I made sure I was at Crossroads by nine the next morning. The vocational school had a beach day scheduled that the boys had anticipated for weeks. The staff and I considered whether to let them go nonetheless, then decided it would do them good. Besides, they'd have a captive audience to hear and rehear their increasingly thrilling triumph over our intruder.

I herded the boys into the vans, waved to Deacon and Willie as they drove to the rendezvous point, then looked for Carey in the locked unit. As I expected, he sat in mute despondency. I could only imagine what we had yet to work through—terror from the trauma, rage at his father, grief over his return to the boy's home the next day. I never would have guessed the true dark cloud that descended upon his mood in a gray drizzle.

"How're you doing?" I edged up to him.

He shrugged. "Doesn't seem fair is all."

"What's that?"

"All the guys get to go to the beach. I'm stuck here all day." After all that had happened, Carey felt left out of a play day. I empathized. Sometimes we need a break from all the emotional intensity.

"I'm sorry," I said, "the school's insurance only covers students."

"Well, it still bites the big one."

I chuckled. "You've been hanging around Virgil too long." He half-smiled. "*We* could do something," I offered.

"Like what?"

"I don't know. It's a beautiful day. What're you up for?"

He looked down as if considering how big he dared dream, then ambushed me with his puppy dog eyes. "We could go to a baseball game—the Giants are playing the Reds."

I had to laugh. "They are, are they? How do you know?"

"Deacon told me."

"Did he."

"Will Clark's going for his one thousandth base-hit."

I knew when I was beat. "Well, we can't miss that, can we?"

"Really?"

"Yeah. We'll see if Ms. Gallagher wants to come along."

As fast as a game-winning rally we were off—we picked up Jen, stopped for mitts, then piled into my truck's cab to beat the crowd to Candlestick.

Few things are more saturated with the restorative bouquet from life's liqueur then taking a kid to their first professional baseball game. Carey was so excited he scarcely noticed the sights along the way. The Golden Gate Bridge, Alcatraz Island, the pyramid pinnacle of the San Francisco skyline all passed by him like chimeral temptations to a saint on his way to the Holy Land.

And Carey knew how to worship.

He hallowed baseball legends and invoked the ways he could catch a foul ball until we pulled into the parking lot and he gaped at the complex like a pilgrim approaching King Solomon's temple. He did not say a word as we scaled the ramps. And when we stepped through the stadium tunnel—the playing field rising like Atlantis from the sea—he stood positively awestruck. Bathed in diamond-bright sunlight, a Major League ballpark glistened. Grown men tossed a ball, shagged flies, and swung for the fences—high priests consecrating the dream of every boy who ever looked to his dad for a game of catch, a tip on a batting swing, a pat on the back as he beat out a single, or a rush of pride when he rounded third and safely slid into home. I put my hand on Carey's shoulder.

He did not flinch.

We indulged in the game with tourists' abandon. All three of us yelled ourselves hoarse during the Giants' six-run outburst in the first, stood up and cheered as Will Clark boomed a double for his thousandth hit, and agonized with Trevor Wilson as he fought through his first outing after surgery removed a cyst from his ribcage a mere month before. We ate hot dogs and drank soda; we shelled peanuts and munched Cracker Jack; we booed the Reds' rallies and cheered the Giants' relievers. Carey stood on his chair to sing "Take Me Out to the Ballgame"; Jen leapt out of hers when an ump made a bad call; we all flashed to our feet when the wave rolled by, and we rode it all the way to a Giant victory, seven to three.

As Carey rushed through the departing crowd bee-lining for the souvenir booth, Jen took my hand. I looked over. Her strawberry-blonde hair complemented the orange letters on her ball-cap. We smiled. Then she squeezed my arm and rested her cheek to my shoulder. It wasn't romantic. Just friendly. But it shot me through with desire. You would have thought we had scored the winning run ourselves, and the home we had slid into was our own.

We took our time getting back. We stopped for dinner in the city, watched the sunset from Crissy Field, then meandered up the 101 like a family reluctant to return from vacation. As we rambled along, we sang. Jen and Carey harmonized; I accompanied on the harp. The highway stretched into the stars. I wished we could have followed it to an Elysian Neverland. But instead, our exit veered right. And we followed that to Crossroads. Jen and I tucked Carey into bed. His souvenir draped the bedside table. A Giants pennant.

Something to hang on his dorm-room wall. A flag of hope in the midst of his Holocaust horrors.

—————

The outing was so tender, Jen scooted next to me as I drove her back to her place. The press of her leg against mine made it difficult to keep two hands to the wheel. I ached to drape my arm over her shoulder or rest my fingers along her thigh. But I didn't want to ruin the perfect day with such a forward advance.

We relished how good Carey was doing and what his return to school would hold. The trace of her perfume mingled with the scents of the ballpark with such sweet promise of play I wanted to pull the truck over and frolic in the fields where coming home yielded fireworks more spectacular than any that sparkle over a baseball game. My God, Jen had no idea what her nearness incited in me.

I parked on the street and walked her to her porch. Jen was chummy enough to slip her arm through mine. Damned if I would offend her with a hand around her waist, I plunged my hands into my pockets, cloaking the effects of her unwitting touch. She let go when we got to the door. Her porch was dark, the only light a distant street lamp, and the gentle wash of moonlight as it caressed Jen's shimmering hair.

"Do you want to come in for a glass of wine?" She couldn't know what she was asking. If I walked through that door I'd want to sip wine all night, then coffee in the morning.

"I better not, Jen. Tomorrow's a big day with the concert and all." Disappointment shaded her eyes. "But I sure enjoyed today. I wish it never had to end." I regretted it the second she looked down. I wasn't respecting her boundaries. No is no.

"It doesn't have to," she said.

"Excuse me?"

She looked at my hand and squeezed it. Then she kissed me. Not friendly. Romantic. Soft, sensuous, and definitely romantic. I could have savored that kiss until the dawn found us still knotted up on her porch. She reached her arms around me and brushed her lips to my neck. My body's every nerve ending throbbed.

"Come in," she whispered. "Celebrate Easter morning with me."

"Are you sure?" I could hardly believe I heard correctly.

"I'm sure."

She pecked my cheek and opened the door. Then she led me in with her hand. As the door closed behind me, seven years of grief and longing surged into voracious hunger. Jen dropped her purse then wrapped her arms around my neck. My back pressed against the door as she pressed her body against mine and searched my mouth with unapologetic desire. I slipped my hands underneath her jacket alert for signs of discouragement. There were none. Without interrupting her foray into my mouth, she spread her arms wide and slipped her coat to the floor. I shook mine off too, and squeezed her close. Her pelvis pressed me tight as she pulled my shirt from my pants. I responded in kind. I slipped through her sweater and lifted free her blouse then slid my hands along the forbidden softness of her bare back. The absence of a bra strap inflamed me.

Jen pulled back. Guilt shot through me. God, I had gone too far. But I hadn't. She smiled with the courtesan confidence I once saw on a seaside bluff. She lifted my shirt over my head. Then she lifted her sweater and blouse off, too. In a single unlayering, she revealed the breasts that have invaded my fantasies since the first day I saw them. I trembled at their sight. Then, I looked in her eyes. Her boldness sparkled. She placed her finger to my lips. I longed to feel her skin against mine. But she was holding the moment. She brushed my lips in teasing seduction. Then she slid her finger down my chest caressing all the way to my pants.

I recoiled as if repulsed.

My rebuff hit her like a bucket of ice-water thrown at her topless body. She clung her arms around herself and stared.

"No, Jen," I begged. "It's not what you think. I want to make love with you, I really do. But I can't. Something's wrong with me. Something horrible is disgustingly wrong with me."

I grabbed my shirt and jacket and left her at the door. She watched me flee still squeezing her breasts. She looked like an intruder had interrupted her in the middle of her undressing. It killed me to see the hurt in her eyes. But how could I possibly tell her?

In the seductive shadows of her midnight foyer, I did not see Jen caressing my chest. I saw my mother.

How could I cleanse myself of such vile fabrications?

———

In spite of the hour, I drove to Petaluma. I hopped the fence and followed my flashlight. The distorted trees could have guarded the gateway to hell and still I would have forced my way through. I had neither food nor sacrifice, but I had a ghost to entice. Seven years had passed since my last divination. I stalked through the cemetery until I came to my mother's grave.

A white rose, nearly a week old, wilted across the base of her headstone. So the bastard was still alive. I ignored his charade and knelt in the grass. My mom's chiseled name stabbed me with shame. What kind of son was I? Desperate to lure her, I stared at the tombstone and pled my case.

"I'm sorry, mom. I must have gotten so close to a patient I've projected his mom onto you. It's disgusting the things she did to her boy; it sickens me to my stomach. I know you would never do anything like that, but I can't get it out of my head. Remind me of how it really was, the way you used to love me—the care in your eyes, the purity of your touch, the affection in your embrace, anything, just a memory, a moment, something that can dispel this repugnant image out of my filthy mind. Please, mom. Help me remember your love. Please, help me remember."

If her ghost lingered beneath the soil, it did not recognize me. Or if it did, it was not enticed by my appeal. I could not conjure even a memory's vapor to sweep my arms through as I tried to clutch it. I was staring at stone. As cold as a mother's rejection.

Who could blame her?

I had one last task while I was still there. An off-chance of reconciling with the other woman in my life. I shined my light on the large stone centering the grave-marker's ring of rocks like a medallion on a necklace. The white crossed veins glittered. I picked up the rock. The black velvet jewelry box was embedded in the dirt where I had buried it seven years before.

I dug out the box and replaced the rock. I brushed off the soil and opened the lid. Jen's lion eye of an engagement ring stared with unmarred beauty. It watched a scrap of paper flutter to the ground like a slain bird. Glancing down, I recognized the handwriting instantly. The scratchy scrawl of an old man writing in a language still foreign to him.

My dad's appeal was direct.

Two words.

'Come home.'

45

I DID NOT EXPECT a fatted calf. I may have been famished, but I wasn't seeking forgiveness. Then again, he wasn't exactly running to greet me.

I had not seen my father since the morning I graduated from high school. I told him not to come to the ceremony; I'd be moving out when it was over. I had a diploma by noon, an apartment by dark.

I parked across the street and stared at the house that so filled me with dread the word 'home' would forever give me chills. It was after midnight, the place as dark as a condemned building. I did not conclude that he was asleep. I never knew my father to lie down. He smoked in the dark living room corner as the rest of us retired, the vigilant seer who shunned all light. He was always gone by morning.

I walked to the porch and knocked. He did not turn on the porch-lamp. He cracked the door and scowled like I was a Bible salesman and his shotgun was pumped. Even in the dark, he recognized me.

"What brings you back?"

"I got your note."

"It's been there for years."

"I don't get there that often."

I could not tell from his scowl if it pained him, or he thought that it served the bitch right. "You coming in?"

"For a minute."

He left the door ajar and returned to his chair in the living room's shadows. As I entered, I noticed the dull glow from the dining room opposite the parlor. The table was set for Passover—china and silver for four, bowls for dipping, glasses for wine, cushions on the chairs, candles burning low in their sticks. The only thing missing was the food. And the people. A museum showcase of a dead Seder.

I stepped into the living room and sat on the couch. My dad cowered in the corner a spit away from the candle's reach. By the ashtray beside him, sat my mother's Catholic Missal. Across it, a single white rose was draped. Beside it, a vintage photo of her as a girl dancing before the Alps.

"Why did you come?" he interrogated.

"To ask you one question." He glared like a man who promised nothing. "Why did you hate my mother so much?"

He took a drag from his smoke. I expected an indignant denial, or a cryptic allusion to an ancient betrayal.

"You always hated me," he said. "I know that. It was the price I paid."

"That's not an answer."

He stared into me as if determining my desire to know.

I guess I did.

———

Your mother, she joined our theater company when she ran away from home. She was six-teen. Her father, he was not a good man. He used her for four years. Promised if Lena would lay with him, he would not touch her younger sister. When one day she comes home and he's with the sister anyway, she plans their escape, and they come to Munich.

The sister, she was zurückgeblieben, *retarded. A few months after they arrive, the Nazis, they gather all the retarded ones into the trucks. They gassed them in the woods. Lena, she was outraged. She joined a protest group, the White Rose, and passed out illegal flyers. And she persuaded members of our company to stage anti-fascist plays. She was irresistible. She could make you fall in love with her, then give your life for freedom. All over the city, she performed like a star, without fearing the risks. She lit up the dead; she made them dream again; she gave them the courage to resist the darkness. Then, she was arrested.*

With six of our Jewish friends, she was convicted of treason, and sent to Dachau. From February 1943 to April 1945, she stayed there. In the camp, the Nazis, they segregated the prisoners—Jews in one barrack, communists in another. Your mother, she would sneak over and talk with our friends. They were terrified. They heard the rumors, everyone had, and they feared deportation. Lena, she was very spirited. Hopeful. She comforted them.

Several weeks, they pass and Pesach neared. Of course, rations, they are nothing, bread and broth. Provisions for Seder are impossible. Matzah inconceivable. Our friends, they de-spaired. The Chosen Ones must celebrate God's liberation of our people. If they are not faithful to God, perhaps God, He is not faithful to them.

Some priests, they were prisoners too. Your mother, she knew one. He smuggled in a small fortune—several dozen communion hosts. Lena received the Eucharist many times, tiny pieces of host so they last. One day, Lena, she lies to him. Tells him she has six Catholic friends sentenced to die who beg God for one last communion. The priest, he consecrates six hosts, and he ordains her to give them to her friends.

On the first night of Pesach, after all are asleep, the women, they huddle in their bar-rack. One, she bribed a cook for a potato. Another, she snuck blades of grass for bitter herbs. Someone else, she stole a bit of candle. But the real miracle, the gift of God, is your mother's unleavened hosts. A mitzvah they declare. A holy act that God will bless.

One woman, she stays by the door; the others, they light the candle, they lay out a cloth, they begin the Seder. They say the prayers. They ask the questions. They tell the story. But midway through, the woman at the door, she panics,

"Somebody, they are coming. Quick, hide the food."

One woman, she wraps up the cloth and she hides it between her legs. Another, she holds the candle in her fist. They wait for who it is that is coming. It is not Elijah. It is three guards. Looking for a quick lay.

The leader, he walks up and down the barrack trying to choose which woman he will take. He does not pass over the right one. As God would have it, he chooses the woman with the meal up her skirt. He orders her to come. She does not move. He orders her again. Then he raises his rifle to beat her. Lena, she jumps forward.

"Take me," she says. "She's having her woman's time."

The guard, he looks at Lena, and he says, "Maybe, I will have you both." He grabs Lena with one hand, the woman with the other, and he shoves them toward the door. The bundle, it falls to the floor. The guard, he opens the cloth, and he finds the food.

"What is this?" he says. "These are hosts. Stolen from a priest no doubt. Surely these women do not mock Jesus by using his body for Passover. No. They have converted. Is that not right, ladies?"

They stare at him terrified. He gathers the hosts, and he acts like a priest. He goes to the woman who dropped the cloth, and he says, "This is the Body of Christ." She stares at him. "Look," he jokes with the guards, "she still does not know how to do it. You say, 'Amen', then you take the Eucharist into your mouth." He repeats, "The Body of Christ."

She looks at the others for what to do. If she refuses, he kills her for her defiance. If she eats, he kills her for her blasphemy. She declines. So the guard, he shoves it between her lips, he takes his rifle, and he butts it into her teeth.

One of the guards, he's a good Catholic boy. He sees the host fall onto the floor, and he rushes to pick it up. "Stop," he tells the leader. "This really is Jesus' body. This is blasphemy." Hah—raping women is one thing. But letting the Eucharist fall to the floor, this is blasphemy.

But the leader, he does not stop. He turns to Lena and he says, "This is the Body of Christ."

He thinks she's a Jew. But of course, she's a Catholic. And she's scared for her life. So she says 'Amen', and she eats the host.

"Very good," the guard says. "The angels rejoice in heaven. Now you, follow her example." He goes to another. But she refuses. So he shoves it into her mouth, and he butts her in the teeth. The other guard, he picks up the host on the floor. The leader, he is enraged. "Look at how you make Markus grovel for his Christ. Eat this." But the next one too, she refuses, as does the next, until he gets to the last, and he says, "No? You will not receive the Christ? Here, I show you how." And he stuffs it in his mouth, and he butts the last woman spitting pieces of host as he screams, "Where is your Jew God now?" He orders the guards to take them out to be shot.

"What is their crime?"

"Smuggling, insubordination, blasphemy of the Christian God." The guards, they round them up. But when they get to Lena, the leader, he says to leave her.

"She will not be shot, a good Christian girl like her. Besides, she already volunteered for another assignment."

The guards, they take the others. The leader, he rapes Lena. Then to punish her for smuggling, he moves her to a brothel across the camp for the SS being trained there. For two years, your mother, she survived Dachau, by serving every desire those Nazi boys could imagine.

You see the irony, no? God passed her over, so she could become a whore.

The story, it has a coda. A couple months, they go by. Your mother, she sees the priest returning from a work detail. She goes to him, and she confesses the whole thing. Always a good Catholic girl, she fears she has committed a grave sin. The priest, he's a compassionate man. He tells her, in the eyes of the church, she has sinned. But in the eyes of God, she has not. God is most pleased to give his body for a Jewish Passover. Your mother, she does not understand. If she sins in the eyes of the church, will she not go to hell? So the priest, he gives her penance. In memory of the women who were killed, she is to celebrate Passover every year of her life.

My Passover. Your mother's penance. Tell me, what possible sense does this Seder have? Who is the lamb and who the slayer? Who is passed over and who left to die? Where is the Promised Land when all ways, they point to Egypt?

I will go to hell not understanding how one person's sacrament is another person's sentence.

———

My father lit another cigarette as I struggled with his story.

"So you hated my mother because, what? She profaned your Passover by trying to do good? Or because she did what she had to, to survive Dachau?"

He winced as if my incomprehension stabbed him.

"You do not understand. I have no use for God. I despise what He's done to our world. I celebrated Pesach for your mother. And for you. Her penance, it helped to keep her away from my son."

"Now we're getting to it. Why would you keep her from me? She was my mother."

He drew his strength from the nail between his lips.

"I barely recognized this woman I found at Dachau. Before, she was a passionate idealist, a girl setting the world on fire. Two years later, she was an old woman addicted to her misery like opium. You must remember, your mother, she was a plaything for men whose fantasies were as perverted as the horrors they committed. When they were through with her, she remembered no other way to be. Each man she saw wanted to use her. And she had an instinct for how to pleasure them. Most times, she did not know she was doing it. Her body was free, but her mind was trapped in Dachau's brothel. It is a terrible burden to be another person's conscience."

"So what are you saying?" I couldn't believe it. "My mother became addicted to prostitution, and you kept her from indulging it?"

"I did what I could."

"That's preposterous."

"Why do you think I watched her so closely?"

"Because you were consumed by jealousy. You treated her like a tramp."

"I had to be strict."

"You were a tyrant."

"Those Nazis, they fucked their way into your mother's head."

"*You* were in her head!"

"I had to keep her away from men."

"Well you did a damn good job."

"Not good enough."

"What're you talking about? The only men my mom slept with were in your imagination."

"Perhaps. Outside of this house."

"She never had men *in* this house."

"I wasn't worried about men here."

"Then what?"

"I was worried about you."

"What in God's name is wrong with you?" It hit me like a rifle butt.

"I did not care if you hated me. But I swore I'd protect you, and protect her from herself. I tried locking her in her room. I tried pleading with her. I tried shaming her. Months might go by, but she always went to you."

"You are lying, you sick bastard."

"I'd find her in your room, by your bed. Maybe she's trying to stop herself. But she can't. She slips her hand into your bed, and she touches you."

"Stop saying that!!"

"Sometimes I'd come home early. Catherine would be gone. And I'd find you . . ."

"STOP IT!! STOP-IT-STOP-IT-STOP-IT!!" I leapt from the couch. "GODDAMN YOU. WHY ARE YOU MAKING THIS UP?"

"I'm sorry, Tony."

"FUCK YOUR SORRY!"

"I did all I could."

I paced the floor beside myself. I wanted to puke; I wanted to bludgeon; I wanted to torch the whole house then stomp on the remains. What kind of a bastard did I have for a father? The Pharaoh who would come off as Moses. I should have known better than to come back home.

"I can't take this," I said. Then I glared at him. "I never want to see your sorry ass again. I hope you die alone."

I started to leave.

"Tony." I turned. He looked like he had already sentenced himself to death. "I loved her. From the day I met her to the day I die."

I was too disgusted to reply. I turned away.

"And Tony." He talked to my back. "I loved you, too."

I made for the door.

"Wait." I stopped. "Take this." Across the end-table he slid my mother's childhood picture. "Remember your mother this way. Inside, this is really her."

I didn't take it. I walked out.

On both of them.

I got to my car but I could not drive. Like shards of glass, piercing images pelted me.

Me in my bed. My mom at my side. My nightshirt spread wide. Her hand sliding down my chest. Me in her bedroom. Her standing beside me. Me in my pajama bottoms. Her teasing snicker. Me lying down. Her in her underwear. Me too tense to nap. Her holding me tight. My hardened excitement. Her amorous drowsiness. My bottoms sliding down my legs. Her rubbing me close. My stare at the door. Her falling asleep. My terror that someone would come. My prayer he would get there fast. Please, somebody, come. Please, don't pass me over. Please, God, save me . . .

Why does God have to be such a monster?

———

I spied the Easter morning sunrise from my parked truck.

The house across the street was once my home.

46

"Did you catch the headlines?" Virgil beamed like he'd swayed the court himself. "'HARRIS GETS REPRIEVE.' How's that for an Easter sunrise?"

I hadn't showered, I hadn't slept, and *my* Easter sunrise brought depravity to light. I wasn't in the mood for a political debate.

"He's going down," I snapped as I passed him. "In two days, he's dead."

"What d'ya mean?" Virgil bristled at my drive-by slam. "All gassing's banned for ten days."

"I'm telling you," I sneered. "Two days. He's dead."

As it turned out, I was right. Forty-eight hours later, after still two more reversals, one after he was already strapped in the chair, Robert Alton Harris was executed by cyanide gas. As the hood came over his head, he stared at the dad of one of his victims.

He mouthed two words.

'I'm sorry.'

———

Carey slipped his Easter surprise under my office door. A homemade certificate of adoption. Construction paper and black marker, a colored-pencil seal in the corner. The State of California granted one Dr. Tony Backman custody of Carey Michael Foster effective immediately. Carey signed the bottom. My signature line was empty. A pen was attached.

I had kids request I adopt them before but none had gone to such trouble. I dreaded his disappointment. Another great start to the day. Best just to get it over with.

He sat in the Box staring at the pennant spread across the coffee table. Whatever balm the pennant offered, it didn't soothe completely. His finger flicked in steady staccato.

"Happy Easter, Carey," I greeted with mustered cheer.

"Happy Easter, Dr. T." He was cautious, like a beau who anxiously awaited a reply to his declaration of love.

I sat down and admired the certificate. "I'm honored by your gift."

"I'm thinking, maybe I don't have to go back at all," he pressed.

I sighed with the bad news to come. "I'm sorry, Carey. I'm not in a position to adopt anybody. I don't even have room in my house."

"I can sleep on the couch, I don't mind."

He wasn't making this easy. "I've grown very attached to you, Carey, really. But there just isn't any way." He looked down like I told him his dog was put to sleep. "We'll still see each other though. I'm suggesting sessions twice a week."

He thought, then spoke directly. "I don't want to go back, Dr. T."

"I know."

"No. I mean . . ." He screwed up his courage. "There's bad people there." I had seen this too. Kids anxious about readjusting once they're released. I sucked up my fatigue and gave him what I could.

"We all have people we don't get along with. You'll be alright."

"It isn't like that." He thought some more. Then he looked up. "Are you sure I can't go home with you? I can ride with you to work and go to school with the boys. I promise, I'll be good."

"It's not about being good," I consoled as best I could. "It's just time to face the world. You won't be alone."

He looked back down and considered playing his trump card. "What if I tell you something?"

"What?"

"Remember the story of the flicking finger?"

"Yes."

"It really happened."

I couldn't believe he wanted to go there now. I forced myself to concentrate.

"Why don't you tell me about it."

He did. "This boy goes to his mom's house to tell her something. He finds her in her room dressed up like a nun. This man's watching her touch herself while she prays. The man sees the boy and tells him to kneel next to his mom. He tells the mom to do things to the boy while he's praying. The man starts breathing real hard. The mom whispers to the boy, 'Don't worry, I'll take care of everything.' Then the man stops. He walks over to the boy and reaches out and touches his worm. Then he says, 'You dirty little boy. You should never have done this.' And he takes his finger, and he flicks the boy's worm. The mom jumps up and says, 'Come here. I kiss all the men I love.' And she kisses him real hard. I pull up my pants and I run. I ride my bike back to school and I hide in my bedroom.

"But later that night he found me. He was all upset. He said he hadn't meant for that to happen, and he wouldn't have done it if I hadn't shown up like that. That a dirty little boy had no right to live. And now he shouldn't have to live knowing I saw him doing those things. So he tied me up, and he cut my arms, and he kept saying, 'Close your eyes. You shouldn't have seen me like that. Close your eyes.' Then somebody came and he hid. But when the boy ran for help, he whispered. 'I'll get you. And I'll get your mother if you ever tell.'"

Even in my exhaustion I wished his dad a long time in hell.

"I'm really sorry, Carey." He nodded like he knew. "And you were right. He came back."

He stopped nodding. "That's just it. Maybe he didn't."

"What do you mean? We caught him."

"Maybe it wasn't my father."

"But you told me earlier you saw your father that night."

"I saw my father later," he corrected, "when I was riding away on my bike."

It sounded contrived but I went along. "So who was the man that cut you?"

"What if he was somebody at Salve Regina?"

"Was he?"

"Would I have to go back if it was?"

"Carey, are you just playing a game so you won't have to go back?"

"I'm just wondering, if I told you, would I have to go back anyway?"

I was so tired my eyes hurt. I rubbed them while I answered. "I don't know. To be honest, you might. But we'd make sure that you were safe."

"Would you put him in jail before I get there?"

"It's not that simple. There'd have to be an investigation, to make sure he really did it."

"What if he says he didn't?"

"That usually happens. But there are ways to find out."

"Like what?"

"If somebody saw something. If he's done it before. Things like that."

"What if nobody was around?"

"It's hard sometimes. That's why the more you tell me the easier it is."

"What if people believe him and not me?"

"No matter what, we'd keep him away from you." He thought the matter over. I still couldn't tell if he was running me around and I was way too weary to guess. "Carey, I need to know. Did someone from Salve Regina cut you?" Carey studied his finger's flick. But he wasn't going to say. Being nervous about returning is one thing. Making a false accusation is another. I didn't push it. "I'll tell you what," I offered, "I'll keep my eyes open tonight. If I see anything the least bit suspicious, I'll talk to Dr. Carter about our options. Okay?"

"Do I have to sing?"

"It's the best way to scope things out, to act like everything's normal. Besides, you want to show them, don't you? No matter what anybody does, they can't keep you down."

"I guess," he shrugged at the table. By now, the pennant's balm had thoroughly dried up. His finger flicked with the anxiety of a psychiatric outpatient having to face contempt back home.

"It'll be okay," I reassured. "I'll be watching the whole time. Nothing bad is going to happen."

I had one last stop before I could sleep. Though I craved her understanding, I feared Jen's ire. I swore I'd give her the explanation she deserved. But first I had to make amends.

She looked like she had slept as little as I had. Her eyes seemed to ache with one more rejection than she could handle. I hoped to God I wasn't setting myself up for the same. I knew it would be one more than I could handle.

"Jen, I am so sorry about last night."

She squeezed her robe tight. She did not invite me in. "What happened, Tony?"

I tried to find words but they wouldn't come. I slept with my own mother for Christ's sake. How could any woman ever hold me after that?

She recognized my clothes from the day before. "Where have you been? You look awful."

I stared into her living room. Her coffee mug sat next to the Sunday paper. My mug should have sat next to hers. "I went to see my dad."

"You're kidding." She got the aberration. "Why?"

I almost cried, but I choked it back by glaring at her mug. "Something struck me last night. I had to find out if it was true."

"What was it?"

Please don't hate me, Jen. "Something bad happened."

"What?"

Please don't be repulsed. "Something really bad."

"Tell me."

I swear to God, I'll die if you're as disgusted with me as I am. "To me, Jen. Something really bad happened to me."

She placed her hand on mine. "What is it, Tony?"

The edges of the mug blurred as water leaked into my eyes. I was damned if I would cry. "You don't understand. It's the kind of thing that damages you so bad no woman would ever want you if she knew."

She squeezed my fingers. "Nothing can damage you like that."

"This can."

She pulled my head to look at her. "You can tell me. I want to know." Her eyes brimmed with care. I stared away unable to hold them.

"I will. I promise. But I have to get some sleep first. I'll fall apart if I tell you like this."

"Maybe that's what you need," she empathized, "to fall apart."

"Maybe. But I at least need to think straight first."

"Why don't you sleep here?" She still held my hand.

"Thanks. But I also have to get ready for tonight. Can we talk after the concert? I know it'll be late. But I want to do this today. If nothing else, I want you to know that this has never been about you."

"Of course," she said. "We'll come here right after the concert."

I reached into my jacket pocket. "I really mean it, Jen. I owe you the truth. This is my pledge." I handed her the jewelry box. She opened it. We both stared at the lion's eye. "I don't know how much you'll be able to hold, but I promise you. I'll let you see all my secrets. And hold whatever you can."

She looked up and smiled. Then she kissed me on the cheek.

"I love you, Tony. Of course, I'll hold it. No matter what there is to see."

"Thanks, Jen. We'll talk tonight."

47

A TRIUMPHANT HOMECOMING DID not greet Carey. No crowds cheered along the lane; no well-wishers rushed our car; no banners hung from the buildings; no red carpet cloaked the sidewalk. He and I scaled the promontory and parked in the lot as unreceived as teenage untouchables crashing a party that didn't invite us.

Carey's good-bye was tepid as well. I tried to alert the boys as we walked through the Commons, but they were too zoned out on sitcoms and comics to register I was taking Carey home. Fast Eddie started a 'See ya kid,' but Shadrach ambushed him for the remote control. The others never looked up. The indifferent farewell hurt Carey's feelings.

"Don't they know I'm not coming back?" he asked once outside.

"The guys are funny that way," I explained. "They hide their feelings by pretending not to care. They're like that with everyone who leaves."

Virgil, however, did come through. He ran out to the truck with a parting gift. The padded-rubber sledgehammer from 'The Night that God Got Nailed.' He inscribed a charge along the handle. "Keep swinging, Carey. Don't let the bastard down for nothing."

Through the entire drive to Salve Regina, Carey shouldered it like a marine would a rifle.

———

We left Carey's gear in the truck and sidled along the recital hall. Singing hummed from the practice room behind. We walked in and found the choir, clad in navy blazers with maroon school insignia, rehearsing for the approaching concert. They noticed Carey but the conductor's direction constrained them from a welcome. Father Ike spied Carey too, and blushed a shade. I imagined relief that Carey had made it. Or irritation that we'd cut it so close.

When the choir concluded the song, Eichler's baton kept the singers poised in place. "Well, boys," he held the moment. "It looks like Master Foster is joining us after all."

Then the boys let loose. "Great to see you, Carey," "You're looking good," and "Boy, do we need you," rose through the ripples of cheer.

Father Ike masked his pleasure and rapped against the stand. "We still have work to do. The concert starts in less than an hour. Carey, why don't you get changed. Your suit is in my office."

Carey looked at me, anxious about our separation. "You're gonna stay, right?" he asked like a toddler would a parent on his first day of pre-school.

"I'll be right here," I reassured. "I'm not letting you down. Promise."

He withdrew through a door at the far end of the room. Moments later he emerged. Once more, a member of the Salve Regina Boys' Choir.

The boys were milling about and people were filling the hall when Jen walked into the practice room. She was beautiful—a black evening dress and heels with an elegant full-length coat for the cold front that was moving in. Her right hand's ring finger glittered with my Easter morning offering.

"How is he?" she asked, a squeeze of my arm as much affection she dared at her workplace.

"Nervous. But the boys are great. They're treating him like nothing happened."

She spotted him and waved. Then she looked at me. "I'm looking forward to tonight."

I winced. "He's not the only one who's nervous."

"I'll hold it, Tony," she assured. "Whatever it is."

Carey left his buddies and shuffled over. "You look very handsome," Jen praised. With maternal instinct she brushed hair off his forehead then caught herself at the touch. Carey savored the attention. "Dear," she fussed, "your lips are chapped from the ballgame." She dug through her pocketbook, found some balm, knelt down, and swabbed them.

"It smells good," Carey said.

"It's cherry." She capped the tube and gave it to him. "In case you need it later."

"Thanks," he said brightened by her care. Father Ike called the choir. Carey's splendor shadowed. He looked to me, stage-fright returning to his eyes.

"You're gonna do great," I encouraged. "We'll be right here the second it's over." He looked like he wished it was over already.

"Carey," Eichler called, "it's time."

Carey gave in and turned. Within two steps he glanced back. "You're going to keep your eyes open, right?" he confirmed a final time.

"Of course," I swore. "I won't let you down. I promise."

He nodded, trying to trust, then turned back.

"Hey, Carey," I called.

He looked.

"How're you going to play it?"

He looked quizzical, then remembered.

"So sad, they weep," he foretold.

That he did.

Jen and I sat along the side aisle about midway back. The audience hushed as Schuyler Peckham, decked out in a charcoal suit with clerics, strutted down the center-aisle, bowed before three judges seated in the front row, then mounted the stage to welcome the crowd. He was uncharacteristically succinct.

"It is my singular joy to welcome you to our annual Easter recital. Once more, I am reminded of how appropriate it is that we celebrate our choir on this day above all others. These boys come to us from broken homes and abusive parents, from callous state institutions and inattentive treatment centers; and at Salve Regina we help them discover their song. Like the miracle we commemorate today, death is defied, and life reborn. Hallelujah indeed. Through music, Christ is risen anew."

The audience applauded as the boys filed in and stood on the tiered platform onstage. Peckham returned up the center-aisle and hovered in the doorway. Without saying a word, Father Eichler stepped to the dais and readied the choir. He flicked his baton. The boys sang.

I had to admit. It was extraordinary.

Their sound soared with such ethereal purity it all but begged for comparison with blue-eyed cherubs accompanying the heavenly choir. No stain soiled those voices, no despair gutted them. They rose with Eden's innocence to remind us, the world, God Himself if He was listening, of the song humanity spoke in before perversion clamored it away. Their music was testimony, that deep in the world's bowels creation's song still sings, steady as a heartbeat nursing life into a loveless planet. Midway through the piece, Jen slipped her hand into mine. It stayed there until the music died.

They sang an eclectic mix, several spirituals, a few hymns, an aria from an opera, an Appalachian piece from Copeland. The music trickled forth without introduction or commentary. Eichler promptly cued the boys for the next piece while the audience applauded the one just completed. He so savored the music his command drew forth, he seemed oblivious that an audience was behind him at all. It came as some surprise then when he turned before the final song, coughed into his lapel mic like a man phobic about public speaking, and, too scared to face us directly, spoke to a spot of floor up front.

"This final selection is Salve Regina's school song." He cleared his throat and fingered his collar. It was painful to watch, like witnessing someone in penitential self-torture. "It was the favorite hymn of our headmaster's mother, and features a solo by Carey Foster. We'd like to dedicate it to her . . . Monsignor Peckham's mother, that is."

Fearing reprisal for the slip-up, he shot a glance at Peckham then mercifully faced the choir. He lifted his baton. But before the music could begin, reprisal came. Though not from Schuyler Peckham. The rehearsal room door slammed open. Phyllis Foster, wearing a virgin white nun's habit, appeared in the doorway. All eyes stared as she sauntered towards a paralyzed Eichler like a cat approaching a cornered mouse. His baton still raised, Eichler looked back at Peckham with a stricken plea for help. Peckham's flush was visible through the doorway's silhouette. He snapped at Shuk to end this instantly. Shuk hustled down the side aisle. Before he could get up front, Phyllis reached Eichler. She threw her arms around his neck and pressed her open mouth against his while grinding her body with a mauling kiss. Shuk grabbed her by the arm. She let go willingly, sliding her hand along Eichler's face then turning with Shuk and shuffling up the aisle. Eichler looked to Peckham for guidance. Peckham, massaging his hand as if it was on fire, motioned to get the boys singing. Shuk had Phyllis halfway up the aisle. A step away from me, she pulled her arm free, leaned down, and hissed in my ear,

"I kiss all the men I love."

Shuk grabbed her again and dragged her toward the door. As she passed Peckham, Phyllis reached to stroke him, too. Peckham caught her by the arm before she had the chance and escorted her out the building. I gazed in their wake with dread in my stomach. I knew. The nun in Carey's story, the guilt in Eichler's eyes, the betraying kiss, the incriminating words, it all came together. Ichabod Eichler was the man who *prayed* with Carey's mother.

"Jen," I gasped. "Call Sheriff Thomas. Get her here immediately."

"Why?"

"It's Father Ike. The one who cut Carey."

"How do you know?" she cried.

"Phyllis was telling me. Quick. You get the Sheriff. I'll get Carey. I want Eichler before he gets away."

Jen hurried out. I stood in the aisle to rush the stage. I could taste my thirst to impale him. The boys were hailing the Holy Queen—their hope in sorrow and woe. Unfortunately, the Mother of Mercy failed to come for Carey. His voice cracked at his first 'Alleluia' then faltered so thoroughly as he stumbled through his solo Eichler drowned him out by augmenting the choir's accompaniment. Carey, defeated, stopped singing. The crowd writhed in compassion. The judges closed their books. With a pitiful crescendo of 'Salve, Salve, Salve Regina,' the song finally died out.

Eichler dismissed the audience, then set his sights on Carey. As the boys loitered on the platform, he scaled the steps, gripped Carey's arm, and whisked him toward the rehearsal room. Carey looked for me in terror. I was all over it. If Eichler thought he was getting away he misgauged my ferocity. I fought through the crowd, crossed the stage, and dashed into the door through which they disappeared. By the time I got there, Eichler was pulling Carey into his office. I raced across the room and kicked the door open. Eichler had Carey backed against the desk, two hands to Carey's shoulders. Carey searched me to save him.

"*Get your filthy hands off him,*" I screamed plowing into Eichler and pulling Carey from the desk. Fearing he might break for the door, I grabbed Eichler with my free hand and pinned him to the desk where he had Carey. "You're not going anywhere," I seethed. "The police are on their way."

I looked at Carey, still gripped in my other hand. "Are you okay?" He stared, too scared to respond. Peckham dashed into the room.

"What's going on?" he demanded.

"Eichler's after Carey," I said. "Here. Take him." I handed over Carey to Peckham. "Get him as far away from this pervert as possible. I'm staying with Eichler until the police cart him away."

Carey gaped at me reluctant to go.

"I know what's going on," I told him. "Trust me. I'm not letting you down. I promise."

When Carey and Peckham were well out of earshot, I lit into Eichler. I was so enraged *I* could have been the boy abused coming back for vengeance. "You sick prick," I fumed. "How could you *do* such a thing?"

"I know," he wailed, shivering with shame. "I can't believe she showed up like that."

"How do you *live* with yourself?" I stormed the room resisting the urge to pummel him with a choir stand. "I hope they throw your ass in jail," I spit, "until you're a very old man."

He shook his head as if his life was over. "Believe me," he moaned, "it couldn't be worse than what I've been through already."

"Than what?" I raged. "Some sorry sense of remorse?"

"Than the Monsignor."

"The Monsignor? He knows?"

"He walked in on me."

"He *caught* you?" The sight disgusted me.

"It was awful. He must've followed me then waited until the worst. God, I can't stop seeing him standing in that doorway."

"He knows about Carey, too, then?"

Eichler looked up. "Carey? What about Carey?"

"*That you molested him too, you pervert, then tried to kill him!*"

"Kill him? Carey tried to kill himself."

"*He told me all about it, Eichler. You attacked him after you abused him at his mother's.*"

"Look, Dr. Backman. I'm a lewd man, but I don't molest children. That's depraved. And I surely wouldn't kill him."

"You're lying."

"I'm not," he pleaded. "I paid his mother for favors, yes, but I never touched Carey. Monsignor caught me, he castrated me, then I got the hell out of there. Carey was nowhere around."

This wasn't making sense. "What do you mean he castrated you?"

He shuddered at the humiliation. "There I was with that woman dressed like that, when I looked up and saw him. He glared from the door with the disgust of God. Then he walked over, cocked his middle finger, and snapped me right in the balls. I couldn't get out of there fast enough."

Jesus fucking Christ. This could not be happening. Carey had been telling me all along. He even drew me a picture of it. The blemish on the finger's hand, it wasn't a nail hole from a crucifixion. It was the stain from Peckham's palm. Goddamn me to hell. I had handed Carey to his killer completely unaware.

And as sure as he would share a place in hell beside me, I knew exactly where Peckham had taken his prey.

48

T HE ARCTIC WIND WHIPPED as I raced through the dark woods. Through flailing skeletal branches, it hissed its displeasure at my trespass, then stabbed me with its icy blasts as I bolted across the black creek. I did not care. The winds could have howled from hell's bitter depths and still I would have slashed through them. In his dead mother's chapel, Schuyler Peckham had Carey.

I slammed through the gate and leapt at the door. The handle was cold and locked. I tore around back. Passing the fountain, I kicked the font free and hauled the concrete over my shoulder. Peckham's muffled yell echoed from the darkened altar within.

"Close your eyes, Goddamn you. Pull up your pants and close your eyes."

I hurled the font through the stained-glass window. Splinters of the Virgin shattered across the floor. Peckham menaced over a kneeling Carey, Carey's pants splayed on the floor. His tiny penis stood erect—pointing up at Peckham in perverse implication.

"He got away from me," Peckham pleaded as he stepped back from the filth. "He ran here with this." He flashed a blade in his stained palm.

"Get away from him," I wailed as I climbed through the window and approached, Madonna glass under my feet grinding into the floor. "Goddamn it. What did you do to him?"

"I caught him defiling himself," Peckham grasped to explain. "It's vile, I know."

"You sick bastard," I came back, knowing better. "How could you?" How could I? How could we both conspire to soil this boy?

"You've got it all wrong," he appealed, lifting his hands in innocence. "He was trying to kill himself again. After desecrating the chapel. I actually saved his life."

Sensing my fury, he kept backing away. I had but one instinct. Get between him and Carey. Then rid the world of his revolting presence.

"I saw you," I seethed, too disgusted to glance again at Carey, too pierced by guilt to hold his humiliation. "You molested an innocent boy."

With maniacal calm, he checked the wrath in his eyes. "You saw nothing. I detest depravity."

"Then what's that stain in your pants?" He stole a look at the wet spot in his crotch. I stepped between him and Carey. He controlled his desperation with demonic coldness.

"That's not . . . what you think."

"No? The police will test what I think."

His defiance hardened. The knife came down. "Nobody tests Schuyler Peckham," he swore.

"They'll test," I swore back, slipping off my jacket in case he lunged. "Your lewdness demands it."

"I am a man of God," he dared. "My chastity is beyond reproach."

"You're not chaste enough," I scorned. "An eleven-year-old boy. How sick can you be?"

He smoldered like a bull calculating a charge. "I loved that boy," he spewed. "I would never have touched him."

"In your own mother's chapel too."

The nerve I struck calcified his rage. "Leave . . . my mother . . . alone," he rasped.

"Why? Did she . . . ?" The unimaginable nearly caused me to retch. Then it hit me. "My God, she did. You were the boy in the story."

For a second, I'm afraid I saw it—a flash of yearning in his eyes. 'What if,' it said, 'could you save me from myself if I was?' But as soon as it flashed, it passed. And with it my humanity. "*Leave . . . her . . . be . . .*"

The truth enflamed my loathing. He had no right. Violating a child is beyond absolution. I didn't care if Nazis raped him. "People get abused," I scathed. "It happens. But God forbid, you don't play it out with your kids."

Through his self-control, his bestial rage boiled. "Close your mouth," he growled.

"You don't fondle your own boy," I implored. "Goddamn it. You protect him from the horror."

He wheezed through clenched teeth. "Schuyler . . . Peckham . . . does not . . . fondle . . . boys."

"Hate her; defame her; piss on her grave for Christ's sake; but you don't abuse another child."

"*I didn't abuse my boy, Goddamn it.*"

"No," I spit. "You prayed with him instead. Just like your mother taught you."

He looked past me, at Carey exposed on his knees. I do not know what he saw. Perhaps the remains of his assault. Perhaps himself, exposed beside his mother. Perhaps only the futility of denial. But whatever he saw, he did not watch long. He dropped his eyes to the floor. He turned his back halfway. He coddled the image for but a brief moment. Then he snapped.

"God despises impurity," he hissed. And raising his blade like a spear, he lunged.

I was ready. I draped his hand with my coat and tripped him to the ground. He shook the coat away but I smashed his wrist with my heel then kicked the knife free with such savage force I could have punted the stain clean off his palm. He grabbed his wrist in agony. My own rage came unleashed. I was repulsed beyond restraint. I lifted him up by his groomed clerics, clamped his face with my hand, and slammed him into the wall, pulled back and slammed him again, and kept on slamming until all resistance drained from his body and he slumped to the floor with a moan. He shook his head in surrender, succumbing to his despair like a plunge through the sea. All I could do was spit. And hope he drowned in the ocean depths. I fell to my knees spent with disgust.

Only then did I turn to Carey. He was still on his knees, still without pants, still staring into darkness, oblivious to the struggle that saved him. Sensing my stare, he turned his head. His mouth was open, his eyes hollow, his face so blanched it seemed to fade. He looked like a ghost-child, floating in crematorium smoke, staring back at his executioners before dissipating into the night. 'Why did you do this?' his eyes silently asked, 'Why did you let this happen?'

He looked at the Monsignor groaning at my side. Then he looked again at me. His eyes not discriminating between savior and abuser, he questioned us both the same.

'Why?' he mutely asked, his eyes deadened from the final indignity he could stomach. 'Why?'

He looked at his bare-skinned belly. Against it, he held erect a sword-length piece of Madonna glass. Blood trickled where his hands clenched the edges. A white fragment of Mary's garment ran with red. He looked back at me, back at the last pair of eyes to ever hold his hope.

They weren't crying.

"No, Carey. Don't," I begged. He plunged the glass into his stomach. The shard pierced. But not far. "Carey, please. We can get through this." He kept staring; he kept asking why; he kept searching me for an answer as he fell forward onto the floor. The shard pierced further. Until it punctured through his back.

I stared at his vacant open eyes. I stared at the boy who sought in vain for someone who would cry for him. I stared at the boy in me who couldn't find tears in a mirror. I stared at every boy abused whose cry for care goes unwept. I stared at them all, bleeding on the floor in front of me . . .

When Schuyler Peckham wept, his eyes stuck on Carey, his face contorted at the horror. "Don't you see," he beseeched through his tears. "God despises impurity." And with his eyes not turning away, he sobbed.

I lost it. A convulsion of madness seized me, a tidal wave of hate. I rose up on its crest, grabbed the sharpest weapon at hand—the crucifix of nails mounted on the pole beside me—and like a demented harpooner, I surged with the wave and gorged the Monsignor in the evil white whale of his belly. I ripped the spear free and I gored him again. And again. And again. And again and again and again.

While innocent blood puddled behind me, I stabbed the man whose face was but the last one in the long repulsive lineup of Carey's abusers. I stabbed the man whose face for me framed the very features of Satan. I stabbed the man whose face in fact mirrored my very own, only mine was devoid of tears.

And I stabbed him, until he closed his eyes.

———

In memory, I watch the rest of the night as if the sounds of the scene are muted. I see that man who looks like me, the curdled acid of his vomit stringing down his chin. But I cannot hear him. His mouth is wide as his primal shriek rips through the world with an irreconcilable refusal. But his shriek does not pierce my deafness.

He rocks amidst the shattered glass and screams as a weeping Jen holds Carey in her lap. He balls himself up against the wall and screams as Shuk dislodges the upside-down crucifix impaling Peckham's body. He cowers in the corner and screams as paramedics approach him with sedatives. And he keeps on screaming, even as he fades into sleep.

———

I've been to the world's bowels.
There is no song, steady and restoring.
Only a scream, convulsive and cold.

———

Unless of course, the scream is the song.

Epilogue

Mother's Day 2000

THE DAWN SWABBED THE night with rose as I left my post for the final time. I had already packed my truck. Paramount's gilded Bronson Gate receding into my mirror, I followed Melrose to the 101, then simply headed north.

I did not know what the day's end would bring. The pulse that got me out of bed for a year had faded with Carey's last breath. I had done what I set out to do. I told his story. I traveled through hell to the bitter depths. I kept my eyes open and watched him die. Then I dwelt in the silence and listened for the heartbeat that pumped life back into the world. A pulse had yet to appear. Whether one would remained to be seen. Or what I would do if the flat-line prevailed. The way out was as dark as Dis' cavern—without a river's trickle to follow. I had only one move within me. Three gifts to deliver, before holing up until the promise of daylight took hold.

———

I reached the cemetery a bit before three. I did not scale the wall—the gates were open. I parked on a lane and proceeded to the grave. At its base, a fresh white rose was delicately placed.

I had nothing to say to my mother. I bore neither forgiveness nor disgust. Only the sorrow of a son who stops by on Mother's Day without bringing flowers of his own.

My gift was for my father. I lifted the rock at the center of the stone-lined border. In the dirt where I had buried Jen's lion-eyed ring, I placed a plastic bag. It contained my mother's Dachau patch. And a note.

> You once asked—
> Who is the lamb and who the slayer?
> Who are the chosen and who the rejected?
> Here's the thing. We're all of them at once.
> Even you. Both Pharaoh and Moses.
> And neither one. Just my dad.'

———

The gates at Salve Regina were open as well. The arched ironwork had been replaced. The name was changed, the motto tweaked.

> Through darkness, light.
> Through sadness, joy.
> Through despair, hope.
> Come. Know life.
> Mater Dolorosa Home for Boys'

The grounds bustled with activity. Sunday afternoon was free time. And visiting hours for the occasional caller. Several groups of boys were clumped here and there—playing hoops on the courts, hackey-sack in the grass, some trading cards on the steps. Grandparents circled the pond with a resident. A woman nursed a baby in solitude. A toddler splashed lilies in the rippling fountain from the safety of his father's arms.

Unwatched from the tower, I walked into the wing and climbed to the second floor. The hallway of classrooms was deserted. As the outdoor buzz seeped in with the early evening shadows, I paced to the last door on the left and stood in its threshold. Jen's classroom was empty. Though I had been there only once, it was as familiar as the memory of one's first-grade schoolteacher. I could not help but wonder. What would have changed if I never knew Jen taught religion at Salve Regina? Perhaps nothing. Perhaps everything.

Without soliciting the light, I stepped to her desk. No pictures adorned it. No hints of her journey through the intervening years since I disappeared to the south. Except the paperback copy of her book. *Gathering a Splintered Almighty: The Presence of a Maternal God within the World's Suffering*. The back cover bore a picture of Jen and a young girl. A short bio accompanied it.

'Dr. Jennifer Gallagher lives with her daughter in northern California. She teaches religion at Mater Dolorosa, a residential Boys' Home for court-appointed youth. There, they look for shards of the sacred together. They help each other find their voice. And once in a while, they hold a few tears.'

I unfolded the opening pages and found her midrash on the Shekinah. I read the story, then closed the book. Next to it, I placed my package. My own attempt to rebind the pieces, with hope that the sacred would come back to life. Bound by two rubber bands crossing at the center, my typed manuscript came with an inscription.

'Seven years late, but I'm keeping my promise. It explains a lot. And nothing at all.'

I stared at the two manuscripts side by side. It was fitting. For years I wanted to know what stories feed life within a suffering world. I had read only two that did not tempt me to rip up the paper on which they were printed. Carey's and Jen's. A callous God unmasked. And a maternal Companion weeping over the pieces.

That's where I live.

Between Good Friday and Easter.

Jesus is dead. New life is but a dream in the dark.

———

My truck's cab harbored my last remaining gift, mounted behind the seat like a rifle in a Confederate pick-up. Carey left it behind. I thought he might want it, now that he had his chance. Hitching it to my shoulder, I followed the path behind the recital hall, retracing Carey's final steps.

The school's din receded as the path became a trail through the woods. I followed the footbridge, crossed the creek, and hiked to the clearing. The sun, nearing the horizon, bathed the chapel in an amber glow. I passed through the gate, left the path, and knelt before the plaque—bordered by flowers—mounted beside the chapel steps. Carey's body had been cremated, his ashes given to his mother. The only monument to his earthly life was the memorial before me. I had written the words from the state hospital, but had never seen them inscribed. The chiseled letters were black with shadow.

His story was his song.
And his song sought eyes that would weep.
May the melody ever sound.
And may all who hear, be moved to tears.

Carey Michael Foster 1981–1992

As I stared at the stone, I listened. I sought for but an echo that his song was alive. Like scenes from a silent movie, I could see him—belting "Take Me Out to the Ballgame" while standing on his seat during a seventh-inning stretch, crooning "Shenandoah" while snuggled between Jen and me during a lazy car-ride home, lullabying an audience with "Close Your Eyes" from the backstage recesses of God's disappearance. I could see him. But I could not hear the music. I strained. As one whose life depended on a whisper of sound to suggest that he was still singing. But I could not hear it. This time, the disappearance was too complete.

"Why are you so sad, Mister?"

I looked up to see a young black girl, no more than four or five, standing on the chapel steps. Her head peeked over the railing that she steadied with one hand.

"This plaque is for a boy who died here," I said forthrightly. "He was a friend of mine."

"Does it make you feel bad?" she innocently asked.

"Yes," I said. "It makes me feel bad."

"I have some medicine that can make you feel better." In her free hand, she gripped a container of orange Tic-Tacs like it was the sum of her life savings. "Would you like one?"

"Yes," I responded. "I would like one very much." She scrunched her face like a doctor squeezing drops from a final vial of serum. Several Tic-Tacs shook into her hand. She set the container onto the ground and returned the extras one by one. Through the bars of the railing, she offered the remaining piece of candy. I received it off her fingertips and placed it into my mouth.

"See," she lilted, "it makes you feel better, doesn't it?"

"It sure does," I nodded. "It does a lot."

"Chloe, leave that poor man alone." A man exited the chapel with several family members and brushed Chloe's shoulder. "I'm sorry she's bothering you," he said.

"No bother," I replied. "She's a precious young girl." Several boys bounded the steps then raced out the gate. "Thank you for the medicine, Chloe."

"Your welcome," she said like it was all in a day's work. Then she followed her brothers down the trail.

I picked up my offering and climbed the stairs. My heart pounded as I entered the chapel. The sun had yet to set. Colored beams streaked through the floral windows. It was as quiet as a tomb. And just as deserted.

Like a ghost drawn to the site of his death, I tread toward the altar. Its back was turned to the scene that had played out behind it. I placed my gift upon the table and, steadied by gift and table alike, I stared at the chancel floor.

The floor was clean. The shards were swept. The blood was washed.

But the nightmare remained. In my mind, glass glittered like streets at Kristallnacht. Two bodies were slumped on the floor. One face down in the splinters, the other speared by a crucifix, their two puddles of blood were streaming into one.

The sun had reached the horizon when I looked up at the window. As the shadows stretched, the colors glowed with dusky light. The splintered pieces of Peckham's Madonna had been recast—the lacework of shards reassembled into a stained-glass twist on the Pietá. The once majestic Queen of Creation—the obliterated portal into Hades' core—loomed now as an all-encompassing Mater Dolorosa. Leaking with tears, Mary's eyes looked out. Cradled in the crook of each arm, two bodies were held—their torsos nestled in separate shoulders as their legs dangled toward each other. A crown of thorns ringed one man's head, a hanging rope the other's neck. Jesus and Judas. Two of her boys. Both had splinters of glass in their bellies. And unlike Vincent van Gogh's depiction, both were held with a mother's care.

I stared at the bodies, then up at Mary. More than a marred mirror of God, her crying eyes pierced me. Carey had found them. Peckham had too. But her gaze reached beyond. Like snow that settles over slum and field alike, her gaze held the whole tangled lot of humanity. Toddlers knocked over by rushing patrons, and moms who swoop them into their arms. Religion teachers questing for God with kids from the courts, and kids rummaging through the ruins in search of their song. Children dispensing candy, to strangers, and dadies shooing them on their way.

Settling in ever-widening circles, her gaze embraced us all. Dachau mothers and protective fathers, sadistic fathers and praying mothers, inspiring mentors, inspired believers, storytelling teens, lewd choral leaders, caroling children, pederast priests, even the man with blood on his hands from villain and victim both.

Seeing us all through compassion's wash, Mary's eyes pled.

'Will you weep for my battered children with me?

'Will you weep for the whole battered world I hold?

'Will you weep for the Jesus and Judas in you, with the tears that restore them both to life?'

I looked into her eyes while she looked into me, grace drifting my soul's every shadow. I looked until pain and rage, shame and guilt, were all well-dusted. Then I looked at the weapon in my hands.

The hammer that nailed an unmoved God rested on the altar. Virgil's words were etched in the handle. 'Keep swinging, Carey.' Of course, he couldn't anymore. 'Don't let the bastard down for nothing.' And the bastard was now in our mother's arms.

I stared at the hammer until I heard the heartbeat. Or at least the trickle that points the way.

Tears splattered the handle like raindrops on stone.

In the light of the splintered Pietá, they glistened like stars.